DEADLY WOMEN

The Woman Mystery Reader's Indispensable Companion

Deadly Women

The Woman Mystery Reader's Indispensable Companion

Edited by:

JAN GRAPE

DEAN JAMES

and

ELLEN NEHR

Carroll & Graf Publishers, Inc.
New York

First Carroll & Graf edition 1998

Carroll & Graf Publishers, Inc.
19 West 21st Street
New York, NY 10010-6805

Library of Congress Cataloging-in-Publication Data

Deadly women / edited by Jan Grape, Dean James, and Ellen Nehr.
p. cm.
Includes index.
ISBN 0-7867-0468-3 (trade paper)
1. Detective and mystery stories, American — Women authors — History and criticism. 2. Detective and mystery stories, American — Women authors — Bibliography. 3. Women and literature — United States — History — 20th century. 4. Women authors, American — 20th century — Interviews. 5. Detective and mystery stories — Authorship. I. Grape, Jan. II. James, Dean (Darryl Dean) III. Nehr, Ellen.
PS374.D4D43 1998 97-21435
813'.087209287—dc21 CIP

Manufactured in the United States of America

Acknowledgments

Thank you to Ed Gorman and Marty Greenburg for making this book possible and to Gail Cross, designer extraordinaire for making this book look fantastic, and to Carroll & Graf for making this book.

(J.G.)

Thanks to Jan Grape who put in many long hours on this project and graciously allowed me to tag along for the ride and handle the cozy side of the street. Thanks to Ed Gorman for adopting me into the family. And, finally, as always, thanks to Nancy Yost, Agent Extraordinaire, for the perpetual smile in her voice whenever we talk.

(D.J.)

Dedication

Dedicated to my mother, Pee Wee Pierce, who often let me read instead of doing my chores. My husband, Elmer, who often let me write instead of doing my chores. In Memory of my dad, Tom Barrow, and my friend, Ellen Nehr.

(J.G.)

To the memory of the one and only Ellen Nehr. Ellen, I'd rather not have gotten this gig the way I did. I hope it's something you would have been proud of. I'll never forget you and all the wonderful writers you recommended.

(D.J.)

Ellen Nehr *Photo credit: Al Nehr*

A Note of Sadness Among the Silliness

Ellen Nehr was the first person to reach out to me from the mystery world. Our rapport began during an interview in 1986 and moved to weekly phone calls, sharing hotel rooms at cons, and exchanging books, galleys, and clippings. She was always willing to share her wisdom with me. When I wondered if a title had been used, she researched it for me. When I asked about a particular book or author, she knew the answer. When I called just to whine, she sympathized (for the most part). Opinionated and outspoken? You bet. Concerned and supportive? Yep.

There's a void now. Whenever I encounter a bit of gossip, I keep hearing myself think, "I've got to call Ellen. She'll love this."

All I can say is that I hope she's found Agatha, Josephine, Dorothy L., and all the other of her idols. I suspect that was her idea of heaven. She deserves it.

—Joan Hess

Contents

Foreword

When Ed Gorman called to ask if I'd be willing to co-edit *Deadly Women* with Ellen Nehr I was ecstatic. "It'll be a fun book," I said and called Ellen.

Ellen said, "With your knowledge of the private-eye and mean streets and my knowledge of historical and cozy, well, between the two of us, I think we've got it covered." But a few months later Ellen discovered other projects more important and left for a higher plane of existence. Sometime after that Ed called and mentioned Dean James as my new co-editor. "Dean's the perfect choice," I said, "I've known him for years and we work well together. He's the most knowledgeable person I can think of to take on the job and I feel sure Ellen would approve."

Many women mystery authors are covered in this volume and many are not. Writers were chosen at random with the only design to try to have a cross-section of styles and a diversity of sub-genres. If that criteria was not met, usually it was because an author was too pushed for time to meet the deadline or someone was unintentionally overlooked. *Deadly Women* is not a definitive word on women mystery writers but meant solely for your perusal and pleasure. We tried to keep errors to a minimum and hope you'll forgive the ones we missed.

No project like this is the work of only one or two people. The many authors involved came through in delightful and superb ways; funny, charming, intelligent, helpful, but always, always with their wonderful creative energy and enthusiasm. So here for them we offer our personal thanks for their contributions. I hope each of you, and especially Ms. Nehr, approves of the final copy . . .

—Jan Grape & Dean James
July 31, 1997

A Brief Look Back

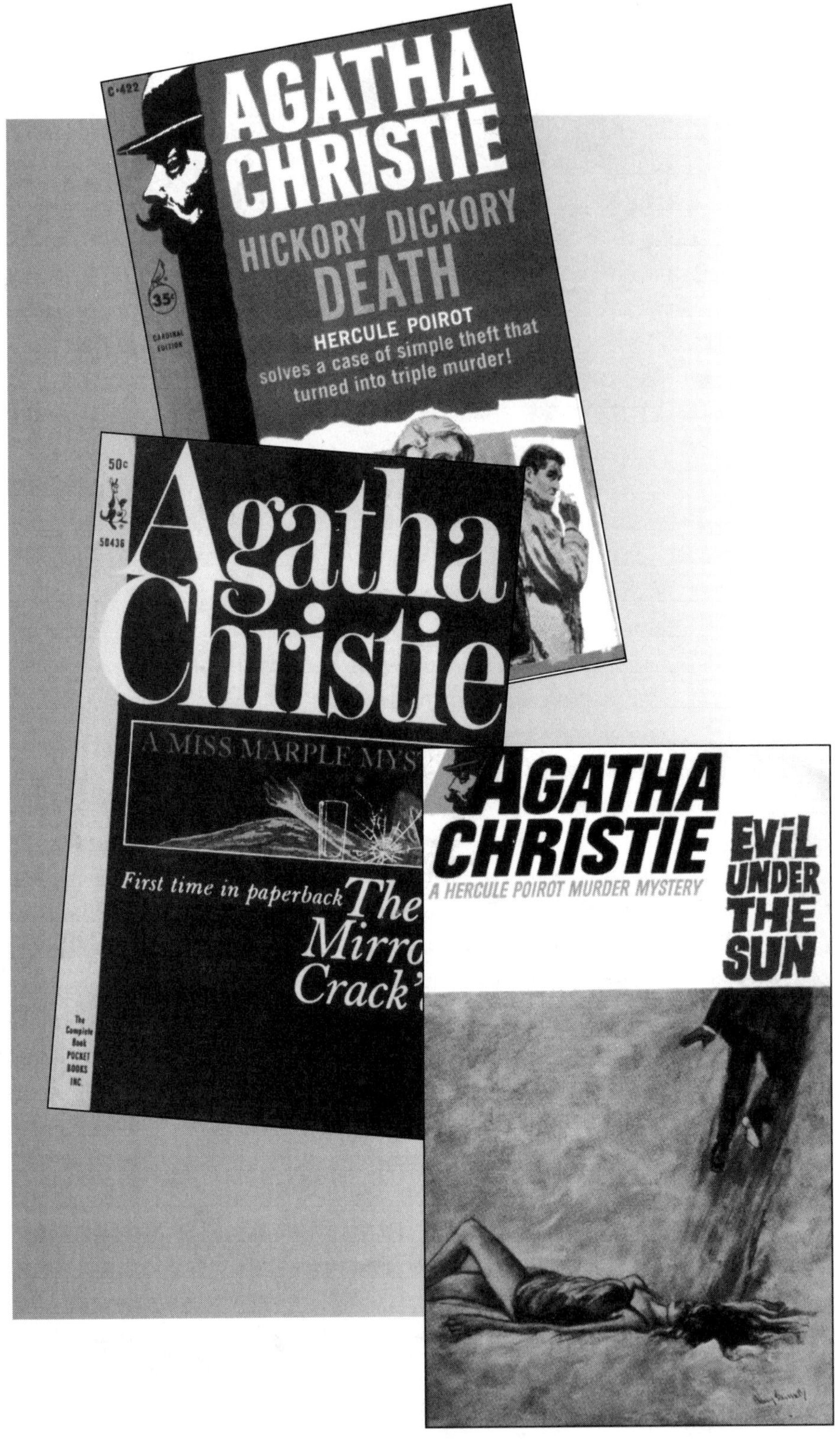

Hickory Dickory Death, The Mirror Cracked, and ***Evil Under the Sun*** by Agatha Christie

O, Pioneers

Charles Champlin

As they did in the twenties, thirties, and forties, when Agatha Christie, Dorothy L. Sayers, Ngaio Marsh, and Margery Allingham in England, and Mignon Eberhardt and Mary Roberts Rinehart among others in this country, ruled over crime fiction, women have again come to prominence in the field.

PATRICIA CORNWELL, SUE GRAFTON, and Mary Higgins Clark have both been atop best-seller lists; Sara Paretsky, Marcia Muller, Mary Higgins Clark, Nancy Pickard, Elizabeth George, and Sharyn McCrumb have made best-seller lists themselves, and England's Ruth Rendell and P.D. James would be on anyone's short list of the best mystery writers of either sex, anywhere.

All the American writers are spiritual daughters of two remarkable women, who launched the tradition of American women writing crime fiction. One of the women, Mrs. Metta Victoria Fuller Victor, is known hardly at all and was not even identified as a mystery writer until recent times. The other, Anna Katharine Green, is much better known, partly because she had the good sense to keep writing and publishing into the 1920s, her career having lasted the better part of a half-century.

Mrs. Victor wrote as Rose Kennedy, Corinne Cushman, Eleanor Lee Edwards, Mrs. Mark Peabody, possibly Louis LeGrand, M.D., and most importantly as Seeley Regester, in which gender-ambiguous guise she wrote what historians of the genre believe was the first murder mystery by an American woman, *The Dead Letter*, published in 1866.

Mrs. Victor had written her first novel, *The Last Days of Tull: A Romance of the Lost Cities of Yucatan* in 1846, when she was only fifteen. She later wrote many paperback dime novels for Beadle & Company, but *The Dead Letter* appeared in hardcover. It has most of the hallmarks of the mystery fiction that was to follow: a murder, several suspects, a detective, the steady pursuit of clues and evidence, deductive reasoning, and a denouement in the library, with the unmasking of the least-suspected culprit.

Then as now, mysteries defy easy synopsis. But let it be said that in *The Dead Letter*, Richard Redfield, a clerk in the post office's dead letter office in Manhattan, finds and reads an undelivered letter dated two years previously. It is bafflingly cryptic and signed "The Negotiator." Could it relate to the murder of Henry

Moreland, the fiancé of Eleanor Argyll, which occurs in flashback in the next chapter? Yes; coincidence was a useful staple in the genre from the start. Redfield, who also reads law with Eleanor's father, has an undisclosed crush on the girl himself, and vows to solve the murder. He hires Burton, a man Mrs. Victor describes as a secret policeman, but who operates entirely like a modern private eye. Burton has devoted his life to being "a hunter on the paths of the guilty," a forerunner of all the knights in plain clothes who work the mean streets.

Burton cleverly locates the hired assassin in a Central American country. But the question then becomes: Who engaged him to do in Moreland? Burton assembles all interested parties in the Argyll library. Then, after some misleading feints at the narrator himself, nails the real villain. The jealousy-wrought wretch cries, "Yes, I did it, Eleanor," and drops to the floor in a swoon. The swoon is perhaps the one element of *The Dead Letter* that did not survive in the mystery tradition.

For eleven years, no one followed Mrs. Victor's lead. Then in 1878 Anna Katharine Green published *The Leavenworth Case,* which became an enormous international success, selling a million copies and wearing out three sets of plates. It was said to have been the favorite reading of British prime minister Stanley Baldwin. On an American tour, Sir Arthur Conan Doyle paused in Buffalo to pay his respects to the author, who had invented her detective a decade before Doyle created Sherlock Holmes. The novel's success established Ms. Green (Mrs. Charles Rohlfs of Buffalo, N.Y., as she was most of her adult life) as the mother superior of all the later generations of American women mysterians. She published into the 1920s, lived until 1935, and is occasionally still reprinted.

She was born in Brooklyn in 1846, the daughter of a lawyer. Crime may well have informed dinner-table conversation from time to time. The family moved to Buffalo when she was three, and there she spent most of the rest of her life. Remarkable for a young woman in her day, Anna Katharine went to Ripley College in Vermont. After graduating in 1866, she went home to Buffalo, determined to pursue the only career she cared about, being a writer.

It took her twelve years, living at home and writing, writing, writing, to break into print. She thought first to be a poet, which her father considered a suitable job for a woman. She began writing what became *The Leavenworth Case* in secret, not sure what her father would say. But she showed it to him when it was half-finished (it ultimately ran to 145,000 words). Her father not only liked it, he helped arrange an interview with George Putnam, who published it, and Putnam's has been publishing mysteries ever since.

The novel was even more prophetic of things to come than Mrs. Victor's. A familiarity with firearms, ballistics, and anatomy come into play. It was a small ball from a Smith & Wesson that penetrated Mr. Leavenworth's medulla oblongata as he sat in the library, the reader is told, and he was dead before he could lift a finger. The library seems to have been locked from the inside, but Green does not pursue the point to create an early locked-room mystery.

What echoes loudest down the years is that Anna Katharine Green created a series sleuth: Ebenezer Gryce, "a portly, comfortable person with an eye that never pierced, that did not even rest on you." (This may have been more unnerving than a piercing stare.) Gryce had a side kick, named Morris but also called Q, as in Query, who often worked in disguise. After *The Leavenworth Case*, the author used Gryce in several more stories and novels, letting him age with the passing years, until he was in his 70s and crippled by rheumatoid arthritis. At one point Gryce says, "I suspect everyone and nobody," a line that in variations has also echoed through the genre.

Suspicion falls on the dead man's two nieces, one of whom stands to inherit his considerable fortune. There are shadowings and impersonations, a mysterious stranger, a suspenseful stakeout in a village upstate from New York, a secret marriage revealed, a whole treasury of misdirection. Once again there is at last a confrontation with all the principals, this time in a gloomy attic rather than the library. Gryce, using a technique of penultimate accusation that has seen good use many times since, makes such a plausible case against one of the nieces that the real killer leaps to his feet and cries, "It is a lie, a lie! Mary Leavenworth is as innocent as a babe unborn. I am the murderer." He does not swoon, but he cries piteously, "I have given my soul to hell for a shadow . . . for a shadow."

Anna Katharine was a moralist, indicating again and again that pride and greed were the engines that drove crime. Greed has not been displaced in the century since.

But inventing Ebenezer Gryce and surrounding him with so many of the ongoing conventions of mystery fiction was only the beginning. Green also invented Amelia Butterworth, a Manhattan spinster who worked with Gryce on several occasions. Green described her as "a woman of inborn principles and strict Presbyterian training." Another of Green's creations was Violet Strange, introduced in a series of short stories in 1916. She's a highborn and feisty young socialite who won't take money from her father but works as a private eye in an agency something like Pinkerton's. But she occasionally cuts costs by riding to assignments in the family's chauffeured limousine.

What Metta Victoria Harper Victor and Anna Katharine Green wrote is significant for the resonances it has sent along the decades since. Yet what seems even more interesting today is that they defied the inhibitions and frustrations of women in mid-nineteenth century times, and wrote not domestic fictions but dramatic tales of murder and the darker passions, all placed in a well-observed real world. Anna Katharine had a keen eye for social nuances. Gryce observes candidly, "I cannot pass myself off as a gentleman. Tailors and barbers are no good. I am always found out. I have even employed a French valet, who understands dancing and whiskers, but it was no good."

The style in both women's prose was operatic and leisurely, the attitude allowing no confusions of right and wrong, no ambiguities (although one of the villains was allowed to leave the country on condition he never return). A condensed version of *The Leavenworth Case* published in 1981 with an introduction by Michele Slung still ran to 311 pages. One of Green's novellas, a clever piece called "The Doctor, His Wife and the Clock" is reprinted in a recent anthology, *The Mammoth Book of Golden Age Detective Stories* (Carroll & Graf). There is apparently no biography of Green, but a very good monograph, "Mother of Detective Fiction" by Patricia D. Maida, was published by Bowling Green University Popular Press in 1989.

More than a century after Anna Katharine Green and Mrs. Victor published their innovating works, both might be astonished, certainly pleased, to see how abundantly their descendants are prospering.

Lady and the Dark: Louisa May Alcott's Literary Double Life

Elizabeth Foxwell

In 1995, the literary world hailed a new novel—a dark tale of treachery and obsessive love between dissolute villain and virtuous heroine against a cosmopolitan background. It hit the New York Times *best-seller list for one week, its translation rights were sold in eleven countries, and a four-hour NBC miniseries was planned for broadcast in 1996—all nearly 130 years after the story was first penned, and over a century after the author's death.*

THE NOVEL WAS LOUISA May Alcott's *A Long, Fatal Love Chase,* a fragment of Alcott's hidden past as a writer of "blood and thunder" tales. *Chase*'s publication, as well as the appearance of several volumes of her thrillers, have forced scholars to revise their estimation of Alcott as the demure author of the classic *Little Women* and its subsequent sequels. Although her alter ego Jo March enjoyed a brief career in this field, Alcott's time was more prolonged, exploring powerful themes in *Chase* and in twenty-nine often lurid tales of deception, tragic love, and dramatic death. On this canvas, she illustrated the underside of human existence in the struggle for domination between the sexes, including such strong subjects as, and her personal experience in, drugs, insanity, and hypnotism/mesmerism. She featured independent, strong-minded women, a reflection of her determined pursuit of her own career and later work in women's suffrage. Through her thrillers, Alcott proved she had a great deal more to say about society in a more sensational medium.

The stories:

"A crowd is the best place for secrets."—L.M.A., "The Abbot's Ghost; or Maurice Treherne's Temptation"

Alcott's mysteries lie in identity—the stripping away of facades, and the discovery of buried secrets and betrayal to reveal a harsher reality. Many of her characters play double roles. The masquerades may be conducted more obviously as in the masked ball in "A Marble Woman: or, The Mysterious Model" where the previously cold husband in disguise seeks a key to his impassive wife's heart—or, as in the intricate "V.V., or, Plots and Counterplots" which turns on several characters playing roles not their own. V.V.'s lover is murdered, and she is forced to flee. A mysterious woman appears in the second part of the story, but Alcott keeps the reader guessing as to her identity and purpose until the final pages. She is likewise adept at masking the hero's identity, as he plays detective into past and present crimes. "Behind a Mask; or, A Woman's Power" features the seemingly demure governess Jean Muir playing a determined charade and bewitching all of the men of the household to punish pride, and establish a safe haven for herself. In "A Double Tragedy: An Actor's Story," the stage is literally the scene as the actor-protagonists perform *Romeo and Juliet* and an equally tragic lover's duet offstage.

"Perilous Play" features a unique twist on drug-taking. Some bored friends follow the suggestion of one of their number and experiment with hashish. The drug causes Mark Done and the icy girl he loves to face their fears and their love. "Heaven bless hashish," Done says at the end, "if its

dreams end like this!"

"A Nurse's Story" is one of the most interesting, and may reflect Alcott's own stint as a Civil War nurse, related in a short book, *Hospital Sketches* (1863) and an experience in nursing an insanity case. Kate Snow comes to nurse a troubled young woman, part of a household under the control of a proud stranger, Robert Steele. Kate, who is able to calm her patient through mesmerism, equally fascinates Steele, awakening his love. She is faced with a hard choice between duty to her charge and honor, and the result is tragic for Steele and bitter for Kate.

Alcott's stories are, most of all, morality tales, consistent with her messages in the Little Women books. The characters whose reach exceeds their grasp come to bad ends, such as Pauline in "Pauline's Passion and Punishment" who is destroyed by her desire for revenge on a faithless lover. In Alcott's world, betrayal is punished, self-sacrifice is rewarded, and love redeems character flaws. But the women in her stories demand equal footing with men; and if they are undone by their pride and selfishness, they at the same time operate fearlessly on their own. "'To you I will acknowledge that I am not worthy to be this good man's wife," Jean Muir tells her former pupil and her mother, "and to you I will solemnly promise to devote my life to his happiness . . . ' Jean seemed to expect no friendly demonstration . . . and to accept their contempt as her just punishment" ("Unmasked" p. 439). Thus, Jean, although she has achieved her objective, accepts the consequences of her actions, a typical Alcott message.

A Long Fatal Love Chase

"She answered not a word, never turned her head, and betrayed no sign of having heard the insult except by, with a sudden disdainful gesture, gathering back the sweeping skirt that brushed him as if he were some noxious thing." *(Chase,* p. 136)

A Long Fatal Love Chase evokes several Shakespearean parallels. References are made to *The Tempest* in the naming of the villain "Phillip Tempest," foreshadowing the heroine Rosamond's future turbulence, and in the casting of Rosamond's grandfather as a feeble Prospero and Rosamond as Miranda.

Rosamond, chafing at her confined life with her grandfather, meets and is seduced by the suave and scarred Tempest and sails off with him. Discovering their marriage ceremony was a sham and Tempest is already married, Rosamond flees. The rest of the book centers on a clash of wills, between Tempest, who is determined not to be bested by his "wife's" temerity in leaving him; and Rosamond, who will not forget betrayal and become a slave. The chase proceeds from England to France to Germany and back to England; from abbey to chateau to madhouse, with Rosamond in many guises finding a better and nobler man along the way. The story's theme is a familiar one for Alcott—a possessive, obsessive love versus a generous and self-sacrificing one, with Rosamond as the prize and ultimately the victim.

Completed in 1866, the novel was rejected as "too sensational" by Alcott's publisher, perhaps because of the "living-in-sin" factor of Rosamond and Tempest's mock marriage, Rosamond's fling with transvestism and sacrilege in dressing up first as a boy, then as a nun; and her true love's vocation as a priest. Readers might find all this a bit tame by today's standards, but Tempest's blind selfishness and pride, Rosamond's sense of entrapment, and the loyalty of Rosamond's small circle of faithful friends are all timeless.

> *"Life is my college. May I graduate well, and earn some honors!"*—L.M.A., journal, March 1859

As Amy E. Schwartz (1994) suggests, Alcott was ambivalent about her "blood and thunder tales"—penning Jo's penitence and renunciation of the genre in *Little Women* on the one hand and yet expressing pride of their ability to support her family, gain her independence, and provide free rein for her imagination. "Wrote much, for brain was lively, and work paid for readily," she wrote in her journal in 1862. "Rewrote the last story and sent it to L. [Frank Leslie, editor of *Frank Leslie's Illustrated Newspaper*], who wants more than I can send him. So . . . I reel off my "thrilling" tales, and mess up my work in a queer but interesting way" (*Journals*, p. 109). Even after the success of *Little Women,* she noted in 1877 after writing "A Modern Mephistopheles" [the first title for *Chase*], "Enjoyed doing it, being tired of providing moral pap for the young" (Ibid. p. 204).

We can be grateful to Rostenberg and Stern, the literary detectives who ferreted out Alcott's hidden works. They have provided a sharper picture of the seemingly decorous Concord resident's double life and her quest for the literary experience that fully exercised her keen perception and vivid imagination.

REFERENCES

Alcott, Louisa May. *A Long Fatal Love Chase.* New York: Random House. 1995.

Louisa May Alcott Unmasked: Collected Thrillers. Edited by Madeleine Stern. Boston: Northeastern University Press, 1995.

Louisa May Alcott: Life, Letters, and Journals. Compiled and edited by Ednah D, Cheney. New York: Gramercy Press, 1995.

The Journals of Louisa May Alcott. Edited by Joel Myerson and Daniel Shealy. Boston: Little, Brown & Co., 1989

Schwartz, Amy E. "From 'Little Women' to 'Blood-and-Thunder:' The Other Side of Louisa May Alcott." *Washington Post.* December 30, 1994, p. A17.

From Honey to Freddie

Robert J. Randisi

HONEY WEST.

There, I said it.

I've noticed over the past few years that books purporting to be complete studies of the female P.I. invariably leave out Honey West.

THEY TALK ABOUT MARCIA Muller being the mother of the Lady P.I. with the publication of the first Sharon McCone novel, *Edwin of the Iron Shoes* (1977), which is true—even though McCone is slightly predated by Maxine O'Callaghan's Delilah West (by virtue of the story in Alfred Hitchcock's Mystery Magazine in 1974). When there are discussions about the P.I. form, however, McCone is given the edge because she appeared in a novel earlier than Delilah West did (*Death Is Forever,* 1980).

However, while everyone is mentioning Marcia Muller and Maxine O'Callaghan, they seem to forget that the first Honey West novel, *This Girl for Hire,* by G.G. Fickling, appeared in 1957, followed—between 1957 and 1972—by ten more.

G.G. Fickling was the joint pseudonym of husband and wife Forest Ellison "Skip" and Gloria Gautruad Fickling. Friends of Richard S. Prather, the creator of Shell Scott, Prather once remarked to the Ficklings that there was no commercially successful female P.I. series. They promptly created Honey West, who was basically a female version of Prather's Shell Scott, in both character and style—a first-person, fast, funny, sexy series. Honey later made it to TV in the sixties in a short-lived series starring Anne Francis.

All of this is by way of saying that I think of Honey West as the first legitimate series female P.I. She was predated by Rex Stout's Theodolina "Dol" Bonner and Henry Kane's Marla Trent, but those characters did not develop into series, and they were created by men. Even Carter Brown's Mavis Seidlitz, which was a series that followed Honey West, was written and created by a man.

By virtue of all this, and with no

offense meant to Sharon McCone or Delilah West, I proclaim Honey West—ahem, in my opinion—to be the mother of the series female P.I.

There, I said it.

So much has been written about Sue Grafton, Sara Paretsky, Linda Barnes, and other established female P.I. writers that I would like to dedicate my limited space to discussing some of the lesser known American lady P.I.'s and P.I. writers who would appear on the verge of becoming—well, *less* lesser known.

So, let's talk about the lady P.I.'s of the nineties:

It's February 1996 as I write this, and to this date Catherine Dain's Freddie O'Neal; is—ahem, in my opinion—one of the most recent significant female P.I.'s to have arrived on the scene. Six books have been published in the series, with *Lay It on the Line* (1992) and *Lament for a Dead Cowboy* (1994) nominated for SHAMUS awards for Best Paperback P.I. Novel.

Another who qualifies as significant is Sandra Scoppettone's Lauren Laurano, who appeared in three novels published by Fawcett Books. They were *My Sweet Untraceable You* (1994), *I'll Be Leaving You Always* (1993) and *Everything You Have Is Mine* which, in my opinion, was the best P.I. novel to appear in 1991.

Also born in the nineties was Janet Dawson's Jeri Howard. The fourth winner of the PWA/St. Martin's Press First P.I. Novel contest Janet's first Jeri Howard novel, *Kindred Crimes,* was published in 1990 by St. Martin's Press. There have been four novels since, all published by Fawcett, all well received. *Nobody's Child* (1995) was the most recent. Janet Dawson has become an important practitioner of the P.I. novel.

Others to come along in the nineties who might make an impact are Sandra West Prowell, whose first two Phoebe Siegel novels, *By Evil Means* (Walker & Co., 1993) and *The Killing of Monday Brown* (Walker & Co., 1994) were published to critical and commercial success; S. J. Rozan, who published two novels featuring her P.I. team of Lydia Chin and Bill Smith, *China Trade* and *Concourse* were published by St. Martin's Press in '94 and '95 respectively; and Gloria White, who copped an Edgar Award for *Charged with Guilt* (Dell, 1995), her third Ronnie Ventana novel.

Other authors to watch for during the nineties are Valerie Frankel, Ruth Furie, Phyllis Knight, Margaret Lucke, Michelle Spring, Valerie Wilson Wesley, Sharon Gwyn Short, and Sharon Zukowski.

In the case of Margaret Lucke, her first novel, *A Relative Stranger* was published in 1991. In between, she and her P.I. Jess Randolph appeared in the anthology *Lethal Ladies* (Berkley, 1996). Her story, "Identity Crisis," was arguably the best in the book.

Others who appeared in *Lethal Ladies* who could make a dent in the genre in the nineties are Wendi Lee, who published her first Angela Matelli novel, *The Good Daughter,* with St. Martin's Press in '94; Jan Grape and Christine Matthews, who so far have written only short stories about their characters, Jenny Gordon and C.J. Gunn of Austin Texas, and Robbie Stanton of Omaha, Nebraska; and Australia's Marele Day, who won a SHAMUS award for Best Paperback P.I. Novel in 1994 with her Claudia Valentine novel, *The Last Tango of Delores Delgado,* published in Australia but distributed here. Her fourth, *The Disappearance of Madelina Grimaldi,* has found an American publisher, Walker & Co., and was published in the U.S. in 1996.

Of course, we expect to continue to enjoy Sue Dunlap's Kiernan O'Shaughnessy, Karen Kijewski's Kat Colorado, Linda Grant's Catherine Saylor, D.C. Brod's Quint McCauley, Annette Meyers' Smith & Wetzon, Barb D'Amato's Cat Marsala, and many of the other fine authors already plying, with great success, their trade in this genre, which is continuing to show a remarkable growth in both quantity and quality.

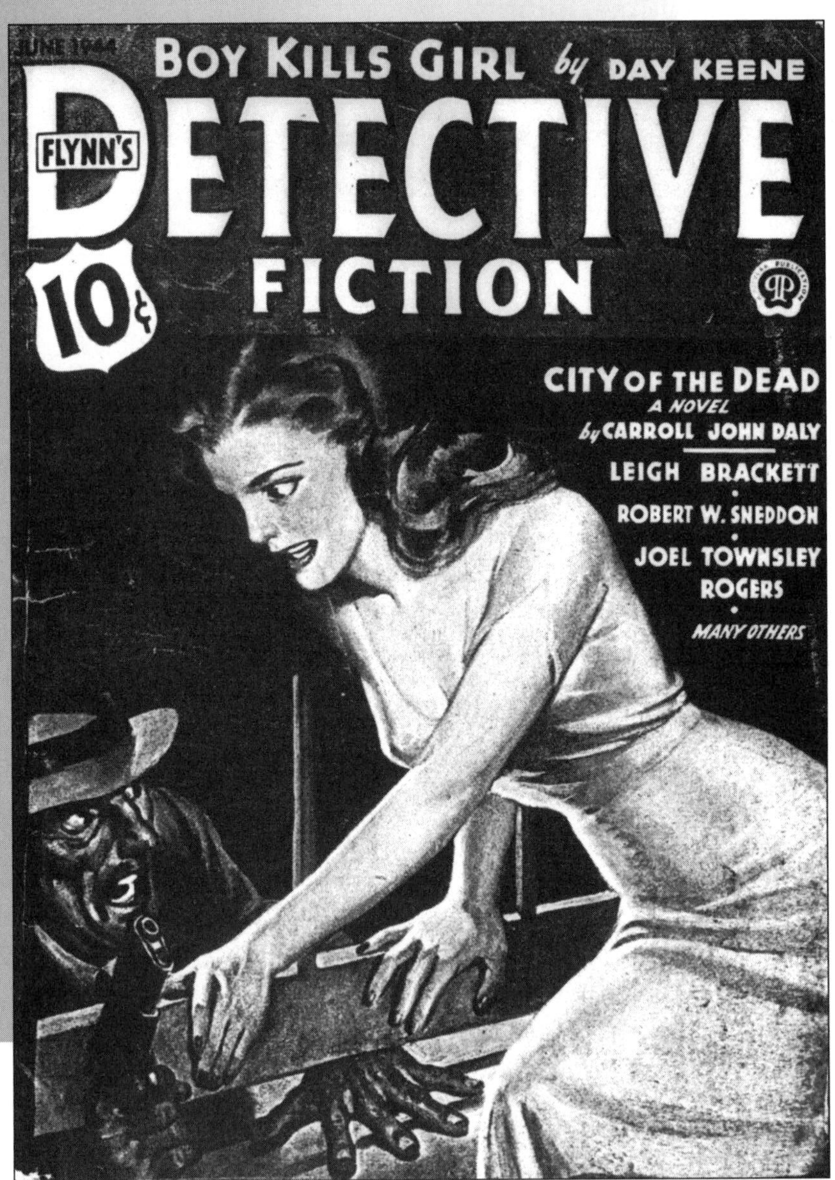

Flynn's Detective Fiction, June 1944

Women in the Pulps

Bill Pronzini

Pulp fiction—the real thing, not the modern Quentin Tarantino sleazeball variety—was the primary source of popular fiction between the two world wars and until the emergence of the paperback original novel and network television in the early fifties. Successors to the dime novels and story weeklies of the nineteenth century, the pulps were seven by ten inches in size and so named because they were printed on untrimmed woodpulp paper.

WITH THE EXCEPTION OF love-story magazines, they were aimed primarily at a male readership; thus, the enameled covers of most mystery, detective, adventure, western, and science-fiction titles had vividly colored artwork depicting scenes of high melodrama. In the cases of the "shudder" or "weird menace" pulps (*Dime Mystery, Horror Stories, Terror Tales*) which featured stories with a sex-and-sadism bent, and the Spicy Group (*Spicy Detective, Spicy Mystery,* etc.) which sold mildly voyeuristic sexual titillation in an action-story context, the covers also emphasized women in various stages of undress, more often than not being tortured or threatened by an array of slavering fiends.

Prior to 1926 and the advent of the hard-boiled "*Black Mask* school" pioneered by Dashiell Hammett and editor Joseph T. Shaw, pulp mystery and detective fiction was relatively sedate. Even *Black Mask,* from its inception in 1920 throughout its first six years, published more than a few mannered, drawing-room style mysteries by both men and women—none of whom, significantly, had substantial literary careers in or out of the pulps. The contents pages of *Black Mask* in its early years are spotted with long-forgotten names, among them such women authors as Florence M. Pettee, Elizabeth Dudley, Sally Dixon Wright, Eliza Mae Harvey, Helen Holley, Wyona Dashwood, and Marjorie Stoneman Douglas.

Other pulps during this period featured stories and novel serializations by much more prominent women authors, including Dorothy L. Sayers, Carolyn Wells, and Agatha Christie. Twenty of Christie's short stories, for instance, had their first U.S. magazine appearances in *Street & Smith's Detective Story, Flynn's Weekly, Mystery Magazine,* and *Detective Fiction Weekly;* and two of her novels, *The Murder of Roger Akroyd* and *The Tuesday Club Murders,* were first serialized in this country in *Flynn's Weekly* and *Great Detective Magazine,* respectively. Another Christie short, "The Face of Helen" rather surprisingly was reprinted in the last issue (July, 1951) of *Black Mask.*

Even after the hard-boiled renaissance led by Hammett and Shaw, and the host of imitators the "new," streamlined *Black Mask* spawned, one long-standing magazine continued to cling tenaciously to the more traditional type of detective tale. This was *Street & Smith's Detective Story,* the very first pulp to be devoted to crime fiction. "Born" in 1915, when S&S converted its dime-novel weekly, *Nick Carter,* to the pulp format, *Detective Story* throughout its thirty-four year life regularly showcased stories by and of interest to women. A number of its contributors enjoyed successful careers as mystery novelists: Christie, Sayers, Wells, Helen Reilly, Elizabeth Sanxay Holding, Ethel Lina White, Margaret Millar, D.B. Olsen (Dolores Hitchens), Sue McVeigh, M.V. Heberden, Zola Helen Ross, Mary Collins, Marty Holland, and Muriel Bradley. Above average *Detective Story* mainstays who confined their output to short stories, and are therefore known today only to pulp collectors and aficionados, include Margaret Manners, Marion Scott, Madeleine Sharps Buchanan, Agatha Gandy, and Inez Sabastian.

From 1930 to the demise of the last detective title in 1957, nearly all the crime pulps were "a man's world" in terms of content, authorship, and readership. A handful of magazines, among them *Mystery Book* and *Two Complete Detective Books,* specialized in publishing abridged versions of hardcover mysteries, quite a few of which were by women. But most publications featured original stories exclusively or almost exclusively, and the best of them—*Black Mask, Black Aces, Dime Detective, Double Detective, Detective Tales, New Detective*—emphasized hard-edged tales told from the male point of view. As a result, few women wrote for them (or read them), and fewer still made significant contributions to the annals of hard-boiled pulp—or novel length—crime fiction. Until the runaway popularity of the female private eye in recent years, the vast majority of women mystery writers evidently preferred their crimes and misdemeanors to take place in surroundings more genteel than Raymond Chandler's mean streets and to be couched in less graphic and violent prose.

The exceptions, of course, are notable. One was Georgiana Ann Randolph Craig, better known as Craig Rice, whose medium-tough Chicago lawyer John J. Malone appears in such excellent novels as *Eight Faces at Three, The Corpse Steps Out,* and *Trial by Fury,* and in a clutch of pulp yarns published in the late forties and early fifties. Another—the woman with the most impressive body of hard-boiled fiction—was Leigh Brackett.

Brackett was an avowed admirer of Chandler and the *Black Mask* school, and her debut novel, *No Good from a Corpse* (1944), a complex southern California tale featuring private detective Edmond Clive, is so Chandleresque in style and approach that it might have been wriitten by Chandler himself. Indeed, Brackett was given the opportunity to write (or rewrite) Chandler's own work when she was hired to co-author the screenplay of *The Big Sleep* in 1946; and twenty-five years later she wrote the script for the Robert Altman-Elliot Gould film version of *The Long Goodbye* (1973). Although limited to seven stories, all published between 1943 and 1945, her pulp detective yarns are first rate. One, the no doubt editorially retitled "I Feel Bad Killing You" (pulp editors had an inordinate fondness for lurid titles, especially those utilizing puns, e.g., "Rest in Pieces"), a novelette which appeared in the November 1944 issue of *New Detective,* is in the same lofty class as Chandler's *Black Mask* stories.

The most prolific woman contributor to the post-1930 pulps was a St. Louis elementary school teacher, Dorothy Dunn. In the forties and early fifties Dunn published more than sixty stories in *Dime Detective, Detective Tales, Thrilling Detective,* and *Black Mask,* among others. The same qualities that distinguish such tales as "Dead-End Darling," Morphine Alley," and "Senora Satan," make her only mystery novel, *Murder's Web* (1950), well worth reading—strong characterization, offbeat situations, and evocative and distinctively gritty prose. ("They all looked alike, these Skid Row bums. Stomachs rotted out, faces a network of broken veins under the dirty whiskers, minds a pickled organ twisting in the alcholic juices of a bell-jar skull.") Other women whose names appeared more than once or twice on the contents pages of the male-oriented periodicals: Miriam Allen deFord (who also wrote as Miriam Allen), Frances Beck, Kay Krausse, Tiah Devitt, and Marian O'Hearn.

The honor of the longest piece of original fiction by a woman to be published in a top-line hard-boiled pulp belongs to Kathleen Moore Knight. Though best known for her traditional Cape Cod mysteries starring Elisha Macomber, Knight also wrote an occasional novel of a moderately tough nature; two in this vein are *Pray for a Miracle* (1941) and *Borderline Murder* (1947), both as by Alan Amos. "Without Benefit of a Camera," a 25,000-word novella of violence and intrigue in wartime Mexico, appeared in the September 1944 issue of *Black Mask.* It is no surprise, given the nature of pulp fiction in those days, that the author's byline was abridged to the gender nonspecific K.M. Knight.

The pulps, alas, are long dead, but their legacy lives on. Women may have played a small role in their heyday, but a case can be made that such contemporary writers as Marcia Muller, Sue Grafton, and Sara Paretsky owe at least a small debt of gratitude to Craig Rice, Leigh Brackett, Dorothy Dunn, and other convention-defying sisters of that bygone era.

Private Eye, July 1953

Paperback Ladies

Bill Crider

Almost as soon as the paperback-original market began to develop, there were female private eyes narrating their own stories.

PROBABLY THE FIRST WAS Eli Donovan, in James L. Rubel's *No Business for a Lady* (Gold Medal, 1950). The back cover of the book says that "Most detectives have angles, but here's one that has curves—Eli Donovan, lady detective. She doesn't ask quarter from any man. All she asks is that he be on the tall side, with muscles and a nice personality." In the complicated plot, it's revealed that Eli's real name is Liza Malone, and the story kicks off when her husband, reportedly killed on Tarawa during the war, turns up in town. He, too, has a new name, but he has more than that; he has a new wife. In working her way through the resulting mess, Ms. Donovan shows plenty of resourcefulness and considerable toughness, even if she does faint after the climactic fight. Unfortunately, the writing in the book is mediocre at best, and the plot is faintly ridiculous. ELi's first case for Gold Medal was also her last.

The next female eye of note was created by the husband-and-wife writing team of Gloria and Forrest E. ("Skip") Fickling. Their byline was G.G. Fickling, and their character was Honey West. The publishers (Pyramid Books) clearly aimed the series at male readers, and Honey's measurements (38-22-36) are mentioned frequently, sometimes even on the covers of the books. Honey spends a lot of time in bathing suits and underwear, and the covers of all the books emphasize her figure. On the front cover, back cover, and spine of *This Girl for Hire* (1957), she is described as "the sexiest private eye ever to pull a trigger." Pyramid Books blithely ignored Eli Donovan and billed Honey as "literary history's first female private eye." Most of the eleven books in the series are marked by police lieutenant Mark Storm's pleas with Honey to leave the thinking to the men, but Honey never listens. She tells her own stories, and she's plenty tough, but she attained her greatest popularity not on the page but on television, where she was portrayed by Anne Francis in 1965–1966. According to Francis, women today tell her that they were very much influenced by the show, which gave them a role model quite unlike the ones provided by Laura Petrie and Harriet Nelson.

Pyramid, recognizing a good thing, published another novel with a female eye, Marla Trent, who first appeared in *Private Eyeful* (1959).

The book was written by Henry Kane, and it's a big improvement over the Rubel and Fickling novels because Kane, now largely ignored or forgotten, was a very good writer. Marla Trent is described as a "private eye with a body to match her brain. Marla Trent knew how to use them both—for business—or pleasure." Kane was an attorney, and his plot is a good one. A convict, brought to court to testify, pulls a gun and kills the prosecutor. Trent's client is accused of slipping the gun to the convict, and she has to clear not only the client but herself. The novel is told in the third person, and it's clever and fast moving. Trent appears again in *Kisses of Death* (Belmont, 1962), along with Pete Chambers, another of Kane's series characters.

But it took a woman to bring a realistic female private eye into paperback, though not many people now know much about Phyllis Swan and the three novels she did in the Anna Jugedinski series for Leisure Books, the first of which, *Find Sherri!*, appeared in 1979. Anna is not alluring in the way that Honey West and Marla Trent are. She's a rape victim who has trouble paying her bills and who knows the streets. Her cases are grittier than those engaged in by her paperback predecessors, and while the writing does not always sparkle, the stories are never less than interesting. Swann deserves credit for creating a female private eye for the paperback market who gets by more on street smarts than glamour; she's a forgotten pioneer.

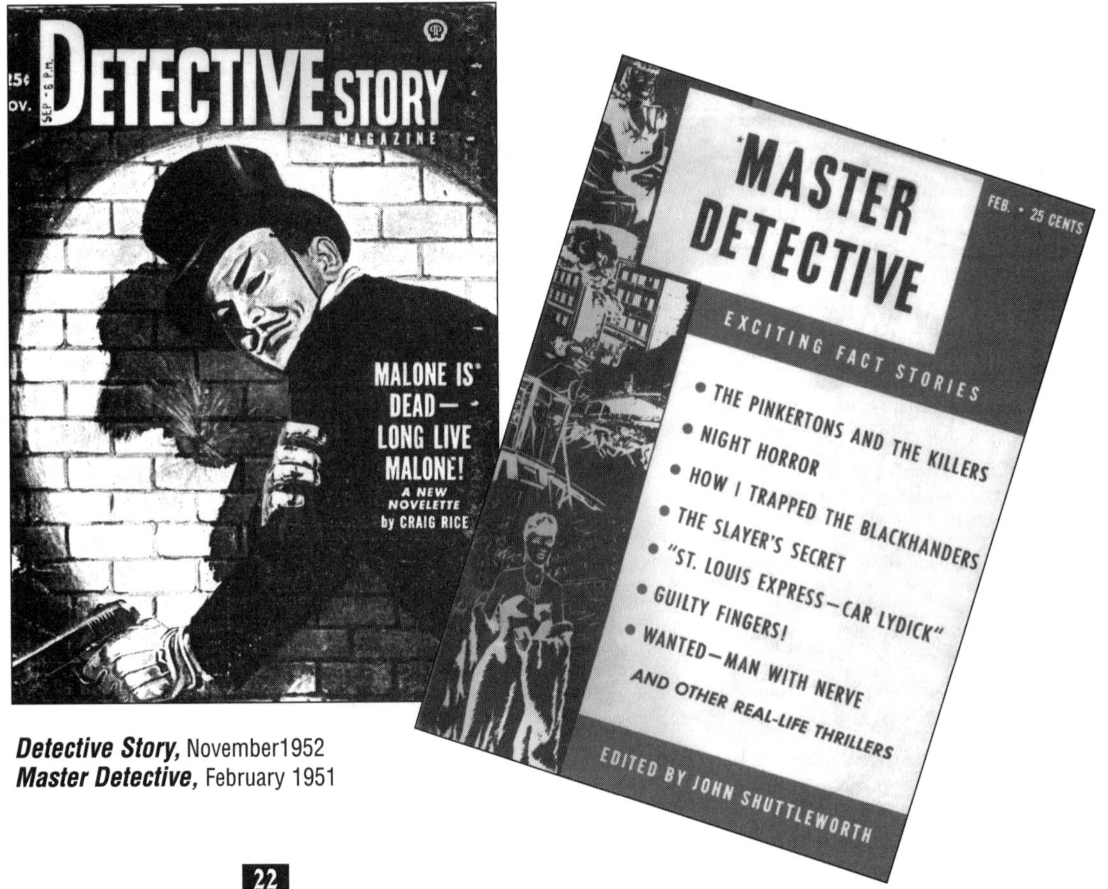

Detective Story, November1952
Master Detective, February 1951

Carter Brown's Fabulous Mystery Babe: Mavis Seidlitz

George Kelley

"Carter Brown" (pseudo-nym of Alan G. Yates, the prolific Australian paperback mystery writer) created a classic "dumb blonde" in a series of a dozen novels written over twenty years featuring Mavis Seidlitz, a partner in Hollywood-based Rio Investigations.

MAVIS IS A MARILYN Monroe/Jayne Mansfield blond bombshell with the IQ of a gerbil. The typical Mavis adventure is modeled on the screwball comedies of the 1930s with bodies popping up unexpectedly and Mavis finding herself in various states of undress. It's all entertaining, politically incorrect, silliness.

The first three Mavis mysteries, *Honey, Here's Your Hearse* (1955), *A Bullet for My Baby* (1955), and *Good Morning, Mavis* (1957, refine the formula for the rest of the books in the series.

In *Murder Wears a Mantilla* (1957; revised edition NAL 1962) Carter Brown puts a spin on that formula by having Mavis vacation in Mexico. Settings are not a strong point for Carter Brown: Mavis's Mexico is about as Mexican as a Taco Bell in Toronto. Mavis is approached by a man claiming he's Luis Salazar, a matador and best friend of Mavis's partner, Johnny Rio. He asks Mavis to do him a favor and naturally Mavis believes every word of the stranger's story.

Mavis goes to the address Salazar gave her and finds a dead body, a suitcase full of money, and a figurine. Before long she's dodging the Mexican Secret Police led by Rafael Vega.

Bullfighting is changed forever when Mavis finds herself in the center of a stadium full of screaming fans and facing a charging bull. It's the book's highlight.

The Loving and the Dead (1959; NAL 1959) marks the first American publication of a Mavis Seidlitz book. Carter Brown's previous American paperbacks featured two characters:

Al Wheeler—a horny lieutenant in the Sheriff's Department of an L.A. suburb, Pine Valley—and a horny private eye, Danny Boyd. Brown specialized in making his books "spicy." A great detail of description is devoted to describing female characters' figures, breasts, garters, and revealing clothing. Mavis even tells us her "vital statistics;" 37-25-36 (which evolve to 38-23-37 in later books). And she is always snapping a bra strap at critical moments.

In *Loving and Dead* we find a story which concerns the terms of a will. In order to inherit part of the Randolph Ebhart fortune, the family members must spend seventy-two hours at the dead man's estate. Mavis is hired to play the role of Clare Ebhart, the eldest son's latest wife. Ebhart's two previous wives had died under suspicious circumstances. Mavis finds the kinky maid, Edwina, murdered in the cellar where Randolph Ebhart kept his whips and chains. The highlight of the book is the scene in which Homicide Lieutenant Frome tries to interrogate Mavis and ends up almost losing his mind as Mavis baffles him with her own special brand of lunacy.

Rafael Vega returns in *None But the Lethal Heart* (1959). Vega is acting as a bodyguard for the president of Mexico's son, Arturo. Vega shoots a man he thinks is an assassin but in actuality is wealthy financier, Jonathan B. Stern. Now he wants Mavis to help him dump the body.

Carter Brown makes the most of the farce of driving around southern California with a body in the trunk of a car, looking for likely spots to drop it off. Mavis is at her nutty best in these kinds of scenes.

Anthony Boucher provided the inspiration for *Lament for a Lousy Lover* (1960) ". . . and one wonders if he (Lt. Al Wheeler) and Mavis will end up in the same book," wrote Boucher in his *New York Times* column on August 30, 1959. Brown obliged Boucher's musing with a double murder mystery. Mavis is hired by a TV producer named Bliss to keep one of his stars from disrupting the filming of the TV western. When the star and co-star are murdered, Wheeler arrives to investigate. He and Mavis get off to a shaky start but finish the book in a predictably erotic position.

The Bump and Grind Murders (1964) reestablishes the partnership of Mavis and Johnny Rio when they're hired to bodyguard a stripper named "Irma der Bosen." Of course, Mavis gets to go undercover as a stripper, "Mavis der Zirkus."

What the success of the Mavis Seidlitz books, as well as the entire Carter Brown oeuvre, owed to the eye-catching paperback cover art work of Robert McGinnis is incalculable. When McGinnis became the regular cover illustrator for all Carter Brown books in the sixties, it gave the series a unique style that helped sell millions of copies. The covers McGinnis created for *Seidlitz and the Super-Spy* (1967) (where Mavis meets a James Bond clone and the blend of spy novel derring-do and Mavis's lunacy gives satisfactory results) and *Murder Is So Nostalgic!* (1972) are among the best covers in the entire Carter Brown series.

Other books in the series are *Tomorrow Is Murder* (1960), which is important in that Mavis goes solo in this one and the final title: *And the Undead Sing* (1974) is one of the wackiest. Mavis gets "girlnapped," escapes, gets drugged, has a black widow spider tattooed to her derriere, is tossed into a brothel, is chased by a zombie, and ends up getting rescued by her partner, Johnny Rio. The series ends with a bang.

A Carter Brown Mavis Seidlitz Checklist:

Honey, Here's Your Hearse! Sydney, Horwitz, 1955.

A Bullet for My Baby. Sydney, Horwitz, 1955.

Good Morning, Mavis. Sydney, Horwitz, 1957.

Murder Wears a Mantilla. Sydney, Horwitz, 1957; New York: New American Library, 1962.

The Loving and the Dead. Sydney, Horwitz, 1959; New York: New American Library, 1959.

None But the Lethal Heart. Sydney, Horwitz, 1959; New York: New American Library, 1959.

Tomorrow is Murder. Sydney, Horwitz, 1960; New York: New American Library, 1960.

Lament for a Lousy Lover. New York: New American Library, 1960.

The Bump and Grind Murders. New York: New American Library, 1964.

Seidlitz and the Super-Spy. Sydney, Horwitz, 1967; New York: New American Library, 1967.

Murder Is So Nostalgic. New York: New American Library, 1972.

And the Undead Sing. New York: New American Library, 1972.

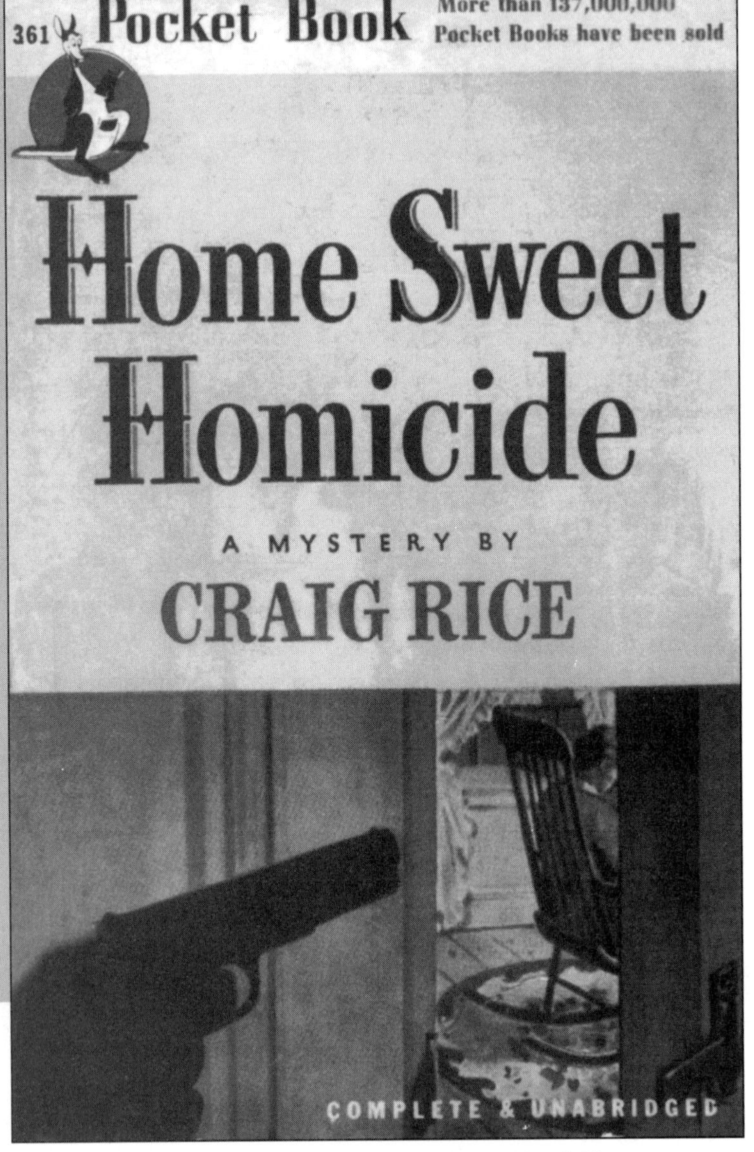

Home Sweet Homicide by Craig Rice

Leave Them Laughing:

The Mysteries of Craig Rice

Jeffrey Marks

Timing is everything in comedy, and humorous hard-boiled writer Craig Rice had the gift. She bounded into the mystery genre between the Great Depression and World War II with the unique ability to lighten America's fears. The culmination of her success came after twelve novels when, in 1946, Time *magazine put her on its cover. She was the first mystery writer to be so honored and one of the few women ever featured.*

NOTHING IN THE UPBRINGING of little Georgiana Craig suggested such future greatness. She was born in Chicago during 1908 to a socialite mother and a painter father, who promptly left their daughter with elderly relatives to return to Europe. The half-sister and her husband, Nan and Elton Rice, adopted the girl after a number of years, and Georgiana grew up in northern Washington State. Struggling through several artistic endeavors after high school, she took a job in journalism. She excelled at writing in a fast-paced environment and quickly moved up at a newspaper to cover the crime beat.

She returned to Chicago and married twice, producing three children before turning to novels. Rice's timing couldn't have been better. Her first novel, *8 Faces at 3* (New York: Simon & Schuster), appeared on the scene in 1939, the same year as Chandler's first Philip Marlowe novel. The book made her a household name and she maintained a grueling pace to keep her audience amused during the war years. Rice suffered from bipolar disorder; she sometimes spent days on end at the typewriter and wrote as many as four full-length novels in a year at her peak. Even President Roosevelt wrote her a fan letter, thanking Rice for easing his troubles after Pearl Harbor.

The subgenre of "mean streets" belonged to the men in the 1940s. Rice melded screwball comedy into the hard-boiled milieu to present a

Chicago where corpses move at will and police serve as straight men. She developed the trio of John J. Malone, a Chicago lawyer with a penchant for booze and blondes, and his friends Jake and Helene Justus, who always involved Malone in their troubles. Rice's cast was rounded out by Joe the Angel, who owned the City Hall bar where many chapters took place, and Captain Daniel von Flanagan, the put-upon police officer. Decades before the advent of the contemporary female private eye, Rice crafted novels that portrayed women as strong, capable characters. Many of her books feature women accused of murder, most of whom play an active role in obtaining their freedom.

In a time where male detectives kept women as trophies, Rice let her female protagonist have her own adventures. Helene Brand Justus drank the lawyers under the table, yet traveled in upper-crust Lake Shore Drive social circles. Helene was the fearless driver who charmed the police with her cool, icy beauty and helped innocent clients escape the law. Reviewers often compared Rice to Helene when the character matched Craig's birth mother better; the real similarities were between Rice and Jake Justus, the hard-drinking jack of all trades who scraped by on his luck and brains.

Rice attempted to create other series characters, but none proved as endearing or enduring as the Chicago threesome. She wrote the first mystery for actor George Sanders and was rumored to have written the Gypsy Rose Lee mysteries. Under her own name, she introduced a detective team of Bingo Riggs and Handsome Kusak, migrant photographers; however, the series never caught on, and Rice ended it after three books.

Under the pen name of Michael Venning, Rice wrote novels of psychological suspense that featured Melville Fairr, a detective whose talents rested in his ability to get through life unnoticed. Rice was once asked by *Who's Who* for a life story of Venning and photos of the author. She dressed in the clothes of Larry Lipton, her husband at the time, and sent in the pictures. They were subsequently published by *Who's Who.*

Rice's most successful non-series work was the very domestic *Home Sweet Homicide.* The story fictionalized Rice's home life with the story of a murder next door to three precocious children and a struggling mystery-writing mother. The book sanitized many of the less seemly details of Rice's life, but the novel was a best-seller and eventually a movie starring Randolph Scott. Magazines in 1945, though, found the children to be a bit too realistic and refused to publish a condensed version of the book in their pages.

Not only did Rice garner acclaim for herself, she took the time to help other mystery writers. Along with Anthony Boucher and Ned Guyman, she was the driving force in establishing Mystery Writers of America and its southern California chapter. When Fred Dannay started *Ellery Queen's Mystery Magazine,* Rice took the time from her schedule to pen stories for the vital first few issues of the magazine.

Sadly, the popularity that had been seven years in the making plummeted after 1946. Lipton squandered her money and filed for divorce, leaving her with a huge debt to the IRS. In the decade following her appearance on the cover of *Time,*

Rice completed only one Malone novel and a book of her collected true crime stories, most originally printed in newspapers. She was fired repeatedly from reporting jobs for her penchant to take up the cause of the accused and for excessive drinking. In a field where hard-drinking men were considered the norm, women who acted like their male peers could not be forgiven.

The years of alcoholism led to a stay in a sanitarium and brushes with the law. Her fifth marriage to the unemployed Paul Bishop, whom she met in the sanitarium, ended with severe beatings that left her with a permanent limp. Visiting New York while trying to revive her career, she fell twenty feet to land on a concrete slab in a freak hotel accident. Several broken bones put her in a hospital for months. Her sole output at the time consisted of short stories that she sold to keep herself in spending money.

She collaborated with Stuart Palmer and his character Hildegarde Withers to create one of the first cross-series detective teams in mystery. The series of Malone and Withers won acclaim from readers and were posthumously published as a collection. Even Palmer's help with the money from the stories and their film rights didn't break the freefall, and Rice died in 1957 after a household accident. A brief but brilliant career had come to a tragic end, but the unique magic of Craig Rice lives on in her work.

A Craig Rice Bibliography

John J. Malone and the Justuses

Eight Faces at Three (Simon & Schuster, 1939)

The Corpse Steps Out (Simon & Schuster, 1940)

The Wrong Murder (Simon & Schuster, 1940)

The Right Murder (Simon & Schuster, 1941)

Trial by Fury (Simon & Schuster, 1941)

The Big Midget Murders (Simon & Schuster, 1943)

Having Wonderful Crime (Simon & Schuster, 1945)

The Lucky Stiff (Simon & Schuster, 1945)

The Fourth Postman (Simon & Schuster, 1948)

My Kingdom for a Hearse (Simon & Schuster, 1957)

Knocked for a Loop (Simon & Schuster, 1957)

But the Doctor Died (Pyramid, 1967)

SHORT STORIES

The Name is Malone (Pyramid, 1958)

People vs. *Withers and Malone,* with Stuart Palmer (Simon & Schuster, 1963)

Once Upon a Time and Other Stories, with Stuart Palmer (Gold Penny Press, 1981)

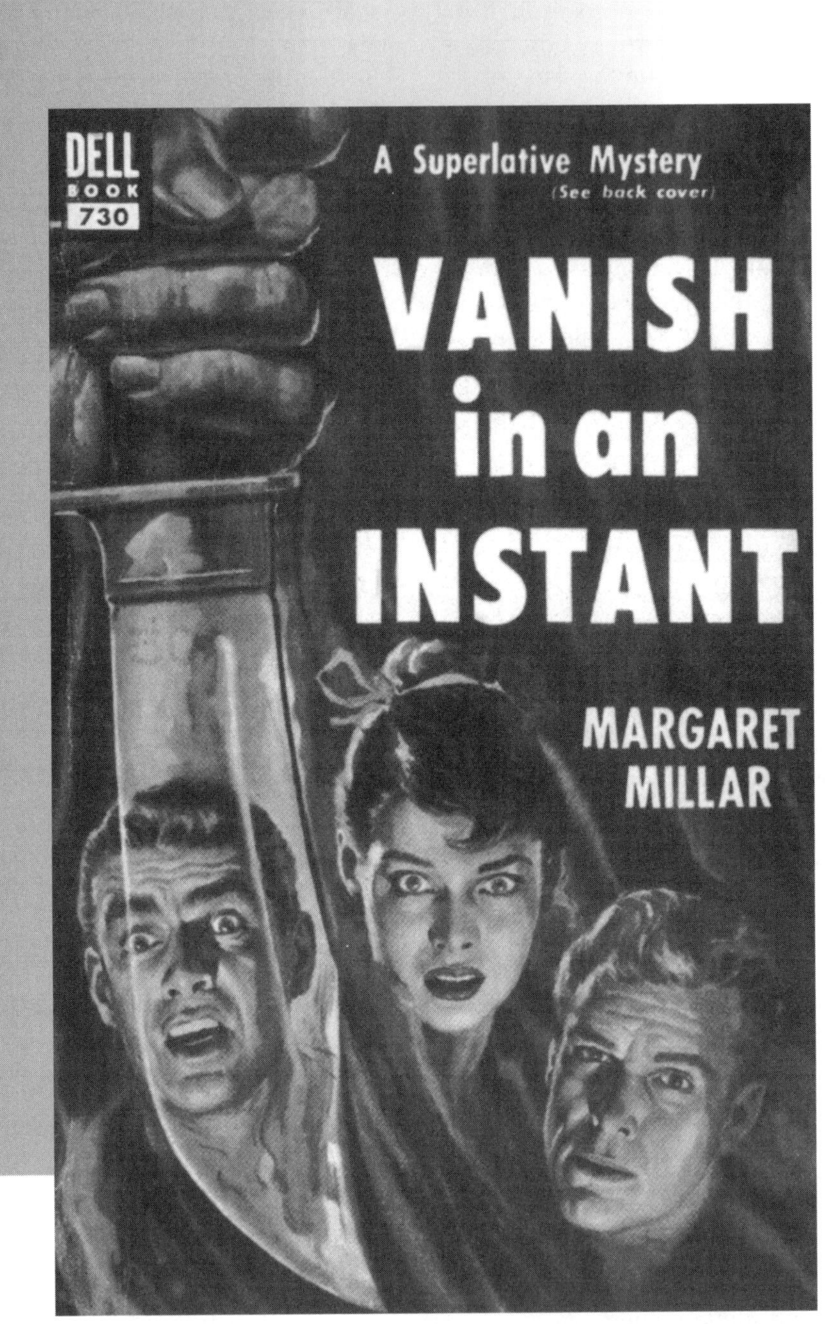

Vanish in an Instant by Margaret Millar

Some Women We Should Be Reading

Ed Gorman

The other day, I got a letter from a woman who reads my novels asking which mystery writers I preferred.
I'm sure my response surprised her.

WHILE I'M ASSOCIATED WITH hard-boiled fiction, I certainly don't limit my reading to that particular sub-genre, nor to mystery fiction itself. I remember reading the advice F. Scott Fitzgerald gave his daughter—the better the material you read, the better the material you will write. The wise writer, I think, reads literature as well as popular fiction.

The wise *mystery* writer, I think, reads in most if not all the sub-categories.

Over forty years of reading mysteries, I've developed a core library of suspense material. Here are just a few of the names in that core, writers too quickly forgotten I'm afraid, but writers who deserve our attention.

Margaret Millar:

Somewhere there's a John D. MacDonald quote saying that there are only two crime writers who could be accused of writing real literature, Simenon and Margaret Millar. These days, I'd add Ruth Rendell. But John D. was certainly correct about Margaret Millar. For me, *How Like an Angel* is not only her best book, but the best mystery novel ever written. I got to know Maggie (as she preferred to be called) over the phone in the last three years of her life, and I frequently asked her questions about "Angel" and how she could be so prescient—in 1961, she saw coming the revolution that hit our society in the latter part of the decade. She said that all she'd done was spend a little time on California college campuses; it was in the air. "Angel" sets out some writerly problems that only a true virtuoso could hope to master, yet master them she did. She wrote a number of books almost as good as "Angel"—*An Air that Kills, The Listening Walls, A Stranger in My Grave,* and one of the most fetching novels I've ever read, the serio-comic *The Murder of Miranda,* which deals with a woman's loss of physical beauty. For me, Millar remains the supreme stylist of the suspense field. She was a better plotter than Christie

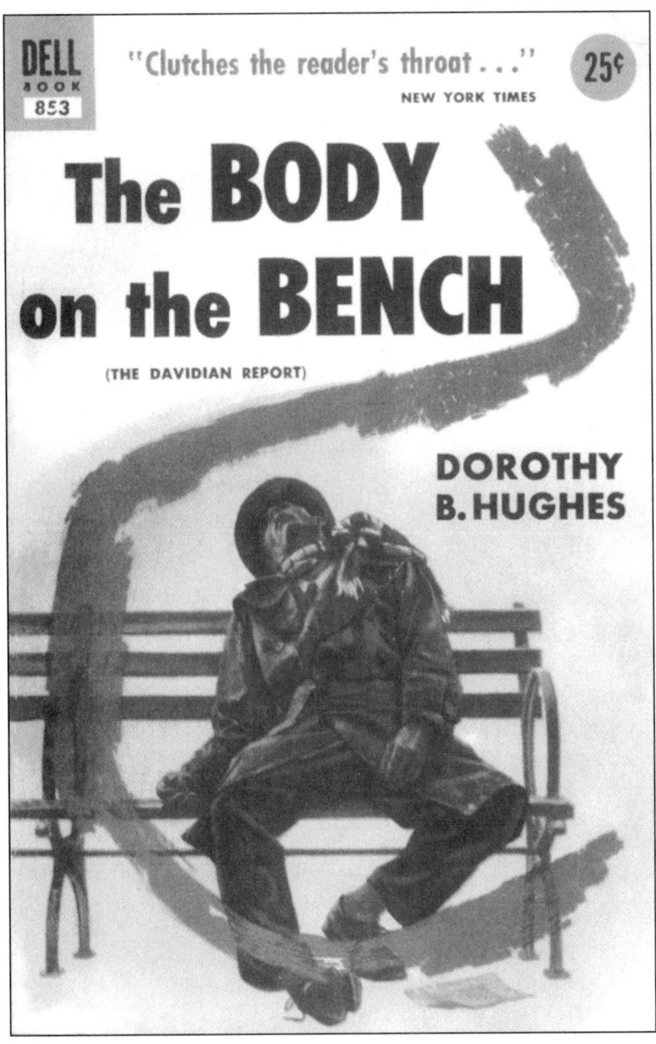

The Body on the Bench by Dorothy B. Hughes

ever was, and a far far better writer. This is heresy, but when she was at her best, she was an even better writer than her husband Ross MacDonald, though the one time I subtly suggested this to her she got very angry, and told me I was being "foolish."

Dorothy B. Hughes:

Dorothy was somebody else I knew slightly. One day when I called and asked how she was, she said that she'd fallen the night before and banged her head on the floor. When she told her neighbors about this, they were worried about her. "Oh, hell, people make such a fuss about everything these days," she told me. Dorothy's novels were just as tough-minded as she was. Dorothy was lucky enough to have three of her books become excellent films—*The Fallen Sparrow, Ride the Pink Horse,* and *In a Lonely Place.* The last one is probably Bogart's best film, and a powerful piece of work. Dorothy's novels were typically about desperate people in deep trouble. She was a lot more skeptical about the world than her hard-boiled counterparts, and she was as stylish a wordsmith as anybody in her generation. Dorothy's people were also one other thing—lonely, always set apart from friends and society, even (or especially) when they seemed to be popular with their peers. *In a Lonely Place* is especially harrowing in this regard. The protagonist Dix is so isolated that he is incapable of reaching out to anybody. Dorothy's best work always reminded me of Chandler—they were both particularly good at setting mood and describing physical realities, but in at least one regard, Dorothy was Chandler's superior. She didn't cop to middle-aged romanticism and sentimentality to avoid looking at the world as it truly is. She reported back just what she saw in the human wars. She didn't gussy up a moment of it.

Charlotte Armstrong:

In a very astute piece on Armstrong, Carol Cleveland noted that "[Armstrong] had a distaste for looking at abnormal psychology in as much depth as Margaret Millar or Patricia Highsmith." What fascinated

Armstrong was the everyday-gone-wrong. She had a very practical, almost chilling attitude toward life, one that was even a bit Darwinian at times. She was on the side of plucky, bright, intelligent people, and eschewed the darker and more self-absorbed folks so in vogue in the fifties and sixties. While her best books are probably *A Dram of Poison, The Turret Room,* and *The Balloon Man,* I've always been partial to *The Unsuspected* and *Mischief,* the former because it's a great example of how to build cat-and-mouse suspense, the latter because, for once, Armstrong did deal with the darker side, and did so with great skill. *Mischief* became *Don't Bother to Knock,* the film in which Marilyn Monroe, as the pitifully disturbed babysitter only recently released from a psychiatric hospital, gives her most compelling and persuasive performance. For all that she disliked the dark side, when Armstrong went there, she went willingly and well. Her story, "The Enemy," about a paranoid teenager, is as nasty and disturbing as anything Patricia Highsmith ever wrote.

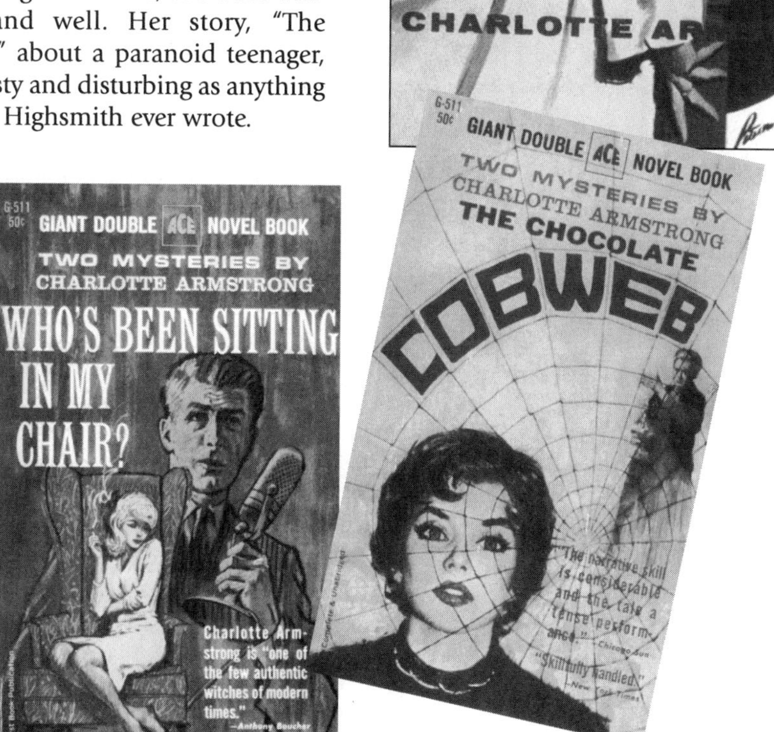

A Dram of Poison, Who's Been Sitting in My Chair? and ***The Chocolate Cobweb*** by Charlotte Armstrong

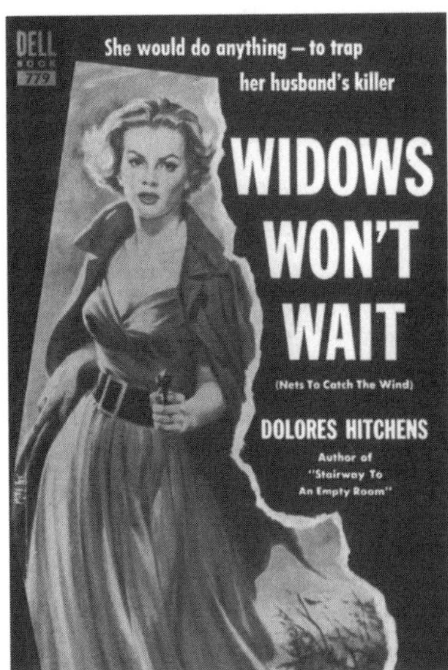

DELL
She would do anything — to trap her husband's killer
WIDOWS WON'T WAIT
(Nets To Catch The Wind)
DOLORES HITCHENS
Author of "Stairway To An Empty Room"

Widows Won't Wait and ***The Abductor*** by Dolores Hitchens

Dolores Hitchens:

When you look up Dolores Hitchens in *The St. James Guide to Crime & Mystery Writers,* you see a long list of utterly forgettable traditional whodunits. From *The Clue in the Clay* (1938) to *Gallows for the Groom* (1947), none of the titles promise much. But what is truly remarkable about the entry by one Fred Dueren is that he makes no distinction between her early and rather formulaic work, and the books she produced in the fifties and sixties. To quote Bill Pronzini: "(Dolores Hitchens's) *Sleep with Slander* is the best private eye novel with a male protagonist written by a woman—and one of the best written by anybody." *Slander* is an astonishingly good novel—rich in character, milieu, and a grasp of the working class rarely seen in crime fiction. Its theme was so shocking to readers of 1961 that a few libraries took it off their shelves. Dueren also overlooks such lesser but still very strong books as *Sleep with Strangers, The Watcher,* and *Footsteps in the Night,* novels that very effectively convey the middle-class realities of the sixties and early seventies. Hitchens had a good ear and a dead-on eye for the various charades played by the human animals. She also wrote a series of railroad mysteries with her husband Bert, *F.O.B. Murder* and *The Man Who Followed Women* being especially strong traditional mysteries. The latter has three of the best opening paragraphs I've ever read:

"By the time the misty, foggy nights of that particular April rolled around, Mr. Howery had been following women for almost a year.

"In the way of most innocent amusements which become compulsions, his had begun idly, almost whimsically. Months ago he had stepped out of a movie into the dark of a night not quite summer, warm with the smell of the city and with some faraway memory-teasers blown on the wind, a hint of clipped hayfields and stubby dusty hills, and out at the edge of the glow splattered by the theater signs he had seen the young woman in the red coat, dropping the candy wrapper in the gutter, and it had occurred to him to wonder where she was going.

"Like that."

Dolores Hitchens coulda been a contender.

Elisabeth Sanxay Holding:

Not many writers get a blurb like this from Raymond Chandler: "For my money she's the top suspense writer of them all. Her characters are wonderful, and she has a sort of inner calm which I find very attractive." Holding was a master plotter and a master stylist. In some ways, she reminds me of Cornell Woolrich. There's a great deal of spiritual turmoil in all of her characters, especially the middle-aged ones who are frequently her protagonists. They feel suffocated by their weakness to cope adequately with their problems, and as terrified of the pasts as they are of their futures. She also reminds me of Woolrich because of her ability to set and sustain mood. In her best books—*The Blank Wall, Net of Cobwebs,* and *The Innocent Miss Duff*—she demonstrates the ability to refine the melodramatics of Christie without in any way lessening the impact of all the twists and turns. Her upper-class people are really people, not just types, and this makes even the most unsympathetic of them interesting. Chandler also commented on the "narcotic" quality of Holding's prose, and he was dead-on here. There is a hothouse quality to all her books, an oppressive quality lurking between the lines, that makes even the romantic moonlight just a bit sinister.

These women should be readily in print. I realize that given today's publishing realities—no backlist titles unless you're a best-seller—this is very unlikely. So it's on to the used bookstores to search out the women and men who've entertained us so much as readers, and taught us so much as writers.

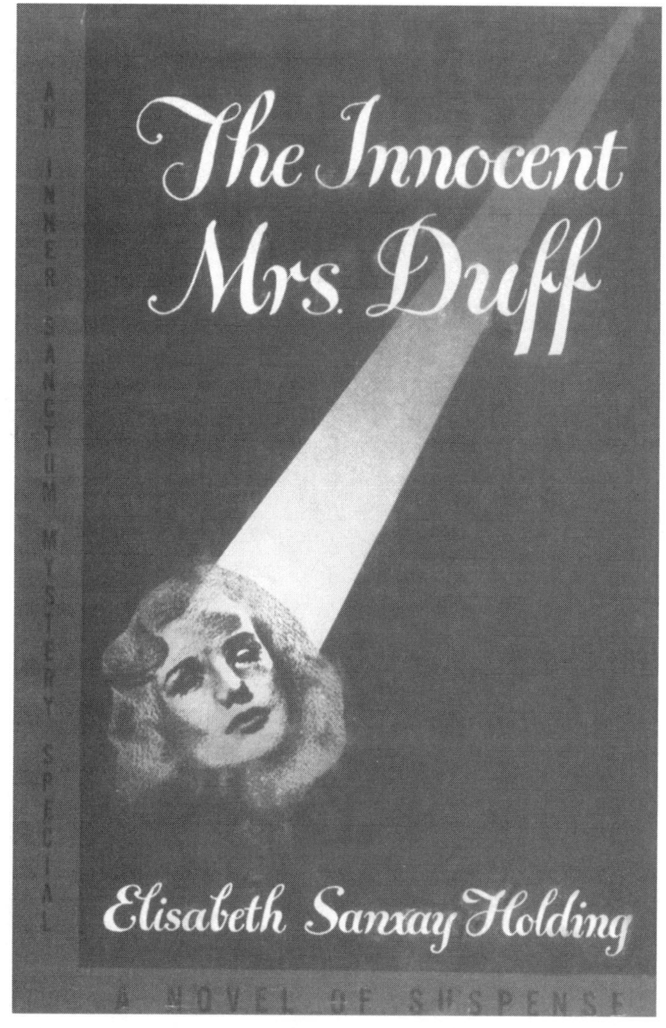

The Innocent Mrs. Duff by Elizabeth Sanxay Holding

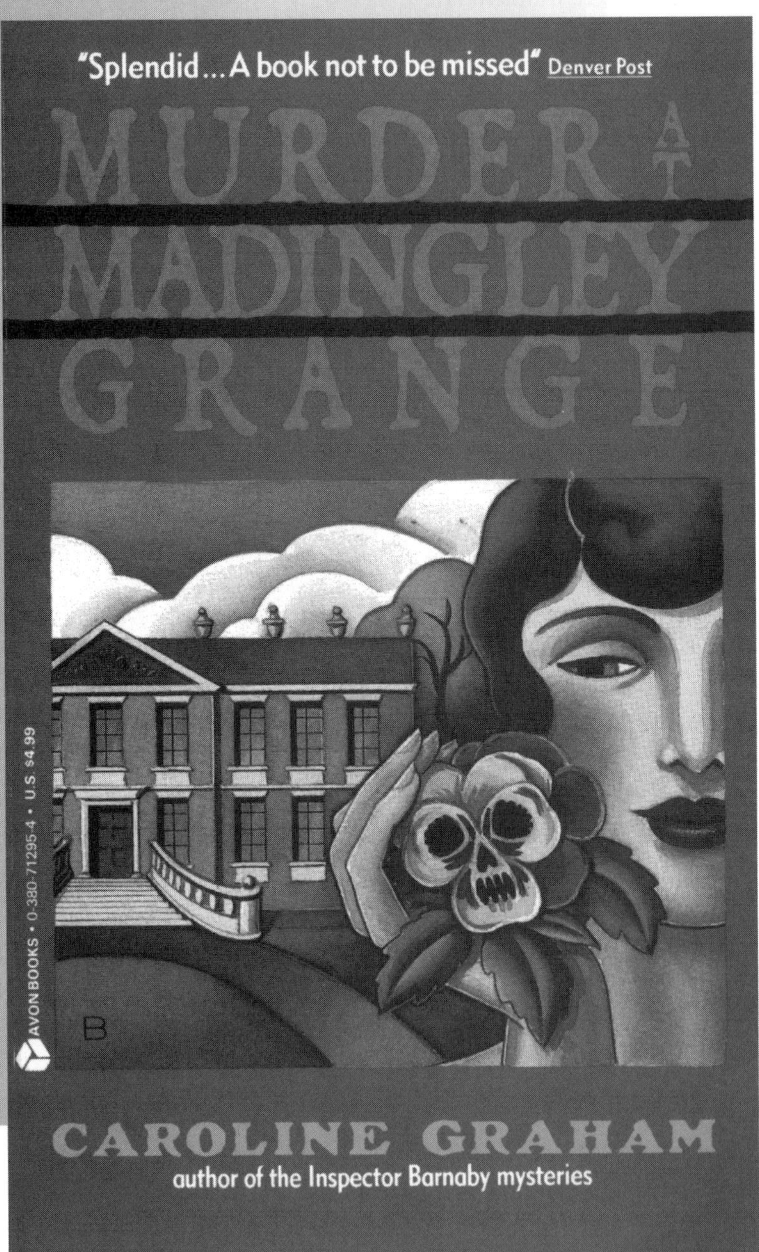

Murder at Madingley Grange by Caroline Graham

Beyond Christie and Kinsey:

The Twelve Best Women Mystery Writers You Never Heard Of

Thomas Leitch

All right, you've already rounded up the usual suspects. You've read every Agatha Christie novel three times, crying each time at the end of Curtain, and you're hot on the trail of Kinsey Millhone's trek from A to Z.

YOU'VE FOLLOWED LORD PETER and Harriet from their first meeting in Holloway Prison to the hymeneal altar and gaped with amazement as V.I. peered down every sinkhole in Chicago. You've tracked Georgette Heyer and Christianna Brand and Craig Rice through the mists of history; you're first in line whenever a new Mary Higgins Clark or Lilian Jackson Braun or Patricia Cornwell hits the best-seller lists; and you've been part of the ride when newer writers like Minette Walters and Laurie R. King and Mary Willis Walker and Nevada Barr and Janet Evanovich have suddenly burst into the stratosphere. Each ad and each interview you see tells you you're reading all the right people, since the same names keep popping up everywhere you look. But your library and your bookstore are chock-full of mysteries you don't know anything about. Where do you go from here?

Don't think for a minute that because you've read the headliners you've covered the field. The publicists who work for best-selling authors and their presses lose sleep every night thinking of new ways to keep the same two dozen names before you wherever you turn, so it's not surprising if they succeed. But your friends—and that includes booksellers and librarians—know the field is much richer than its classics and superstars. If they know anything about your tastes (British or

American? puzzle or thriller? Jane Haddam's festive holiday celebrations or Sharyn McCrumb's shivery evocations of history? Amanda Cross's civilized academics or Ruth Rendell's doomed antiheroes? Linda Barnes's rain-slick city streets or Joy Fielding's deceptively smiling suburbs?), they'll be happy to lead you from familiar faces to new pleasures, since nothing else gives mystery fans the thrill of introducing their friends to some new or underappreciated author or reintroducing a forgotten face from the past. In the spirit of that camaraderie, here are a dozen suggestions, ranging from the virtually unknown to the too-little-known, to help you get your RDA of R.I.P.:

—1—

Though she's been toiling in Australia since the 1960s, some of **Patricia Carlon's** best books have been slow to make the trip to the U.S. Two vintage titles finally burst into American editions in 1996. *The Souvenir* (originally published in the U.K. in 1970), which reviews the fatal consequences of two teenage girls' hitchhiking trip across Australia, is a model of how baffling a writer can make a whodunit using the bare minimum of characters. *The Whispering Wall* (1969) displays an equally powerful mastery of creeping menace in its presentation of a paralytic witness to a murderous plan she can do nothing to stop—a plan whose agents soon realize that she's on to them. Both novels offer stellar evidence of just how much room for evil there is in the most civilized formulas.

—2—

Sarah Dunant started with a fast, nasty tale of cocaine smuggling and vengeance (*Snowstorm in a Hot Climate,* 1988) before settling down with British shamus Hannah Wolfe—if "settling down" is really a phrase you'd want to use for Hannah, whose astringent, self-lacerating wit and antiauthoritarian attitude makes her one of the detectives you'd least want to live with, and one of the crew you're most grateful to be able to visit in the pages of *Birth Marks* (1992), *Fatlands* (1994), and *Under My Skin* (1995).

—3—

Imagine P.D. James with a wild and wicked sense of humor, and you'll have an idea of the poisoned bonbons **Caroline Graham** has served up in the four mysteries she's set

Chief Inspector Tom Burnaby. Titles like *The Killings at Badger Drift* (1988) and *Murder at Madingley Grange* (1991) hint at Graham's fondness for the traditional British closed-circle whodunit, but don't begin to suggest the zany behavior her suspects are capable of. In her most recent mysteries, *Death in Disguise* (1993) and *Written in Blood* (1995), Graham uses the mechanics of farce to deepen conflict and character with an audacity that would make Joe Orton proud.

—4—

Donna Leon began her career sedately enough with *Death at La Fenice* (1992), a mystery at Venice's Teatro La Fenice squarely in the upscale domestic tradition of Agatha Christie and Ngaio Marsh. Since then, however, she's gradually broadened her social canvas to include the cover-up of an American serviceman's murder (*Death in a Strange Country,* 1993), the political and financial shenanigans behind the killing of a prominent banker found dead in a red dress and high heels (*Dressed for Death,* 1994), and the big-city corruption behind the murders in *Death and Judgment* (1995) and *Acqua Alta* (1996). Her police detective Guido Brunetti's affectionately detailed home life will make you yearn to live in Venice instead of just visiting.

—5—

Not all of **Patricia McGerr's** books are memorable, but two of them are unlike anything you've ever read, if only for the inspired changes McGerr rings on the question of whodunit. In McGerr's masterpiece, *Pick Your Victim* (1946), a torn newspaper clipping makes the murderer obvious from the beginning; the challenge is to use the slender clues to identify his victim. McGerr is equally inventive, if not quite as successful, in *Catch Me If You Can* (1946), in which a woman who has killed her husband tries to figure out which of the other characters is the detective on her trail. Either novel is a great antidote to the detective-story formula that ends up showing you just how flexible that formula can be.

—6—

If **Sena Jeter Naslund** had never written anything but *Sherlock in Love* (1993), she would still have the distinction of having produced the finest Sherlockian pastiche of all—a novel that not only resurrects Holmes and sets him an unusually

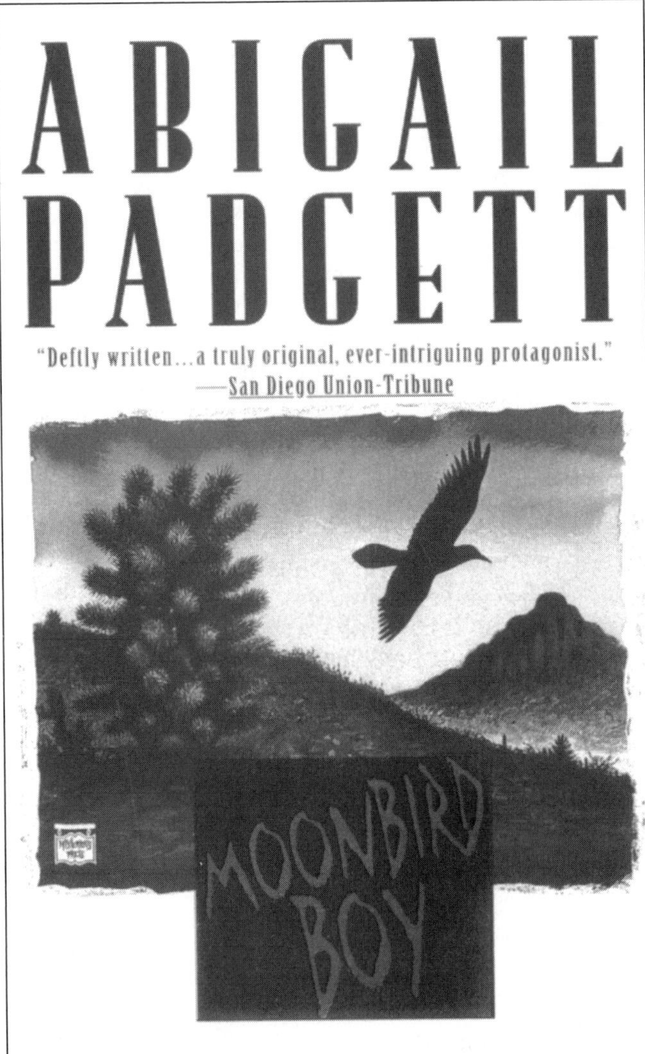

Moonbird Boy by Abigail Padgett

clever problem to solve, but puts the whole Holmesian myth to startling new uses, revealing the problems of love and power at its heart. More than just a nostalgic return to Baker Street, this is a bold reimagining of what it means to be Sherlock Holmes.

—7—

Bo Bradley, the San Diego social worker whose work with children **Abigail Padgett** has chronicled, is the most original new detective to appear in many years—not because of her profession, though it does give her a unique insight into the seamier side of families and the government agencies that try to rescue them from themselves, but because of her manic-depression, which makes her perspective painfully, even pathologically, empathetic. Compared to Bo in *Child of Silence* (1992), *Strawgirl* (1994), *Turtle Baby* (1995), *Moonbird Boy* (1996), and *The Dollmaker's Daughters* (1997), any other detectives who tell you they really feel their clients' pain are just pulling your leg.

—8—

Though they haven't got the publicity of Lindsey Davis' stories about Roman gumshoe Marcus Didius Falco, **Lynda S. Robinson's** Egyptian tale. which trace intrigues at the heart of an even older civilization, are in their way even more fascinating. In her Lord Meren's striking debut (*Murder in the Place of Anubis,* 1994), Robinson manages to bring out a very modern kind of political corruption behind the crime while still keeping the techniques of detection appropriately primitive and maintaining a welcome decorum of manners and language. *Murder at the God's Gate* (1995) is scarcely less impressive, and *Murder at the Feast of Rejoicing* (1996) is a tour de force—a wholesale transposition of the English country-house murder to the cradle of civilization. In her latest, *Eater of Souls* (1997), Robinson again strikes out in a new direction, beginning a trilogy in which Lord Meren struggles to solve the murder of Queen Nefertiti.

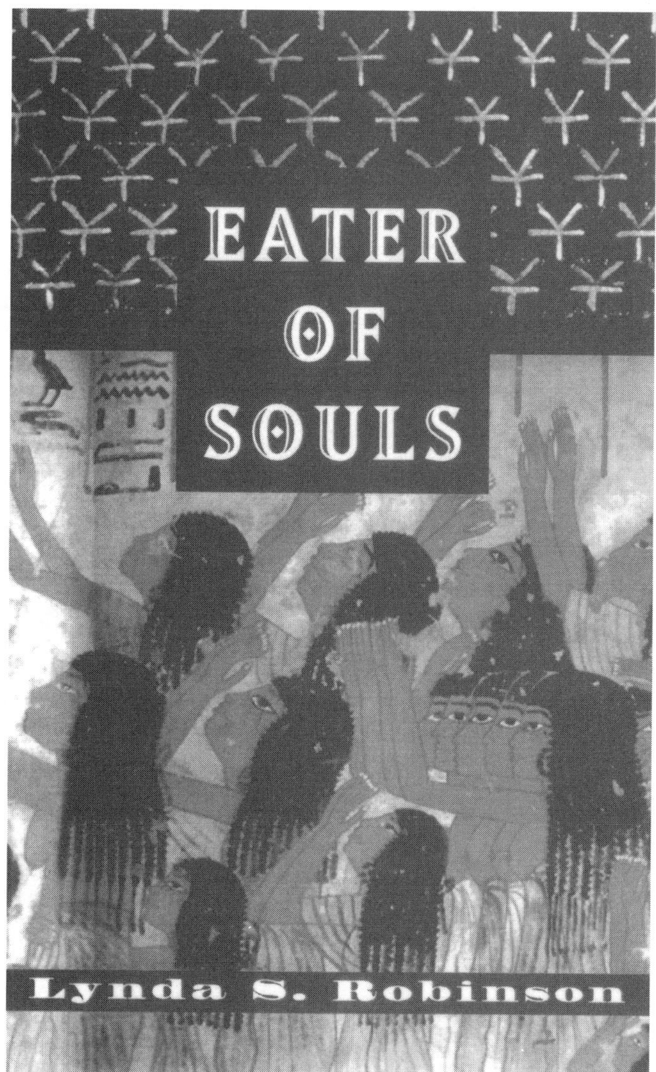

Eater of Souls by Lynda S. Robinson

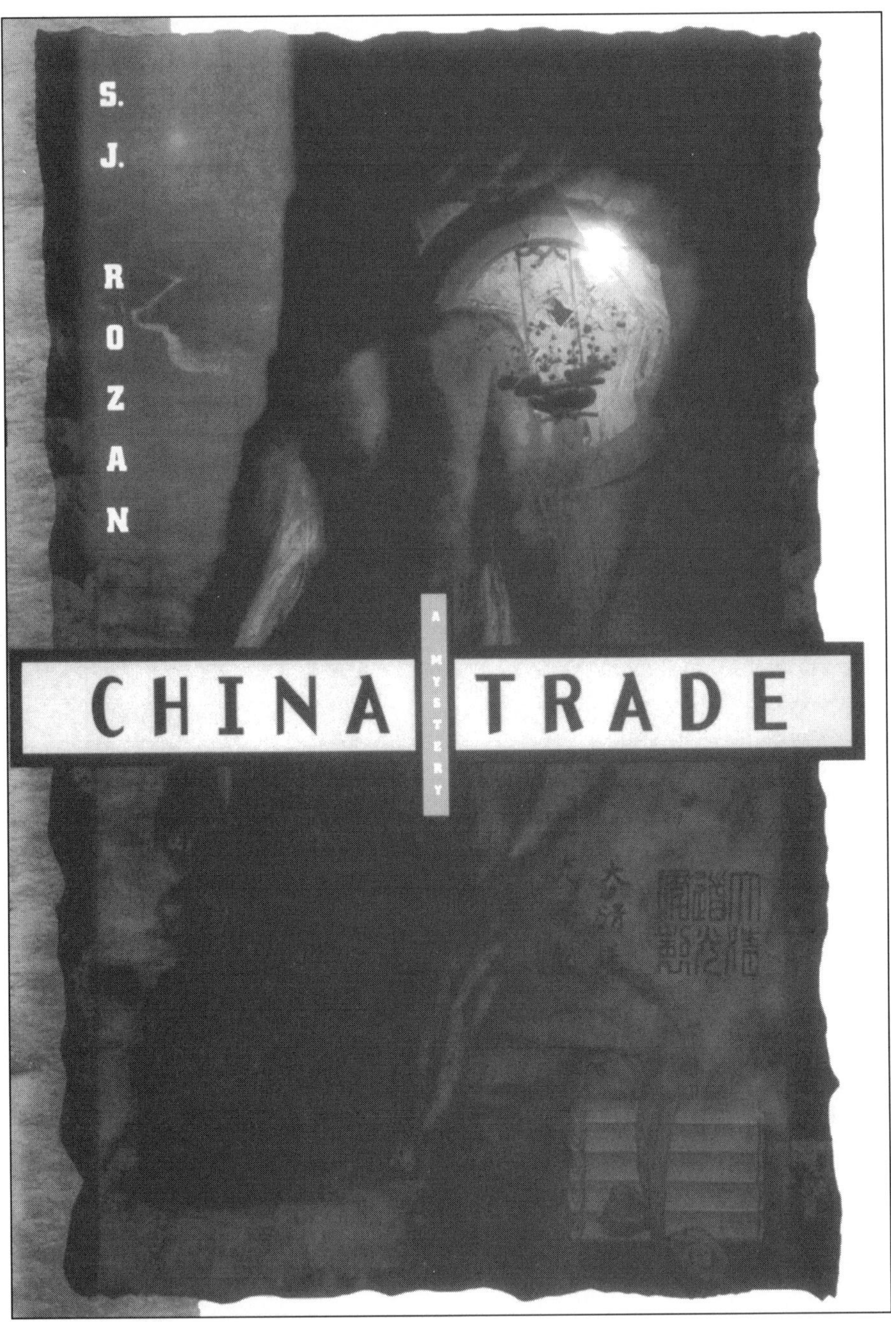

China Trade by S.J. Rozan

—9—

Flashforward a few millennia to the British historicals of **Kate Ross.** Even if Ross's hero, Julian Kestrel, is a Regency rake a little too good to be true—has anyone who took this much care over his dress ever had such a razor-sharp mind and such a heart of gold?—the spirited mysteries his author sets him are vintage stuff, and his Cockney valet and amanuensis, the perpetually bemused Dipper, is a suitably racy and resourceful guide. Ross's first novel, *Cut to the Quick* (1993), which introduces Kestrel to a family knee-deep in motives for killing an inconvenient young woman, is still her best, but fans(and there will be many—will want to continue on to *A Broken Vessel* (1994) and *Whom the Gods Love* (1995).

—10—

Legal novels, like real-life courtroom proceedings, tend to drag interminably, unless their author is **Carolyn Wheat.** Whether it's Wheat, herself an attorney, or her heroine, Brooklyn lawyer Cass Jameson, who pulls off the miraculous stunt of wrapping up each of Cass's complex legal yarns in less than 250 pages, the stories never stint on the kinds of devious twists you may have thought only came wrapped in an extra pound of pages. The best of Wheat's four novels since her debut (*Dead Man's Thoughts,* 1983) is *Fresh Kills* (1995), which offers a series of dizzying spins on an on-again-off-again adoption. But even better news may be the appearance of her latest, *Mean Streak* (1996)—this time showing Cass defending her mob-defending ex-lover on a murder charge—which holds out the hope that Wheat may be stepping up the pace of her all-too-meager output.

—11—

Since winning as Edgar for her very first novel, *The Suspect* (1985), **L.R. Wright** has gone on to create a series of novels that combine several unlikely strengths: psychological penetration, acerbic humor, unpredictable (often zany) plot twists, resonant landscapes of Vancouver and its environs, and a shrewd, likable detective, Sgt. Karl Alberg of the Royal Canadian Mounted Police. In *Fall from Grace* (1992), Wright balances Alberg's domestic romance with librarian Cassandra Mitchell with a disturbing portrait of the magnetic charmer Bobby Ransome; *Mother Love* (1995), equally warm in its handling of Alberg, turns its gimlet eye on one of those harrowingly dysfunctional families echoed again in her latest, *Strangers Among Us* (1996). Wright holds your hand so reassuringly that she can have you neck-deep in vipers before you know it.

—12—

Fans of Julian Symons and Ruth Rendell have never raised **Margaret Yorke** to the same level of sales and public recognition, maybe because so many of Yorke's patient, deadpan studies of middle-class British angst stick to a single pattern so closely. But what a grand pattern it is, and how cunningly Yorke spins it out! After publishing four novels about the amateur Oxford detective Patrick Grant, Yorke turned to the psychopathology of everyday life in *No Medals for the Major* (1974) and has been uncovering frightful secrets in this little patch of land ever since. Among Yorke's three dozen novels, one particularly good example of her quiet, deadly power—*Almost the Truth* (1995), about a well-meaning but disconnected father's attempt to avenge his daughter's rape—shows that Yorke's obviously studied her remorseless weaving at the foot of Madame Defarge, or the three Fates.

If your friends have put you on to these writers already, take the plunge into the work of some equally talented newcomers. Try Jo Bannister's agonized cops-and-arsonists procedural, *A Taste for Burning* (1995), or S.J. Rozan's she-said-he-said series about Chinatown shamus Lydia Chin (*China Trade,* 1994) and her partner Bill Smith (*Concourse,* 1995), or J.M. Redman's slam-bang adventures of lesbian New Orleans private eye Micky Knight (*The Intersection of Law and*

Desiree, 1995), or Gini Hartzmark's fast, funny take on corporate litigation-cum-homicide (*Bitter Business,* 1995), or Kate Clark Flora's psychological slugfest *Death in a Funhouse Mirror* (1995), or Lynn S. Hightower's war of nerves between a female cop and a female psycho (*Flashpoint,* 1995).

Or looking to the past instead of the future, beat a retreat to your local library to dig up some neglected classics by a pair of former MWA luminaries. Margaret Millar is not exactly unknown—after all MWA named her a Grand Master in 1983—but her work is often overshadowed by the very different novels of her husband, Kenneth Millar, aka Ross MacDonald. Millar pioneered the tale of suburban menace taken to such different directions by Marilyn Wallace and Patricia MacDonald. In Millar's hands, slightly off-kilter details are the key to monstrous horrors under the California sun, often leading to dazzling surprises at the very end. Try *Beast in View* (1955), *An Air That Kills* (1957), *A Stranger in My Grave* (1960), *The Fiend* (1964), and *Beyond This Point Are Monsters* (1970). Millar's spell is equally potent in the creepy short story, "The People Across the Canyon" (1962).

Like Millar, former MWA president Helen McCloy is less well-known than her husband, David Dresser, alias Brett Halliday, and her books, most of them out of print for many years, have never been reprinted as a paperback series, perhaps because her detective, the psychologist Dr. Basil Willing, is too inveterately rational to be very interesting himself. But Willing's cases have all the sparkle he lacks. *Cue for Murder* (1942) is still the best tale of murder on stage ever written; *The One That Got Away* (1945), with its well-drawn Highland landscapes, is remarkably ingenious in its ways of getting you to overlook the obvious; and *Through a Glass Darkly* (1950) actually manages to improve on McCloy's spooky short story about a woman and her fearsome Doppelganger to create an atmosphere of growing terror as a counterpart to Willing's logic. The paranoid wartime fantasy *Do Not Disturb* (1943) still holds up fifty years later, as do two peerless short stories, "Chinoiserie" (1946) and "The Singing Diamonds" (1949)—models of how tightly packed a short story can be. McCloy's evergreen work, like that of her more recent colleagues, is a testament to the joys of the road less traveled.

Mary Higgins Clark *Photo credit: Bernard Vidal*

A Conversation with Mary Higgins Clark

Jan Grape

MARY AND I TRIED to do this interview late last fall and again shortly afterward, but in late November she had marriage plans and soon the Christmas holidays were upon us. Eventually, on a cold rainy raw January day in both New Jersey and Austin we had a long telephone conversation and this is more or less how it went.

JG: Tell me about John. And how's married life?
MHC: He's absolutely great. As one of his friends wrote to his daughter (she was a woman who had worked with him for many years at Merrill-Lynch), "Tell Mary, now she has everything." Isn't that lovely?

JG: That's great. I'm happy for you. Well, shall we start? I read somewhere you wrote poetry as a child, did you try to write stories or books at that age?
MHC: Not at age seven, no. But I was also talking stories. Friends would stay over or I'd stay over with them and I'd say, let's tell scary stories . . . let's turn out the light, just have one candle and tell scary stories. And I was writing plays and skits and I made my brothers perform and I remember once my little brother asking "can't I just once be the star." And I said, "No." And in the garage, we had just a single garage and it was under the house, and I got the old velvet draperies and I had a stage and wrote plays for the neighborhood kids and charged them two cents to watch.

JG: Oh, great.
MHC: So I was always talking, writing . . .

JG: And telling stories. Do you think story-telling was the influence of your Irish background?
MHC: Oh, yes, the Irish are storytellers. It's just part of what goes into their makeup. They never say anything simply . . . they have a lyrical way of speaking and a cadence in their voices, and I'm completely Irish. My mother was born here, but all my grandparents were born in Ireland and my father was, too. So it's that ingrained.

JG: That gift of gab?
MHC: Yes, that gift of gab. Do you know what they say about the

Irishman who has kissed the Blarney Stone? (And I did twice) *He could sell a dead horse to a mounted policeman.*

JG: Who influenced you as a young writer?

MHC: In suspense? Well, I always, always loved to read. To me the best gift at Christmas or my birthday was a book. I really was a voracious reader. And what I read for just curl-up pleasure was always suspense. I started with Judy Bolton and Nancy Drew, then went on to Agatha Christie, Josephine Tey, Ngaio Marsh, and Mingon Eberhart—I loved her writing. Charlotte Armstrong—these were the writers I thoroughly enjoyed.

JG: A what point did you decide to be a writer?

MHC: It's decided for you, Jan. I mean the ones who become professional writers. Obviously you have to have some talent. But besides the talent and the desire, it chooses us, we don't choose it.

JG: Who influences you now? Or who do you read now?

MHC: I'm still eclectic. I think Anne Tyler is one of our finest contemporary writers. I think she's a fabulous writer. I like to read a really broad spectrum of nonfiction as well and I like to reread the classics.

And of course I'm always doing so much reading for what I'm writing. Last year I read books on burial customs for *Moonlight Becomes You.* I read Greco Roman burial customs—*Bury the Past, Down to Earth, The Etiquette of Funerals* from Emily Post and Amy Vanderbilt. *The History of Newport,* I had to read all the histories of Newport because of the setting.

Right now I'm reading maps of Minneapolis, and things that pertain to what I'm working on, like the newspapers because I have scenes where my girl goes to Minneapolis in the federal witness protection plan.

JG: Funny I was going to ask you about researching later but we've segued into it which is fine. I was wondering, when do you research?

MHC: I do it as I'm writing the book. I know where I'm going, like when I was in Minneapolis for Bouchercon . . . I had been there, many times so I knew Minneapolis. I had even owned property there. But it's been a while so I needed to know street names and which way you would drive to go to certain places and what hotel a killer would stay in and where the girl's apartment would be. And all of this is important.

Sometimes you get great information from other writers. I meet with a group (The Adams Roundtable founded by Clark and the late Thomas Chastain) every month in the upstairs room of a Manhattan restaurant. We often talk about research and one night Whitley Streiber said something that helped me. He said "When I'm writing a book about a city, I get a subscription to that city's newspaper."

JG: Good tip.

MHC: It's a very good tip. Because you get the prices of houses and groceries and what's going on in that area—the politics, the entertainment.

JG: What sparks a new book for you? Makes you feel you've just got to write this one?

MHC: Well, for example in *Moonlight Becomes You* I was interested in the fact there are so many nursing homes you see where people are being overmedicated or being so badly treated and I thought what is the reverse? What about in the upscale ones? About then there was a big article in the *Times* where people would buy their apartment units but when they die the space reverts back to the company. So here's a half-million-dollar unit that's supposed to revert back after you die and you're only supposed to live seven years or they're losing money on you. I just thought what an interesting concept. Here are people who can well afford to pay for care for themselves and yet they may very well be in danger. Often the people who died didn't have any family looking out for them. Look at poor Doris Duke, one of the richest women in the entire world. When she died she had a doctor overdosing her and a butler methodically stealing from her and a nurse pocketing her antiques. Those were the three people surrounding her.

JG: Poor thing. I think that book touches a chord in us because we all have a fear of something like that happening. I enjoyed reading all those funeral customs. It was a subject I was not too familiar with.
MHC: It's fun to read a subject you would not necessarily go out looking for.

Now the stories in *My Gal Sunday* (which of course is tongue-in-cheek of that old radio show and always intrigued me) instead of the richest, the most handsome nobleman, suppose you had a ex-President. And suppose he married this young congress woman . . .

JG: A Great concept.
MHC: I think they're marvelous fun.

JG: Oh, I can tell you're still having fun with your writing and that's great after so many books. And it's wonderful because it gives you a break from the more serious things you've done.
MHC: Yes, and they've done very well. But some people were looking for psychological suspense. I got a letter from someone yesterday who said she read the first story and threw up.

JG: Good grief. (laughter)
MHC: Well, she just didn't like that kind of story. I've also gotten some very nice letters. But I laughed out loud over that one and thought, oh my gosh, honey, that's a bit drastic.
JG: Are you planning more Sunday and Henry stories, I hope?
MHC: Oh, yes. I owe Otto Penzler a story and so I'm going to do a Henry and Sunday story when I finish this book.

JG: It's great that you still enjoy writing.
MHC: I do, but I'm not going to try to do two books in a year again, that's too tight. And because I do want to smell the flowers at some point. And that way I can continue on writing indefinitely.

JG: The great thing about writing is being able to continue—no matter what our age—until we're in our coffin, right?
MHC: Of course. Just put a pad and a couple of pens and a glass of wine (in my coffin) and I'll be all set. (laughter)

JG: Okay, back to our task . . . several of your books (especially *Loves Music Loves to Dance*) have scared me when I was reading and I wondered if sometimes you scare yourself when you're writing?
MHC: Oh, yes. And yet I love the idea of somebody freezing a body and

then dancing with it—there's something rather sweet about it . . . (laughter)

JG: You're a sick person . . . (more laughs) So how do you research that?

MHC: I had heard the FBI Director at the International Crime Writers Conference discussing cases. I was the chairman of the conference and kept running back and forth from room to room trying to see if there were enough chairs set up and if there was water at the speakers' table and if the mikes were working, but when the director began talking I sat down. He had pictures of these seven young girls—their hands bound and their mouths taped and their young eyes terrified. He said he'd taken the pictures. Seven young girls killed over three years. And the common denominator was they had all answered a newspaper ad. They were answering the ad of a psychopath serial killer. And the thought just walked into my head "Loves Music Loves To Dance."

JG: Wow. The title just walked in and sat down.

MHC: Right. And now on the one I'm doing I have a young woman in real estate, upscale real estate, selling condominiums in Manhattan and she witnesses an murder. She brings a guy in to see a property one morning. Later in the evening she comes back to see the woman owner and she lets herself in and calls out to her, "Isabelle?" Suddenly she hears a scream and a shot. But she has the presence of mind to slam the front door (pretending she left) and jumps in the closet. Now she must get into the witness protection plan because the killer was a mobster.

JG: Sounds good, I'll be looking for that one. You often write about things that are current in our lives: like serial killers and nursing homes and burial customs . . .

MHC: And the multiple personalities, in vitro fertilization was another. I really try to do something different and they have to be more than entertaining.

For instance: In this book you see a young woman who has to lie about everything and she's not a liar. She lies about her name and where she came from and what her background is—everything is a lie. But she has to do it or the killer will find and kill her.

JG: And how would you remember all the lies—keep them all straight?

MHC: Right, and you know the old saying, *"Some people would lie when the truth would serve them better."* In this case she has no choice.

JG: Next question—who has the nerve to critique you? I mean you're *Mary Higgins Clark.* Only your editor or agent?

MHC: I have a couple of family/friend readers, like my sister-in-law I often hand pages to. For the legal stuff, my daughter, Marilyn, is a judge and my son, Warren, is a lawyer and municipal court judge. I get the legal stuff from them or they tell me it's not legal in New Jersey. If they don't know they can tell me where to go.

Yesterday I spent half an hour on the telephone with a retired detective finding out where evidence could disappear in a precinct. And what is the difference between a U.S. attorney and the New York P.D.

And finally my daughter, Carol, is a wonderful, wonderful critic. She was always good at critiquing me even when she was typing my manuscripts in college.

She didn't mind telling me I couldn't do something. In fact, she was the one who said you can't kill off ***Elvira.*** But I said, "She's gotta go." And Carol said, "She's too much fun and people will hate you." And she was right. *The Lottery Winner* was a number-one best-seller.

JG: Thank goodness you listened, right?
MHC: And now Carol says she should get the royalties from it. (laughter)

JG: Some nerve, huh? Do I dare ask, have any of your books ever been rejected?
MHC: *Where Are the Children* was rejected by two publishers. They said people don't like to read about children in jeopardy. You have to remember this was twenty-three years ago and they thought murdering children was too much of a problem.

JG: Which brings me to when you were raising five children and writing about child killers, did you ever get paranoid about your own children?
MHC: My children were in their teens when I wrote those. But once when we moved and our youngest was three, this house was near a lake. I had been very worried about moving near water. Water is always a problem when you have children. And my God, the very day we moved in—Patti turns up missing. And all I could say was "get to the lake."

And you know where she was? Asleep on the couch. It was turned around facing the wall and you couldn't see her. She'd gotten tired, got her security blanket, curled up and had never heard us screaming for her.

And those emotions and feelings all came into play in my early books. That and a true case of a woman who was accused of the deliberate murder of her two children.

JG: Okay, tell us what your writing day is like?
MHC: I get up early. When I have to I've gotten up at four o'clock for this book. But I find when I do that I don't get enough out of it because then I'm so darn tired by one in the afternoon so I'm not sure that serves me well. I like to get started by seven, seven-thirty. I work all day when I'm on deadline. Yesterday I worked nine hours straight. The housekeeper brought me up a sandwich and I ate at my desk.

JG: I was going to ask if you have an office at home?
MHC: I have a lovely, lovely tower office. We added a second floor and a third-floor gallery. I don't work neatly which is why I wanted a place that I could just walk away from. The office is gorgeous and has huge windows and a skylight so that it's very open and sunny.

JG: What do you think you would be doing today if you weren't writing mysteries?
MHC: I have no idea, no idea at all. Well, I would have been working because I was widowed, you know. Maybe I'd be retired by now and going on a bus to Atlantic City to gamble. I did some radio script-writing when I lived in New York. I probably would have been working in an advertising agency, but here again—it would have been writing.

JG: Any words of wisdom for writers?
MHC: Write. And I think it's wise to

somehow be connected to the community of writing. I tell beginning writers "take a course." It's not just having the talent, you have to learn the craft.

JG: Okay, now we'll do the more lighthearted questions—isn't it a kick to be a question on *Jeopardy?*
MHC: Oh, it's a riot. You know I was a *Jeopardy* question three different times and the one I love the best is when they said, "Her name is Carol Higgins Clark, her first book *Decked* was published in 1992—who is her mother? And there were three blank looks and finally somebody pressed the buzzer and said 'Who is Agatha Christie?'" We loved it.

JG: And speaking of Carol, how is it to have a daughter who is now a successful suspense writer?
MHC: It's wonderful, really I'm so pleased for her. And she's suffering just the way I am and we're on the phone every day moaning to each other. She's writing *Twanged* right now.

JG: *Twanged?*
MHC: It's a country music . . .

JG: . . . Obviously. Maybe she needs to call and talk to me to get that twang down in her head just right.
MHC: Oh, that's right. Well, she's working her fanny off on that one, she's got her deadline and of course my deadline is the here and now and we're both working trying to get finished.

JG: Who would you like to be stranded with on a desert island?
MHC: My husband.

JG: If you could live anywhere in the world, where would it be?
MHC: Right here. I love to travel, but it's like a yo-yo, I always want to come back.

JG: What music do you like?
MHC: I love classical, but I don't know it like John does. I never really had the time to learn. I like the forties kind of music. The Big Bands sounds—always loved that.

JG: What's you favorite color?
MHC: (a brief pause) I'm looking at red walls right now. It's not that I wear red all the time, but I think it's one of the brightest most fun colors.

JG: And it looks great with your hair and eyes.
MHC: And I like red because it's cheerful. But I wear black a lot and the dress I wore for the wedding was green and gold. You know, I guess I like strong colors.

JG: What does your best pal say about you?
MHC: Probably that I'm easy to be around. And I try to be as good a friend as they are to me and we have fun.

JG: What is your greatest success?
MHC: My family.

JG: Tell me a secret about Mary Higgins Clark.
MHC: I'm as open as apple pie. I don't have secrets.

JG: Somehow, I knew that already.
MHC: What do you want to know? Ask me and I'll tell you. Some people will try to sidle up to you and try to ask something and I'll say, "What do you want to know?" Don't waste your time trying to worm it out of

me, I'll tell you.

JG: I know you get interviewed often and are asked the same old questions—what do you wish someone would ask? Then consider that I asked it and you can answer.
MHC: I wish someone would ask me about my fan mail. Sometimes I'll get a letter like—"Dear Ms. Clark, I was sick and in the hospital and someone gave me one of your books and for the next four hours I forgot my aches and pains." And I've gotten a letter from someone who said, "My little boy was sick and hospitalized and I'm a single mother and for weeks I was by his bedside and I got through it by reading your books." That's lovely and very flattering.

JG: Makes it all worthwhile then, doesn't it?
MHC: Indeed. And since I don't deal with sex and violence, I'm on the reading list from age twelve and up all over the country and I get letters from kids saying "I never liked to read but I liked your book and now I think reading is fun." Those are the kind of letters that make you feel great.

Then I always keep one that I really love, love, love. "Dear Mrs. Clark, I am twelve years old and I've read the first half of *Where Are the Children*. You are a wonderful writer. Someday I hope to read the second half."

JG: Oh, that's priceless.
MHC: Isn't that great?

JG: Listen, Miss Mary, I appreciate your time and . . .
MHC: I'm sorry we weren't able to do this sooner.

JG: No problem. Take care. And thanks again.

A Mary Higgins Clark Checklist

Where Are the Children?

A Stranger Is Watching

The Cradle Will Fall

A Cry in the Night

Stillwatch

Weep No More My Lady

While My Pretty One Sleeps

The Anastasia Syndrome & Other Stories

Loves Music Loves to Dance

All Around the Town

I'll Be Seeing You

Remember Me

The Lottery Winner

Let Me Call You Sweetheart

Silent Night

Moonlight Becomes You

My Gal Sunday

Pretend You Don't See Her

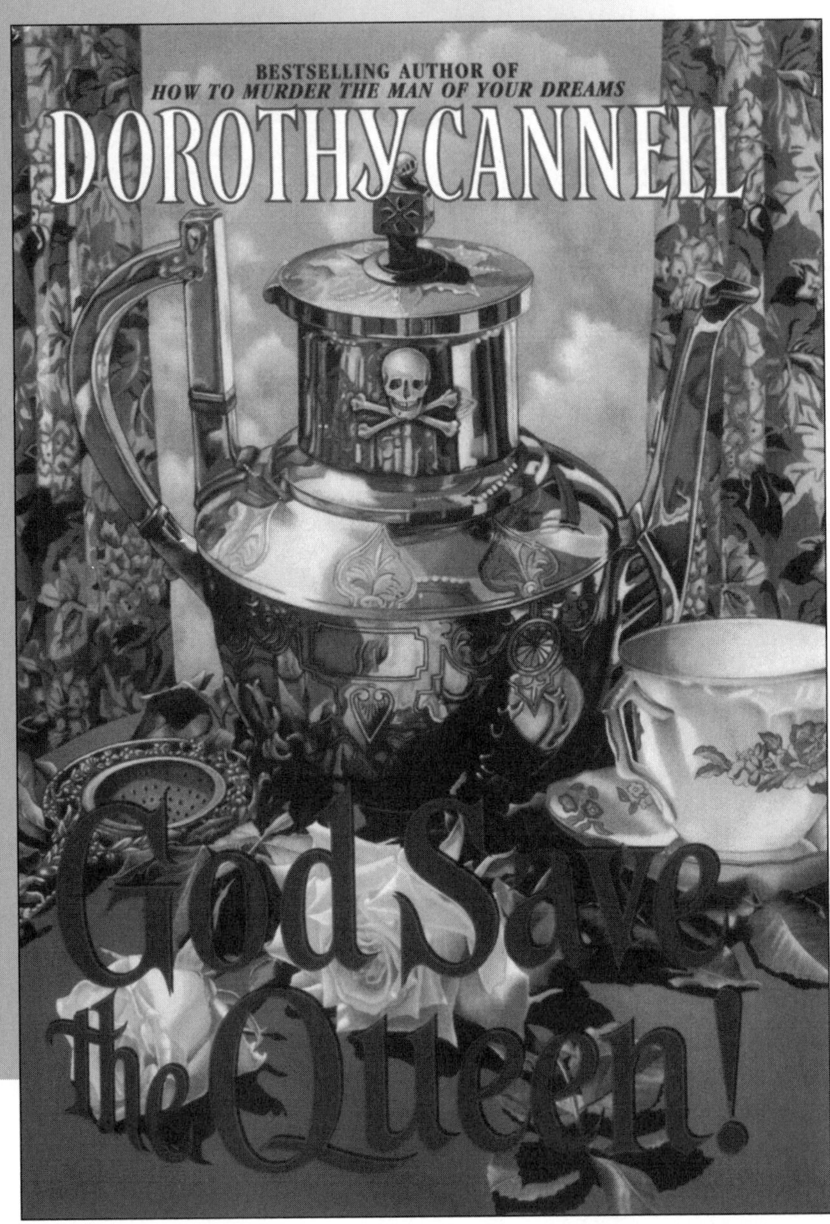

God Save the Queen! by Dorothy Cannell

Interview with

Dorothy Cannell

Dean James

Every once in a while, a book comes along in the mystery world and very quickly comes to be regarded as a classic. Dorothy Cannell, an Englishwoman long resident in the U.S., authored such a book. Her first novel, The Thin Woman, published in 1984, immediately received a warm reception among mystery-lovers for its charm, humor, and appealing characters.

DOROTHY CANNELL HAS SINCE that time published seven additional novels, five of which feature the heroine of the first novel, Ellie Simons Haskell. *The Widow's Club* was an Agatha Award nominee for Best Novel, and at Malice Domestic earlier this year, Dorothy Cannell won an Agatha for Best Short Story for her Regency spoof, "The Family Jewels." Though Dorothy Cannell modestly proclaims in public that she's not funny, canny listeners will note that she does so with a wicked glint in her eyes. In person she is much like her books, warm, generous, and charming, and any extended conversation brings forth the subtle wit and unerring eye for satire which is also a trademark of her fiction. I recently corresponded with Dorothy from her home in Peoria, Illinois, and the following is the result.

What role did macramé play in the beginning of your writing career?

Thank you, Dean, for asking that exceedingly important question. Twenty-some years ago, I did hope to find fulfillment as a woman and an artist creating macramé wall hangings of museum quality. But I discovered that rope wasn't my medium. I created a knotty monster that took over the basement and threatened to move upstairs and strangle the entire family while we slept. Instead our house was struck by lightning one midsummer night and burnt to the ground (the age-old curse of the macramé gods). After which rude awakening, my husband suggested I embark on a new hobby, and I decided to write a book.

What do you worry about most when you write: plot, character, or humor?

I don't worry excessively about any of the three, mainly because I am one of the laziest people alive. Without undue humility I don't believe I am a great plotter. The theme of a book comes more easily, and I have to admit it interests me more. Finding a character's core occupies much of my planning time, and I am only satisfied when I can see and hear the person and get inside his or her head. Humor is the easiest part of writing for me, I just let it happen from the situation or the character's reaction.

Your first novel, *The Thin Woman,* is already regarded as a "classic." Has the reception for your very first novel affected you adversely with your later novels?

Writing *The Thin Woman* was magic in a way that perhaps no other book will be for me because it was the first, and I was operating entirely on dreams. When it sold I was euphoric. It was enough to know it would find its way into the hands of even a few readers. I certainly never expected *The Thin Woman* to be so warmly received, and that did make it harder to write the next book, which was *The Widow's Club,* because *Down the Garden Path* was already done. It wasn't until *Femmes Fatal* that I stopped trying too hard and losing out on some of the joy of writing.

One of the important threads which runs through all of the books about Ellie Haskell is the way in which Ellie tries to deal with her insecurities. Does this make it more difficult, sometimes, to write about Ellie? Why is it important for you to write about a character like Ellie who worries about so many things?

Ellie was a character who came alive in my head one day as if I had known her all my life, and yet in some ways she continues to surprise me in the way that one's real-life friends often do. I have never tried to provide Ellie with insecurities as a means of making her a more interesting character. They are simply a part of who she is, and no sooner does she straighten herself out in one emotional area, when another demon rears its grizzly head. But because Ellie and I share many of the same interests and concerns, I do get to address subjects that matter to me through her.

Your main characters seem, in a sense, to be searching for their identities, This is particularly true for the heroine of *Down the Garden Path,* but in a way I think it's also true of Ellie. Would you agree with this? If so, why?

Tessa Fields in *Down the Garden Path* was searching for her birth mother, a topic close to my heart because my two daughters are adopted. And I will admit that through Tessa I was able to explore my feelings about all the ways in which one can be a mother and the intense need we all have to belong. Ellie is particularly intent on self-exploration and is frequently tripping over some new side of herself. This happens because I believe this is real life. I don't think I have ever set out to make Ellie grow as a character; it is one of the inevitabilities of a series, and what helps to make writing hopefully new and exciting.

You grew up in England, but you've lived in the United States for a little over thirty years now. How did a nice young English girl end up in Peoria?

My husband, Julian, grew up in Peoria and lured me here with promises that it was the garden spot of the U.S. And after thirty years it is hard to imagine living anywhere else.

Has living in the U.S. for all these years given you a different perspective on

writing about England and English characters?

Absolutely. I think that in my case distance has made the heart grow fonder, and the England I write about is lavishly painted with nostalgia. At the same time, I think I have gained a perspective that would be missing if I had never left. I haven't any plans as yet to set a book in the States, partly because I'm afraid I wouldn't get the voices right, and mostly because I like being able to sit down at the word processor, press a couple of buttons, and be back home again.

Several of the Ellie novels are "about" various issues confronting contemporary women: the "total woman" movement in *Femmes Fatale,* finding Mr. Right in *How to Murder the Man of Your Dreams,* for example. Obviously your eye for satire finds some very rich targets in contemporary culture. How do you decide to work such topics into a novel?

I select topics that needle me. In *The Thin Woman* I chose an overweight heroine who would not only find a man who loved her for herself but who would beat the odds against living out her own private fairy tale. My starting point in *The Widow's Club* was the topic of women who are dumped in middle age by their spouses, and who end up feeling like losers. Basically what I do is get angry and then say let's have some fun with this while still having my little say.

Your Agatha-winning short story, "The Family Jewels," was a wicked take-off on Jane Austen and the whole Regency-novel genre. Have you thought about an entire novel in this vein?

I am not sure I could sustain that sort of charade for an entire novel, but I would love to try some day. Imitating Jane Austen is like trying to play a minuet with one's toes.

Rumor has it that you are taking a break from Ellie and company for your next book. Is this true? If so, can you tell us anything about the new book? Will it be the first of a new series? If so, will you alternate between series?

The book I am writing is outside the Ellie series, but I know I will hook up with her again before too long. She can get on without me much better than the other way around.

Who are some of your favorite writers? Are there any whom you would consider have directly influenced the type of fiction that you like to write?

Jane Austen first and foremost. Charlotte Bronte, Dickens, Daphne DuMaurier, Mary Stewart, P.G. Wodehouse, and lots of people that aren't big names, all of whom have influenced me in one way or another. When it comes to today's writers, Barbara Michaels has had the most direct impact, because reading her books was not just a joy in itself but an inspiration to keep trying to do better in the hope that one day I could produce a book that some reader would love as much as I did hers. And when *The Thin Woman* came out I did secretly hope Barbara would recognize me as a fan. I won't mention any other favorite current mystery writers because there are so many and I might miss somebody out, and they would refuse to autograph their latest book for me.

Heroines Are Born and Influenced

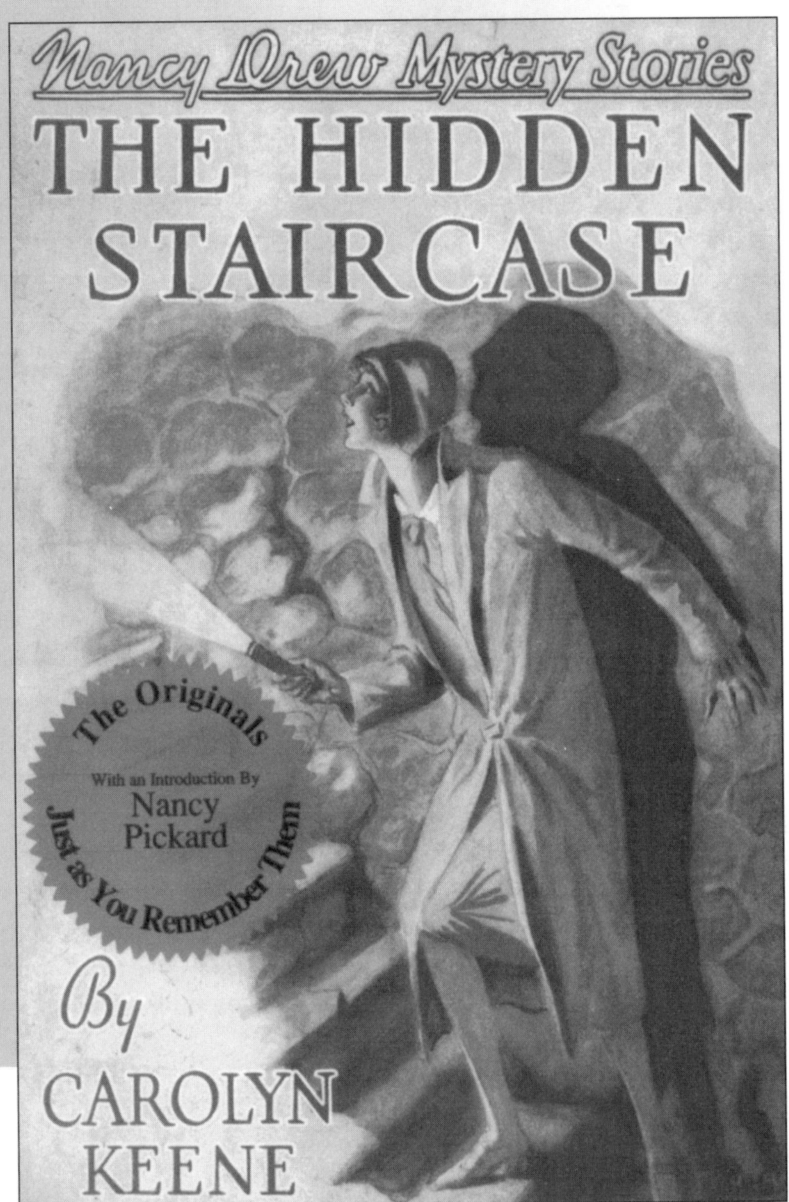

The Hidden Staircase by Carolyn Keene

I Owe It All to Nancy Drew

Nancy Pickard

When I was ten years old I wrote, "I will be happy if I can have horses, solve mysteries, help people, and be happily married." In that order.

FOR THIRTY YEARS AFTER that, I forgot on any conscious level about that wish list. When I finally came across it again, I was forty years old, married to a cowboy, doing volunteer work, and writing murder mysteries.

The child was, indeed, the mother to this woman.

It's easy enough to figure out why I wanted to "have horses"—doesn't almost every adolescent girl dream of riding Black Beauty? Growing up in the fifties made it de rigueur for me to want to be "happily married," and being a college student in the sixties made it nearly obligatory for me to want to "help people." But whence the desire to "solve mysteries"?

That's easy, isn't it?

I read Nancy Drew, didn't you?

Sometimes I think I owe it all to her—my career, my amateur sleuth heroine, most of whatever finer qualities I may possess, even my blond hair, blue eyes, and my name. Nancy Drew was (almost) everything I wanted to be when I grew up: intelligent, self-confident, incredibly courageous, honest, straightforward, kind, courteous, energetic, successful, and independent. I confess that I also wished I were well-to-do and beautiful, just like Nancy. It's possible that she could have used more of a sense of fun and humor, and it cannot be denied that in her language and attitudes she reflected the white, middle-class, Christian prejudices of her day, but I'd rather blame those failings on her creators. I like to think that had Nancy but known, she never would have thought, spoken, or behaved in those ways.

Recently, for the first time since I was a girl, I read the original version of *The Hidden Staircase*. First published in 1930, it may be the most famous and the most fondly remembered of any of the Nancy Drew mysteries. In 1959, the story was republished in a rewritten edition that drastically altered both the plot and the characters. If I had a daughter, this original version is the one I'd want to pass on to her. It is the edition I will give to my son.

I think it is not overstating the case to maintain that the original Nancy Drew is a mythic character in the psyches of the American women who followed her adventures as they were growing up. She may have been Superman, Batman, and Green Hornet, all wrapped up in a pretty girl in a blue convertible.

This original *Hidden Staircase* is a rich and nutritious feast of psychological archetypes, so that it assumes the quality of fairy tale and myth. Nancy herself, in this version, is quite a heroic figure, one that in our culture we're more accustomed to seeing portrayed as a boy than a girl; she's incorruptible, honest, steadfast, and courageous, a veritable Sir Lancelot of a girl, off on a quest to rescue the fair maiden who is, in this case, her father, and to recapture the Holy Grail, which in this case is a silver spoon, a pocketbook, a diamond pin, and a couple of black silk dresses.

We'd have to go back to ancient goddess mythology to find an equivalent female of such heroic stature, back to a figure such as Innana, who was the chief Sumerian deity, a woman who went to hell and back on a rescue mission. Such journeys into the "underground" are viewed in psychological terms as descents into one's consciousness; it is believed that a person must bring the contents of the unconscious into the light of consciousness in order to fully integrate one's psyche. In *The Hidden Staircase,* Nancy symbolically does just that, by tumbling like Alice down a black hole and then by journeying deeper and deeper into a really quite frightening tunnel where she perseveres with remarkable courage until she finds a way to ascend once more into the light. In doing so, she solves all mysteries and reunites everyone and everything that have been wrongfully separated. This is, at heart, no "mere" adventure story, this is myth.

In this original story, Nancy works alone, facing every terror on her own, although with the support, encouragement, and appreciation of the grown-ups. It reminds me of the mythic initiation rites, where the young person is challenged, with the full backing of the adults to prove herself. Nancy's father, in this version, is an ideally archetypal figure who approves of everything his daughter does and praises her unstintingly. He's so proud of her he could bust, as proud as fathers are said to be when their sons make the winning touchdown in a football game, as proud as Zeus was of Athena. In this version, Nancy is a marvel of decisiveness and resolution, and she gets to experience a full personal triumph.

Do you remember how you felt when you read this story?

I remember exactly how it was for me.

I was scared and had gooseflesh, and my stomach clenched, and the hair on my arms stood on end, and I tucked my feet beneath me so the boogeyman under the bed couldn't grab them, and when Nancy was in the tunnel I could hardly bear to turn the page for fear of what might happen next, and yet I couldn't help turning the page to see what happened next. Oh, it was wonderful! It was delicious. It was spooky and mysterious and creepy, and I was there falling down those stairs with her, praying the flashlight wouldn't go out, feeling my way along the dark, damp walls of the tunnel, almost plunging through the wood where the stair was missing, breathing a sigh of vast relief when Nancy pulled the iron ring and the other door opened . . .

All of that is still here.

The faults are still here, too—the racism and anti-Semitism—and they make for painful reading now, just as they did for their victims back then. I hope they'll inspire us to examine our own "historical context" for the prejudices we don't know we have.

Do you want to know another truth? I miss her.

I miss the sheer joy of reading a "Nancy Drew."

Evidently millions of other women do, too, because they're turning in record numbers to read the new breed of adult fictional women sleuths whose undeniable progenitor is Nancy Drew. It is surely no coincidence that my own detective, Jenny Cain, has a name that matched Nancy's syllable for syllable, and that she's slim, blond, and blue-eyed, too. My Jenny is as good as motherless, like Nancy, and she's smarter, braver, and more resourceful than her own father, like Nancy. More than one reviewer has referred to her as "Nancy Drew all grown-up," which I take as truth and compliment.

The real Nancy Drew mystery may be the Mystery of the Appeal of Nancy Drew herself, and of her phenomenal attraction to successive generations of American girls.

I believe the solution to that mystery is this . . .

Nancy Drew, especially the Nancy of this original story, is our bright heroine, chasing down the shadows, conquering our worst fears, giving us a glimpse of our brave and better selves, proving to everybody exactly how admirable and wonderful a thing it is to be a girl.

Thank you, Nancy Drew.

This art inspired by a Judy Bolton cover.

"What Sharon McCone Learned from Judy Bolton"

Marcia Muller

"Hey, Judy . . . get your nose out of that book and come to the mailbox!"

Judy Bolton, girl detective, took her nose out of the book and stuck it into her first adventure, The Vanishing Shadow *(1932). I, on the other hand, stuck mine into the Judy books, where it intermittently remained for twenty-some of her thirty-eight cases.*

THE BOLTON NOVELS, AUTHORED by Margaret Sutton, were an absolute delight, dealing with things that were sure to fire a young girl's imagination. Haunted houses, disasters both natural and unnatural, robbers, crystal gazers, bootleggers, evil Indian spirits, jewel thieves, and mysterious strangers—they all graced the pages of the series. The books had mystery, intrigue, and romance. But most of all, they had Judy.

Judy, who possessed all the virtues I aspired to: courage, strong convictions, sharply honed logic, independence. But she was no paragon on a pedestal; she also had faults and problems that I could identify with. Stubbornness. Social insecurity. A spoiled brother upon whom the family doted. Ostracism by the snobby girls in high school, because egalitarian Judy insisted on making friends with the mill workers. Two attractive men who pursued and confused her. People constantly telling her to stop being unladylike. But what the hell—the chief of police frequently consulted with her, and she couldn't even go on her honeymoon without becoming involved in a mystery.

I didn't want to be like Judy, however. I wanted to be like her creator. Even at the tender age of ten—although I didn't know it at the time—I was learning the craft of mystery writing.

The Judy books were extremely well written, and from them I learned how to write. Nuts-and-bolts, such as where the quote marks go in dialogue. More complex aspects, such as creating character and atmosphere. Plot. All the elements that make a series really work. A rereading of a number of old favorites in preparation for this article revealed to me that Sutton was an even stronger influence on my work than I'd previously thought.

Take Judy herself: She is, if anything, more egalitarian than Sharon McCone, standing up to social snobbery and injustice. Like McCone, her temper often gets her into trouble. They both sometimes adopt holier-than-thou stances, only to call themselves on it and question their motivations. And they are fiercely independent and often unresponsive to authority.

Throughout the course of the series, Judy aged and changed—something I've incorporated to the McCone novels. Unlike the stable of writers at Stratemeyer Syndicate, who turned out the formulaic Nancy Drew books, Sutton allowed her protagonist to mature, to graduate from high school, have a career, settle into a solid marriage, and become a mentor to younger girls and boys. Interestingly, in reading the books in order, I was aware of the same odd compression of time I see in my own series: In the early books, Judy's world is very much that of the 1930s; the cover of the last entry, *The Secret of the Sand Castle* (1967), depicts her in a miniskirt—although in series time it's only a few years later. Similarly, when Sharon McCone first appeared in 1977, she described herself as "a child of the sixties." At the rate she's aging, she'll soon have to describe herself as a child of the eighties!

The Sutton books also had a large ongoing cast of characters, and Judy never operated as a loner. Initially she had her family and a small set of friends, but quickly she attracted others, picking them up at an average of one per case. I well know the problems this must have posed for the author, as I, too, have difficulty keeping McCone's cohorts straight, and periodically have to send the less interesting ones off to exile in farflung places.

Other influences I've gleaned from Sutton's work? Spooky trappings? Oh, yes. I'm probably one of few writers to attempt a gothic private-eye novel. Flying? Definitely. McCone became a pilot when she acquired a pilot boyfriend. I'd forgotten it, but damned if I didn't open *The Ghost Parade* (1933) and find Judy soaring high in a open-cockpit biplane with one of her suitors! Relatives coming out of the woodwork with odd requests? So far, Sharon has been hired by one sister, a brother-in-law, and has (reluctantly) shared the detective work with a brother. Could this be because *The Secret of the Musical Tree* (1948), in which Judy rescues her cousin from a gang of kidnappers, is my all-time favorite in the series?

While other young girls worshipped actresses and pop stars, I worshipped writers. I can vividly remember saying, at the age of ten, "I'd just *die* if I could meet Margaret Sutton!" That opportunity finally presented itself in 1977, shortly before my first McCone novel was due to be published. Sutton was speaking to a class at the University of California, and I was allowed to sit in. Afterward I went up and told her how much the Judy books had meant to me—so much that I had now sold a mystery of my own. Sutton graciously replied, "I would very much like to have a copy."

Now, wouldn't the ten-year-old me have just *died* if she'd known that one day Margaret Sutton would be reading *her* words?

APRIL
7
8
9

Nancy Lies about Her Age

Mary Blount Christian

Nancy Drew was born before I was—even before "The Star Spangled Banner." I mention this right off because I have a sneaking suspicion that she lies about her age. Not even leap-year babies can claim to be eighteen sixty-five years later. By the time I came along, voracious reader that I was, a stack of her mysteries had been published.

THERE WAS SOMETHING ABOUT the pride of ownership that made me give up sweet treats so that every other month I had enough coins in my little pig to ride the bus to town with Mother and pick out my next title.

The open-cage elevator creaked its way to the third floor so slowly that I tapped my Mary Janes impatiently, unable to contain my eagerness. Before the door had opened with a full clank I'd bolt from the elevator, straight past the Storybook Dolls to the shelf of bright-colored spines emblazoned with such magic words—Secret, Mystery, Hidden, Ghosts. On alternate months, I stood in the aisle of Foley Bros. surreptitiously reading until Mother called me or the saleslady chased me away.

Nancy was every mother's ideal daughter—moral to the point of boring, hair and clothes meticulous, never a dilemma about right and/or wrong. She was every little girl's ideal—a doting father who valued her opinions, gave her free rein, and always arrived to save her from peril. Ned, her unassuming boyfriend, had the personality of a wet dishrag, so there was no mushy stuff to gag a girl still at the age when she thinks boys are a mishap in the lab of a mad scientist.

The mysteries were pure—no personal problems stood between the reader and the solution.

Nancy, forever young, gave us the reassurance that, like Peter Pan, we would never grow older. She traveled to exotic places, and we vicariously went, too. Best of all, she was independently mobile with her blue convertible. (In my own fantasy it was a red roadster; blue was simply not bold enough.)

She had everything a girl could

want, except cleavage, which I certainly aspired to at eight. For that I read Brenda Starr, Reporter. Those two females, with Rosie the Riveter, formed my earliest opinions of limitless potential for women. Nancy taught me that curiosity, despite the grown-ups' constant reminder that it killed the cat, was an honorable thing, because it brought answers. And answers brought solutions (of which we are short at that age!).

Brenda was my first indication that I could stop spying on my neighbors and harness my natural, overactive curiosity into a newspaper career.

I read them all, but they never quite caught my imagination like Nancy and Brenda. The Hardy Boys?—they were, after all, boys. Dana Girls?—I preferred to work alone. The Bobbsey Twins—I liked the idea of an only child.

I never confused any of them with literature. It didn't take a ten-year-old to tell the difference between the writing of Keane and Twain, Swift or Stevenson. But Nancy and Brenda filled a need that none of these masters of literature did. Those stories put strong women into the main roles. It would be so easy to make fun of Nancy stories; they aren't literature. But they answered a need. What good is any writing if it doesn't fill a need? The greats could inspire me to read, but the unintimidating, ordinarily written stories could inspire me to write.

Would I have become first a reporter, then a mystery writer, had there been no Nancy or Brenda? Probably; after all, I never became a riveter. But I think my life would have been less rich without them.

This article was to be about the influence of female characters in mysteries on real-life females. I'm not so sure that it isn't the other way around. Nancy's perpetual teen age gave her the perfect excuse to have less supervision, to be more mobile, to take more responsibility for her actions. Her fictional world hasn't changed that much, even though she's finally reached college and observes periphery, contemporary problems.

While real-life parenting continually evolves from authoritarian, through indulgence and democratic to time-out for misbehavior, writers struggle to create characters who are similar to their readers but unhampered by grown-ups. Parents are in comas, trapped in avalanches, cut off by flooded rivers, alcoholic, drugged, or too neurotic or work-driven to tell their kids to be home by ten on a school night.

I personally like the trend toward supportive parents who dole out freedom and responsibility in equal portions. Not all mystery readers grow up to be detectives or writers. But they will have developed a talent for sorting through all the possibilities and alternatives and settling on the best answer. That can't be a bad thing in life. Any life.

My attitudes have probably changed, because while I have retained that child I once was, I am also parent and grandparent. (All right, so I'm not *that* much younger than Nancy!) I like the new trends of real kids with real problems, kids who learn something about themselves while they are solving mysteries. They even learn something about many subjects—art, government, environment, computers, what-have-you.

It's a nice combination. It makes me wish I was a kid again. Somehow, when I open up one of those mysteries, I am.

Writer's Bookshelf

Margaret Maron

I am a mystery writer. I write of exit wounds and blood splatter patterns, of fingerprints and tire treads, of alibis and aliases. So when I read for inspiration, I must read The Anarchist Cookbook, The Handbook of Poisons, *and* Practical Homicide Investigation, *right?*

WRONG.

MY NOVELS USE a classic mystery form: there is a crime, there is someone to solve that crime, and in the end, justice appears to be done. (This last, incidentally, does not mean that good is automatically rewarded nor that evil is automatically punished.) To some writers, such structure might seem too limiting, but it limits me no more than the sonnet or sextain limits a poet . . . which brings us to why *The Collected Poems of Edna St. Vincent Millay* is one of the two books I consider indispensable. (*Pride and Prejudice* is the other, simply because it is funny, elegantly plotted, and has a universal tale hidden beneath a facade of seeming frivolity; but that's another essay altogether.)

I discovered Millay when I was eleven, and she made me want to write. She took me through the heartbreak of adolescence, she consoled me through deaths and disappointments as I grew older, she sustains me now in middle age. (The next time someone you love has a near brush with death, read "Thanksgiving Dinner" and feel the exaltation of her words "and did not.") The sonnet did not limit Millay. It was the form through which she could soar.

As a lyric poet she cared about meter, complex rhyme schemes, and poetic images; yet her language is very clear; she uses homely images chosen from nature, and she is completely accessible, which is probably why she's dismissed and undervalued by so many academics. (Like the King James Bible, she requires no priestly interpreter.)

Her poems quickly spring to the universal, but they are rooted in the particular. A flower is not a flower. It is a spiked larkspur, a yellow violet, a specific blue flag in a bog. It isn't the scent of generic herbs, it's tansy or sweet basil or old-fashioned sage and it brings me immediately into her garden, into a sensuous landscape I can taste, touch, hear, see, and smell.

The mystery form is but the framework upon which I hang my concerns for the passing of a culture, the despoliation of our region, the pollution of our coastal waters, the use of art as a commodity, etc.

I am told my books have a strong sense of place.

If so, I learned it from Millay.

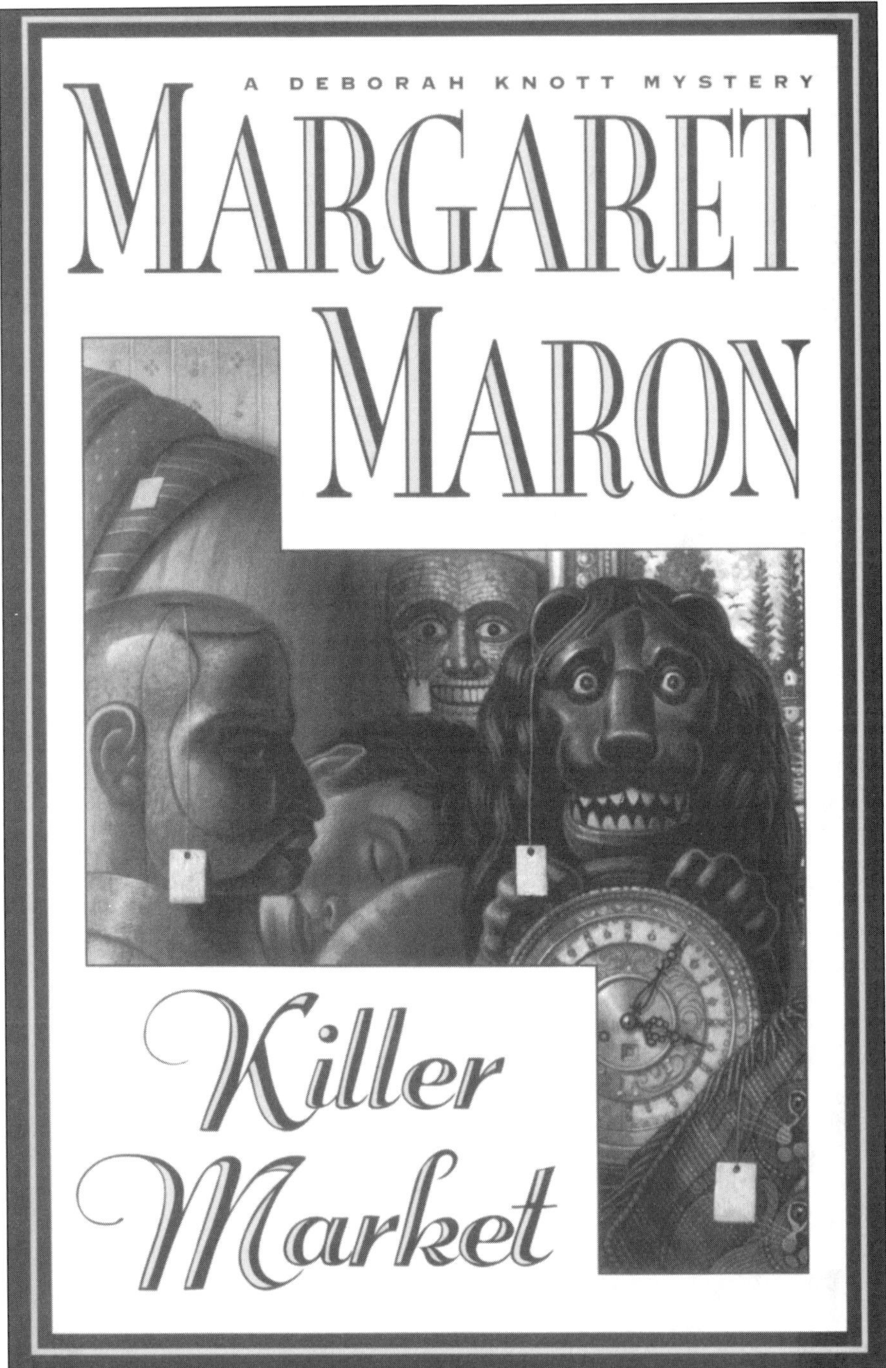

Killer Market by Margaret Maron

The 10 Best Pieces of Writing Advice I Ever Received . . .

1. *from Mom: "Write as often as you can."*
2. *from Fawn Hall: "Learn to type." (Six weeks at a night school or community college will make you a touch typist for life.)*
3. *from Dick and Jane: "Read." (In and out of your field.)*
4. *from Black & Decker: "Don't read ONE how-to-book; read a dozen." (So you'll understand there's more than one way to build a house—or craft a book.)*
5. *from Moses: "Rewrite." (Even when your words are engraved in stone, they aren't engraved in stone.)*
6. *from Mrs. Johnson, 2nd Grade: "Neatness counts." (And sloppy manuscripts signal a nonprofessional.)*
7. *from the Marquis de Sade: "Submit." (No work ever sold sitting in a file cabinet.)*
8. *from William Tell: "Don't aim too low." (Target the top markets in your field and submit there first.)*
9. *from (a tie) Pandora: "Hope"; and Tinkerbell: "Believe!"*
10. *from Ann Landers: "Use it or lose it." (Write!)*

. . . **Margaret Maron**

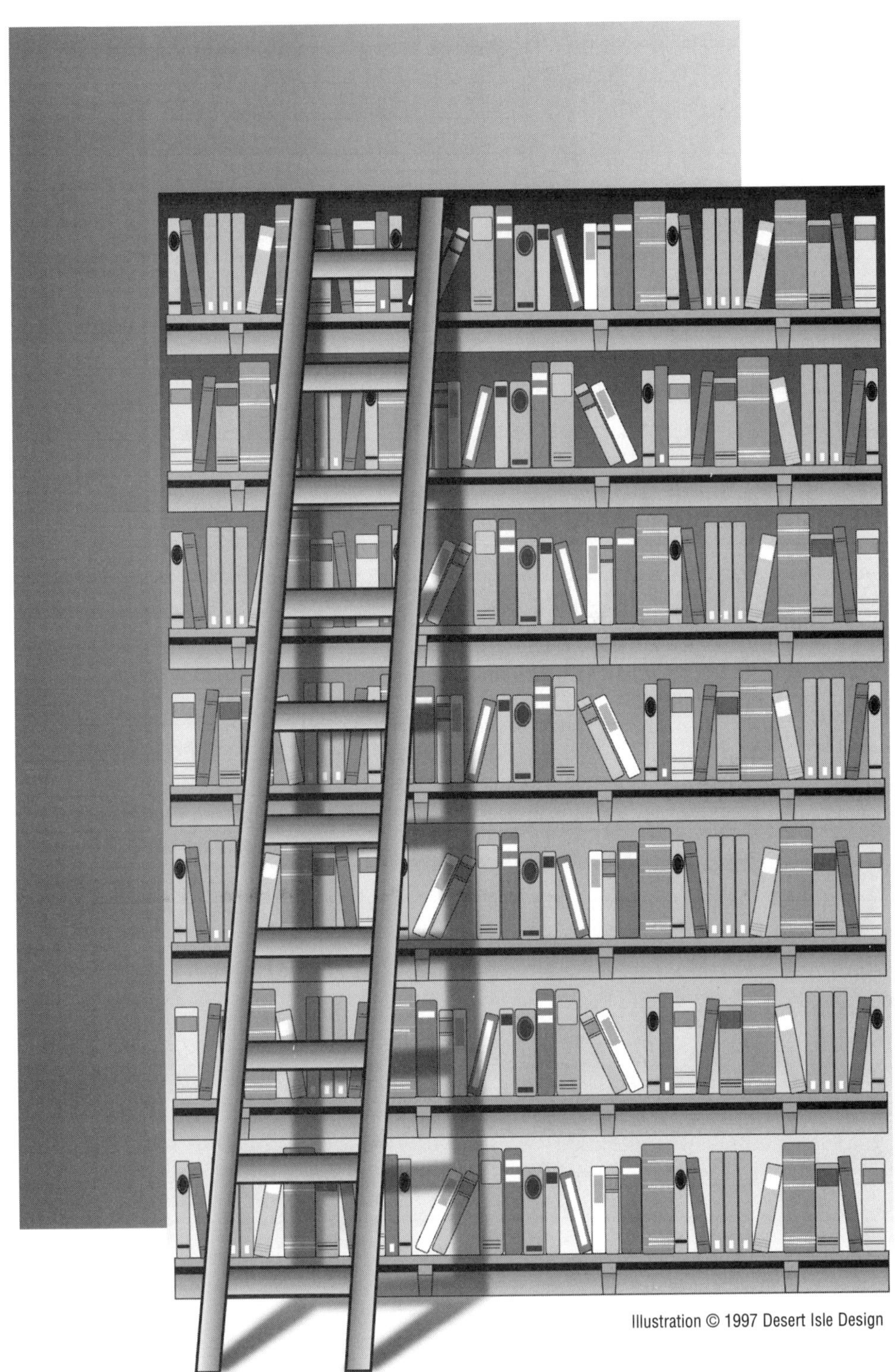

Illustration © 1997 Desert Isle Design

Drifting Through the Library Stacks

Sharon Zukowski

My parents made reading an important part of our lives. From cereal boxes to newspapers to books—the five Zukowski kids read anything and everything. The rules were simple: we could read at breakfast and lunch, but not dinner. Reading at the dinner table was a treat reserved for "special" occasions.

NOTHING WAS OFF-LIMITS. If we could carry it home from the library, we would read it. This reading "free-for-all" allowed me to drift through the library stacks, pulling down whatever looked interesting.

Edgar Allan Poe. Arthur Conan Doyle. Agatha Christie. Dorothy L. Sayers. Ellery Queen. These greats are often included on a mystery writer's list of early influences. Not mine. I didn't read Poe until forced to by a high-school English teacher—and I did not enjoy the experience. I never read a Sherlock Holmes story until a year or two after I graduated college (and then only because I was dating a guy who was a Sherlockian fan). *Ten Little Indians* is the only Agatha Christie book I read (until much later in life). Sayers and Queen never sparked my imagination.

My early influences varied. After a brief flirtation with Nancy Drew, I devoured biographies. George Washington Carver and other inventors fascinated me. From bios, it was an easy slide to history. My fascination with World War II, especially Hiroshima, lasted for a few years. Then I started reading the books my older brother and sister brought home from school. When they finished a book, I'd borrow it and read.

As a result, I read books like Stephen Crane's *The Red Badge of Courage* while still in grammar school. I liked the book—but didn't know why. It wasn't until a few years ago that I reread *Red Badge.* My adult eyes saw things the child skipped over because she didn't understand.

High school opened new reading worlds. Along with Shakespeare, Steinbeck, Sinclair, Fitzgerald, Lewis, and the standard classroom fare, I discovered "popular" books such as James Michener's *The Drifters,* Betty Smith's *A Tree Grows in Brooklyn,* John Updike, and Raymond Carver.

When I entered college, I also

entered the world of drama. Surrounded by friends who loved the theater, especially Eugene O'Neill, I suddenly felt uneducated. My high school, while giving me a great background in early American theater, had somehow completely skipped over the man who may have been America's greatest playwright. I made up for this oversight by immersing myself in O'Neill. After reading all his plays, I read his bios. From there, I went to his influences: Shaw, Chekov, Ibsen, Strindberg.

How did these influences affect my writing? Not at all—because I wasn't writing while drifting through the library stacks. My writing career didn't begin until 1987 when I started *The Hour of the Knife* (published in 1990 by St. Martin's Press).

But by 1980, I was looking for something different to read. Something that was well written with a story. I was tired of reading popular fiction, books where "nothing happened." I wanted good characters, I wanted a good story. I wanted action.

If I close my eyes, I can picture the book that set me off into the mystery world as first a reader, then a writer. It was a paperback collection of short stories featuring the "great American Detective."

Dashiell Hammett, Raymond Chandler, Sara Paretsky, Nancy Pickard, Robert B Parker, and above all others, John D. MacDonald.

These are my early mystery influences.

Early Influences

From Annette Meyers:

I DON'T KNOW WHO turned me on to the *New Yorker*, probably a teacher who knew I wanted to be a writer, but whoever she was, she changed my life. As Toms River, New Jersey, was a small town in every sense of the word, the sophistication of the *New Yorker* was exotic and thrilling. And inspiring.

The *New Yorker* taught me how to write. I was profoundly influenced by two of their regular contributors. J.D. Salinger and S.J. Perelman. The *New Yorker* "style," for better or for worse, is still in my work.

Another major influence on me as a writer was Melville's *Moby Dick*. It opened my mind to the metaphysical. It has haunted me and my work in the best of all possible ways.

My mother belonged to the Book of the Month Club, and although she would hide the "torrid" books, I'd usually find them. So I read Hemingway's *For Whom the Bell Tolls* and there were those wonderful clean, spare sentences.

Salinger, Perelman, Melville, and Hemingway. I was blessed.

From Wendy Hornsby:

MY EARLY INFLUENCES: FOR mystery; Margaret Millar, Raymond Chandler, Ross MacDonald, Ross Thomas, Agatha Christie, Edgar Allan Poe, of course. As a kid I read my way through Dickens, a huge influence on a budding hard-boiled writer, and Mark Twain who is the master of characterization, and Ambrose Bierce because he was so wicked.

From John Lutz:

EARLY INFLUENCES?

A VARIETY of people. Many of them short-story writers.

Hemingway, Saki, Graham Green, Ray Bradbury, Flannery O'Conner, Irwin Shaw, Dorothy Parker, Steinbeck, Fitzgerald, London, Maugham . . . and closer to our field: Ross MacDonald, Cornell Woolrich, Jack Ritchie, Stanley Ellin, John D. MacDonald, and of course, Poe, Doyle, Hammett, Chandler, Christie, the people who influenced those people previously mentioned.

Other influences: Benham, Hutter, Dannay (both as editor and writer), Sullivan, and more recently Hutchings and Jordan, by virtue of what they would or wouldn't buy as editors.

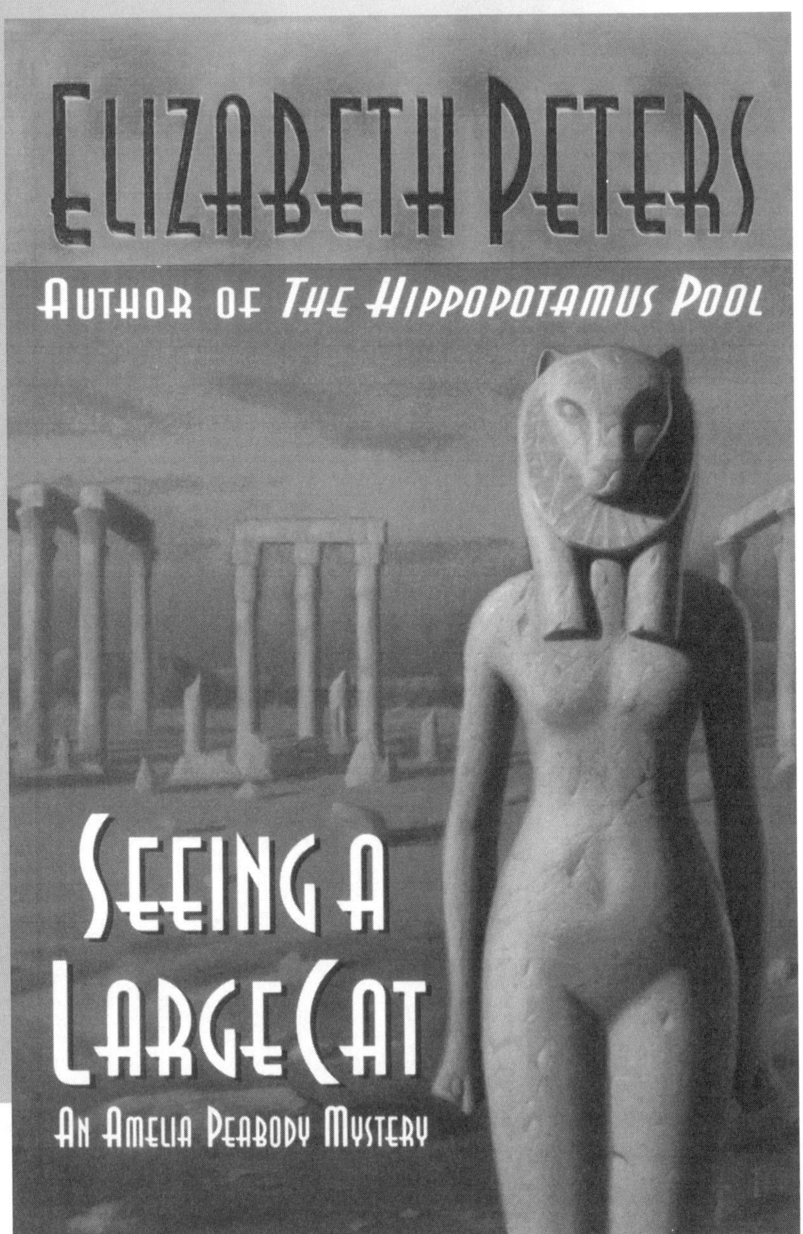

Seeing a Large Cat by Elizabeth Peters

Interview with Elizabeth Peters

Dean James

IN 1966, A YOUNG writer named Barbara Mertz published her first novel, *The Master of Blacktower,* under the pseudonym of Barbara Michaels. Two years later, she published her first novel under the name of Elizabeth Peters, *The Jackal's Head.* In "real life," Barbara G. Mertz earned a Ph.D. in Egyptology from the famed Oriental Institute of the University of Chicago, and she published two very popular nonfiction works on the political history and the daily life of ancient Egypt. In the three decades since the appearance of her first novel, Barbara Michaels has become a best-selling writer, and Elizabeth Peters's books fly off the shelves as well. Michaels became known primarily as a writer of "romantic suspense" in the tradition of writers like

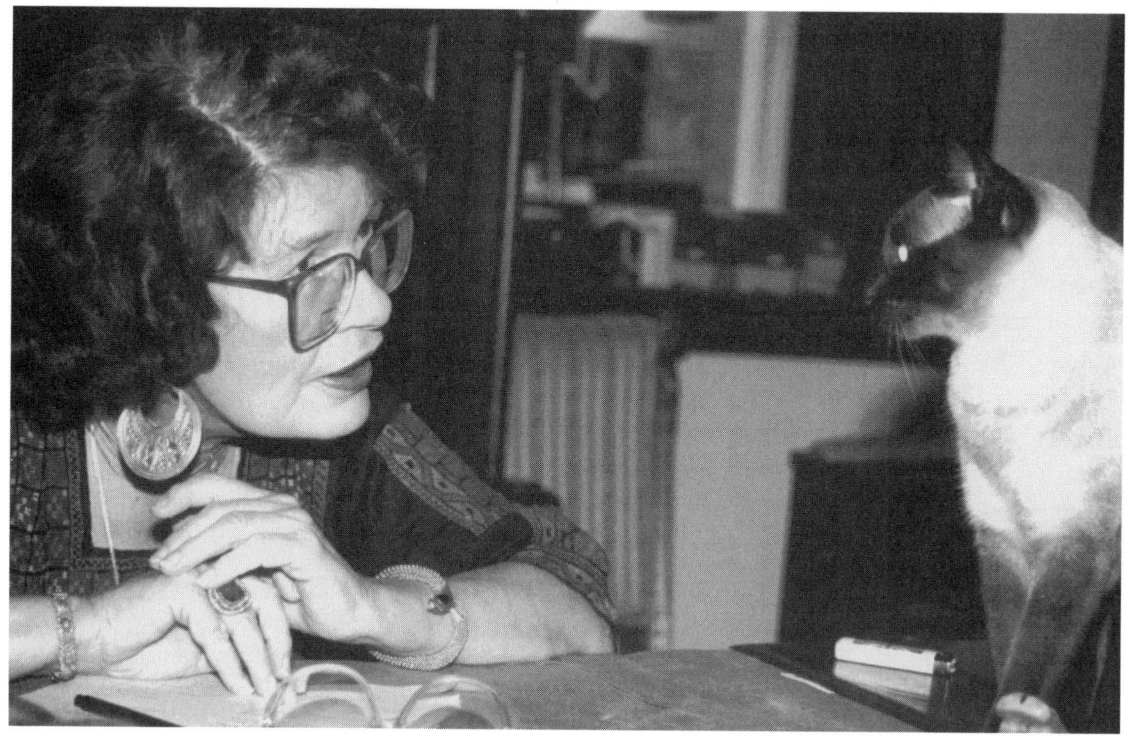

Elizabeth Peters *Photo credit: Osmond Geier*

Mary Stewart and Phyllis A. Whitney. Often mixing elements of the supernatural with more mundane terrors, Michaels can spin a web of suspense that keeps her readers sleepless. The books of Elizabeth Peters, on the other hand, are more akin to traditional mystery novels. Although her early novels were also cast in the "romantic suspense" vein, Elizabeth Peters soon invested her work with a healthy sense of humor and some rather innovative notions about the abilities of women and their relationships with men—ideas that were quite radical for the mystery and romantic suspense fiction of the time. From their very beginnings, two of Peters's mystery series characters, Jacqueline Kirby and Vicky Bliss, defied the conventional wisdom that any single woman in a mystery novel had to marry a "hero" at the end of the book. If either of these women ended up with a man at the end of a novel, it was by her choice and on her terms; and if there was no man around at the end, well—that worked, too. Several years before Marcia Muller launched the "rebirth" of the female sleuth with her novel *Edwin of the Iron Shoes* (1977), Elizabeth Peters and Barbara Michaels were busy writing about liberated and intelligent women confronting and tackling challenging situations with their own capable hands. The very first Guest of Honor at Malice Domestic, Barbara Mertz has won many honors in her career, including a lifetime achievement award from Bouchercon, an Agatha Award for Best Novel for *Naked Once More*, and an honorary doctorate from Hood College, as well as the unabashed adoration of her legions of fans, both male and female, around the world. She took time out from a busy writing schedule, immersed in the continuing adventures of Amelia Peabody Emerson, to allow "Elizabeth Peters" her say in her own inimitable fashion.

What writers and/or books influenced the type of fiction that you wanted to write?

If I wanted to be pompous, which I often do, I would say (truthfully) that every writer I've ever read has influenced my work—and then I'd give you a list, starting with Plato. The strongest influences, obviously, are from writers of thrillers and mysteries. I never read Nancy Drew, went straight to Agatha and Dorothy, Chandler and Ellery Queen—and to the fantasy writers my dad favored. It may have been Lovecraft and the other Weird Tales crowd who began my interest in horror stories. And of course there were H. Rider Haggard and John Buchan, from whom I borrow unashamedly.

When did you first realize that you were funny? And was there a conscious decision to make humor an important part of the Elizabeth Peters books?

Am I funny? I hope so. As one of my characters once remarked, "Laughter is one of the two things that make life worthwhile." (Actually, I would make that "four things"—adding gin and chocolate.) In fact I had a hard time convincing my then-editor that I could get away with humor in a mystery context. *The Camelot Caper* (1969) was the first book in which I let myself go, and the poor man was extremely dubious about the whole thing. People seemed to like it, so I was allowed to proceed from there. I still don't understand why he reacted as he did. Male writers had been producing comic mysteries for some time. I guess maybe it was, at that time, a new venture for women.

Is there any truth to the rumor that you are the illicit love child of H. Rider Haggard and Dorothy L. Sayers?

Make that illicit *grand*child, if you don't mind.

Did readers and critics notice, back in the 1960s and 1970s, that Peters heroines like Vicky Bliss and Jacqueline Kirby weren't the standard issue suspense-novel heroines?

Some readers did; I can't remember that any critic was perceptive enough to notice I was being innovative, brilliant, and ground-breaking. The first Vicky, *Borrower of the Night,* which was published in 1973, was, I believe, the first "liberated Gothic." I can't think of an earlier mystery in which the heroine turned down both ardent suitors and blackmailed another guy into giving her a job. (This is where we miss dear Ellen Nehr, isn't it? She probably could think of one.) I'm proud of that, and I am still slightly annoyed at being overlooked by feminist critics. Thanks for asking, Dean!

Did you feel you were taking any risks by writing about such unusual women in a convention-ridden genre? Weren't you pretty much a "lone voice crying in the wilderness" for most of that time period?

Thanks for asking that one, too. I don't believe I thought of myself as being a lone voice—though for a good many years, I guess I was—or of taking chances. I did my thing and luckily for me, I found an audience of receptive readers who have been incredibly supportive and loyal. And, at the risk of sounding vain (something I constantly avoid) I think the books can be enjoyed on several different levels. It's only *very* clever critics like yourself who notice my subtler techniques.

In your career, there have been some significant changes in mystery publishing. What do you think are the best changes? The worst?

The great thing that has happened with mystery publishing is the expansion of the definitions and limits of the genre. The classics of the first Golden Age were almost all puzzles—whodunits. The second Golden Age produced writers as diverse as Reg Hill, Joan Hess, Charlotte MacLeod—the list is endless, and the additional richness such writers have contributed is vast. The worst thing? Take your pick—the excessive concentration on publicity, especially book tours, which I hate—it takes time away from writing, which is, after all, the point of the whole thing, and puts an additional burden on the beleaguered author—or the recent focus on blockbuster best-sellers, to the detriment of good solid so-called "midlist" writers. We're losing potential talent because publishers want instant gratification and big profits and they aren't willing to let a writer develop at his or her own pace.

Has Elizabeth Peters traveled to all the marvelous and exotic places that her characters have in the books?

Yes, lucky creature, she has. And plans to go on doing so as long as her strength holds out. When it fails she will be carried around in a litter.

[Ed. Note: may I go ahead and put in my application right now as Chief Litter-Bearer?]

What are the most endearing characteristics of your three series heroines, Vicky Bliss, Jacqueline Kirby, and Amelia Peabody Emerson?

Hmm, well, some people would claim they have no endearing characteristics. All I can do is give you my opinion. In some ways Jacqueline is the least sympathetic of the three; she is inhumanly competent, sharp-tongued, and cynical. I like her because she *is* sure of herself and not about to take any crap from anybody. The same thing could be said of Vicky and Amelia, but they have weaknesses Jacqueline hasn't demonstrated—and it is their weakness I enjoy as much as their strengths. Vicky is over confident and too quick to leap to conclusions. "Sometimes I am wrong," she admits—and that's endearing, I think—not only that she is wrong sometimes, but that she can admit it. Amelia seldom admits she is wrong, but the perceptive reader will notice that she is very insecure on some levels—and the discrepancies between what she says and what she does make her, for me, both comical and attractive. Of course, the main thing about all three is that though they are ardent feminists, they all adore men. Especially certain men.

What are their most exasperating qualities?

My dear, they have no exasperating qualities. I modeled all three to some extent on myself.

Is any of them more difficult to write, for some reason, than the others? Jacqueline and Amelia are particularly strong-willed, I think. Vicky is stubborn, too, but in a different way.

It all depends on the mood I'm in, and on the plot possibilities that come to mind. Some plots demand certain characters. I do Vicky when I'm feeling sentimental and romantic—or when a delicious scam comes to mind—but I guess Amelia is the one I find easiest to write about. Which leads us on to—

Amelia seems the nearest and dearest to your heart these days. Why? What is it about her that appeals more to you as a writer?

It's true that at the moment I am more engaged with Amelia; I think it is in part because my interest in Egyptology has reawakened—it was always there, to some extent, but I've made three trips to Egypt in the past five years, and every time I go I become more hypnotized by the country and the subject. The second reason is that I had, recently, one of those breakthroughs that sometimes (only too rarely) occurs with a writer—I now have clear in my mind the general plot outlines for the next four books—even the titles. This has never happened to me before. I can hardly wait to see how it is all going to work out.

What are the particular challenges in writing the Amelia books? What are the easy bits, if any?

The challenges are also the rewards. Avoiding anachronisms and getting the background details right is a lot of work, but I enjoy that kind of nit-picking research. Perhaps the greatest challenge arises from the fact that I pinned the books and the characters down in time. I didn't do that deliberately, because at the beginning I didn't intend to write a series. If I had intended to, I might have finessed the dates and the ages of the characters, and—above all else!—not given Amelia and Emerson a child who was bound to get older with each passing year. Ramses is twelve in the latest book. [Ed. Note, *The Hippopotamus Pool.*] He will be sixteen in the next—nineteen in the succeeding volume—and so on. I have to make him a believable (well, more or less) adult and yet retain his distinctive characteristics. The same is true, to a lesser extent, of the other characters. It's enormous fun! The easy bits relate to the relationship between Amelia and Emerson. I can write their dialogue when I'm half asleep. (No comments, please.)

The latest Amelia novel, *The Hippopotamus Pool,* introduces a new character, David, whom we all hope to see again. Will we see further complications to the Ramses/Nefret relationship in upcoming books? *The Hippopotamus Pool* also brought back Evelyn and Walter Emerson; will we get to see more of them?

You will indeed see David again. One of the things I enjoy about these books is the cast of supporting characters. I've gotten to know many of them quite well; I think about them, worry about them, and wonder what is going to happen to them. With Evelyn, for instance, it seemed to me quite reasonable that—devoted mother though she is—she would be a little envious of Amelia's adventurous life, so I gave her a parasol and a chance to have a few adventures of her own. I use these characters as I need them, but I have a certain fondness for them. Kevin O'Connell, the young journalist, has been frustrated in love several times; I think he needs a wife, and one day I may give him one. Abdullah is getting old; what am I going to do about the dear fellow? (I have an idea.) Ramses and Nefret . . . I know how that relationship is going to turn out, but there are a good many complications for them and me to work out before the culmination. And what about Sethos, the Master Criminal, my favorite villain? Is he really dead? Who is (or was) he, really?

What's next for Elizabeth Peters?

You should have a pretty good idea, from the above, what is next for Elizabeth Peters. I want to do another Vicky one of these days—not only because she and John still have a long way to go before they can straighten out their relationship, but so that I can play a particular joke involving a certain famous fictional detective who specializes in art thefts. However, my major concentration for a while will be on Amelia and Co. I am having almost as much fun with these books as some of my readers appear to have, and although I know in general terms what is going to happen I can't wait to see *how* it will happen.

As a "scoop," Elizabeth Peters gave us her titles for the upcoming new volumes in the adventures of Amelia Peabody Emerson and crew:

Vol. 9: *Seeing a Large Cat (1997)*
Vol. 10: *The Ape Beside the Balance (1998)*
Vol. 11: *Serpent on Your Brow*
Vol. 12: *Thunder in the Sky*

[Ed. Note: There are no publication dates yet for these, but fans will be awaiting them eagerly. Just like me.]

An Elizabeth Peters Checklist

VICKY BLISS SERIES

Borrower of the Night (1973)
Street of the Five Moons (1978)
Silhouette in Scarlet (1983)
Trojan Gold (1987)
Night Train to Memphis (1994)

JACQUELINE KIRBY SERIES

The Seventh Sinner (1972)
The Murders of Richard III (1974)
Die for Love (1984)
Naked Once More (1989)

AMELIA PEABODY EMERSON SERIES

Crocodile on the Sandbank (1975)
The Curse of the Pharaohs (1981)
The Mummy Case (1985)
Lion in the Valley (1986)
The Deeds of the Disturber (1988)
The Last Camel Died at Noon (1991)
The Snake, the Crocodile, and the Dog (1992)
The Hippopotamus Pool (1996)
Seeing a Large Cat (1997)

NON-SERIES BOOKS

The Jackal's Head (1968)
The Camelot Caper (1969)
The Dead Sea Cipher (1970)
The Night of Four Hundred Rabbits (1971)
Legend in Green Velvet (1976)
Devil-May-Care (1977)
Summer of the Dragon (1979)
The Love Talker (1980)
The Copenhagen Connection (1982)

Ten Favorite Mysteries From Barbara Mertz

(aka Elizabeth Peters and Barbara Michaels)

"These are not *my all-time favorites—how could anyone limit herself to ten? They are ten* of *my favorites. The distinction should be evident." Barbara Mertz*

1. *The Woman in White* - Wilkie Collins
2. *The Daughter of Time* - Josephine Tey
3. *The Family Vault* - Charlotte MacLeod
4. *Through a Glass Darkly* - Helen McCloy
5. *The Dark Place* - Aaron Elkins
6. *Strong Poison* - Dorothy Sayers
7. *If I'd Killed Him When I Met Him* - Sharyn McCrumb
8. *Urn Burial* - Patrick Ruell (Reginald Hill)
9. *Thus Was Adonis Murdered* - Sarah Caudwell
10. *The Plague Court Murders* - John Dickson Carr

Interview with Sharan Newman

Dean James

HISTORICAL MYSTERIES HAVE BECOME a very popular part of the mystery genre as a whole, with writers like Anne Perry and Ellis Peters becoming bestsellers. The two periods which seem to be the most popular for writers are the Middle Ages and the Victorian era. One medievalist who is writing mysteries is Sharan Newman. Currently completing her dissertation for a Ph.D. in medieval history from the University of California-Santa Barbara, Sharan Newman has the academic credentials to enforce her historical fiction. The author of a novel for young adults and of a trilogy of Arthurian fantasy novels, told from the point of view of Guinevere, Newman has also published three novels in her critically acclaimed series about a young French woman, Catherine LeVendeur. The first novel in the series, *Death Comes as Epiphany,* was an Agatha and Anthony nominee for Best First Novel, and it won the Macavity Award in the same category. In this first appearance, Catherine LeVendeur is a novice at the Convent of the Paraclete in twelfth-century France. Presided over by Heloise, the Paraclete was a famous monastic institution of the time. Real people like Heloise, Peter Abelard, John of Salisbury, Abbot Suger of the Abbey of St. Denis, and Bernard of Clairvaux mingle with the characters Newman has created to tell her stories of murder and mayhem in the twelfth century. The second and third novels in the series, *The Devil's Door* and the recently published *The Wandering Arm,* continue the story of Catherine and her family. Readers looking for quality historical fiction ought to add Newman's name to their lists of must-read authors. In addition to providing readers with a vivid look at life in France in the twelfth century, Newman also offers absorbing stories with well-drawn, sympathetic characters.

Thanks to our respective Internet connections, Sharan and I were able to conduct this interview via cyberspace. Here's what Sharan had to say about her work.

Before turning to mysteries, you had written one juvenile/young adult novel, and a trilogy of historical novels about Guinevere. How did you decide to switch to historical mysteries?

I switched to historical mysteries when I discovered that mysteries were what I was reading most. Then I happened upon a minor tidbit of history that intrigued me and formed the basis for the first book, *Death*

Comes as Epiphany.

Isn't the Guinevere trilogy going to be reprinted soon?

The Guinevere books will be published late in 1996 in paperback. They are historical fantasy based on the legends of King Arthur and set loosely in Late Roman Britain.

Why did you choose the twelfth century for your series? And why France?

I chose the twelfth century because that's the area I was most interested in for my academic work. France particularly because I know where I want to go on research trips.

I've heard you remark, on a number of occasions, that you often feel more at home in the Middle Ages than in the twentieth century. Why is that? How do you think it affects your fiction?

I do feel more at home in the twelfth century, in a way. I've lived with it so long that I feel I know many of the people and events better than current ones. I know that I would have to do just as much research if I wanted to write a contemporary mystery and would probably make more mistakes. I suppose that affects my work in that my characters are not historical figures to me but friends and neighbors.

You're writing about an intelligent, forceful young woman who lives in a period in which most lay persons think women had little freedom. Is this a popular misconception? If not, how far can you push the limits and remain accurate in your portrayal of the period?

Women in twelfth-century France had more freedom than most people assume; certainly more than in later periods in European history. Their ability to act independently varied according to social class and individual family circumstances, just as it does today. One confusion is because there were rules about what women could do, or at least a number of men writing in an attempt to keep them from doing things, but records indicate that these rules were largely ignored. Women were not priests, nor master masons, nor usually warriors, but that's still largely true for every time up until the last thirty years.

This is a complex issue which has to be looked at in the context of the medieval concept of freedom and the restraints and obligations put on all of society. You don't really want the full lecture here. I will say that I can give examples of women just as intelligent and forceful as my heroine (or more so) living at this time.

In the first novel, *Death Comes as Epiphany,* Catherine uncovers a previously unknown bit of family history, that she has Jewish relatives. Why did you decide to give Catherine a partly Jewish family? How does this "dual perspective" of Catholicism and Judaism affect the characters and the plots?

The story of the Jews of northern Europe in the Middle Ages is another that has been either distorted or ignored. I became interested when I realized how little I had been taught about this community even in graduate level classes. The conflicts between this group and the majority in power provides a great deal of subject matter for a mystery. Also the little noted but indisputable fact that individuals within both groups interacted on a friendly level interests me a lot. The "dual perspective" allows me to show some of the diversity of belief and opinion in this time and also, on a practical note, lets me explain things that might be strange both to one set of characters and to my readers.

In the second novel, *The Devil's Door,* violence against women plays an important role in the story. Were medieval attitudes about domestic violence significantly different than modern attitudes?

Were medieval attitudes about domestic violence significantly different from modern ones? Not different enough.

What aspects of the Middle Ages do you find it most difficult to portray in the novels? (e.g., what aspects of the Middle Ages do you think are most difficult for modern readers to get a true sense of?)

I think that it's difficult for modern readers to understand that there was a wide variety of opinions and beliefs, both social and religious, in the Middle Ages. At the same time, there are concepts we take for granted, such as personal freedom as opposed to personal responsibility, that would have been totally alien to most people then. My major problem is trying to portray both the universal emotions that are part of being human as well as the cultural beliefs that belong to this time and place and still make them comprehensible to the modern reader. This isn't that difficult as long as the reader is willing to throw out previous misconceptions about the time.

As you've been working on the novels, you've also been coping with graduate school. How do you manage both?

I have no idea how I manage. Not as well as I'd like to. Any suggestions would be appreciated!

Are there any writers who have influenced you, in what you write, etc?

I'm influenced by Heloise, John of Salisbury, Bernard of Clairvaux, Peter Abelard, Terry Prachett, and that incredibly prolific writer, Anon.

Are there any types of information that you need to know but have difficulty finding out? How do you find out obscure things, like what people used for toilet paper in the twelfth century?

I have friends with very strange dissertation topics.

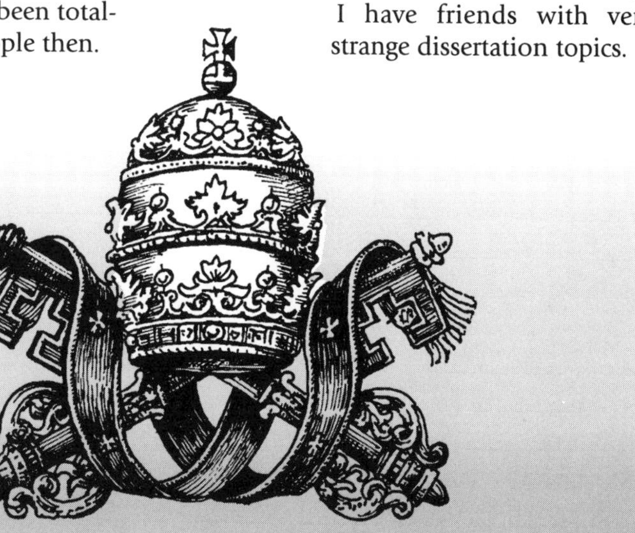

You've Come A Long Way, Baby

Murder at the Feast of Rejoicing by Lynda S. Robinson

Women's Roles in the Ancient Mystery

Lynda S. Robinson

The farther you go back in time, the harder it becomes for a writer to make a woman the major detective in a mystery due to the limitations most societies placed on females. Why?

I WOULD LIKE TO ANSWER this question first by saying that I'm often asked why I chose the male characters of Lord Meren, confidant of King Tutankhamun, and his adopted son Kysen as my detectives. The characters are in fact based on my reading in Egyptology, where I came across a short discussion of the fact that pharaohs often had confidential inquiry agents called the Eyes and Ears of Pharaoh. Such an official in ancient Egypt would have been male. In conjunction, one of the primary reasons I chose to make my detectives male was because, in the ancient world, women weren't as free as men. Women simply couldn't move around in society as freely as men did. In addition, most women didn't play major roles outside the home. There are exceptions, but these are statistically rare.

I had to have a detective who could move freely through various divisions of Egyptian society without comment. I also needed a detective who could play a commanding role in government and at court. Women might be vendors in a market, might be weavers, dancers and priestesses, or queens, but seldom (perhaps never) did they hold any kind of position in government such as vizier, minister, or tax collector. Neither did they seem to hold power positions in the great temples.

There are of course instances of women taking power and a role usually reserved for men, such as Hatshepsut, who ruled as a female king. However, she did rule as a king. There was no concept of a queen regnant in ancient Egyptian culture. Such cases as Hatshepsut seem to have been the exception. Thus it would have been inappropriate for me to show a female detective investigating embalmer priests, royal scribes, noble ministers of pharaoh, or even the more humble tomb-workers of the Valley of the Kings.

Such limitations based on gender seem unfair, and perhaps they were. However, Egyptian females were also among the most free in the ancient world. They could own property, make contracts, divorce, take property with them from a marriage, own a business.

From where do these limitations derive? This is an important question that should be answered if one is to understand why writers of ancient and historical mysteries make their female characters behave as they do. A brief exploration of the nature of male and female roles in the human species will illuminate.

In preindustrial societies the most basic and common division of labor is along gender lines. In hunter-gatherer societies (the simplest) this division, along with age, constitute the basic criteria by which bands of people organize themselves. This means that women are responsible for food preparation, gathering of plants, fruits and nuts, and child-rearing. By virtue of their responsibilities, especially that of child-rearing, women are therefore less mobile, although no less essential to a group than men.

Contrary to the biased imaginings of male scholars and Hollywood, man the hunter could not survive without woman, the gatherer. Anthropologists have, at last, studied the actual results of hunter-gatherer survival strategies and realized that no such group can survive on the yield of hunting alone. This is because, in most environments, hunting isn't nearly as successful as we urban dwellers would like to think. It isn't uncommon for the hunt to be unsuccessful for many days and for men to come back empty-handed. When this happens, the band's survival depends on what the women have gathered.

As societies become more complex, the roles people play also become more complex. However, until well after the Industrial Revolution, the work that women did was labor intensive and time consuming, unrelieved by such modern inventions as frozen food, mass production of staples such as bread, the sewing machine, and so on.

In addition, without modern science, pregnancy and childbirth were extremely risky, resulting in high mortality rates for both mother and infant. As with other species, a low survival rate necessitates a high birth rate, thus further risking women's health. All of these factors tended, until recently, to limit the time women could spend away from their duties. These factors limited their mobility, limited the length of women's lives. There used to be a lot

more widowers than there are now.

Nevertheless, these limitations shouldn't obscure the vital role of women in ancient and historical societies. Indeed, one can be misled by the misogynistic tendencies of some societies such as ancient Greece and Rome or Victorian England. Any writer of historical mysteries can tell you that the historical and archaeological records are biased. This is because, until recently, scholars were mostly men, and men study those things that are most familiar to them. The majority of them in the past have discounted women and their lives as uninteresting or unworthy of study.

After all, all the important inventions in history, all the great art, all the great writings have been done by men, with a few exceptions. Right? Well, let's think about it. Who do you think is more likely to have discovered the use of fire—a male who is out hunting, or a female who needs to cook food for her family? Who is more likely to have invented pottery—the male who uses spears, bows and arrows, or the female who needs pottery with which to cook? Also, men in the ancient world made records of their own contributions and interests because they were most often the ones holding the clay tablet and stylus or rush pen and papyrus.

In addition, we of the twentieth century tend to forget just how vital women's roles were to preindustrial cultures. In ancient Egypt, for example, there was no Social Security. Social Security came in the form of one's children. Offspring took care of the older generation and yet needed their parents to pass on essential skills. The children women bore and raised weren't luxuries; they were indispensable to survival.

What are the solutions to the limitations placed on women in the ancient/historical world in which so many exciting mysteries are being set? Anne Perry has done an excellent job of creating a husband and wife team of detectives from Victorian England, Charlotte and Thomas Pitt. Her considerable talent hides the effort to which she must go to place her female detective in a position in which she can justifiably involve herself in the investigation of crime.

Victorian women simply weren't policemen; they weren't judges; they weren't sheriffs or private investigators. But they were married to all of the above (Thomas Pitt is an inspector), and their male relatives held such positions. In many cases Perry skillfully devises plots close to home and family so that Charlotte can be

Illustration © 1997 Desert Isle Design

brought on the scene. Her upper class connections also give her an advantage.

However, there are some things that Charlotte cannot do, such as chase someone around the slums of London. Thomas does that. The farther back in time one sets a mystery, the less likely it is that Perry's ingenious solutions will work. This is true in my case because many of my stories involve political and diplomatic intrigue at the highest levels of ancient Egyptian society. This is not to say that highborn women weren't influential. Nefertiti, consort of the heretic Akhenaten, seems to have held a great deal of power. But it is probable that she did so through her personal relationship with the king rather than through her official position as queen.

Despite the limitations discussed above, I create major female characters in my Egyptian series who, like Anne Perry's characters, wield power in informal ways. I believe that, like most disadvantaged groups, women sought paths around the obstacles put in their way. This is why, for example, traditional women often seek to influence men through emotions. Such activities would most likely leave no trace, no written record, no formal body of knowledge. However, it is a logical deduction to make, because the human species hasn't changed that much in three thousand years.

Writers of ancient and historical mysteries must constantly challenge themselves to understand the ways in which women contributed to past societies and show these contributions in their stories. Thus, the daughter of my detective, Lord Meren, is slowly working around her father's prejudice against her involving herself in his work. In doing so, she goes against the accepted women's role in her society, just as did Hatshepsut before her.

Few of us realize how much women's contributions and lives are and have been discounted because it is a bias with which most of us are raised. This bias discounts, ignores, and unfortunately often denigrates the importance of and contributions by women to the four-million-year history of the human species. Luckily, scholars and writers are beginning to reverse this long-standing bias. This move toward the more realistic and respectful treatment of women extends to fiction as well, especially mystery fiction.

Tough Girls, Hard Cases:
Strong Women in Mystery

Susan Wittig Albert

Until the early eighties, the American mystery was a male-dominated domain, the books soaked in guts and gore and peopled by hard-boiled P.I.'s whose idea of a tender moment was a quickie on the office floor. But things have changed dramatically—and, many readers believe, for the better. In the past decade-plus, a new crowd of writers has brought life and breadth to the genre that traces its beginnings back to the macabre fiction of Edgar Allen Poe, charging it with a brand-new feminine energy.

WAIT A MINUTE. WHAT was that word again? Feminine?

You bet.

Women have been writing mysteries for years, but the best known of these tended to be British. Their main characters, moreover—like Sayers's Lord Peter Wimsey and Allingham's Albert Campion—tended to be male, or if female, then frail, elderly, and modestly nonassertive, like Christie's Miss Jane Marple. On the American side, we find Mary Roberts Rinehart's perennially jeopardized heroines, Mignon Eberhart's conventional Nurse Keate (who played a secondary role to police detective Lance O'Leary), and Phoebe Atwood Taylor, whose main characters were male. Looking back on these early mysteries, we can see how clearly the female characters reflected women's restricted social roles. They might be sturdy helpers, diligent caretakers, and potential or actual victims, but they lacked the strength to stand alone.

In the last quarter of this century, though, women's mysteries have become something else entirely. Beginning with Marcia Muller's Sharon McCone (who made her first appearance in 1977), Sue Grafton's Kinsey Millhone (1982), and Sara Paretsky's V.I. Warshawski (also 1982), the strong woman detective has emerged as a major player in modern genre fiction, giving women writers and readers an opportunity to flex their considerable muscle. Twenty years after Sharon McCone cracked her first case, the strong woman is still on the job, and getting stronger every day.

But in women's crime novels, "strong" has many meanings. These new female protagonists have the intellectual strength and professional training required to cut to the heart of complex problems in criminal logic—and the stamina not to become emotionally involved. Patricia Cornwell's forensic detective, Medical Examiner Dr. Kay Scarpetta, is a case in point. Winner of the Edgar, Creasy, Anthony, Macavity, and Gold Dagger, Cornwell's character works closely with the FBI and the police department, but does the brain work herself, remaining aloof from involvement in the often gory crimes she investigates. Another brainy sleuth is English professor Kate Fansler, created by Amanda Cross (Carolyn G. Heilbrun).

Other new-breed female detectives have reserves of physical strength, like Susan Dunlap's diminutive former gymnast Kiernan O'Shaughnessy, or Carlotta Carlyle, a six-foot-one cab-driving ex-cop P.I. (created by Linda Barnes), or Liza Cody's Eva Wylie, a female wrestler and junkyard security guard. If you are a criminal, these are not women you care to mess around with in a dark alley.

Still other strong women may not have much physical strength, but they have an inner strength born of wisdom and lived experience. Crusty, ascerbic Henrie O., for instance, is Carolyn Hart's seventy-something reporter, whose first adventure won Hart an Agatha. "I may sometimes be a soft touch," Henrie O. acknowledges in *Scandal in Fair Haven;* "I'm not a damned fool." Other nobody's-fools are seventy-plus Sister Mary Helen, the creation of Sister Carol Anne O'Marie, and the forgetful but astute Peaches Dann, an older widow brought to life by Elizabeth Daniels Squire.

A different kind of strength—the strength of deep inner insight—belongs to professional psychic Theresa Fortunato, featured in Kate Green's often spooky mysteries, and professional astrologer Jo Hughes (*Blood of an Aries*) by Linda Mather. Then there are women who have the courage to stand on feminist principle in a man's world: among others, the protagonists in *An Unsuitable Job for a Woman,* by P.D. James, *Southern Discomfort,* by Margaret Maron, and *Everything You Have is Mine,* by Sandra Scoppetonne.) And still others have enormous emotional depth and resilience: Jenny Cain, for instance, Nancy Pickard's award-winning sleuth.

In fact, many of these new female protagonists are distinguished by their emotional strength. In a genre that has traditionally emphasized plot over character and where violent action has often dominated the narrative, these new crime novelists are different. Creating characters who often seem to belong in mainstream fiction, they display a deep fascination with human motivation, with the searing emotional drama of splintered relationships, with the corrosive friction between the individual and society. Theirs are complex, thick, *dense* novels, rich in the mystery of human experience.

And while in early detective fiction the detective remains essentially aloof from human experience (symbolized by Nero Wolfe's physical isolation and Sherlock Holmes's seven-percent solution to the unsolvable riddle of human emotion), these new women protagonists are drawn into the depths of the mystery, and are profoundly changed by their experience.

Sometimes these changes are a product of the character's changing life situation, which is often based on real-life experiences women recognize and understand. P.M. Carlson's Maggie Ryan, for instance, is a college student in her first case (*Murder is Academic*). She later marries, then becomes a mother. Elizabeth George's Scotland Yard character, Sergeant Barbara Havers, must care for an unbalanced mother; Havers's emotional capacities grow as she struggles to deal with her mother's diminishing mental capabilities. Deborah Knott has to learn how to separate herself from the compromised past of her father (*Bootlegger's Daughter* by Margaret Maron), while newly named Deputy Martha Ayers, in Sharyn McCrumb's award-winning *She Walks These Hills,* must learn how to separate herself from her mentor and lover and be her own woman.

But the central character seems to undergo the greatest growth when she becomes psychologically connected to the crime (something that almost never happens to male detectives), usually through a deep inner link, real or imagined, with the victim. In this situation, she is led to an often frightening encounter with the darkness in the deepest pit of the soul, exposing her (and our own) misconceptions about the nature of order and justice in human society, making her vulnerable to human evil. In *Death in a Tenured Position,* for instance, the death of a female professor challenges Kate Fansler's too-easy understanding of her own place in the male-dominated academic world, fundamentally altering her facile, unquestioning acceptance of the privileges men grant themselves in such prestigious institutions as Harvard and Columbia (where the author is an English professor). In *I.O.U.,* Jenny Cain's understanding of obligation and responsibility—the duty we owe to others in the community—is deeply challenged when she solves the mystery of her mother's agonizing illness and death. Jenny's confrontation with greed and evil, intensified through her identification with her victimized mother, make it impossible for her to continue to live and work as she had before.

Other female protagonists are profoundly changed by their encounters with the dark side of human nature. Jill Smith's feelings about her live-in lover are altered by what she learns in *Death and Taxes* (Susan Dunlap). Two women—Kate Shugak in Dana Stabenow's Alaskan series and Anna Pigeon, Nevada Barr's U.S. park ranger—discover the depths of their resources in confrontations with human evil in a wilderness setting. Lauren Laurano, Sandra Scoppettone's lesbian detective in *Everything You Have is Mine,* faces the dark side of the big city.

Whatever the character of the evil that confronts them, these new women detectives are risk-takers, afraid but able to face their fears, vulnerable but refusing to be victims. Their greatest strength emerges from their willingness to be afraid, to be vulnerable, to grow. Their greatest appeal to us as readers lies in what they learn about themselves as they confront the mysterious depths of evil and the unknown—the world of the shadow that lives in all of us, honest citizen and criminal alike.

The serial form of the contemporary mystery—a form that many women writers exploit with extraordinary depth and creativity—affords a unique opportunity for moral growth and psychological development. Some writers (Sue Grafton, for instance) appear not to realize the potential of the series form, so that each book, however well done, is simply another chapter in the continuing adventures of the detective. In the hands of a masterful writer like Sharyn McCrumb, however, the series itself becomes a mega novel with its own mega plot. In McCrumb's Ballad series, for instance, an over-arching plot that is woven out of the linked lives of Sheriff Spencer Arrowood and Deputies Joe LeDonne and Martha Ayers connects all the books. Readers watch, fascinated, as all of McCrumb's central characters, women and men, grow and change from their first appearance in *If Ever I Return, Pretty Peggy-O,* to their most recent in *Rosewood Casket.* Readers who take the books out of sequence are struck by the degree to which the characters have grown.

Taken altogether, it is their complex humanity that sets these new detectives apart from earlier protagonists, who were not only emotionally unassailable but also physically invincible, logically unerring, and morally certain of the distinctions between right and wrong. These are psychological luxuries the new female detective cannot easily afford. Groping for meaning in a world rendered meaningless by violence, she suffers pain, makes logical blunders, confesses her confusion and moral uncertainty. Understanding that human actions grow from many different roots, she often mistrusts her reconstruction of the crime—and even doubts her solution to the mystery.

And because she stands on the outskirts of the male-dominated world of law and order, where principles of right have long seemed absolute and unassailable, the woman detective may also question the long-held assumption that solving the crime will somehow restore order and justice to a society that is only temporarily out of kilter, only waiting to be defended and rescued by the detective. Indeed, the new crime novels by women suggest that our society may be much more radically out of alignment, that the task of the detective is not to bring justice and enlightenment but to enter the darkness, and that it is more important to be compassionate than to be morally correct.

And if you ask me, that's exactly what makes these new women so strong.

The Lesbian Detective

Ellen Hart

Mystery novels are, in a broad sense, social documents, reflecting the society in which the author lives and works. As one reads a favorite writer, cultural values and prejudices quickly become apparent, whether these values and prejudices are examined or unexamined, stated clearly or merely implied.

THIS PAST CHRISTMAS, MY local Ballantine rep invited me out for a wonderful dinner at a very expensive local restaurant. As we were chatting over appetizers and wine, I mentioned to him that if this were ten years ago, I wouldn't be here—he'd be having dinner with someone else. Prior to the mid-eighties, no major publishing house in the U.S. had ever published a series featuring a lesbian sleuth. Ten years ago, with few exceptions, the only gay and lesbian characters you found in mysteries were either sick (perverts) or dead (victims). Being gay was an indication of a person's pathology, a twisted secret that had to be hidden at all costs.[1]

Enter the modern mystery novel with positive gay characters.

Society has changed a great deal since Eva Zaremba published her first lesbian mystery with a mainstream Canadian paperback house back in 1978. Entitled *A Reason to Kill,* this book introduced Helen Keremos, a hard-boiled lesbian private eye. At the time of the book's publication, Zaremba felt her books were apolitical, though few today would argue the immense political significance of presenting an average, hard-working, middle-aged lesbian, comfortable with her sexuality and her life. Addicted to all manner of mystery novels herself, Zaremba simply set out to produce a mystery squarely within the tradition of the genre.

Several years later, Barbara Wilson added feminist politics to this new mix. Her protagonist in *Murder in the Collective,* Pam Nilson, tracks murder among a small closed

[1]*Editor's note. The only notable exception was Joseph Hansen's series about gay insurance claims investigator, Dave Brandstetter.*

circle of acquaintances (a typical mystery convention) but, giving it a political twist, Wilson makes this group a business collective. Indeed, all of the novels in this series focus on injustice toward women explored within the context of feminist values.

Katherine Forrest, creator of homicide detective Kate Delafield, began her series about the same time as Wilson. The fourth in the series, *Murder by Tradition,* centers on the grisly slaying of a young homosexual restaurant owner and the subsequent trial of the most likely suspect. While not yet completed, a movie featuring Forrest's Kate Delafield may well be the first lesbian mystery ever produced for the silver screen.

Over the next ten years, small presses led the way in the U.S., providing emerging lesbian mystery writers with an opportunity to publish in this new and growing subgenre. Virtually staking out this territory alone, these presses, in conjunction with feminist and gay and lesbian bookstores, helped create a market where once there was none.

During the eighties and early nineties, many new authors became popular as the word got out: Lesbian mysteries were a great read. While it is beyond the scope of this short piece to name them all, some of the most successful writers have been Sarah Dreher and her "Stoner McTavish" series, Elizabeth Pincus, creator of the "Nell Fury" series, Claire McNab and her Australian Detective Inspector "Carol Ashton," Lauren Wright Doughlas and her Canadian sleuth "Caitlin Reece," Jaye Maiman and novelist-turned-private-eye "Robin Miller," and Kate Allen and her "Marta Goicochea" series.

The stylized form of the mystery has often lent itself to parody and satire. Dancing with the expectations of the genre, two lesbian mystery writers have staked out this fertile territory with unusual humor and insight. First came Mary Wings and her wonderfully over-the-top Raymond Chandler send-up in *She Came Too Late* and *She Came in a Flash.* And second, Mabel Maney has emerged as one of the funniest new voices in mystery fiction. Set in 1959, *The Case of the Not-So-Nice Nurse* is a parody of two popular girls' fiction characters, nurse/detective Cherry Ames and that epitome of young ladyhood—well-groomed, well-mannered and well-spoken"—Nancy Drew. Maney re-creates a world in which wearing the wrong shoes, in and of itself, can be a crime.

The genre's first mainstream, hardcover lesbian detective, Lauren Laurano, arrived in 1991 with the publication of Sandra Scoppettone's *Everything You Have Is Mine,* followed two years later by *I'll Be Leaving You Always.* Since then, several other authors have been picked up by major houses, including myself, J.M. Redmond, and Katherine Forrest. New York's interest in the lesbian sleuth is an indication of this growing sub-genre's health and vitality.

When I began writing my first mystery, *Hallowed Murder,* in 1987, I knew nothing about the realities of modern publishing or current market trends. What I did know was that I wanted to present a story that encompassed the full landscape of my own life. For me, that meant my sleuth, Jane Lawless, would be gay. Having spent a good part of my life in the closet, I knew that truth operates on two important levels—the spoken and the unspoken. Because of that, and because I felt strongly that the private and the public self need to merge for a person to live honestly in the world, I wanted my two main characters, Jane and Cordelia, to be out of the closet, matter-of-factly going about their lives, living and moving in the larger world—not just what some have termed the gay ghetto. Perhaps even more importantly, I wanted them to be people my readers could identify with, laugh with, struggle with, and finally, be proud to call friends.

As I travel around the country doing readings and signings, one of the questions I'm most often asked is, why are gay and lesbian mysteries so popular? While there is perhaps no definitive answer to this, I believe gay mysteries are popular for the same reasons any mystery is popular. First and foremost, these books are wonderfully entertaining. Ever since humans began to gather around campfires, we've wanted to hear

Illustration © 1997 Desert Isle Design

good, well-told stories—stories that reflect our lives. The growing appreciation of human diversity in today's society—whether it be cultural, religious, sexual, political, or ethnic—underlines that point. Also, in a world filled with problems and tensions, the mystery has become an oddly comforting morality tale. Truth and lies fight it out, and, while we don't necessarily move from sadness to happiness in each book, we do achieve a certain resolution. In our everyday lives, we seldom find much of that.

And finally, in my mysteries, I do have an agenda beyond entertaining my readers with a good story. Very simply put, I want to build a bridge over which the larger society can walk toward a more mature, informed understanding of what it is to be gay. I've always felt my books could be read and enjoyed by everyone who appreciates a traditional mystery, and much to my delight, the market has borne that out. Some of the best mystery writing today is happening with the lesbian sub-genre, and I invite you all to take a look. You'll be fascinated by what you find.

A Reader's Checklist of Lesbian Detectives

by the Editors

CHARACTER	AUTHOR
Terry Barber	*Jane Meyerding*
Helen Black	*Pat Welch*
Hollis Carpenter	*Deborah Powell*
Kate Delafield	*Katherine V. Forrest*
Poppy Dillworth	*Dorothy Tell*
Nell Fury	*Elizabeth Pincus*
Maggie Garrett	*Jean Taylor*
Tyler Jones	*Joan M. Drury*
Alison Kaine	*Kate Allen*
Virginia Kelly	*Nikki Baker*
Mickey Knight	*J.M. Redman*
Jane Lawless	*Ellen Hart*
Lauren Laurano	*Sandra Scoppettone*
Stoner MacTavish	*Sarah Dreher*
Royce Madison	*Kieran York*
Robin Miller	*Jaye Maiman*
Alix Nicholson	*Sharon Gilligan*
Pam Nilsen	*Barbara Wilson*
Cassandra Reilly	*Barbara Wilson*
Lil Ritchie	*Phyllis Knight*
Sydney Sloane	*Randye Lordon*
Amanda Valentine	*Rose Beecham*
Emma Victor	*Mary Wings*
Nyla Wade	*Vicki McConnell*

POLITICAL CORRECTNESS

Mind your P's and Q's

gay and lesbianism

racism

CULTURALLY SENSITIVE

PC Hits the Mystery Scene—and Gets Hit in Return

Kathy Phillips

Soon after the 1994 publication of his novel The Night Manager, *in an interview with NPR John LeCarré took the opportunity to voice his virulent antagonism to "PC."*

HE SAID, IN EFFECT, that this American invention stands as the single greatest adversary to the contemporary artist; it is the McCarthyism of our age, subversive censorship and an attempt to control the author's thought.

While it is unfortunate that LeCarré didn't define what he meant by "PC," it has become fashionable to attack PC, without defining what it is, assuming the audience will understand, implying a complicity with the audience in an attack on the "forces of political correctness," whatever that or they are. Joan M. Drury, author, editor and publisher (Spinsters Ink, a small Minneapolis house) has written that when they questioned the use of a racist term, they were accused of being "politically correct." While feminists had poked fun at themselves about being politically correct, she says, they gave the term a positive spin. "Politically correct was synonymous with being culturally sensitive—and who would want to be less than that?":

> These days, the far right, the not-so-far-right, the moral majority, the academic/intellectual nazis, and any number of other folk who fall into a range from conservative to "good" liberals are all rallying against, railing about the concept of politically correct ... "Politically correct" was curtailing *their* rights ... was interfering with freedom of speech, freedom of choice, freedom to be all the things these people apparently aspired to be ...

Including a racist or bigot, apparently. She goes on to define "politically correct" as being "culturally sensitive . . . being respectful of all individuals and groups. . . old-fashioned courtesy, manners."

The British, possibly seeing "PC" as a uniquely American invention and having lumped it in with their equivalent, "ideologically sound," tend to most distrust anything which they believe smacks of or may be gathered under the umbrella of "PC-ness." Any proposition, no matter how innocuous-seeming, may be put into question and may be summarily discredited as being "PC" and, therefore, the product of political pressure. Political correctness, English-style, is examined in *The War of the Words: The Political Correctness Debate* (Virago Press, 1994), a brilliant collection of essays which take both sides of the issue and debate whether PC is about tolerance or about power. The editor, Sarah Dunant, television personality and author of an insightful, sophisticated mystery series featuring private investigator Hannah Wolfe (*Birth Marks, Fatlands, Under My Skin*) writes in her introduction, "to call someone PC is less a description than an insult, carrying with it accusations of everything from Stalinism/McCarthyism to (even worse?) having no sense of humour."

So it is with trepidation that one points to a satire that takes on political correctness and says, to paraphrase a little boy upon seeing an emperor, "it isn't funny." Political satire was born in an age when the object of the scorn was a class in power, a class of persons who would subject the writer to penalty, up to and including death, if he was found out. Risk was implied. Part of the humor was the element of risk, the fact that both the reader and the writer are engaged in a conspiracy. While the relative positions of the people and those in power have been ameliorated to some extent, certainly the pointing out the foibles of the monied, leisure classes, or the incompetence of bureaucracy can be amusing.

Ruth Dudley Edwards does just that in her mysteries as social satire, including *Corridors of Death* and *Clubbed to Death* (St. Martin's Press) in which she and her hero Robert Amiss took on the English government offices and the gentlemen's clubs. They are very funny and quite engaging as mysteries. On the other hand, *Matricide at St. Martha's* (St. Martin's, 1995) may present an accurate picture of life in the modern English university, but Edwards develops this picture in a bath of such extreme political correctness that it isn't at all funny. She defines the field of play and political correctness as so absurd that no one could be so ridiculous as to adhere to its principles. Nor, God forbid, to have sympathy with its proponents.

Our hero/antihero Robert Amiss, formerly member of England's civil service, is drafted by his friend Ida "Jack" Troutbeck, Bursar at St. Martha's, a failing and fading Cambridge college. The College has come into a hefty bequest from an old girl and the dons are contentiously parrying on how it should be used. The groups array themselves in three distinct cadres, the Virgins, the Dykes, and the Old Women (who are, in fact, the men).

The Mistress, Dame Maud Theodosia Buckbarrow, leads the Virgins who would dedicate the funds toward serious scholarship;

the Old Women would lay in some decent wine in a new cellar; and the Dykes want a center for Gender and Ethnic Studies—as Jack says, the "minxes and vipers" who want to "get the DWEMs (Dead White European Male) off the reading list and bring on the one-legged black lesbians."

Each group is represented by extreme examples of "the types," and, needless to say, the feminist-lesbian Dykes are particularly unpleasant. Framed in this way, who can win any ensuing argument. In the course of the battle to allocate the funds, Dame Maud is murdered in a most ingenious if improbable way, and the Dykes are implicated. As it happens, of the three Dykes, the attractive African-American from Minnesota is only a lesbian feminist activist because it is politically advantageous and, bisexual by choice, she seduces Robert. The leader of the Dykes, it turns out, is not a lesbian at all and has a fellow on the side (a bit of rough trade) but found it convenient and politically expedient to be thought to be a lesbian. The only Dyke who is, in fact, a lesbian is the murderer.

In the course of setting up the plot, Edwards gives each faction its day in court, proceeding through meetings which, in all likelihood, would have occurred in similar circumstances. And each party in each faction says what they would be presumed to have said. It may be accurate as to its implications, but it is extreme. Furthermore, the words used to describe the factions may be more than sufficient to this end, particularly the word "Dyke" which is still found offensive in some quarters. Ultimately, therefore, with the exception of Jack and Amiss, whom Edwards genuinely seems to care for, the characters are little more than stereotypes, caricatures.

David Berlinski wrote a book (*Less Than Meets the Eye,* St. Martin's, 1994) that attempts to do much the same thing in a California university where the African-American minority takes a place analogous to that occupied by the Dykes. Berlinski's book isn't funny either, but he hasn't got Edwards's obvious talent for establishing plot and sense of place. In both cases, the objects of derision are populations whose chief sin seems to be—to borrow a phrase—"getting uppity." The kind of people who are attempting to benefit from change in society, lesbians and blacks, are painted with a PC brush, set up as extremists, and made the subject of ridicule. The conclusion to be drawn seems to be that members of these groups should make a point of keeping their heads down and not ruffling any feathers—or, roughly, to go back to their former places.

It is easy to make fun of people who aren't real people, just as it is easier to say things in writing about people that would be much more difficult, if not impossible, to say to their faces. By reducing people to types, to something less than human, to something *other*—a "not-I"—we make it easy to justify saying things about them we wouldn't say about or to someone we know, or treating them in ways we wouldn't want to be treated. Including being subjected to ridicule. Incivility is bred in the absence of the human interaction, including the injection of the humanity into a fictional character.

That universities function in a world all their own is a given, and certainly university administrations efforts to comply with affirmative action dictates have produced some unintended results. In Sharyn McCrumb's *If I'd Killed Him When I Met Him* (Ballantine Books, 1995), the humor inherent in affirmative action arises in a genuine funny way. Heroine Elizabeth McPherson has come home to engage in some healing of her own while she thinks to help her mother deal with divorce by a man who's taken off with a younger woman. She discovers, instead, that her mother is doing quite well and living in an apparent state of marital-type bliss with Phyllis Casey, an assistant professor of English at the local college.

After the initial shock of the possibility that her mother may be gay, Elizabeth discovers that her mother is helping Casey with a charade; Casey had found it to her advantage to be thought to be a radical lesbian feminist in a department that had become uncomfortably radicalized. The humor is a twin bill: not only is the English Department, men who choose to use "multiculturalism" and "inclusion" in furtherance of their own political agenda, bamboozled in its own tongue, and, no matter that she is relieved of the actual event, Elizabeth is forced to anticipate accepting her mother as a lesbian. One doesn't have to see through to McCrumb's political position, to agree or disagree with it, to find the set-up and the punch line wonderful.

Returning to *Matricide at St. Martha's,* it is curious that the murderer is the only one of the Dykes who is really a lesbian. Knowing Ruth Dudley Edwards as I do, I can discount homophobia, but can insensitivity also be discounted. Or, rather, an assumption fostered by a generalized cultural expectation. In other words, this is an "other"—no further motive needs to be presented for everyone to agree that she could have perpetrated the deed. No matter how illogical their propositions, movies like *Basic Instinct* and *Fatal Attraction* and Michael Crichton's *Disclosure,* further the notion that a woman who is extreme in any segment of her life may, if confronted with the opportunity, commit the most extreme of acts elsewhere in her life.

Selma Eichler's paperback original novel, *Murder Can Stunt Your Growth* (Signet, 1996), puts a slightly different twist on the proposition. Eichler's heroine, the short and plump Desiree Shapiro, is a new investigator who takes breaks with Ben & Jerry instead of Jim Beam, and she's had two further amusing, paradoxically lightweight encounters with homicide (*Murder Can Ruin Your Looks* and *Murder Can Kill Your Social Life,* Signet). In this latest in the series, Desiree is hired by the grandmother of an asthmatic who has died just short of her tenth birthday, apparently of natural causes associated with her condition. The grandmother thinks the girl was murdered since she had only just avoided being hit by an out-of-control car, and "sick people get murdered, too, you know."

It turns out that the youngster was tickled to death with a feather duster by her older sister Barrie's lesbian lover, Saundra, who wants to take part in a family inheritance which could have been defeated if the grandmother caught on to their relationship. It's as though Martha killed the tattling kid in *The Children's Hour* before the girl had told her grandmother the critical lie.

Except in this case, apparently, it would have been the truth. These are New York liberals, so the right stuff is spouted—Barrie's ex-husband confesses that he left because she was in love with Saundra, but even if he was upset, he now believes that she could have done better. Pshaw. Eichler makes Saundra something other than human, and Barrie doesn't come off too well either. Which isn't to say that a book can't feature a murderer who is a lesbian, but if you make the character truly human, it becomes difficult to set her up as the cold-blooded killer of a child. If you create a character who is fully human, it is difficult to make her the butt of a nasty joke or the object of derision or the subject of PC backlash.

Not long ago, on television and in the movies, any character with an Italian surname was presumed a villain, at the very least associated with the Mafia, the so-called "Mob." Protest from the Italian-American community brought changes, and there was no objection to the intrusion of "thought police." Revisions were made throughout the 1950s to the decades-old volumes of Nancy Drew and Hardy Boys to delete unsavory, insulting, and stereotypic references to Jews and African-Americans.

Now women in general and lesbians in particular are pointing out that the same kinds of slanders exist in our books and in our language and that, far from anything being done about it, the very fact of their being heard creates an anti-PC backlash. Certainly there are extremists who would have "womyn" substitute for "women," but we would ignore even their contributions at our peril. As Sarah Dunant writes, language reflects an underlying attitude, and while changing language may not in fact change attitudes, may not change anything, it may start a change in thought.

It is ironic that, having been discriminated against in life and the subject of stereotypic fictional atrocities for generations, women and lesbians should have to apologize for asking to be addressed by and in their own terms. But although it is no longer fashionable to be either misogynist or homophobe, it is de rigueur to be anti-PC, and women, gays, and lesbians may simply have to wait for a shift in the fashion.

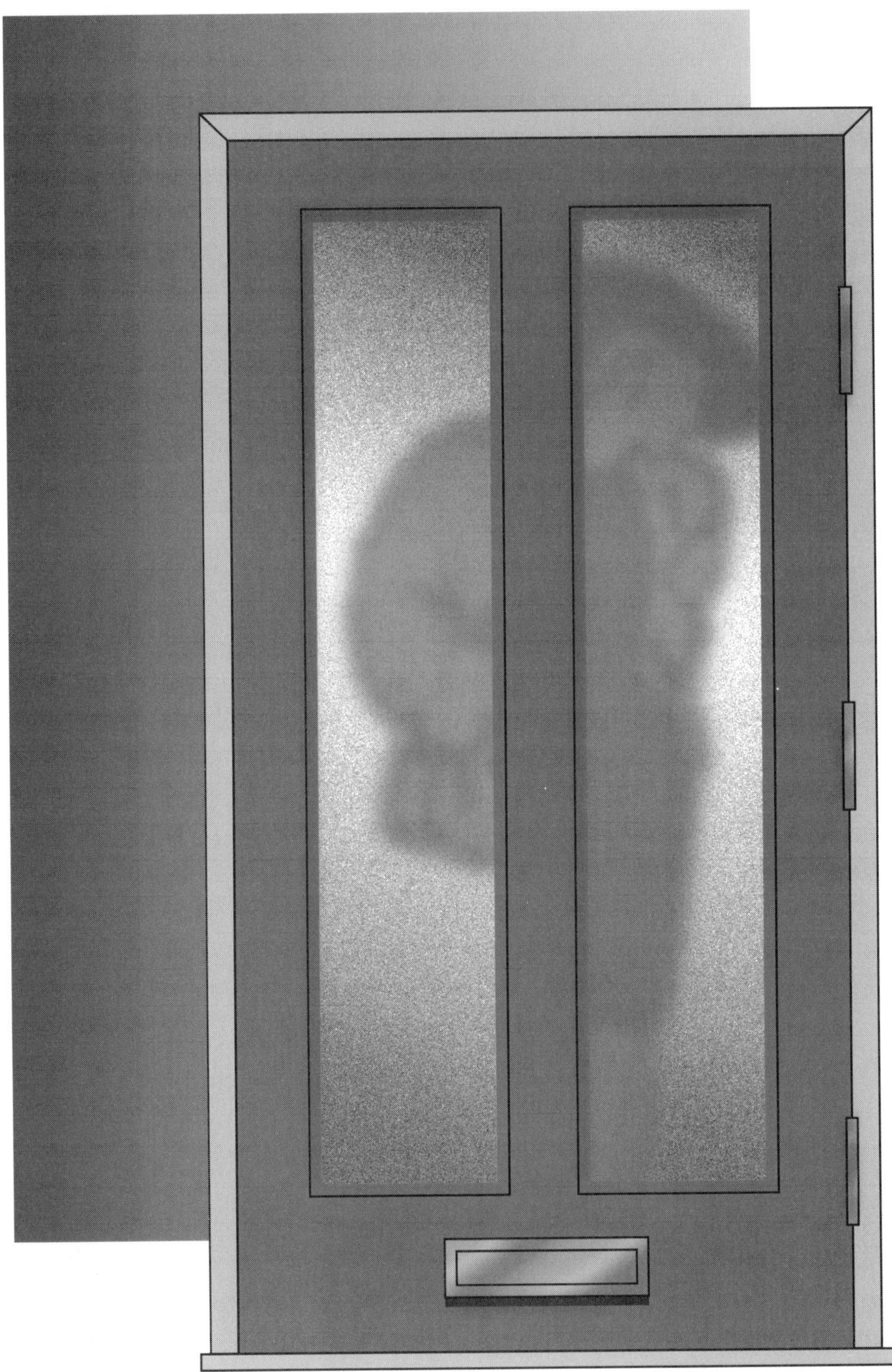

Interview with
Val McDermid

Jerry Sykes

JS: To start with, can you tell us a little about your background.

VM: I grew up in a small town in an area of Fife dominated by the coal mining industry. My family were working class—mining, shipbuilding, engineering in the last couple of generations, fishing and crofting before that. I was lucky enough to go to a school that was fiercely academic and encouraged its pupils to escape the confines of their backgrounds through education. We lived across the road from the local library, which was probably the single most important factor in my becoming a writer.

I went on to read English at St. Hilda's College, Oxford—their first ever undergraduate from a Scottish state school. I had a ball as a student, throwing myself with equal energy into partying, politics, and polemical arguments about English literature. I also realized there how difficult it was to make a living as a writer and I foolishly thought that if I became a journalist that would be the next best thing. It took a while for me to realize the two jobs are about as closely related as a charcoal burner and a wood sculptor—only the raw material is the same.

JS: After Oxford you were a journalist for many years. Were you on the crime beat?

VM: No. I worked principally in the Manchester office of a national Sunday tabloid and our team was too small for any of us to be specialists. I did everything from soap stars' sex lives to heavy duty investigations. I did work on some major crime stories—The Yorkshire Ripper, Ian Brady's revelations of fresh bodies in the Moors Murders, the Lockerbie bombing. And I spent a lot of time working as the northern end of the investigative team on everything from fraudulent diets to illegal sweat shops and abusive old people's homes.

JS: Your first novel, published in 1987, featured a journalist, Lindsay Gordon, as an amateur sleuth. Was she based on yourself and your own experiences?

VM: I think crime writers tend to create protagonists who are either alter egos or imaginary friends. I'd had some early success as a playwright, but by the time I wrote *Report for Murder,* my confidence was at a very low ebb. But my conviction that I wanted to be a writer was still strong so I decided to write a crime novel because I'd always read a lot of crime fiction and I reckoned I understood how the form worked—there had to be a murder, a detective, suspects, and some sort of resolution at the end. I also reckoned that if I made my detective a journalist, I'd also be on safe ground—I knew how journalists worked, what their lives were, what were the stresses and the rewards. With that awareness acting as the foundations, I figured it would liberate me to focus more closely on the details of the plotting and the other characters. So Lindsay acquired a lot of superficial similarities to me, although in many respects, she's a very different personality. In practical terms, she applies her skills as an investigative journalist and interviewer to the subject of murder; her aim is to expose what has happened, and her preferred investigative method is to develop a theory and test it to extinction.

Also, I'm too lazy to do the research involved in having a police officer as a series character. Oh, and I never had enough respect for the police to want to center my creative life in their world.

JS: Had you been planning to write fiction for a while?

VM: I'd always wanted to write for a living, ever since I sussed that somebody actually made a living out of all those books in the library. If I hadn't been a journalist, my first protagonist probably would have had some other profession. But I'd have written regardless.

JS: After four Lindsay Gordon books you created Kate Brannigan, P.I. Did you feel that having a P.I. as your main character would give you a greater range?

VM: Actually, I started writing the Brannigan books after the third Lindsay Gordon and I went back to her after *Kick Back*. There were several reasons why I went down that road. First, I'm a Gemini and I have a very low boredom threshold. I wanted to do something different, something that wasn't a Lindsay Gordon novel, something that explored another area in the crime fiction field. I wanted to experiment with the first person rather than the third person, and I need the sense of challenge that writing something different provides. Also, I had begun to feel that readers have probably higher expectations from writers now than they used to and they, like me, were probably starting to feel that Lindsay was falling over rather too many corpses for an amateur. Besides, the Lindsay Gordon novels were originally conceived as a trilogy, and I didn't have any strong feelings about how I could develop the character beyond that. But Sod's Law being what it is, as soon as I'd turned my back on her, she started kicking down the door at the back on my mind and demanding to be paid attention to.

Brannigan being a P.I. means she is routinely involved in the investigation of nefarious doings, which gives me scope to have fun with all sorts of scams. In the LG books, the starting point is murder. With KB, she's investigating all sorts of other things—fraud, missing persons, theft—and the murder happens almost incidentally, and usually a long way down the story. So the books are very different in their scope and style, but I still enjoy going back to Lindsay from time to time—I've just finished the fifth, *Booked for Murder*, out in October from The Women's Press.

JS: The Brannigan stories are, as Warner Bros. used to say, *torn from the headlines.* For example, in the latest, *Blue Genes*, you delve into the murky

waters of human fertility. Is this the journalist's eye for a good story?

VM: Chicken and egg. Was I a good journo because I could smell a good story a mile off or can I spot a good story because I was a journo for years? I just love a good tale. I remember one editor I worked with remarking that he wanted his paper to have the CFM factor—he wanted people to pick it up and say, "Cor. fuck me, that is amazing!"

JS: Did you do a lot of research for *Blue Genes?* Presumably, as the story touches on illegal experimentation into human fertility, there was not much literature about the subject around.

VM: My attitude to research tends to be "if it can't be done over a decent curry and a drink, it won't get done." The genesis of *Blue Genes* came one boozy night when I was staying with an old college friend who is now a research gynecologist. I was asking her about something altogether different when out of the blue she announced that she'd been reading about experiments where they had produced baby hamsters from the eggs of two female hamsters, and how there was no real reason why one couldn't do the same thing with humans. I spilled my drink. That's how good it was.

A couple of lunches with the tape recorder running on the table, and I'd cracked it. I sent her the book in draft to check it over, she made one or two corrections and result is . . . *Blue Genes.*

JS: The Brannigan novels have a very clear sense of time and place—Manchester in the nineties. How important do you think this is in the modern crime novel?

VM: For me, it's crucial. I think all my novels have a strong sense of place, and they give me a sense of being rooted in reality. I wanted to write about Manchester from the day I arrived there in 1979, because there was a buzz about the place that screamed to be used. The best crime fiction has always painted a picture of its society and its landscapes—think of Conan Doyle's London, Chandler's Los Angeles, Ruth Rendell writing about practically anywhere—and I think its focus on social history and the relationship between people and their landscape is one of its great claims for a relevance and significance the literary world has always been reluctant to grant it. I always feel most satisfied by novels that give me a strong flavor of a place, whether real or fictional—John Harvey's Nottingham. Ian Rankin's Edinburgh. Sara Paretsky's Chicago. K.C. Constantine's Rocksburg.

JS: And yet you chose to set *The Mermaids Singing* in a fictional city.

VM: Sometimes a novel won't work in a real city for a variety of reasons. In this instance, there were practical geographical problems in setting it in Manchester which I couldn't readily resolve, so I made it an amalgam of Manchester, Bradford, Leeds, and Sheffield. The moors outside the city, for example, are very much Yorkshire moors. The other reason for choosing a fictional city was that I was writing about very specific people—an Assistant Chief Constable (Crime), a clinical psychologist, a murder squad Superintendent, the crime correspondent of the local paper. None of these portrayals were entirely flattering. My representation of the behavior and attitudes of particular police officers and the force in general was in several particulars at odds with the realities in Manchester. And since I didn't want to spend the next couple of years getting arrested every time I exceeded the speed limit, it seemed diplomatic to set the book in an unreal city.

JS: *The Mermaids Singing* told the story of the hunt for a supposed gay serial killer. You were writing this at the time when there was a real gay serial killer around. Did that affect the book in any way?

VM: In a bitterly paradoxical way, it reassured me. One of the things I wanted to explore was the differences that would develop in a serial killer investigation where the victims were men rather than women, particularly if they were assumed to be gay. I assumed the police would be reluctant to take it seriously, even to the point where they would shut themselves off from the possibility of there being one killer rather than copycats. That view was vindicated by the Met not admitting publicly there was anything for gay men to be worried about until the frustrated killer himself contacted the press and revealed what he was doing. It was appalling, but it told me I was thinking along the right lines in the assumptions I was making. Not that that made me feel any better about what happened to the real victims.

JS: In view of the fact that the book won The Gold Dagger for best crime novel of the year, are we likely to see more of the characters from that book?

VM: I'm about to start work on a second novel featuring Tony Hill, *Falls the Shadow*. Which I would have written regardless of the Dagger. It's not going to be a series, though—just two books. Honest!

JS: Last year you published *A Suitable Job For A Woman*, a non-fiction book of interviews with real life female P.I.s, both in the U.K. and the States. How did the reality strike you? Was it a surprise or as you expected?

VM: The women were more diverse than I expected; their attitudes on certain subjects more unanimous than I had anticipated. I came away with a lot of respect for these women and the integrity they bring to their work.

I know this is a short answer—but the alternative is a very long one. Best thing I can suggest is that anyone who's interested in the subject should read the book . . .

JS: Has the experience altered the way you look at your fictional creation?

VM: Inevitably. It's made me more aware of where the limits are.

JS: What did the P.I.'s think of Kate Brannigan?

VM: Those who have expressed an opinion seem to like her a lot. They've said they like the way she's always got more than one case on the go, that she doesn't have an unrealistic approach to physical violence. They like the humor and they tell me that the investigative stuff is pretty accurate too. And they all want to know where they can find a man like Richard . . .

Interview with Patricia Cornwell

Paul Duncan

WHILE AT THE CHIEF Medical Examiner's Office, Patricia Cornwell wrote three unpublished crime fiction books—full of poisonings, buried treasure, and wills—in which Dr. Kay Scarpetta was a minor character. One of the editors who rejected her advised her to write about what she knows, and to let Scarpetta take center stage. Patricia was looking for a story for Scarpetta. Around that time, a serial killer was raping and strangling professional women in Rich-mond. Patricia was separated from her husband, living alone, frightened, and bought her first gun for her own protection—and this became the kernel for *Postmortem* (1990). The book became an immediate worldwide success, winning all five major mystery awards.

Paul Duncan met Patricia at the Waldorf Hotel. Patricia's words were accompanied by the theme to *Gone With The Wind* endlessly repeating in the background.

PD: Where does the character of Kay Scarpetta come from?

PC: I have a suspicion that—and this may sound bizarre—one of her genetic coils is from my own relationship with Ruth Graham when I was growing up. She is a very powerful woman, very beautiful and very, very kind. She has a heart of gold and is a compassionate person but, in her own way, is reserved. She was certainly a heroic character to me at a period of time in my life when I had no power, when I was very young. That's the sort of person you want to come save you when something bad happens.

When she was five, Patricia's parents broke up. Two years later she moved with her mother and two brothers to Montreat, a small town in North Carolina, just two miles from the home of evangelist Billy Graham. Growing up, she heard many stories about the kind things Billy's wife, Ruth, did. One Christmas, Patricia's mother had a nervous breakdown and tried to give her children to Ruth. Ruth got the children accommodation with local missionaries for three months, until Patricia's mother was well again. Later, Patricia became friends with Ruth, who became a sort of surrogate mother and a great influence on a troubled teenager with low self-esteem. Patricia was encouraged by Ruth to write short stories and poems. In 1981, after winning an award for her crime reporting at the Charlotte Observer, Patricia had to leave to move with her husband to Richmond, Virginia, where he studied for the ministry. It was here that she wrote a biography of Ruth Bell Graham called *A Time for Remembering* (1983).

PD: Kay is not similar to anyone?
PC: It probably has something to do with the fact that I didn't have anyone in mind when I came up with her. Also, because I'm so rooted in reality—to the real professionals and the real cases—I tend to get somewhat removed from literary, TV, or film characters. They, to me, are not reality, so they have no bearing on my work. This means I have a difficult time trying to explain my characters because people like to categorize them by comparing them to other characters.

PD: However, having created this popular character—a female medical examiner who works for the FBI at Quantico—all sorts of variations of her have started to appear in the past five years. The most notable is probably Dana Scully in *The X-Files*, who has expressed some of the same ideas and thoughts as Kay Scarpetta.
PC: This is one of the reasons why Peter Guber and I are not wasting any time in producing the first Scarpetta film. Unfortunately, my books are the inspiration for other people to come up with other strong female protagonists, particularly in the FBI or medical fields. I won't even watch or read these other things that people tell me about because they'll probably just aggravate me.

One of the reasons I've been fortunate enough to have access to a lot of places and information is because I have a platform of legitimacy from my profession and background. You also earn your credibility through word of mouth and by meeting people. I can't continue to enjoy the world these people live in unless they know they can trust me. They read the books, think I'm okay and the doors open.

PD: You work to get the facts right?
PC: It's an unforgiving world. If you get something wrong, people turn off you just like that. Besides that, I want to get it right for myself, keep it honest. It's very important to me personally, to get it right, to know what if feels like and to experience it as much as I can.

PD: With access to all this information, and with her two years experience as an award-winning crime reporter for the *Charlotte Observer*, I would have thought that Patricia would be writing fact, not fiction.
PC: Sometimes fiction is truer than fact. Actually, I do both, because the scaffolding of all my stories is fact, whether it is a procedure, or the type of case, or the kinds of individuals. It is all rooted in experience and research. That's the fact. The fiction of it is the way that I want the characters to work the cases.

People have asked me over the years why I don't write True Crime and I tell them that I could not bring myself to victimize people all over again. If you have a son or daughter murdered in what turns out to be a sensational crime about which books are written, and you have been on the side of the fence where I have been—seeing relatives sitting in the waiting rooms and the looks on their faces as they come to find out what's happened to their child—I don't want to write about things in gory detail that could upset those relatives all over again. There are cases where people find it cathartic to write about their experiences, and I don't bump the people who do it, it's just that I couldn't, and I don't want to.

PD: The books have very little violence in them. All we see are the effects, both

physical and emotional, of violence committed off-screen.
PC: That's because that's all that Scarpetta sees. It's very rare that Scarpetta will witness a violent act unless she herself commits it, as she's had to do in several books when she's had to defend herself. I only show violence when the bad guys are getting it, not when the victim is getting it.

PD: Is that planned, or is it just the way it's worked out?
PC: That's the way I feel. Violence is a reality to me. I mean, I've had my hands on these dead bodies, I've been to the murder trials, I've been to the crime scenes. I've seen people roll through doors who've had their lives viciously ripped from them. I have no use for the people who commit those kinds of acts. My sympathy is for the victims. That's why I'm very comfortable with Scarpetta because she is their defender. That's the way I feel. I couldn't do it any other way.

PD: Scarpetta is very single-minded. She's on a crusade.
PC: I'd say she and I both have lives consumed by what we do and what we believe. It's that I express mine in a different way than she does. She actually works the cases and I tell the story of the cases. I have said many times that what I really consider myself to be is a scribe to the people out there doing the real work, whether it is the forensic pathologists, the FBI agents, the police, the scientists, the prosecutors . . . Someone needs to tell their stories, go in their labs and find out exactly what they're doing today. "Well, I'm using a gas chromatograph to do this . . ." or ". . . the scanning electron microscope to determine which element this is . . ." They need someone like me to do that, and that's really what I consider my job.

PD: She is so driven or obsessive about her job that it seems, perhaps, sad that she has so little life outside her job.
PC: It's not so much obsessive or driven as it is being devoted. For one to say that Scarpetta is obsessive or driven is like saying that a priest is. It's like a calling. She has taken on a mantle to help people who have no power. She's like a missionary, or a minister, or priest to the people who can no longer speak in a language that other people can understand. That's the way I regard what I do too.

People can also say the same thing about me. I'm divorced, I haven't remarried, I have no kids, you never read in the papers about me dating someone, and so on. It's not that I don't have a private life, or friends, and attachments—I think I have a very rich life in that way—but I deal with people in snatches. I can't have weeks on end with people I like unless I happen to be working with them. It's for the same reason. I'm not driven to be the number-one crime writer in the world—it's not an ambition of mine—it's just that I'm devoted to what I'm doing as she is to what she's doing.

In the same way, I have to be as devoted to her so that I can tell her story and always learn the latest advances in technology or medicine that would be applicable to what she does so that I'm knowledgeable enough to deal with it in a book. And that takes a lot of time.

PD: Certainly, the temptation is to compare Patricia and Kay.
PC: We're the same, but we're different. Certainly, some things are the

same—how could they not be because they're coming out of me? So we probably share the same genetic code, by and large, but we're not exactly the same people. Maybe she's another manifestation of what I would be like if I did what she did for a living? Certainly, there are parallels.

PD: I think it would be difficult to write about somebody like her if you didn't share some of the same qualities. Like, for example, a devotion to justice, integrity, and decency, fighting for people who can't fight for themselves, trying to make the world a little better.

PC: You can't fake that. You either feel it or you don't. I couldn't make you feel what she feels if I didn't feel it.

For each book, I come up with a case I want her to work and then I go through the pilgrimage with her, and I simply put things down pretty much the way I see them, and the way I know them from reality. In reality, of course, nobody is pure good and nobody is pure bad, but there are certainly good and evil people. Without a doubt Temple Brooks Gault is evil. That doesn't mean that he doesn't have good qualities. I don't know what they are and I don't care what they are, and I'm sure Kay doesn't care what they are either.

If you work in these professions, when people do things which are this heinous, you're not interested in their good qualities. You just want to figure out enough about them so that you can catch them, or at least give them a name so you can find them.

As far as Kay is concerned, she is not perfect, but she is purely good in terms of her integrity and morality where justice is concerned. She is having an affair with a married man, Benton Wesley—that's not moral. That's not even smart. She knows it too and she has trouble with it. She's not always done the right thing with Lucy, and she knows it. And Lucy knows it, too. But Kay tries.

I think it's on the personal front that it's more difficult which, I think, is true for most of us. You will never catch me being dishonest in the business world or even in my profession, but sometimes I might be dishonest in my personal life because I don't say something I should say because it's too hard for me to say it. That's where Kay's weaker.

PD: Reading *Cruel and Unusual, The Body Farm,* and *From Potter's Field,* these books read as a trilogy.

PC: In those three books, as a matter of fact, I was trying very hard to get Kay to loosen up a little bit. I think you see that because she has more emotional situations on her hands.

PD: So there was no design for the three books?

PC: No. I start each one with a case and I never know where each will go. For instance, *The Body Farm* was a really hard book for me to write because I set it in my own childhood, in the foothills of western North Carolina. In a way, it was almost like killing off myself as a little girl, by putting myself imaginatively in that environment.

If you're a little girl with no power, like Emily Steiner was, buried beneath the cold earth and people don't know the truth about your death, who would you want to find out who did it? You'd want Scarpetta.

She can't make the child alive again, but she can make her talk. Kay can do something for the living, to make it easy for them to cope with this evil which has occurred—that's really what she does in each of her books.

Maybe we see it more and more in subsequent ones because it becomes more defined to me what her mission is. After all, just like you, I get to know her better each time. I know her a whole lot better now than I did in *Postmortem* and, I suspect, three years from now I will know her even better than I do now.

PD: I wouldn't be able to attend an autopsy. I would see the bodies as people and think of their past lives and emotions. I would find that too upsetting.

PC: That is why you would probably be a good forensic pathologist. That's exactly what the good ones do. They don't look on the body they're cutting as a thing—the bad ones do because it's easier to divorce themselves from their humanity. The dead won't talk to you if you don't know them as a person.

If you really want to hear what they have to say you have to believe in their humanity. Yes, it is a sacrifice because it takes a lot out of you, but I think it takes more out of you not to do that because I think a part of you dies by degrees if you refuse to give a person their humanity. Even if they are dead.

I think one of the reasons that people stay with Scarpetta for four hundred pages is because she does give people their humanity—she gives them names. She went through the whole of *From Potter's Field* determined to give the dead woman her name. When the man was beating his horse, she went up to him and asked him the horse's name and then asked him, "Do you beat Snow White every day, or just on Christmas Day?" She always gives a name to the victim, whether it's a horse or a bald lady found in Central Park. That's what a good forensic pathologist will do. So you might be surprised at yourself. You might do better with it than you think.

I mean, it's not fun, but quite honestly the only way to endure some of the most difficult cases is if you give them their humanity. For example, one day I was with my friend Dr. Marcella Fierro, who's now the chief medical examiner—she's one of the best forensic pathologists in the world, and I've been very lucky to have her as a mentor. We were going down to the morgue in the elevator and there was this horrible smell from a body we had found in the river. It had been there for several weeks in the middle of summer. I had smelt bodies before, but this was the worst. It was really, really wretched. I was going down to help, to scribe the labels. I looked at Marcella and said that sometimes I really didn't know how she could stand this. She looked at me and said that she just tried to remember who he was.

And when you think of that, suddenly you no longer see this bloated, hideous corpse but a man wearing a hat, T-shirt, shorts, and tennis shoes, and he's out on the river fishing with his son. I saw him for the rest of the morning and I was a good trouper and I did my job. If you cannot give that much humanity back to that person, why in the world would you want to spend that much time with what's left with him?

It's All Part of the Writing Game

Why Do They Call Them Cozies?

Ellen Nehr

If a jacket designer wants to put the "kiss of death" on a book, just use either the term "cozy," stick a cat or two or three on the cover or add a teapot. I would suspect that half the people who would pick up such a jacket and put it back down again don't even know where the word "cozy" came from, wouldn't know what one looked like and certainly not how to use one.

NO PERSON WITH A degree of hard-boiledness will pick such a book up even if the author's names were Erle Mickey Chandler or Otto MacDonald Hammet. Add a vase of flowers, a fancy tablecloth or a tea cup and "that's all she wrote" as far as prospective reader is concerned. Sweeping generalities? Well, a bit exaggerated perhaps but the possibility that many readers would be seen reading books in this category is slight. But do they know what they are missing?

Since the amateur sleuth has a long and illustrious history as does the "novel of manners" within the mystery field and their strength is based on the variety of characters that have been integrated into the subject matter. After all there are just so many ways authors can portray police officers, private detectives, postal inspectors, sheriffs, lawyers, firemen and government investigators. Lately we've had a plethora of books, good ones too, by authors who have caught onto the fact that books with novice characters who become involved in the solution of a crime for a variety of reasons ranging from being accused of performing it, or as a victim of an outrage, in an effort to protect someone or just in the performance of everyday duties.

Let's assume that you were told that books featuring the following characters, all amateur sleuths, were coming out quite soon and you are unaware of the author's gender or that of the principal character, their sexual orientation, or the locale/setting. Would you consider reading about a computer programmer, librarian, bookstore owner, park ranger, TV critic, investigative reporter, medieval physician or advertising executive?

Can you believe that the content, the ability of the author to convey emotion, excitement, atmosphere and, of course, a believable plot, should take precedence over the gender of the characters being written about or the one doing the writing? Adopting such an attitude might certainly broaden many people's reading interest.

Why I Don't Write Hard-Boiled

Carolyn G. Hart

Because the mean streets aren't my beat.

I'M INTERESTED IN WRITING about the people you went to school with, your next-door neighbor, your family. I want to write about why Sam makes you mad, why you love Elinor, why you hate Bill.

And yes, I write mysteries.

But what is the mystery and what is this tension that many perceive between hard-boiled and traditional mysteries?

My strong feeling is that we are talking about two entirely different kinds of books, the crime novel and the traditional mystery, and that both are deserving of respect and admiration.

Crime novels and traditional mysteries are categorized murder mysteries. And yet, I would insist that murder is not the focus of either.

The crime novel is the story of an honorable woman—or man—who tries to remain uncorrupted in a corrupt world.

The crime novel is the story of the protagonist, *not* the story of the murder that is solved within those pages. Today's private eye is the white knight who will never, never, never betray his or her code of honor. These books explore society's ills, attempt to right society's wrongs. These books are about the quest for honor.

The traditional mystery is the story of intimate relationships skewed by anger or jealousy or fear or cruelty.

I always enjoy the opening segments of the Agatha Christie television mysteries because they capture the essence of the traditional mystery.

In the opening segments, a figure peers out a window into the street and two women with sly faces are in close conversation.

There is an air of secrecy, covertness, and, most of all, intimacy.

Neighbors watch. Friends—and enemies—gossip. There are lies and deceptions, misunderstandings and misapprehensions, passion and pain, fear and fury.

This is the world of the traditional mystery.

Agatha Christie once compared the mystery to the medieval morality play. It is a brilliant analogy. In the medieval morality play, the trades-fair audiences saw a graphic presentation of what happens to lives dominated by lust, gluttony, sloth, and all the deadly sins.

This is precisely what readers of today's traditional mysteries are offered in a more sophisticated guise.

The traditional mystery provides the readers with parables. The distant mother creates a child who cannot love. A tyrannical boss engenders hatred and frustration. Slyness evokes distrust. A man who cheats on his wife—or a woman who cheats on her husband—cannot be trusted in any relationship. If this, dear reader, is how you live . . .

So, you see, murder is *not* the focus of the traditional mystery.

The focus is fractured relationships. In trying to solve the crime, the detective searches out the reasons for murder by exploring the relationships between the victim and those around the victim. The detective is trying to find out what caused the turmoil in these lives. What fractured the relationships among these people.

And readers, being the intelligent creatures that they are, extrapolate the lessons observed in fiction for their own use, their own lives.

When readers observe the lives around them, they can see the torment of an abused wife or husband (and abuse can quite often be mental and verbal rather than physical), the despair of an unloved child, the hatred of a spurned lover.

Usually these emotional dramas do not end in murder. In fact, they do not end. The violent emotions created by fractured relationships corrode the loves of every person involved. Often forever.

This is what the traditional mystery is all about.

The traditional mystery reveals the intimate, destructive, frightening secrets hidden beneath what so often seems to be a placid surface.

The crime novel has an entirely different and equally valid focus. It celebrates a detective who will not succumb to temptation, who will remain true to his or her code of honor, who will remain uncorrupted in a corrupt world.

The crime novel explores how society can wrong its members. The crime novel is the determined quest for justice, a demand that the rules be observed, the continuing saga of David versus Goliath.

So mystery writers explore the realities of the worlds about us, whether they be violence in the mean streets or the equally destructive but quieter forces of passion in our homes and offices.

Readers experience the brutality of the mean streets in their morning newspapers and they want to believe that there are forces of good trying to keep this world decent. To these readers, the detective novel offers an affirmation of decency in the midst of trauma.

Day-to-day living involves readers in moments of stress and confrontation with those around them. Readers know the jealous mother, the miserly uncle, the impossible boss, the woman who confuses sex with love, the selfish sister. These are the realities of life with which they must cope.

So this is why both kinds of books—crime novels and traditional mysteries—answer a great need. They reaffirm the values of our society and illustrate what happens in lives given over to evil.

As a writer, I find my fascination in the everyday world in which most of us live, the world of work and home. I see the abuse of power among people and this fascinates me. I want to explore why anger and fear disrupts our lives.

We live in an unjust world. I write mysteries to find justice.

Readers read mysteries to find justice. It is the only justice we are ever likely to know.

This is my passion. And perhaps I make it most clear in a passage from *Dead Man's Island.* Henrie O. heeds a call for help from a voice out of her past. She travels to a private island where murder and a hurricane threaten the stranded guests. Toward the close of *Dead Man's Island,* Henrie O. awaits the return of the storm.

"As I stood, fatigue washed over me. It would be so easy to drop down beside Valerie and close my eyes, let the warmth of the sunlight touch me with fingers of life and let my mind drift, taking memories and thoughts as they came.

"But anger flickered beneath exhaustion.

"I suppose I've always been angry. That's what drives most writers, and the hot steady consuming flame of anger against injustice and dishonesty and exploitation, against sham and artifice and greed, against arrogance and brutality and deceitfulness, against betrayal and indifference and cruelty.

"I would not give up."

That passage says everything there is to say about Henrie O. About me. About, I truly believe, all mystery writers.*

*Some of the material in this essay has appeared previously in the Introduction to *Malice Domestic 4* published by Pocket Books in 1995 (CGH).

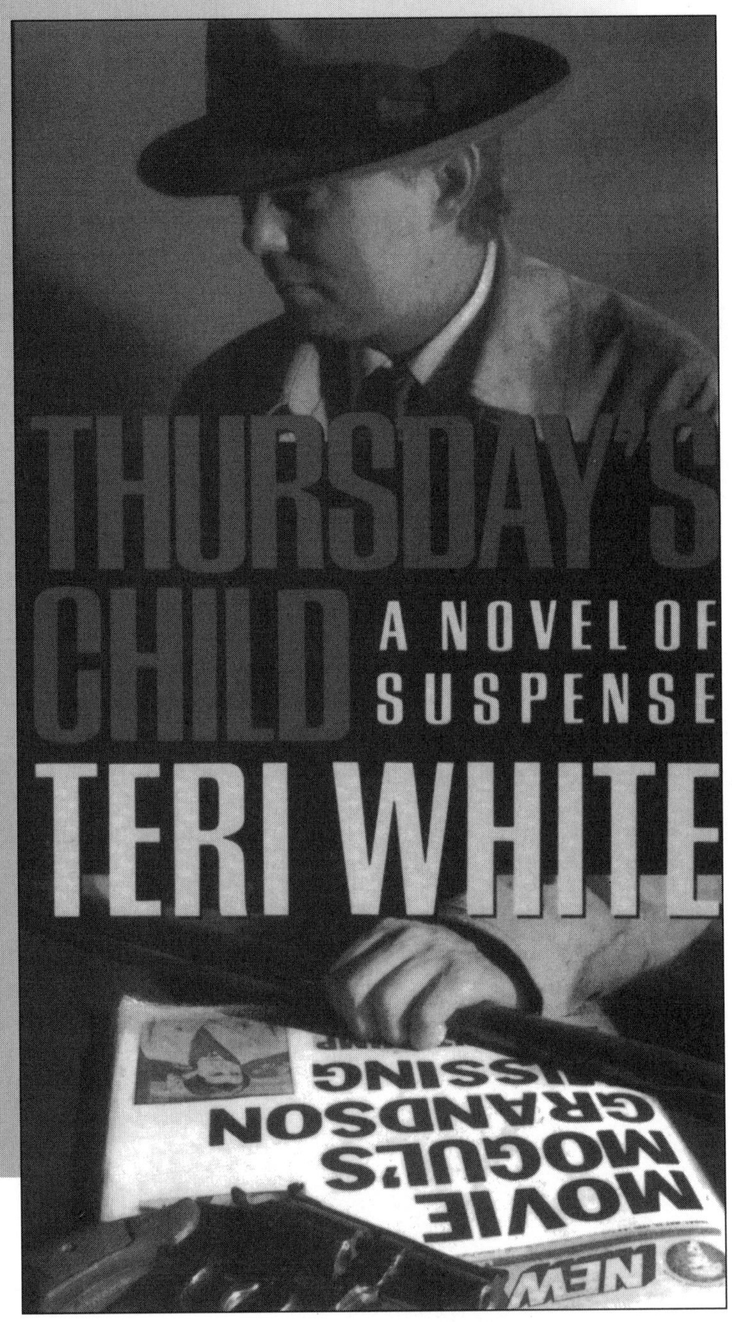

Thursday's Child by Teri White

Why I Don't Write Cozies

Teri White

Before getting down to the serious business of this essay, let me confess that, in person, Teri White is not quite the hard-boiled dame that my books might lead one to think I am.

OKAY, I HAVE BEEN known to have a cancer stick dangling from my lips as I bend over a hot computer keyboard. And although I don't keep a bottle of cheap whiskey in my desk drawer, a nearby refrigerator is nicely stocked with ale and (alcoholic) cider. I have even been known to swear, under provocation.

On the other hand—I love afternoon tea with cucumber sandwiches, scones with clotted cream, and Earl Grey sipped from my flowered Royal Albert china. My teddy bear collection grows ever larger. And—horrors!!—I have even been known to read a dead-body-in-the-library tale on occasion.

But somehow when I sit down to write a mystery, the mean streets seem a much more natural scenario for me than a village in the Cotswolds.

Why?

A professor of critical writing once stressed to the class I was in the importance of defining the terms we used in our work. Since I have always been a believer in following the rules, at least when I couldn't think of any halfway legitimate reason not to do so, that seems as good a place to begin as any.

Term one: Murder.

The unlawful and malicious or premeditated killing of one human being by another; to kill, slay, assassinate, destroy.

Term two: Cozy.

Snug, warm, sheltered.

Now maybe it's just me, but I don't really see those two concepts belonging together.

Not that I necessarily subscribe to the popular theory that hard-boiled writing is more real than the cozy variety. Let's face it—Sam Spade is no more likely to exist than is Miss Marple. (And an argument might even be made that he is less so.) So reality does not really enter into it. The appearance of real life, however, might pertain. Somehow, in my mind, the detective or cop prowling the dark alleys of a big city come to life more fully than a sweet little old lady or a plucky librarian-museum worker-housekeeper-nosy neighbor when it comes to solving a crime and/or tracking down a serial killer.

(The above assumes, of course, good writing in both cases. A rash assumption, admittedly.)

Perhaps what it boils down to is what the reader (me, in this case) is looking for at any given moment. If I'm in the mood for complete escape, a sort of mindless fun, I am more likely to pick up a cozy. (No offense is meant by the use of word mindless, by the way. I have a great respect for those things which simply entertain me.)

But when I write a mystery, I am, for better or for worse, trying to accomplish something else, not simply for the reader, but for myself. I am looking for a way to explain the world around me. To deal with the problems that occur with such wearisome regularity on the front pages of the ten or so different newspapers I read every week. Not to solve said problems—I'm only a writer, after all—but to understand them and maybe help others to understand them, as well.

Lordy, but that sounds pompous and I don't mean it to.

Maybe the only real answer to the question Why don't you write cozies? is the same answer I give when someone asks a similar question: Why do you write the kind of books you write? The response is not original with me—and unfortunately, I have forgotten the source—but I reply, simply, "Why do you assume I have a choice?" I write what I must.

And who knows? Maybe one day, while sipping my tea and nibbling a scone, an idea will come to me and I might find myself doing a cozy. Complete with little old lady. Country vicarage. Warm and jolly murder among nice people.

I wouldn't count on it, though.

The Darker Side of My Life

Billie Sue Mosiman

Like most other people I experienced a childhood filled with bright, lovely moments occasionally dimmed by tragedy and dreadful drama. Did the small darkness creep into my soul and mold me into a novelist of dark suspense? I'd guess, yes, probably. Why other people with similar backgrounds don't become writers isn't something I know how to answer. All I know, and then not with absolute certainty since even the most honest will accidentally invent or misinterpret, is the clay of my own life.

THERE WERE TYPICAL TIMES in childhood with endless sunny southern days when pine trees were castle spires and fairies danced beneath the bloom of purple wood violets. Most of the time, when living with my grandparents in South Alabama, I was surrounded by aunts, uncles, and cousins. There were great-aunts, great-uncles, and people so far removed from the family tree that I had no idea how much kin we were, how much blood we shared. They were everywhere, all these people, varied and wondrous. They sat at my grandmother's table, slept in her beds, reclined on the porch chewing tobacco or pushed the porch swing into rhythm while sipping lemonade. They hunched before the fireplace, dug wells, plowed fields, planted and gathered food from the garden, hunted for rabbit, squirrel, and deer. Home was always a busy place with people talking, telling tall tales, sharing memories.

When I slipped away to my woodland playhouses or went exploring clear, ankle-deep creek beds, imagination provided the voices and the people to keep me company. I fought alongside knights, climbed the vines with Tarzan, raced the wind with Superman, and flew through starry skies with Peter Pan.

Those were the good times. Times so perfect they're like butterflies caught in amber, preserved forever. But in every family there are the bad pennies, the relative who tipples, the petty gossip who brings only harm, the arguments, divorces, and the deaths.

I must have been five when a favorite uncle died. Someone lifted me up to see him in his casket that sat on an altar in the center of the church. I knew instinctively—without the word "death" being spoken—he was gone from me. He was silent, too still, all his lively being had escaped and left a stranger with folded hands, sleeping the long sleep on white satin.

It was one of my early impressions of loss. But not the first. Earlier there had been not a death, but a separation that felt like one. My mother fell ill and was disastrously misdiagnosed. One day she had to be forcibly taken from the house by men in white jackets, her weeping body tied down onto a stretcher. She had been pregnant with twins, but one was growing in her fallopian tube and three doctors would not believe her until that day she lost them both in a bloody flood.

I might have been three or four. I understood very little, but I understood one important lesson: People we love face tragic problems and sometimes our loved ones will be taken away from us, weeping. When they return, they might not be the same as they were. There are many degrees of separation, some of them just as chilly and permanent as death.

By the time I was nine years old and an aunt and uncle had been murdered while on a little road trip with a stranger along the panhandle of Florida, I was almost a veteran of the ways the world has of surprising us. It would take fire and the death of my firstborn to seal the pact, to make me know for sure that life is precarious. It's not necessarily cruel, but punctuated with random violence and departure all the same.

How did these events get me interested in the psychotic, the serial killer, the mind that is diseased or lost or fatally warped? They led me the way, down the path where I hunted knowledge of what makes for sadness and madness, what makes for survival and triumph over tragedy. By writing I would delve deeper, go further, find more answers. The lessons had not been wasted on me. If I had time and I paid strict attention and I plumbed my own feelings and imagination, I would know something at last about the human condition. Just the search was enough, even if no answers were forthcoming. Along the way I'd share what I uncovered with my readers and together we might be able to say: Ah, so that's how it is, that's how it feels, that's why we persevere when it seems that all is lost and life is not worth living.

You might say I have used suspense as therapy, but you would be wrong. We all accept the darkness that touches us because if we don't, there's no going forward. It wasn't acceptance I have searched for or any printed confession to purge the soul. It was understanding I have been in pursuit of that eludes even as it beckons. To understand humankind and to understand self, wasn't that the ultimate goal of every person? It has been mine.

There in the beginning, in the early eighties, I had an agent who tried derailing me from my chosen path. "Leave behind this hairy-scary stuff," he advised. If he had known me better he never would have made such effort to turn a budding suspense writer into a cheerful writer of happy stories where the sky is always baby blue and love conquers all. I knew that world could exist for only short periods and thunderstorms came up unexpectedly. Was I going to lie to my audience and pretend ignorance of what we both knew as the real truth? I was not.

I had come from the piney woods where village people took up their guns to stalk wild monsters whose paw prints could not be identified by even the most wizened hunter. I had come from a place of light and dark where family took care of its own and sometimes meted out justice beyond the prying eyes of the law. I had seen beloved uncles and aunts buried too soon, a beautiful and talented mother wrestle demons, watched people despair, rebel, and be thwarted. And I had listened for the patter of a child's footfalls that would never come again.

Would I be deterred from writing the kind of story that came from those forests, asylums, funerals, and dark quiet rooms from which everyone has gone? These were not just "hairy-scary" stories. These were not stories written to market or to cash in on some prevailing genre or trend. These were the only stories I had in me, and if the agent didn't understand that, we would always be at odds.

Not long after I found an agent who knew I was writing what I wrote best, what I cared about. He began to sell my novels to editors who found something worthwhile in what I had to say. If I perfected this art of storytelling, I'd one day perhaps even know my own mind, or at least know enough to depend on compassion when wrong gets done and events go awry.

What has driven me was passion and what I have derived from the darkness I brought forward into the light of print for all to see. I did not write of my dear dead ones or of some of the living who had lost the way of the straight and narrow, the way of the sane. I wrote of phantoms, pieced together from research, interviews, newspaper headlines. But whom I write about and what I write about is so intertwined with who I am that there is no fine, thin ruler anyone could slip between the two.

In the end, it's not the darker side of my life that I give to the world. It is hope that I carry forward into story form. Hope that even at the darkest dawn, there's a sun to follow. Hope that when I tell you about the life struggles of my characters in the novels, you will remember how much alike we all are and how very far we have to go to reach perfection.

There are still sunny days for inspiration, life to be lived, works to be written. We, the fiction writers who mine the shafts where it's coal black and there are small lanterns, do this work without apology and sometimes without as much explanation as I've been able to write about here. You know how some writers will tell you they don't choose what they write, the writing chooses them? I don't think they're lying to us. It's the only real explanation I have to offer.

Midnight Louie: From Science Fiction to Feline Fiction

Carole Nelson Douglas

If I were a bridge player instead of a writer, I'd bid "no trump" every time. It's a tossup which genre dominates among my thirty-three published novels: science fiction and fantasy—nine; mystery—twelve; romance and women's mainstream fiction—twelve. My novels often blend several genre elements, too, so categories never tell the full story.

STILL, MY SOJOURN IN science fiction and fantasy, beginning with *Six of Swords* in 1982, was an omen of cat characters to come when Felabba, a white cat modeled on my own Galadriel, appeared from nowhere to converse with *Six*'s human protagonists.

Talking animals are an ancient tradition of fable and fiction, and especially of fantasy fiction. I'm hardly the first writer to have found an animal viewpoint ideal for satire of things purely and impurely human. Animals teach humans empathy; without empathy, humans are less than animal. Most serial killers begin by abusing animals. So no one can persuade me that writing from the feline point of view is a lower form of communication.

Enter Midnight Louie, the feline Sam Spade of contemporary Las Vegas. Long before his first official "Midnight Louie Mystery," *Catnap*, in 1992, Louie had a real-life existence as a stray cat I gave voice to in a 1973 newspaper feature. I later recruited Louie to narrate his own miniseries: four short romances with a continuing mystery element sold in 1985 for late '86 publication. (But the purchasing romance editor got cold paws when she saw the unbridled Louie: "too much mystery, too mainstream, upmarket and sophisticated," she declared. Then she cut the four books up to 37 percent each, held them from publication until 1990 and moved them low on the mainlist totem pole. That's when

Midnight Louie snicked out his claws and moved into mystery pure and simple.)

I suspect, though, that a narrative, first-furperson detective voice would have been rejected by editors or even readers before the nineties. Lilian Jackson Braun's beloved Koko and Yum Yum detect, but keep their palaver to the usual Siamese, if you please. That my science fiction/fantasy publisher also prints my mysteries perhaps explains why Midnight Louie arrived at all as a crime-scene personality.

Yet the renaissance of the mystery of manners, of the amateur detective and the humorous mystery, allowed the ancient fountain to freshen, with creative new characters and settings bubbling over into print.

Among them, much indignant at getting his feet wet in this upwelling of invention, was Midnight Louie.

One thing must be said: Midnight Louie does not "talk." Especially and on principle, he refuses to talk to humans. Felabba the fantasy cat not only talked, she had ninety-nine lives and could perform magic.

Louie's no magician, although he harbors a psychic streak, and his anthropomorphic persona has realistic limitations. He does nothing physically that a large, smart cat couldn't do. I always say that if cats had opposable thumbs, humans would be in trouble. Cat lovers testify that felines open some doors, and would open all doors with the proper equipment. So Louie favors French doors with levers he can pull down. He'll "hitch" rides on buses, trucks, and in cars. Sometimes he has to walk a long, long way.

The only talking in Midnight Louie's chapters is when he reports human dialogue, or when animals converse: their "remarks" are in quotation marks. But are human readers benefiting from a translation? For these are characters of which one can truly write "he purred" or "she hissed."

In a fantasy or science fiction novel, I wouldn't pussyfoot so warily around the believability of animal actions and communication methods.

Yet Midnight Louie is basically a fantasy construct whose characterization spoofs the homo sapiens gumshoe: not as young as he used to be, but still the rampant ladies' man by his own report; a cynical loner treading the mean streets, operating by his purrsonal code, no matter the cost.

Louie apes a politically incorrect human model, so he's a politically incorrect cat, unlike any of my six neutered, house-bound cats. He is free to roam through an always-open

window. Like the original Midnight Louie, he was long homeless and is not "fixed." (Louie asserts that he "comes with four on the floor and fully equipped from the factory."

As a responsible animal lover aware of the miserable lives of feral cats and horrendous pet overpopulation problems, I find that Louie's fictional propensities cause the author as much angst as they amuse the readers. So into the storyline on little cat feet has crept Midnight Louise (born of a typographical error in my local newspaper). Louise is conducting a parent search for the dirty dog who abandoned her mother after a one-night stand. She is, of course, the very model of a modern female gumshoe: fixed, liberated, and hard on poor old papa. She even inherits Louie's former job of house detective at the Crystal Phoenix Hotel. If there is one thing on earth and in Las Vegas that makes Midnight Louie quail, it is not human or canine or killer, but Midnight Louise.

By his seventh adventure, *Cat In A Flamingo Fedora,* Louie is forced into the politically correct condition while still retaining his macho charms. A neat trick that keeps Louie the utterly unique cat detective he always was; if only human sex lives could be so handily managed.

In the Midnight Louie mysteries, the quandaries of contemporary life the four major human characters face (and their doings occupy most of the novels) are mirrored in a growing underworld of cat characters. Karma, the psychic Birman. Ingram, the Thrill 'n' Quill mystery bookstore cat. The Divine Yvette, Louie's Persian ladylove who belongs to fading film star Savannah Ashleigh, and Yvette's suitor Maurice, a one-time shelter inmate now a television pitchcat.

In my fantasy novels, the journeys my human (and animal) characters take are metaphorical, veiled in Jungian imagery welling from the subconscious.

In mystery, the issues are more calculated, upfront, and personal. That's why I call the Midnight Louie books "cozy-noirs," seeing both terms as needing of reinvention. (Oxymorons often best describe the genre-blending and issue-addressing tensions in my work.) When I told a reporter that the Midnight Louie series was "really" about "the dilemmas of sexual responsibility in the nineties," I watched his jaw drop and saw the unasked, unthinkable question: Can a mystery series set in Las Vegas featuring a feline sleuth as a part-time narrator possibly deal with such a serious issue?

You bet your best set of company whiskers. And that's no fantasy.

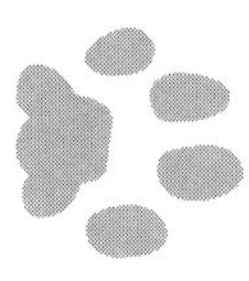

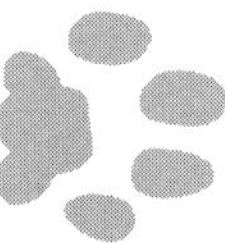

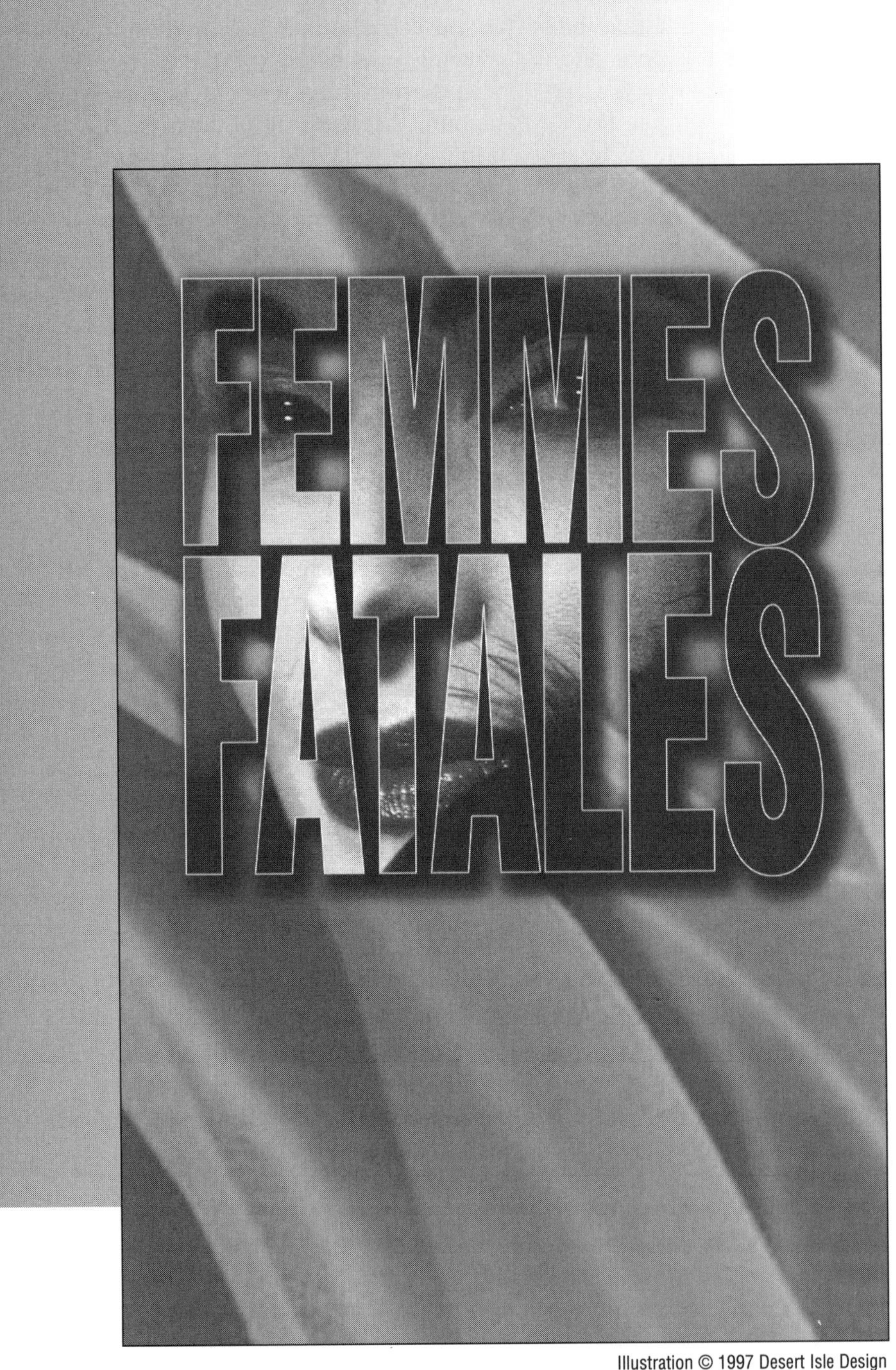

Illustration © 1997 Desert Isle Design

The Strange and True Story of a Woman Who Wrote Pulp Fiction

Gayle Lynds

I realized how unconventional my writing career had been when the head of a prominent publishing house rejected my novel, Masquerade, *because "no woman could have written this." If fact, the publisher demanded "evidence" I was female.*

AFTER MY SHOCK SUBSIDED, and I finished laughing, I saw she had a point: *Masquerade* is an international thriller, and that field's been the domain of male authors for some twenty years. That was the problem.

The answer began back in 1983 when I faced divorce. Once a reporter and editor, I hadn't had a job in a decade. Instead, I'd been a stay-at-home mom, sending my husband off to his law office, sitting on PTA boards, and, yes, baking great cookies. I had no job, few prospects, and two small children who'd grown accustomed to eating.

I'd also begun writing fiction, and as my divorce hurtled toward finality, literary journals published two of my short stories. But I was "paid" in journal copies. Although wonderful, they weren't nutritious. I needed to make money.

So when a friend asked whether I could write pulp fiction paperbacks for men, I lied. I said, "Of course." I'd read a few and found them intriguing. Surely I could learn to write them, and I saw a way to put green leafy vegetables and nine-grain breads into the mouths of my delightful children.

Nick Carter is America's version of James Bond, and many men have written some five-hundred paperbacks published about him. My friend (male) had a contract. He developed an outline. I set aside the literary novel on which I was working, and instead I wrote *The Day of the Mahdi, Nick Carter #190.*

I crossed my fingers.

The novel pleased the publisher, and he sent it to his other writers: This is the kind of book we want.

I was relieved, and my children were fed. I also began editing magazines, which supplied a steadier (and higher) income. But I liked the Carters so much that I wrote four more, creating the ideas and outlines for the last three. Why? Because I was learning. I was exploring characterization, suspense, plotting, and style, and I was being paid for it.

Traditionally, pulp paperbacks have provided a training ground for men. Some—like Dean Koontz, Nelson DeMille, and Martin Cruz Smith—went on to become highly respected authors. Why couldn't a woman?

Over the next seven years, I wrote eleven pulp novels, all with male leads, all aimed at male audiences, most with international settings. Men who write for or about the male pulps tell me I'm unique, that no woman in their memories did as much as I.

Even in nonfiction, I continued the pattern. When I wrote a self-help book about how to create happy, successful relationships, I used the viewpoint of the psychotherapist who was my primary source. He was a man.

Then as the 1980s ended, I was bedridden with back surgery. I finished the last of my book contracts, and I contemplated what to do with my life. The answer was obvious, where I'd been heading all along—international thrillers like those of Robert Ludlum, Frederick Forsyth, and John Le Carré.

By then, Sue Grafton, Marcia Muller, Mary Higgins Clark, and a host of other fine female authors had proved women could hold their own in mystery and suspense.

Why not in international thrillers, too?

I'd been studying genre novels written by men. Now I studied those written by women. And what I discovered affirmed everything I'd hoped to be teaching myself: A central character, whether male or female, is most effective when not only strong but emotional, and that insight, logic, and understanding permeate the best writing of both sexes. Female novelists had pushed the mystery and suspense envelope. No longer would readers accept James Bond bimbos and passive princesses as their favorite female leads. Readers wanted their characters to be three dimensional, and so did I.

Meanwhile, in international suspense, male novelists had been struggling with this same issue. A few were trying to reinvigorate the field by writing books starring women. Those books quickly found a large reservoir of readers. Obviously, it was time for female writers to stride through the glass doorway.

With that in mind, I began research for *Masquerade,* which is based on an actual CIA "black" program in mind control. I was convinced readers would find a strong, brainy woman caught up in an international suspense story fascinating, especially if brought to them by a female writer who'd trained in the male pulps while remaining decidedly a woman.

I've been fortunate. *Masquerade*

was ultimately bought by the president of Doubleday and published as their lead hardback in February. In terms of sexism, I find it interesting that the president who turned down *Masquerade* was a woman, and the one who bought it was a man. Never once did Steve Rubin, Doubleday's chief, question whether a woman could have written *Masquerade.*

How do I feel about it now? Proud. Amazed. Grateful. Because of the pulps and my literary background, I not only learned to write, I learned to "think" like both a man and a woman. And I had some strange moments: A New York senior editor refused to use my real name on my three young-adult mysteries because "boys won't read books written by girls." Yet, for quite a few years, I received fan mail from not only boys but girls. All were addressed to Mr. ——(one of my pen names). I wrote back without noting their error, but I enclosed a photo. Then I smiled, contemplating their surprise when they discovered "Mr." was "Ms."

Even today, people still occasionally ask why I wrote for the male pulps. How could I have done it? My answer is always the same: I didn't know I wasn't supposed to.

Julie Smith *Photo credit: David Spielman*

Life with Ed

Julie Smith

*The original Edgar, by all accounts, wasn't the most cheerful guy in the world, but the one who lives with me is as festive as Mardi Gras. The book for which he was awarded (*New Orleans Mourning*) happens to be about that season, so I got him some Mardi Gras beads and a rhinestone tiara.*

HE SITS ON A properly ornate, gold-painted pedestal beside my desk. Above him hangs a watercolor of Faulkner. Surrounding Bill and Ed are photographs of Tennessee Williams's New Orleans home and my other hero, Eudora Welty. Any self-respecting Chinese or African would instantly recognize the grouping for what it is—an ancestors' shrine.

I mention this to help convey the respect in which I hold that little ceramic bust. Surely it goes without saying that, short of a seven-figure contract, winning the Edgar is unequivocally the best thing that can happen to a mystery writer—it is an honor of gargantuan, international proportions. It is one of the very few literary awards Americans have seen fit to offer.

It can lead to respect and riches. In my particular case, it pulled a moribund career out of the toilet—I was literally ready to quit writing after fifteen years of simply not making it, when suddenly I *was* making it.

Now it could be argued that the Edgar didn't do that, the book for which it was awarded did. However, that would be spurious.

The book, *New Orleans Mourning,* was rejected something like twenty times in proposal form. It was at last bought by a publisher that promptly decided to discontinue its trade division, the ms. was bought back, and reoffered in completed form to another twenty editors, who also rejected it. Finally it was bought by a second (brilliantly perceptive) editor at a house that had already spurned it.

Many of the editors who saw the book wanted to buy it, but due to past sales figures, were simply unable to. Thus it wasn't the *quality* of the book, it was the salability of the book that saved my career, and the Edgar provided that.

Now one expects that in business. One reason for wanting the Edgar is to become more attractive to publishers. That happened to me, and I'm eternally grateful. I love Ed to death and I would consider it a great honor to kiss the feet and trim the toenails of every member of the kind and wise committee that awarded him.

But all that should be obvious. Having said it, I hope I may muse a moment without seeming to whine.

A funny thing happens when you actually get an Edgar. Sure enough, you get what you think you deserve—better contracts and more respect. Invitations arrive. Reviews improve.

But while your head is spinning, you start to ponder our cultural obsession with symbols—I don't say "American" obsession because, sadly, I think it may be universal.

Many kind people from whom I hadn't heard in months or years called with congratulations and I found that utterly heartwarming. But when a woman I'd been seeing at parties for twenty years suddenly fell all over me, I simply had to ask if she really didn't remember meeting me before. And no, she certainly didn't—though we'd seen each other maybe forty times and been introduced fifteen. Since then, this has happened repeatedly in one version or another.

Well, really! Did I deserve twenty years of snubs for not having an Edgar?

Still, I wanted respect, and I knew Ed could bring it.

Thanks, guy, but no wonder you were so morose when you lived here on Earth. There's something a little bald about human nature in the raw.

Edgar Award
Photo credit: Jan Grape

Marti MacCalister: Tough Cop—Tender Heart

Eleanor Taylor Bland

I've known Marti McAlister since she was a child. She introduced herself to me as a precocious five year old who wanted to play the tuba in a marching band instead of taking piano lessons.

AT THAT TIME I was attempting to write a vocational series for young children. Marti wanted to join the circus and become a lion tamer when she grew up.

Instead, Marti went to college and studied Sociology. However, her sense of adventure led her to a less traditional occupation, which was lucky for me. She joined the Chicago Police Department. As Marti explains in *Slow Burn,* "I don't want to abuse power, but I don't want to be excluded from the exercise of power either." She loves everything about policing—except the paperwork. When I decided to write a mystery series about a homicide detective, Marti volunteered. To her, homicide victims are the most helpless and solving their deaths the most challenging.

Living with Marti is relatively easy, except when I'm busily working at my nine-to-five job as an accountant. One day, while I was completing an audit, she said, referring to our third book *Gone Quiet,* "Belle is the only one who loved him." It was several weeks before I found out what she was talking about.

Marti is always several chapters ahead of me. She loves the puzzle as much as the solution. Although she maintains her professionalism, she isn't afraid to become emotionally involved. Marti is a survivor, and has had to come to terms with large doses of reality. Like so many women I know, she is strong, even in the weak places. She is compassionate, She wants to help make this a better, safer world. She has experienced the loss of her husband. She is doing whatever it takes to raise her children. She worries. She's uncertain.

She gets lonely. She feels guilty when she can't do everything she thinks she should. She gets frustrated when her best isn't enough and pushes herself to excel. Although she's comfortable being tough when she has to, she's not afraid to be sensitive and caring. She recognizes and accepts her contradictions and is pleased with who she is.

There is nothing more pleasurable for me, as a writer, than to immerse myself into my characters. Marti and I are so much alike, and I've known her for so long, that she is very easy to write about.

I have a cast of thousands inside my head. Sometimes they impatiently beat on my forehead, demanding to be freed. Often, there are many things that I know about my characters that I never tell the reader because it isn't important to the story. Sometimes, it takes a while before they tell me their secrets, or reveal characteristics and mannerisms.

Occasionally, as in the case with Marti's partner, Vik, another character tells me why someone thinks or behaves as he does. In *Dead Time,* I knew who Vik was, but not why, until a retired newspaper reporter who knew Vik and his family explained. Invariably, I bring at least two or three characters on stage and set them up as the killer, only to be told, "Sorry, I'm not the one," while the real killer, already on stage, cleverly withholds motive or other critical information.

How do I create characters who interest me and engage my attention? By intently observing the people around me. By seeking out and enjoying and being enriched by people who are different, unusual. By asking questions and learning about other cultures, other places, other people in relationship to place. But enjoying and being enthusiastic about the wealth of diversity all around me.

I listen intently when others speak, attentive to accents, speech patterns, regional differences and new ways of saying things. I study body language which often contradicts what is being said and tends to be a truer indication of feelings and attitudes. There is a richness of expression, both verbal and non-verbal, that is fascinating to observe.

Although there is a great deal of time and effort involved in my writing, for me, there is no greater satisfaction than bringing characters to life and letting them tell me their story.

The Older They Get . . .

Elizabeth Daniels Squire

Characters of all ages tend to talk to their authors. And, because characters live inside our heads, they have access to everything we know. On top of which they know even more than we do about themselves. Which makes them uppity or else helpful, as the mood suits them. Or even philosophic.

SO I WASN'T SURPRISED when Peaches Dann, my fifty-eight-plus absent-minded sleuth, looked me straight in my mind's eye and said: "You don't know how lucky you are to write about a well-seasoned wiser sleuth like me."

Now, I knew Peaches's on-off, on-off memory had nothing to do with age. She made that quite clear back when she first appeared in *Who Killed What's-Her-Name?* Furthermore, with the passage of time she's learned the memory tricks that help her solve murders. So she says.

"Every age is interesting," I said, not wanting this older-wiser thing to go to her head.

"Exactly," she said. "And it's great to have lived through all the earlier ages plus the present. You are all of yourselves rolled into one—the young, the middle-aged, the well matured. I mean, look at Henrie O. She tells Carolyn Hart all sorts of ways that her earlier experience as a newspaperwoman can help her solve crime, right?

"Or take Mrs. Pargeter," Peaches said, switching to the British detecting scene a la Simon Brett. "Mrs. P. admires the fact that her late crime-lord husband believed in honor among thieves. She knows how to use his underworld connections to solve crimes-without-honor and actually make the world a better place. So even experience of a very dubious sort can be used with wisdom. And sometimes compassion."

Peaches had a point. "What I like about an older sleuth," I said, "is the same thing I, the author, like about being older myself. You reach an age where you're willing to do what works best for you even if it looks eccentric to other people. Where you respect the real deep-down differences in the way people's minds work, including your own. And if some folks think that's outrageous, so be it."

"I, myself, am not outrageous," Peaches said firmly. "I'm a pragmatist, pure and simple in every book."

"Except perhaps the time your dinner guests found an upside-down bowl with two toilet paper rolls on it and at the very top a half-eaten apple, all on the kitchen counter," I said. "You know folks always come in the kitchen."

"Temporary Found Sculpture!" Peaches cried. "Made of what came to hand, to remind me to take the rolls out of the oven at eight-thirty. Because my timer broke. And as soon as I explained that the apple half eaten meant half after eight as in a-t-e, they all reminded me when the time came. Temporary Found Sculpture works. So it's not eccentric."

To spare Peaches's feelings, I talked about her peers. "Well, how about Dorothy Gilman's Mrs. Pollifax. She's sixty-something, and she outwits Bulgarian terrorists, African assassins, Albanian thugs, and other dangerous types with totally unconventional ploys. Like the time she substituted a can of peaches for a can of uranium and thus prevented mayhem."

"Don't give away plots," Peaches said. "It's not fair."

"And how about Father Brown? I said, to get more classical. "He was a Roman Catholic priest, and yet he solved crimes by stepping in the killer's shoes. What was it he said? Something like 'When I'm quite sure I feel like the murderer, I know who he is.' What would the Vatican think of that?"

"And how about Miss Seeton, who has already outlived one author despite her senior status?" I asked. "Miss Seeton doesn't even bother to find out why her sketches contain clues that help other more-law-enforcement-minded folks solve murders. She just draws cartoons and there the clues are. Now, how is that for odd?"

Peaches retorted. "It's wise. You do what you can to be useful. And by the time you are fifty or sixty or seventy, you have learned all sorts of surprising things because you've had to. And anything you've learned can be helpful if you can just figure out how. That's the mystery. How to use it."

But Peaches isn't like Henrie O., who covered murders and wars and other disasters as a reporter. She's not even like Stefanie Matteson's Charlotte Graham, an older Oscar-winning actress turned sleuth with all sorts of fancy connections to help her out. When Peaches worked, she helped her first husband run a North Carolina mountain craft shop—hardly apprenticeship to find killers.

"Of course you collect memory tricks," I said, "But aside from that . . ."

She felt my skepticism. "My experience," she said, "is partly in figuring out what makes people tick. Back in my craft shop days, I could tell—just by the clothes they wore—a customer who would want cute little carved wooden mice from one who wanted lovely traditional pottery. Mice go with ruffles. Men rarely buy cute mice, except when kids demand it.

"And," Peaches continued, "since I forgot things, like who I put aside the toby jug for, or who I should know by name because they came in last week, I have more know-how in getting around what I don't know—in figuring it out. What else do detectives do? I have learned how to get folks to tell me what I need to know without letting them find out I don't already know it. Older sleuths have had to learn all kinds of things like that."

"You mean," I said, "that just as Miss Marple could solve any crime by comparing the killer's motive with some point of psychology in an English village, every older sleuth has the equivalent of a village. A community of experience he or she can draw on."

"Of course," Peaches said. "You might say I draw upon the confederation of the absentminded." (Peaches knows how to make even foolishness sound good.) "Because since my adventures as an absent-minded sleuth have been written up in books, everybody sends me their tricks. Did you know that 83 percent of Americans believe they have bad memories for names? A scientific study showed that. And over 60 percent believe they have trouble finding things like their keys or their glasses. But that's Americans of *all ages.* And I, being older, have collected and developed more memory coping devices over the years. I am an expert!"

Good grief! Peaches is getting as full of herself as senior-citizen Hercule Poirot who brags about his little gray cells! Can getting around spacey gray cells be something to crow about? That takes nerve!

Amazing what kinds of experience older sleuths draw on. Of course, ex-police-chiefs like Susanna Hofmann McShea's Forrest Haggarty can detect, especially with the help of other small-town-Connecticut seniors. But how about D.B. Borton's Cat Calaban saying she's a better sleuth because she's been a mother! I guess lots of mothers

Illustration © 1987 Dynamic Graphics, Inc.

would agree.

"O.K., O.K.!" I said to my own sleuth. "But you older sleuths have limits. Admit that Peaches! You can't have a convincing fistfight or sword-battle or get seriously beaten up and be back at work in two hours."

"Poo!" said Peaches. "Some of us are in great shape. Fannie Zindel, who's so full of energy she needs two authors, is a five-times tennis champion. And anybody who lives in the mountains like me has to walk up and down hills." (Peaches is rather proud of still being a size twelve.)

"But I'll admit," she said, "that mostly we are forced to battle with our wits—right? Give me an older sleuth any day for surprise twists and unexpected insight. Take Nero Wolfe. He hardly moved out of his chair, but he solved all sorts of exotic crimes with snakes and poison and I forget what else. He was a great detective, all with his mind.

"But I'm not jealous of him," Peaches went on. "I'm jealous of the senior sleuths who get to travel. Such as Dottie and Joe Loudermilk in their RV van. Since they're retired, author Gar Haywood takes them to the Grand Canyon to solve a murder. Why can't you take me there? There's one advantage of an older sleuth that you've ignored," she accused. "We aren't tied down. Or not as much. We can go places ! Any place you like. We're ready!"

"So what's the drawback with being an older sleuth?" I asked. "It can't all be perfect."

"The drawback," Peaches said, "is for you, not for me. With every book, I get older. Suppose I get so old I can't detect anymore? Then what will you do?"

I just laughed. "You forget—I get older, too. And in the meantime I'll just follow the motto I learned from Mrs. Pollifax: 'Adapt, adjust and catch your breath later.'"

Long silence from Peaches. "I don't suppose," she said, "that you'd consider getting your motto from me?"

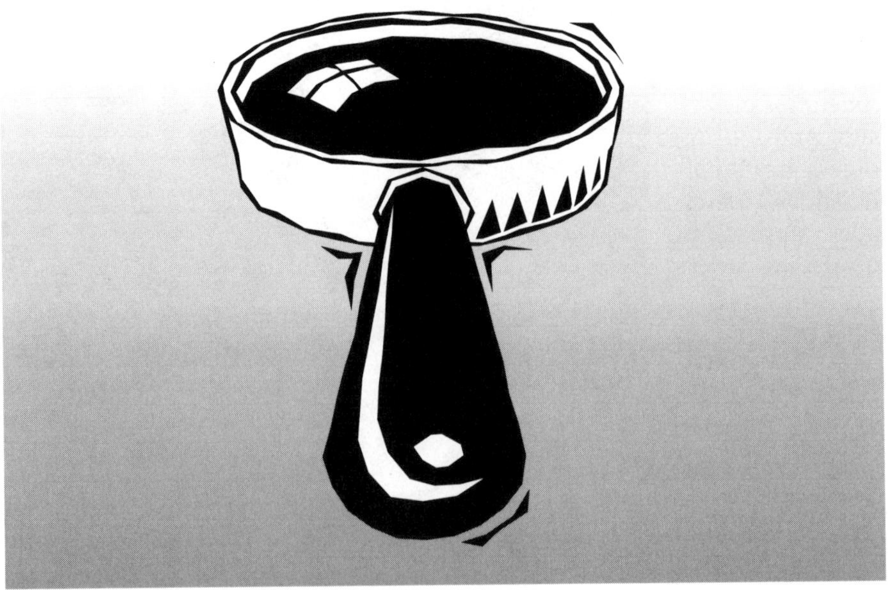

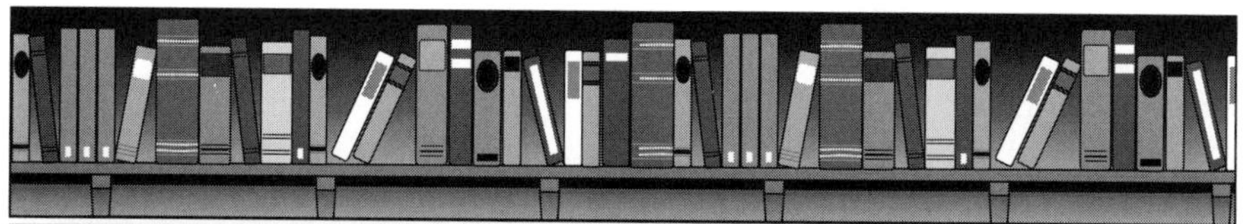

A Reader's Checklist of Older Women Sleuths

by the Editors

CHARACTER	AUTHOR
Angela Benbow	*Corinne Holt Sawyer*
Amelia Butterworth	*Anna Katharine Green*
Cat Caliban	*D.B. Borton*
Emma Chizzit	*Mary Bowen Hall*
Henrie O. Collins	*Carolyn G. Hart*
Mary Alice Crane	*Anne George*
Peaches Dann	*Elizabeth Daniels Squire*
Jane Amanda Edwards	*Charlotte Murray Russell*
Clara Gamadge	*Eleanor Boylan*
Charlotte Graham	*Stefanie Matteson*
Lavinia Grey	*Kate Gallison*
Patricia Anne Hollowell	*Anne George*
Lil Hubbert	*Gallagher Gray*
Dewey James	*Kate Morgan*
Tish McWhinny	*Barbara Comfort*
Rachel Murdock	*D.B. Olsen*
Emily Pollifax	*Dorothy Gilman*
Eugenia Potter	*Virginia Rich*
Lady Margaret Priam	*Joyce Christmas*
Sister Mary Helen	*Sister Carol Anne O'Marie*
Penny Spring	*Margot Arnold*
Betty Trenka	*Joyce Christmas*
Caledonia Wingate	*Corinne Holt Sawyer*

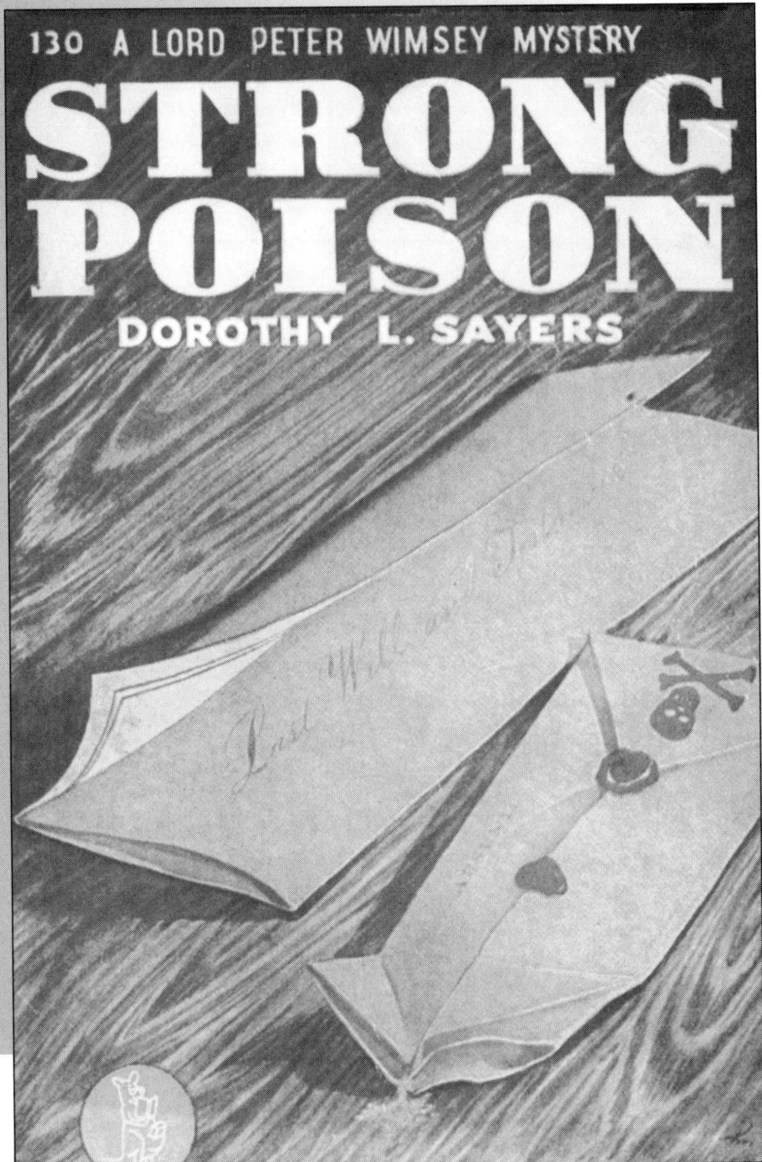

Strong Poison by Dorothy L. Sayers

Something to Love and Laugh At (The Aristocratic Sleuth)

Joyce Christmas

Some years after she created that most lovable of man-about-town aristocratic sleuths, Lord Peter Wimsey, Dorothy L. Sayers remarked in an essay, "The Importance of Being Vulgar" (1936), that a lord is "something to love and laugh at."

WHILE THE IDEA OF a body discovered in a bathtub wearing only a pince-nez (*Whose Body,* 1923, Lord Peter's first case) is mildly amusing, Lord Peter, himself, in the series that features him, does not, in my opinion, inspire great rollicking gales of laughter.

Perhaps Sayers was thinking that the whole business of upper-class society, its pretensions and snobbery, was worth a chortle or two among her less than upper-class readers. Perhaps the conceit of Lord Peter—a bit dippy and asinine on first appearance, though growing more serious with time—engaged in tracking down murderers was a silly enough idea to inspire laughter. (In my experience, English peers would not consider crime-solving quite the done thing.) If Sayers was laughing, she was also certainly loving her Lord Peter, and for three quarters of a century, mystery readers have loved him as well.

My series character, Lady Margaret Priam, the daughter of the Earl of Brayfield, is a resident of New York City (but with ties to the family estate in England, Priam's Priory). She solved her first murder in *Suddenly in Her Sorbet* (1988), where the overbearing chairlady of a benefit gala dinner-dance meets her end face down in the lovely cassis sorbet. (I thought it was funny.) I have tried to make Margaret likable, if not lovable, and I hope the laughter comes from the people around her who are enamored of her title—the society ladies and their consorts, all of them ripe for satirization. They are social climbers who imagine themselves to be aristocrats. Even if they believe they have "arrived," they are always fighting to retain their social clout, their wealth, their marriages, their social glow. Their pretensions to being America's aristocrats is indeed something to laugh at.

Influenced by E.C. Bentley's creation, Philip Trent, the subspecies of mysteries featuring English aristocrats as detectives was created between World War I and World War II by Sayers, Margery Allingham (Albert Campion, possibly of royal birth, whose mother is so distinguished that her name cannot even be spoken), Ngaio Marsh (Roderick Alleyn, a policeman to be sure, but also the younger son of a peer), and Michael Innes (Sir John Appleby, another policeman, but one with a knighthood). Nicholas Blake's (poet laureate Cecil Day Lewis's) Nigel Strangeways is equally upper class, as are Anthony Berkeley's Roger Sheringham and a number of others.

The well-born sleuth (and one ought to pay respects to the very genteel world of Christie's Miss Marple) with nothing better to do than enjoy his fine art, music, and wines, and the society of his era (plus the occasional murder) is a recurring character who is often found in his natural habitat, the English country house, where murder seems a more common occurrence than even along Raymond Chandler's "mean streets." Here dwell not only titled detectives but blue-blooded victims and, of course, the servants—the ponderous and solemn butlers, the simple maids sent into blubbering hysterics by the crime, the no-nonsense cooks who continue to set out a proper tea and meals at the appointed times, regardless of the bloody events rocking the place. And certainly, no self-respecting progeny of a peer, intent on tracking down the villain of the piece, could cope without a devoted manservant to chat up the sniffling maids and backslap a suspect chauffeur who might harbor a clue.

Where did they come from, these foppish, dilettantish geniuses at crime-solving? Why were they popular?

One may speculate that, between the wars, the typical middle-class reader picking up the latest Sayers or Allingham was entertained not only by the plots, the characters, and the puzzle of the mystery, but also by the purported inside look at the lives of the titled and moneyed, very much as they are today entertained by the doings of the Prince and Princess of Wales and the scandals of the upper class.

Much has been written about the roots of the "gifted amateur," and scholars have ruminated on the rise of a large middle-class reading public in the earlier years of this century, who took Sherlock Holmes to their hearts and were hooked on a craving for crime fiction that seems clearly to exist to this day.

The upheavals of the First World War perhaps caused the public to look back at the stable, settled picture of Life As It Ought To Be, where Everyone Knows His Place, with the aristocracy at the top, with the money, the leisure, the brains and the education to meet and face down any situation, even murder. Indeed, it is often said that a pleasure of reading mystery fiction is knowing that by the end, the proper order will be restored.

The sleuth himself, for it is invariably a man (except for Baroness Orczy's Lady Molly Robertson-Kirk of Scotland Yard, and Anne Perry's well-connected upper-class Victorian Charlotte Pitt, there are almost no aristocratic female detectives), is often presented as vaguely idiotic (class prejudice at work?) and surely owes a debt to The Scarlet Pimpernel (1905), Sir Percy Blakeney, the foppish Englishman who bravely rescued aristocratic victims of the French Revolution, and to P.G. Wodehouse's Honourable Bertie Wooster, who, while not a detective, surely epitomizes the reading public's view of the upper classes: a silly, comic figure, often in need of rescue by practical and wise Jeeves, someone who is more or less like the public themselves.

America's lack of a hereditary aristocracy made if difficult to transplant the Lord Peter type to these shores. Yet S.S. Van Dine's Philo Vance (*The Benson Murder Case,* 1926), with his English butler and rooms full of art treasures, and cafe society's (and Dashiell Hammett's) Nick and Nora Charles (*The Thin Man,* 1934), awash in martinis, are approximations of the English upper class engaged in detection.

Although some English aristocratic detectives lived on through the Second World War and after, one critic has stated firmly, "The heyday of the absolute amateur, the man-about-town for whom detection was an agreeable hobby, was the period between the two world wars. The type has now vanished completely, and must be, surely, impossible to resurrect—other than through the medium of the pastiche or the historical detective story." (T.J. Binyon, *Murder Will Out: The Detective in Fiction,* Oxford University Press, 1989, p. 132.) It seems impossible indeed to resurrect Lord Peter and his fellow aristocrats as the millenium ends. Certainly not in the American mystery. And yet . . .

When I decided to try my hand at mysteries, I faced the problem of creating a sleuth who was sufficiently "different" to stand out in the highly competitive marketplace for mystery fiction. I wanted a woman, but the suburban housewife was not my preference, although she detects happily, an "absolute amateur" in most cases, through many series. At the time, I also did not want to settle for that other

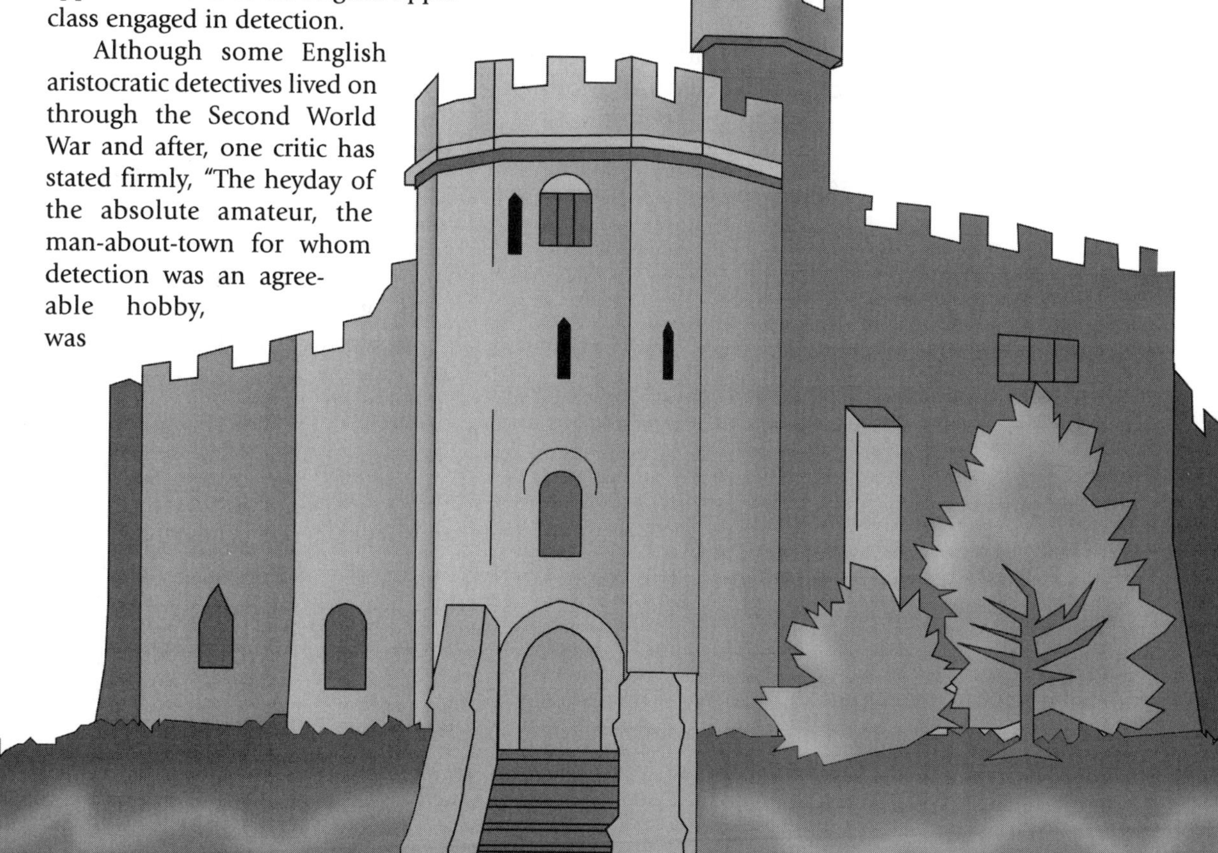

exemplar of traditional English mysteries, the benign but clever little old lady a la Miss Marple, although I have since started writing a Little Old Lady series. For my first book, I looked back to the mysteries I had enjoyed, the works of Sayers and her contemporaries, and the detectives I loved the best, Lord Peter and his ilk. I made a conscious decision to borrow the concept.

Thus Lady Margaret came into being. I had a model for her, a titled British expatriate who, by virtue of her title as well as many admirable personal qualities, is beloved by what passes as the "upper class" in this country, the painfully High society of New York. Deprived of royalty other than media-made stars and glamorous political families, Americans are peculiarly enamored of English titles. Moreover, we love to read about the sordid tales that lie behind the extravagant galas, the glittering charity balls, the social marriages whose demises fill gossip columns. It's a world that seems to exist somewhere beyond normal workaday life. And it can be funny, as I learned during a stint of promoting all those tiresome gala parties.

Because of her title and self-assurance, Lady Margaret can don both noblesse oblige and a designer frock and talk to anyone of any class and get them to talk to her. Very convenient for crime solving. Still, Lady Margaret is not a complete steal from the old days. She isn't silly, but an earnest, youngish woman, who is offended by situations like murder. True to her heritage, she knows it isn't done, and no one should be allowed to get away with murder.

There aren't many lady aristocratic sleuths, except for the aforementioned Lady Molly, but even at this late date, the male of the species hasn't "vanished completely," as solemnly predicted, and oddly, American writers are the ones who are doing the resurrecting, with earls in particular in abundant supply. American Elizabeth George sets her mysteries in England and features Scotland Yard Inspector Thomas Lynley, the eighth Earl of Asherton. His sidekick/assistant is the lower-class Detective Sergeant Barbara Havers, and much of the tension in the books lies not between the upper classes and those who aspire to emulate them, but between the aristocratic Lynley and the resentful, class-conscious Havers. Their relationship is pure class warfare, at least on Barbara's side. It certainly isn't the mellowed-out world of the Dowager Duchess of Denver, no matter how beautifully dressed and well comported Lynley's fiancée, Lady Helen Clyde, and it isn't Lady Margaret's world of moneyed New World social climbers.

Martha Grimes, another American, has also found a place for an earl in her mostly England-set mysteries. Scotland Yard Superintendant Richard Jury's sidekick is Melrose Plant, the eighth Earl of Caverness, along with Plant's American Aunt Agatha, who fancies herself an aristocratic sleuth by virtue of marrying a title.

Interestingly, titled policemen are not something Sayers would have understood. In her day, in Sherlock Holmes's day, the police were as resolutely lower-class as is Barbara Havers. Professor B.J. Rahn has pointed out ("Ngaio Marsh: The Detective Novelist of Manners," *Armchair Detective*) that when Marsh's Roderick Alleyn burst onto the detection scene (*A Man Lay Dead*, 1934), "the police force was a declassé career choice. The Golden Age was the heyday of the well-born gifted amateur sleuth, and such policemen as appeared in the genre were never aristocrats." Alleyn, she says, "was a transitional figure combing the traits of the pre-World War II, gifted amateur gentleman sleuth with the rank-and-file postwar professional policeman." When Marsh created Alleyn, reforms in police recruitment policy instituted in 1931 by Lord Trenchard, commissioner of the Metropolitan Police, were beginning to attract men of Alleyn's educational background, and to some degree, of his class.

As long as an Anglophile still breathes and can read, the aristocratic sleuth won't vanish. The Golden Age mysteries will still be read, and Lord Peter will be loved. And I hope the laughter in my Lady Margaret books will continue to be heard.

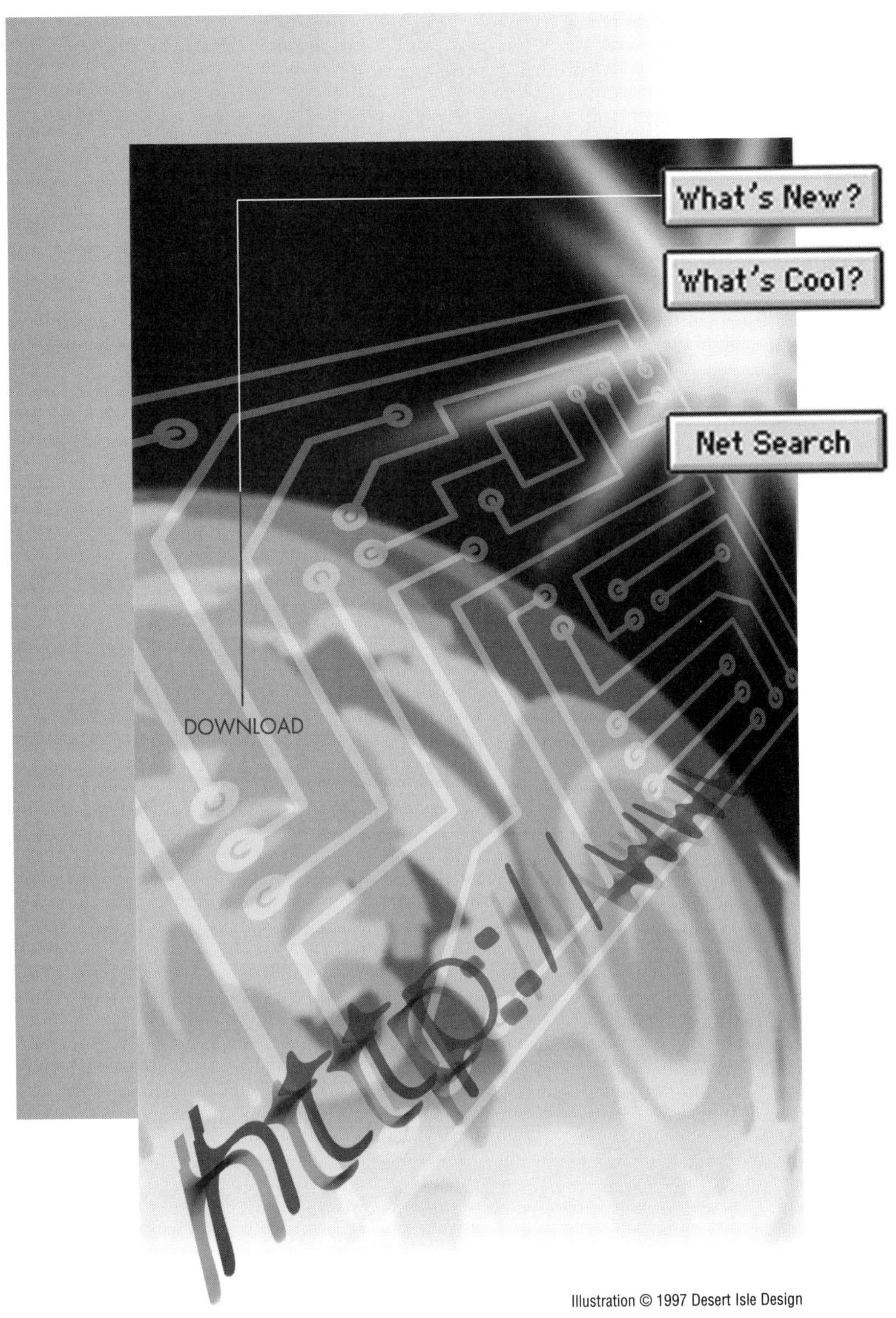
What's New?
What's Cool?
Net Search
DOWNLOAD
http://www

How Cyberspace is Changing the Writer's Life

Barbara Paul

It's already made a number of changes for those of us online. Foremost is the wealth of information available at the click of a mouse; I don't know how many trips to the library I've been saved by having access to the Internet and the commercial services.

THE IMMEDIACY OF ONLINE communication is also a boon; things get done *fast* instead of dragging out forever. But what drew most of us online in the first place is the stimulus of belonging to a community of writers, the almost daily contact with like-minded people.

But this is old news. What lies in the future? There are several possibilities; let's take the small stuff first.

World Wide Web is going to affect almost every aspect of the writer's life. The day may not be far off when writers upload their completed manuscripts directly to their publishers' web sites. No more printing out! No more mailing of disks! All the copy-editing can be done onscreen and then checked by the writer without any mailing back and forth of heavy paper manuscripts.

Once certain in-the-works security measures are instituted, all business transactions can be done electronically—including signing contracts and transmitting payment. A lightpen signature will be encoded and thus function much like a fingerprint; no one can duplicate it.

Writers will find it no longer necessary to tour every time a new book comes out. The PR opportunities of a web page will not replace promotional tours entirely (seeing an author in person can still spark sales), but writers will be able to reach more people through the web than through touring and do so with less effort and expense. A successfully done author's page can draw thousands of readers the first month alone. Compare that to the number who show up at a signing and the advantage is obvious.

It's possible that web pages will one day replace publishing houses, and readers will download books instead of buying them in stores. That's bad news for booksellers; but selling books via download does have its advantages.

For one thing, it will put an end to book-stripping. For another, publishers will no longer be at the mercy of the paper-suppliers; the readers' money will go the writers and the publishers instead of paying for pounds of overpriced paper as well as for distribution expenses. And downloading books will have one remarkable benefit for the writer: *Your book will never go out of print.*

But who's going to go to the trouble of printing out an entire downloaded book just to save a trip to the bookstore? Nobody, probably. So books on paper aren't the answer; the downloaded book will have to take a different form, most likely that of a highly compressed file that can be transferred to an ultra-small disk or even a chip. Those horrible handheld computer/readers you've heard about? They're going to become commonplace. The reading machine will be lightweight and no larger than a paperback book; pop in the chip or disk of the book you want to read and you don't have to lug around a couple of pounds of paper with you.

If publishers decide not to make books available via download but instead distribute them on reading-machine chips, think what a boon that would be to booksellers. Dozens of copies could be stored in the same volume of space now occupied by a single hardback book.

A lot of people—and I'm one of them—will miss the tactile pleasures a printed book has to offer. But the technology is headed in the direction of mechanical readers, and it's hard to put the genie back in the bottle. It might not be as bad as it sounds, though; already a flexible screen has been developed, and by flexible I mean roll it up and put it in your pocket. The associated electronics are small and light, so eventually the screens of mechanical readers will be visually identical to a printed page. No eyestrain from staring at glowing phosphors for hours.

I've saved the biggest change—and the most potentially disturbing one—for last. And that is the way books are actually written. Especially fiction. And *especially* mysteries.

Stories published electronically are already taking advantage of hyperlinks . . . a way to jump from what appears on the screen to a related file. In a strictly linear story, this pause to read related material is an interruption. A distraction. So some writers have begun to ponder the problems of writing nonlinear stories, stories in which the endings are *not* inherent in the beginnings: they could branch off in a number of directions depending on which link the reader chooses. Such a story would have room for side bars—collateral information, author commentary, additional scenes that are not part of the plot but contribute to the story in some other way. A major scene could be written from as many points of view as there are characters in the scene.

Writers of this cyberficiton (I don't know what else to call it) will need to stop thinking in terms of beginning a story at one point and following a path—either straight or meandering—to a clearly defined endpoint. They'll need to think instead in terms of constructing museums, where readers may pause wherever they wish, skip parts if they feel like it, and still emerge feeling satisfied with what they've read. And then perhaps come for a return visit.

Expect to find chapters in which text is accompanied by graphics and sound; the book of the future may well be a multi-media event. Say a character in a story is shown to be entranced by a Rembrandt painting or a Mozart opera: linked files would let the reader see the painting or listen to the music. Writers may find themselves seeking out collaborative enterprises, with artists and composers creating new work specifically for a novel.

The danger of this approach is obvious: the bells and whistles could drown out the words. Much of this multi-media work will have only novelty appeal and won't last; but it *will* leave its mark if a truly nonlinear form of story-telling is developed because of it. But no one has yet figured out to write a nonlinear mystery.

Personally, I don't think it's going to happen. There have been attempts in the past to get away from beginning-middle-end plotting, some of them spectacularly successful—James Joyce, for instance. But none of these other forms of story-telling have ever *replaced* linear writing, and I suspect nothing ever will.

I could be wrong. But whichever way it goes, we're in for interesting times.

A Conversation with
Marian Babson

Carol Harper

MARIAN BABSON, AUTHOR OF over thirty books, has been a published writer for over fifteen years. Born in Salem, Massachusetts, Marian says she has always wanted to be a writer, "ever since she realized that someone actually wrote those books." When she took a holiday to Ireland with a friend, she already had started a collection of rejection slips, stored in a suit box, back in the family home. She stopped counting, eventually, at five-hundred, before she finally moved to London. The Ireland trip was coupled with an eight-day stay in London where she discovered that Londoners "were on her side" and immediately set her cap for living abroad. After all, she liked the place and the people, and London was a publishing center, ideal for breaking into the business. She returned home "to pay off the loan for the holiday" and returned at a later date.

There are two problems with being an ex-pat in Britain—you can't get a job without a work permit, and you can't get a work permit without a job! However, Marian could, with her skills as a wizard typist, get a job in a typing pool and, after earning her resident's permit, she went temping. As you can read on the jackets of her books, she has worked as secretary for architects, a law firm, a Soho club, the British Museum, a visiting (American) superstar, and various companies. She even did a stretch as Secretary for the Crime Writers' Association. And she started going "door-to-door" to publishers to sell her books. (She didn't have an agent then, but she does now.) Marian says she made a conscious decision not to write police procedurals—the British Police structure is very complicated and procedure changes far too frequently for books to stay current (at least three major changes in procedure have been introduced since Marian came to Britain: the abolition of capital punishment; implementation of The Police and Criminal Evidence Act, PACE; and introduction of The Sheehy Report, all of which changed the way police and courts handled cases). What was left was to write the books she wanted to read, books that required less technical details and more character, wit, and plot. More research into the who and why than the how. "After all," she says, "if I didn't write to entertain myself, I wouldn't write at all."

Her first sale was to Collins in 1971: *Cover-Up Story. Cover-Up Story* was followed by a book about how a sleuth acquired his or her cat! After all, lots of mysteries seem to feature cat-owning sleuths, but no one ever actually introduces cat to sleuth in any series. So was born *Murder on Show* (Collins, 1972; as *Murder at the Cat Show,* St. Martin's, 1989), where Perkins and Tate, protagonists of *Cover-Up Story,* meet Pandora, the "orphaned" Siamese cat who takes over their lives in subsequent books. Thus, also, was born the Perkins and Tate public relations series. Trouble was, Collins, after buying *Murder on Show,* didn't seem to be interested in a series, and rejected the next two (subsequently published by St. Martin's, *Tourists are for Trapping* in 1989 and *In the Teeth of Adversity* in 1990, later by Chivers in large print). Marian, therefore, began a career in writing "one-offs." *Pretty Lady* (Collins, 1973; issued in paperback by Warner in 1992) introduced a "heroine" who tries to con a retarded man into killing her rich husband for her, thus freeing her from the marriage while ensuring that she gets all the man's money. This book introduces her characteristic "voice," which is a curious mixture of suspense (and underlying evil) with, later in her career, a bit of humor dropped in for leavening. From that point on, one-offs have seemed "more natural." After all, you really do have to create a situation where the amateur sleuth encounters the crime, and how many professions or life-styles (other than police or private investigators) allow multiple crimes to litter one's life? "Would you invite Jessica Fletcher to tea?" as the classic question asks.

So a series of non-series, psychological suspense novels followed. In each, there is a vein of suspense and "terror" underlying the otherwise "cozy" story. Books like *The Stalking Lamb* (Collins, 1974) and *Past Regret* (Collins, 1990). *The Stalking Lamb* features a terrorized American student while *Past Regret* follows an amnesiac American college student in her year abroad at a London University. Both of these books illustrate another of Babson's signature themes: the use of American characters in a British setting.

In the present mystery-writing climate, there has been some controversy about Americans writing "British" novels (rarely do the British reciprocate, perhaps having little experience with an "American

voice"). Marian handles this problem by making her protagonists in many books be American or have strong American connections. In this way, if there is a mistake in the use of language or a misinterpretation of custom, and the editor doesn't catch it as being too American, then the errors can be explained away as having been perpetrated by a stranger to Britain! However, perhaps Marian has been in Britain long enough to have adapted more fully than she realizes to British language and mores. She tells me that one book was rejected by a British editor because the editor didn't believe her Americans!

Like many authors, Babson writes what she "knows." Therefore, there are books featuring catering (*Death Warmed Up*, Collins and Warner, 1982), painting (Guilty Party, Collins, 1988), theater (numerous, from *Cover-Up Story* through her Dolan and Sinclair series), and even mystery-writing (her forthcoming *Miss Petunia's Last Case* which was being finalized almost as we talked)! Her settings in the theater and the movie industry are perhaps related to being introduced to the theater and film by a cinema-buff father. He always regretted that Marian and her brother were born too late to have seen the classic films, so he took them, as children, to all the Boston theaters where revivals of classic films were being shown. Marian recounts one theater where the film was followed by a stage show. She tells how, while everyone else was admiring the footwork of the chorus line, she was watching the looks on the dancers' faces and their apparent interactions with each other. Even then, she "was looking behind things." At any rate, this love of the theater led to participation in an amateur theater group (in Boston) that never got past rehearsal of its first play, where Marian learned the backstage details as well as the on stage interplay. And this love of the theater has induced her to return to one continuing series, the aforementioned Dolan (Trixie) and Sinclair (Evangeline) series, where the American film and stage stars of "a certain age" travel about looking for work and creating mayhem for hapless Inspector Heyhoe in five books so far (*Reel Murder*, Collins, 1986 and St. Martin's, 1987; *Encore Murder*, Collins, 1989; *Shadows in Their Blood*,

Collins, 1993; *Even Yuppies Die,* Collins, 1994; and *Break a Leg, Darlings,* Collins, 1995).

Another recurring theme in her books are cats. Marian say this is because she "knows cats." She doesn't "know dogs." Cats figure large in many of Marian's books, most notably in the recent *Nine Lives to Murder* (St. Martin's, 1994) and *The Diamond Cat* (HarperCollins, 1994; St. Martin's, 1996). Even the new book has cats in it (one mystery writer protagonist has two—"Had I" and "But Known" while another, hard-boiled author has a tough tom named "Roscoe"). They also figure large in Marian's flat, with figurines of cats in various guises scattered over the mantelpiece. St. Martin's has purchased the rights to the books featuring "Babson's Cats," and these books may be rereleased at some future date.

There is one notable dog, however; an Irish wolfhound named The Semtex which Dolan and Sinclair meet at a poetry reading at an Irish pub called The Green Colleen in *Break a Leg, Darlings.* The Semtex follows them home and is subsequently the center of a confrontation between the poet and his pub mates, Dolan and Sinclair, and a gypsy cabdriver named Nova. She may not "know" dogs, but Marian offers a marvelous send-up of one in The Semtex!

And this leads us to humor and wit. Any good crime or suspense tale is more suspenseful if the tension is relieved by a little light byplay. And Babson is expert at this. Witness the above-mentioned Irish wolfhound. Or the odd gathering of family, waiting to hear about the new will the rich, old patriarch is likely to make (*A Fool for Murder,* Collins, 1983; Walker, 1984), only to find that he has brought home from America a seventeen-year-old bride. Some souvenir!

As to what does Marian read? Besides research for her books—her flat is filled to overflowing with books on various useful topics, dictionaries, and newspaper and magazine clippings. Well, she won't name names, but she will admit to reading "a bit of everything," tending toward "the optimistic kind, anything with humor." And the stacks of crime fiction mixed in with the research material attest to that!

Marian says she probably won't ever move back to the States. After

all, she says, "I can't drive. I hit things!" and that means that life in London with its extensive and convenient bus, tube, and train transport is much more feasible, if not safer! However, she spends several weeks of each year visiting friends in the U.S., especially in connection with mystery conventions, and brings back more Americanisms to portray in her witty and well-written books about Americans in Britain.

My Mama Told Me There'd Be Days Like This

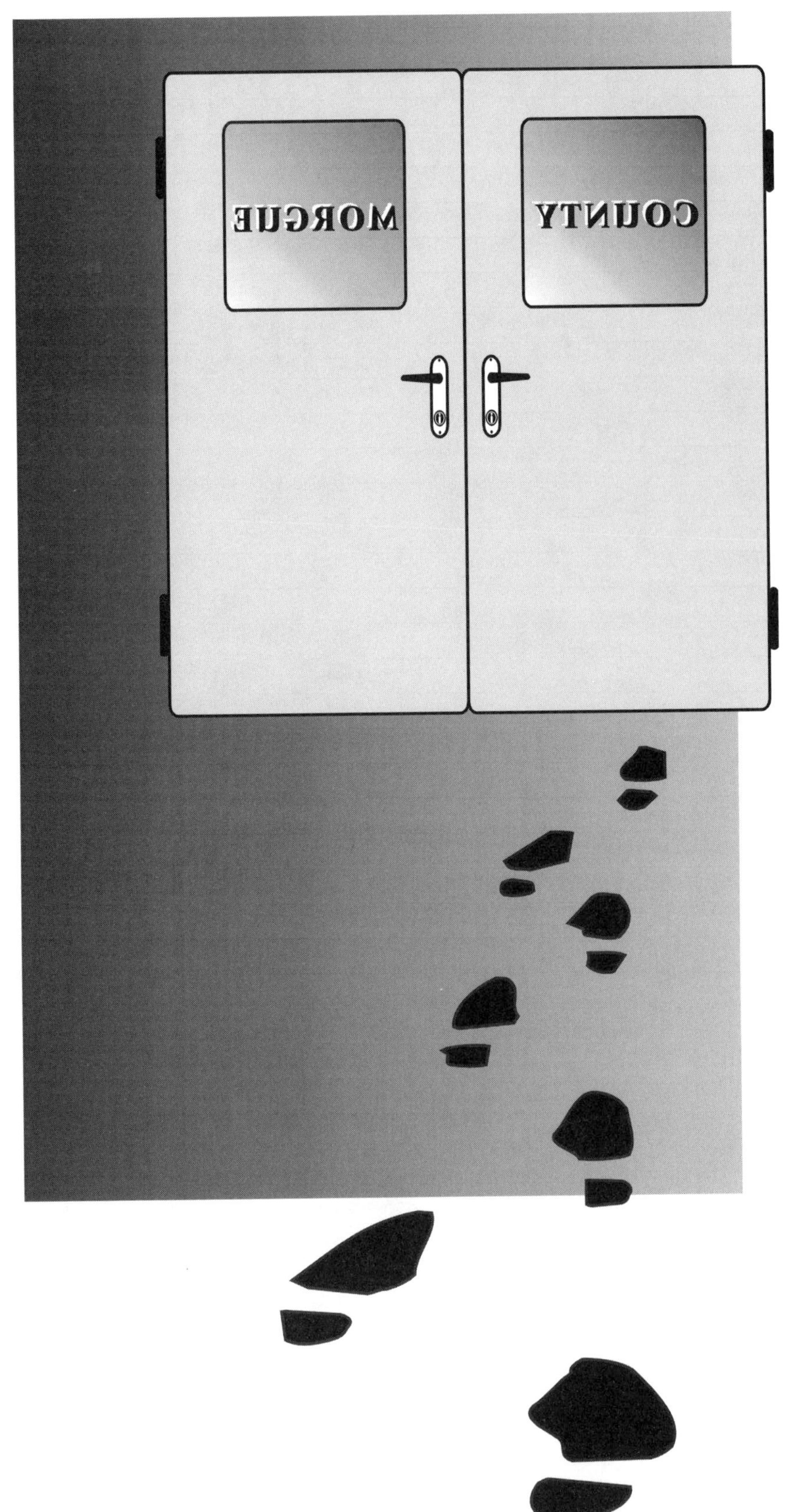
MORGUE
COUNTY

Wendy Goes to the Morgue

Wendy Hornsby

There is a big difference between writing a tough, graphic murder scene, and seeing the product of the real thing up close.

I WAS WORKING ON *Telling Lies* (Dutton, 1992, Onyx paper April 1993), the first in my mystery series with filmmaker Maggie MacGowen. At one point in the story, Maggie has to go to the Los Angeles County morgue to look at a body. For the book, for you, I wanted to get it right both visually and emotionally. I had to go to the morgue.

The first thing you need to know is, Maggie is a lot tougher and braver than I am. "Soft-spoken, genteel college professor" was how National Public Radio introduced me recently. As much as I hate that description, it really is not far off the mark (but I'm working on it).

So, one smoggy summer day my consultant on things police, Detective Dennis Payne, LAPD Robbery-Homicide Division, called and said he had to go to the morgue to pick up some "property" (don't ask). Did I want to come along? I dredged up sufficient bravado, and went.

In the first place, the L.A. morgue is nothing like the TV show *Quincy.* No shiny stainless, no view windows or sleek offices. The real thing is housed in a square, dull-gray, four or five story building on the downslope corner of the massive L.A. County-USC Hospital Medical Center grounds. The surrounding neighborhood is wrecking yards, the Lincoln Heights Jail, railroad switching yards, a couple of freeways, a McDonald's and a Holiday Inn that needs some paint.

While he parked his city-issue car—the only green four door in a lot full of government mud-brown Chevys (that's California mud-brown)—Detective Payne gave me some tips:

The morgue isn't tidy. When the door opens, what you see is bodies, everyone in the county who dies under questionable circumstances. First thing when you go inside, he said, is take a deep breath, get used to the smell in a hurry.

He also warned about touching anything. No problem there.

"It's not like the movies," he said, "not sheet-covered bodies with toe tags sticking out."

"No toe tags? I asked.

"No sheets," he said.

Forewarned is forearmed, right?

Dennis opened the big door, I took a handful of his tweed upholstered elbow, and drew in my deep breath. A big mistake; the death smell is like nothing else.

The long hallway inside the morgue is little more than four gurneys wide, with occupied gurneys lined up along the sides sometimes two and three deep. The dead aren't laid out with hands neatly folded on their chests. Tumbled out comes closer.

Except for Dennis's shoulder ahead of me, there was no place I could look without seeing the violently dead. I took it in small snaps, focusing on the wholish parts of those we passed. When Dennis turned to check on me, I smiled—even the genteel and soft-spoken can lie with their faces. I was feeling about stage-two panicky, but I didn't want him to know it, decide I was a wimp and not invite me along on other adventures. He didn't seem affected by the place. Old hat: Homicide detectives routinely attend the autopsies related to their cases.

Dennis stopped to show me an especially nice example of a gunshot entrance wound. He very thoroughly explained the characteristic cruciform tearing in the flesh, demonstrated how to find the direction of entry from the pattern of bruising. It was fascinating as long as I focused on the wounds and not on the man lying there, looking back at me.

The bodies in the hall were waiting their turns at one of the two big autopsy rooms where about six bodies can be processed at once. The autopsy rooms, in contrast to the hall, are brightly lit and full of activity. Again, there is no clinical gleam. The standard tools are garden shears and soup ladles. Don't call and ask me about it. In *Telling Lies* Maggie goes into the details for me. She handled the entire experience better than I did. I will tell you this, though. After an autopsy your victim can't be dressed in decolletage for the funeral.

I had difficulty with faces, but I managed to hang in without disgracing myself or Dennis. Until we passed a corpse with no face at all. When I realized what I was looking at, I said to hell with bravado, gripped Dennis's arm in another place and seriously studied the weave of his tweed jacket. Nice jacket. Next time I hope he wears plaid.

By the time we got to the X-ray room, I had all that I needed for Maggie's trip to the morgue. All five senses were certainly covered (when the top of the skull is removed, it pops like a champagne cork.) I had the emotional stuff in hand, too. True to form, though her stomach gave one leap, Maggie was a brick at the morgue. She even managed to speak coherently.

I love hanging out with Maggie. Since the morgue, we have seen Skid Row late at night, federal housing projects on payday, the police academy bar, the lockup at Parker Center, figured out DNA and blood-spatter patterns, watched women officers boxing, heard the talk and walked the walk. Next to royalty checks, doing practical research is far and away the most fun aspect of writing crime fiction. Another time, I'll tell you what I did for *Midnight Baby,* Maggie's second adventure, coming out in May (Dutton, 1993). It was certainly more fun than the morgue. Trust me.

One last thing. You know what

Detective Payne said to me as we emerged from the morgue and out into the smog again?

"So, shall we get lunch?"

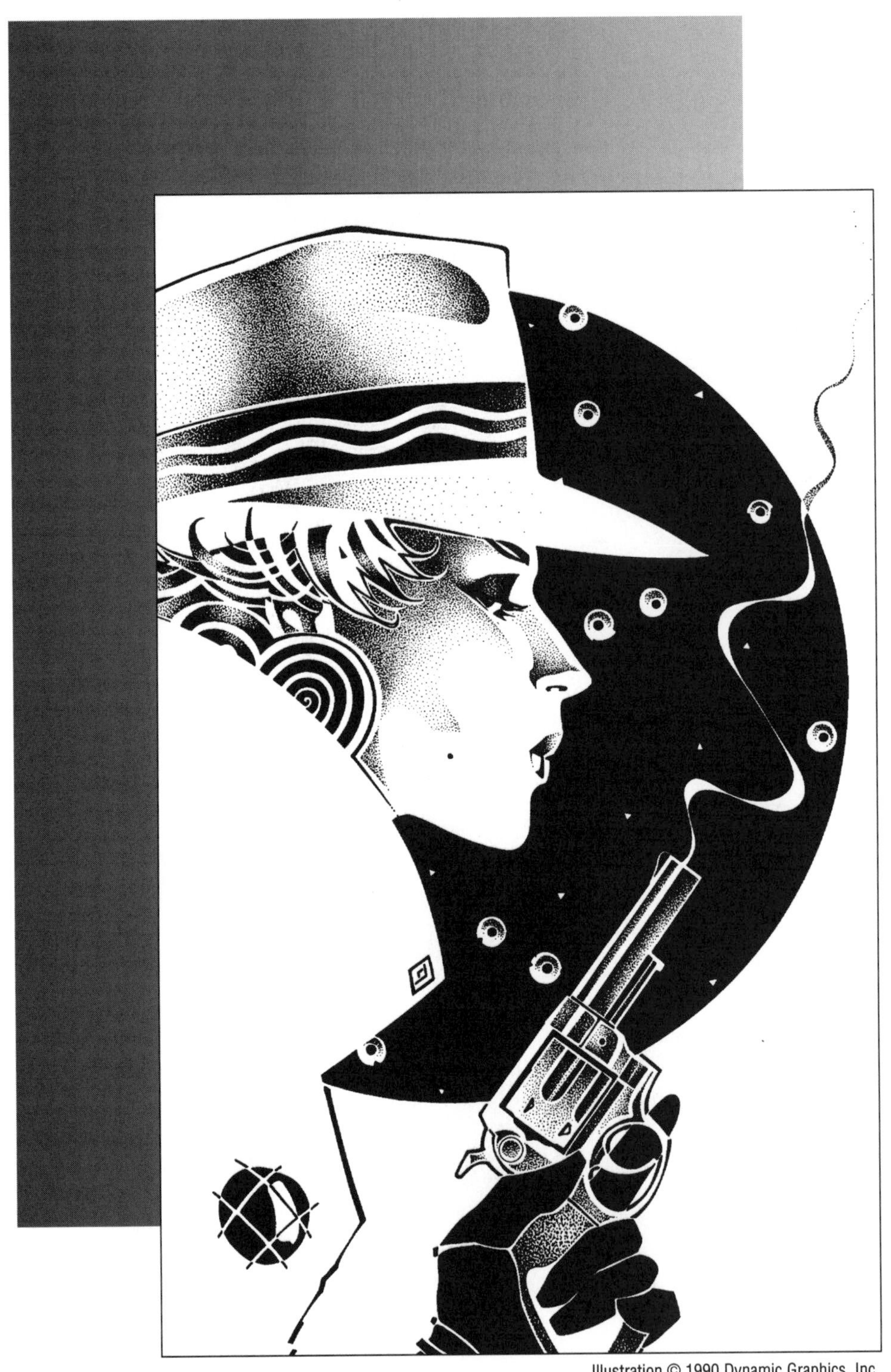

Where Dottie Came From

Gar Anthony Haywood

Did you ever scare yourself writing?

I did. I wrote a mystery from the perspective of a woman and pulled it off.

I PULLED IT OFF! PEOPLE really think of Dottie Loudermilk, my female protagonist and narrator of *Going Nowhere Fast* (and the ensuing *Bad News Travels Fast*) as a woman. A fifty-something wife and mother-of-five.

I am none of these things. I am not a woman. I am not fifty-something. I am no one's wife, and I am most certainly no one's mother. I should have tried this literary stretching exercise and fallen flat on my face.

Instead, I just reached back for Dottie Loudermilk and there she was. In the flesh.

Scared the living hell out of me!

You can't imagine how creepy it is for a macho guy like me to discover after all these years that Dottie Loudermilk has been lying dormant inside me, just waiting for the right book contract to come along to reveal herself.

What did I do wrong? How did I get so in touch with my feminine side? I watch ESPN twenty-four hours a day. I wash no dish nor pair of underwear before its time. I eat Domino's pizza right out of the box, and drink beer right out of the bottle. Does this sound like sensitivity training to you?

Don't get me wrong, I wanted to create a believable character. I was hoping my agent and my publisher would like Dottie Loudermilk and the book that revolved around her. On a conscious level, I was hoping this. But on a subconscious level . . . well, I don't know. I think maybe, just a little bit, I was hoping to hear a few words of criticism. Something along the lines of, "Dottie's a sweet girl, Gar, but she no more sounds like a woman than Dick Butkus with a chest cold."

Wouldn't that have been the ultimate certification of my masculinity, making an absolute spectacle of myself attempting to speak in a woman's voice? I would have turned on the Playboy channel, popped the top on an ice-cold Bud and saluted my unbridled manhood, free to cry at the end of E.T. without ever again having to wonder if I was running dangerously low on testosterone, or something.

Only, I didn't make a spectacle of myself.

What I did instead was succeed. Receive kudos for a job well done, and countless expressions of surprise and amazement that I, a lowly knuckle-dragging, non-ovulating, *All My Children*-detesting male of the species, could write so accurately about the world as seen through the eyes of a woman. How did I do it, everybody always wants to know? What's my secret?

So help me, I don't know.

True, by some weird coincidence, my mother was a woman. That might have something to do with it. And I used to live with a woman, once. She was a wife (mine) and a mother (to our children); I suppose I could have picked up a few things about a woman's lot in life that way. But . . . there has to be more to it than that, right? Something I did, or saw, or overheard in conversation one day prepared me for this screwball form of gender reversal. Whatever it was, it changed my way of looking at things profoundly, lending me a view of men and the way they deal with women (and each other) no man should really be privy to.

And . . .

I think I've just figured out what it was. Sitting right here in front of my computer, right now, this very instant. I've got it.

It's so obvious, I don't know why I never thought of it before. It happened in the wee hours of the morning, as I recall, so I practically slept right through it. But now I can see the magnitude of the event's actual significance. It happened just before I started in on the first Loudermilk book, and in retrospect, I can think of no other experience that could have helped me better appreciate what it must be like to be a woman in a man's world.

I sat down on the toilet with the seat up.

The Life and Loves (and Twisted Fantasies) of a She-Writer

Joan Hess

Come sit down by me, my precious little ones, and I will tell you what it's like to be a rich and famous mystery writer. Yes, right here on this bale of hay, where I can see your chubby pink faces in the soft glow of the forty-watt bulb.

IT ALL BEGINS WHEN your agent calls . . . How do you get an agent? Not now, dearest—ask me on a panel some day. The telephone rings, and anticipating a stern computerized message about a delinquent car payment, you hesitantly pick up the receiver, and in a disguised voice, say, "Yeah?"

"You'd better sit down," your agent says.

"I am sitting down," you say petulantly.

You are informed that your manuscript, that incredibly brilliant work of literature that has estranged you from your friends and family, has delighted you by day (am I funny or what?) and haunted you by night (but why would the murderer steal the cat in the first place?), has served as a three-hundred-page tribute to

Joan Hess *Photo credit: Jack Edmiston*

the death of the rain forest—yes, that bundle that was sealed with a kiss and sent away a month ago—has sold. An advance of six figures is mentioned. You say nothing, and your agent demands to know why you're not screaming. You explain that you've rehearsed this moment so often that it's actually rather stale.

No, sweet children, those flickers in the shadows will not harm you. Move closer, if you wish, and I'll tell you what happens next. Within minutes, your editor calls all the way from New York City to say your book is the best he/she has ever read, and each word, sentence, paragraph, scene, and chapter is exquisite. Your title alone will sell thousands of copies, and there is no doubt in anyone's mind—in the entire publishing house (everyone's read it and loooooved it!) that it will hit the best-seller list before it's shipped.

He/she goes on to say they haven't decided how many hundreds of thousands of copies will be printed, but he/she will tell you the exact figure as soon as it's available. He/she will also keep you informed as to the publication date and the advance sales. After all, it is your book. You and the publishing company are a team, and all the players want to do whatever is possible to encourage sales.

What am I drinking? Water, darling, water. Now comes an idle period, in which you are encouraged to write your second novel so the reviewers will be in a position to point out that your second effort is even better than your first (if such a thing could happen), and that you've shown an increase in the mastery of your craft and are now established as one of the most talented voices in contemporary fiction.

I told you it's water, damn it. Please don't whimper. Reviewers are thoughtful people, not to mention well-versed in the genre and eager to give praise where praise is due. What? No, we mustn't worry about that. If a reviewer dislikes a certain type of book, he/she would never savage it out of idle amusement, nor would he/she ever allow even an iota of personal prejudice to discolor the opinion. A reviewer is proud of his craft, and is as pleased as punch to see his/her name at the bottom of the final paragraph. Be snide about it because it contains humor? Poppycock, you'll see that everyone is quick to acknowledge that writing comedic fiction is as challenging, if not more so, than writing violent, humorless so-called realism. Reveal the plot? Oh, I forget what naive little creatures you are, but it's refreshing to be able to assure you this never ever *ever* happens.

But there's no time to dally when the production process accelerates. Here comes your manuscript from the copy editor, who's gone over every word to check your spelling and catch those pesky typos. Who is this dedicated copy editor? Oh, generally, a mature, well-educated individual with a background in mystery fiction and a true fan of your unique style. There might be a query (or flag, as we call it; let's all repeat that three times) to determine if you intended to use the phrase "hog-nosed bigot" twice on the same page, and perhaps a gentle comment that your approach to punctuation, albeit impeccably correct, differs from that of the publishing house. No, sweetums, those are suggestions. Remember, your editor loved your manuscript, and had there been any reason to revise it, would have called you for a long talk. The copy editor would never dream of rewriting your book.

Our next moment of excitement comes when you're asked if you like the cover. Oh, I'm so very sure you will, and you'll clap your wee little hands with joy. Just once, and this was a long time ago in a galaxy far, far away, an author viewed a preliminary sketch and ever so tactfully murmured that she did not especially care for it. Would you like to know what her editor did? Why don't you guess and I'll tell you if you're right? Yes, your answer is on the button. The editor told the art department to do another cover that adhered to the author's concept. The art department, after carefully rereading the galley, happily complied. Isn't that clever?

They'll also want you to have your photograph taken at a fancy studio . . . unless they send someone to your cottage. I have no idea, how much is costs, my pretties, and you won't either, since your publisher will pay the bill. All you'll do is pose those dimply hands beneath your chin and gaze dreamily into the camera.

And now it's the jolliest fun of all! Your publicist calls and asks if you're willing to do a promotional tour. She, for it often is a bright young woman, says that she's arranged for you to be on the major talk shows across the nation. You'll be going to so many cities your little head will spin and spin and spin. Will you get lost? Of course not, my fuzzy bunny. The publishing house will send someone with you, and that person will handle your luggage, make sure that the big shiny limousine is there, and deal with the hotels and bookstores. Your only assignment will be to be as fresh and sparkly as a daffodil in the morning dew.

This very same publicist will ask you to whom to send review copies so that she can get right on it lickety-split. She'll make sure your hometown newspaper is as excited as she is about your new book—and gee whiz, does she love it! Why, she's going to be mailing press releases, publicity kits, book marks, photos, and everything else she can dream of to absolutely everyone. What? Of course there will be a great big ol' ad in the *New York Times Book Review* section. How quaint of you to ask . . .

And then, you bright-eyed moppets, you'll start receiving copies of all the glowing reviews. *PW, Kirkus,* and *Library Journal* will sing your praises. I get all shivery when I think what the *New York Times* will say in its review. No, dear one, I don't need a blanket. Even though the wind is howling through the knotholes, I'm toasty with pleasure.

Your editor will be calling often to tell you how sales are going, and when the time comes (it will! it will!), he/she proudly will announce that your book has gone into a second printing. Hip, hip, hooray, we'll shout together. You'll hear about foreign sales, book club sales, and even—let's take a big breath—a movie option for zillions of dollars. How often will he/she call? Every time he/she hears something, silly. Editors know how very important it is to stay in touch with their beloved authors. After all, they're keenly aware that the author is the most significant person in the chain.

No, not the food chain, honey. That comes when your publisher flies you to New York to escort you to the MWA banquet. But first you'll go to lunch, where you'll have the chance to ask questions and make plans that concern your future. Will this be a sober and dignified affair? Yes, dear, it's a tradition. Your agent will be there, too, to help you with the funny French words on the menu.

Later you can look forward to the ABA, the ALA, whirlwind appearances in mystery bookstores (publishers do everything possible to cooperate with those hearty souls), and even, dear novices, the Frankfurt Book Fair. Yes, yes, you'll need a passport for that one!

Then, some day in the future, when you've been mainstreamed and been given oodles of respect (not to mention oodles of dollars!), you can snuggle by the fire and read your royalty statements. Dull reading? Heavens no, my winsome children, royalty statements are fascinating. On those very pages are the actual figures of how many books were printed and sold—and when—along with a clear explanation of the reserve against returns. You'll giggle to yourself as you discern all those details that trace your book from creation to bookstores and airports and malls all over the country, and finally to rest. Why did I sigh? Well, each time a novel is remaindered, the author gets a gray hair. The women, that is. The men seem to lose one from atop their shiny heads.

But no more talk of this, my wee ones. You must scurry away to your word processors. Myself? I must hunt for the last of my food stamps and go buy another fifth of water. Then, I think, I'll quietly lie down with a cool compress until the exorcist comes.

The Proper Study of Mankind is Woman?

John Lutz

When Pope wrote that "The proper study of mankind is man" he didn't have mystery writers in mind, and he was using "man" to mean "human being." But if we were to take him literally, we would have to add that the proper study of womankind is woman.

IF A WRITER WANTS to create a mystery novel or short story from the point of view of the opposite sex, he (in this instance we are mainly talking about male authors writing from the female POV) needs to know something about that sex. And the way for male writers to learn is to observe those wonderful and mysterious creatures—women. (I know this sounds like the introduction to a Tony Randall-Jayne Mansfield comedy, but bear with me as I drift into conflict with armed feminists.)

Writing fiction from the opposite sex's viewpoint need not be intimidating. The rules for creating any fictional character transcend gender; the problems are basically the same. The idea is not simply to describe your character in detail but to make the reader experience on some level what your character is thinking and, more importantly, feeling. Your main character needs to be sympathetic and believable.

Believability used to be a problem with the female protagonist in the mystery, especially when it came to the private eye novel (Miss Marple and her ilk aside), but gone are the days when a female fictional P.I. was a novelty. In the contemporary world of mystery fiction, the female detective—professional or amateur—is firmly established. So, one down. The male mystery writer no longer has the problem of explaining how a nice girl like that found herself in such a sordid affair or line of work.

The task of the male writer is to get inside the female mind and heart, at least to the extent that the reader will take for granted that the voice of the novel or story really *is* female. And the male author's name on the book's dust jacket or cover isn't a handicap. There are a number of contemporary male mystery authors who write successfully from the female point of view. While there are women's studies sections in most bookstores and libraries, and a plethora of research material on how women think and feel (an advantage female writers working from the male POV don't enjoy), the most useful approach is still simple and careful observation. The female in fact rather than theory. (The musical number, with Marilyn Monroe and Jane Russell.)

Like writers of either sex, I've observed the people in my life with a conscious or unconscious eye for fiction, including the women, and in the various stages of *their* lives—grandmothers, mother, sisters, friends, nieces, cousins, aunts, romantic interests (clouded observation), wife, daughters, and granddaughters. Conclusion: we male and female homo sapiens are more alike than we are different, but we *do* think and act differently. (*The Vice Squad*, or any creator of erotic art, will attest to this. Enter Dennis Franz and Candide Royale.) Whether these differences are genetic or socially structured is irrelevant for our purposes. What matters is that at times we think and behave in ways typical of our gender. In a novel or short story, a female character may do almost anything or display almost any characteristic—in fact, any fictional character must possess some of the qualities of both sexes to be a thoroughly wrought creation. But for plausibility she must also act or think in some ways so that she registers on the reader as genuinely female.

And of course what your other female characters are doing is also important. Obviously, all or most of your fictional females shouldn't look forward to watching pro football on Sundays, or to changing the car's oil. Just as all or most of your male characters shouldn't spend much time in the morning color-matching their outfits, or holding long phone conversations with friends they intend to meet for lunch within an hour. In times of crisis or action, they might act and react similarly, but not hour by hour, minute by minute—or page by page.

The thing to keep in mind is that the sexes are virtually alike in most ways that relate to fiction, such as basic fears, or sensations of cold, warmth, taste, smell, touch, etc. The broad strokes used to delineate character are the same for both male and female; what we're talking about here are nuances, and they are important.

So be alert to what *most* women do that *most* men wouldn't do, and that you might use to strike life into your fictional characters. I'm not the first to observe that men are interested in physical matters while women are more attuned to relationships, even at an early age. When my four-year-old granddaughter Ellen, skillfully playing family politics, bit herself on the arm and accused five-year-old brother Andrew of biting her, the frustrated and furious Andrew bit his own arm and invited his parents to compare tooth marks. Ellen (a young Linda Blair), caught in a blatant lie, suffered one of her few embarrassing moments. She'd been concentrating on family dynamics and how to shed phony tears and sell her story. Relationships. It never occurred to her that Andrew would be thinking about physical evidence. Something for the writer's notebook.

A few years ago, a male writer friend (a guy who knows a thing or three about women—middle-aged Errol Flynn) went to dinner with my wife Barbara and me. After ordering, Barbara excused herself and left the table. Twenty minutes passed before she returned and matter-of-factly told us that while in the lavatory a woman she'd never met had told her of romantic problems and asked her advice as to how she should treat her fiancé. My friend pointed out that this sort of thing would never happen in a men's room, where the only sounds are those of running water and the occasional clank of the towel dispenser. We looked at each other. Here was something we could use.

So, two examples of the different approaches of male and female. While of course such defining characteristics aren't present in all women or men, the writer needs to use some of them to create nuances that make characters of the opposite sex ring true.

The women in my life have taught me that anyone is capable of anything. Neither gender conforms to anyone's model, nor should it. The way to create a plausible protagonist of either sex is to give him or her a primary character trait, secondary traits, and consistency. And mixed in with that, some actions and reactions that provide the reader with a firm sense of your character's gender. There is more to this than simply substituting a male or female name for one of the opposite sex. Your fictional men and women must be very much alike, but also very different.

Vive la différence! Observe *la différence!*

Writing Like a Girl

Wendi Lee

"Jefferson Birch inhaled deeply of the fragrant posies clutched in his hand and thought of Meg. Meg. Just conjuring up her face in his mind made him feel all warm inside. Cactus, his horse, nudged Birch and whinnied softly, bringing him back to the here and now."

MY HUSBAND PUT DOWN the manuscript, took off his glasses, squeezed his eyes shut, and rubbed the bridge of his nose.

"Well?" I asked. "What do you think of it so far?"

"You want the truth?"

"I guess," I said reluctantly.

He put his glasses back on. "You write like a girl."

That's what my husband kept telling me through my first three novels, all traditional westerns featuring Old West private eye, Jefferson Birch—"You write like a girl."

I was finding it hard to master Jefferson Birch's voice—after all, he's a guy and I'm not. What would I know about writing from a man's point of view? But by the third book, I had become pretty comfortable with Birch and his world.

That was about the time I began writing from Boston P.I. Angela Matelli's point of view: "I slammed the phone down so hard that the desk shuddered. Okay, if that's the way he wanted to play it, we'd meet and play it his way. I strapped on my holster, checking my gun to make sure it would fire seven rounds straight into the bastard's chest."

I reread the copy and realized I'd been writing from a western male point of view a little too long. I sat back and began to think about the differences between a nineteenth-century character and a twentieth-century character—besides the obvious differences in living conditions, of course.

For a start, Birch's demeanor was different from Angela Matelli's, and as a man who lives in the 1870s, he would have many differences from a 1990s man. When I sit down to write a story set in the 1800s, I have to put myself in that setting, which is alien to my lifestyle. Research always helps me set the tone and "build the stage," so to speak. But it's harder to do the sort of research needed to create a character of the opposite gender.

What I've discovered over the years of writing from a male point of view is by no means always true, but here are some general observations that distinguish a male character from a female character: Men tend to leap into action more quickly than women do. Women will think about the consequences of the action before leaping, sometimes second guessing themselves.

Neither way is better than the other, but they do have different consequences, and a writer has to deal with the results. For instance, in *The Good Daughter,* Angela is looking for evidence in her dead client's house, when she hears an intruder entering the place. Even though she is a capable woman, she is an ex-Marine and assesses her situation. In the end, she errs on the cautious side and doesn't confront the stranger. Instead, I had her hide under a bed.

If Birch were in a similar situation, he would probably confront the intruder, maybe first making sure that he had the advantage if he had to fight.

Dialogue is a big telling point. Men and women talk differently. A man talks in specific terms: "Let's get something to eat, then see what's playing at the Bijou."

A woman might speak in less specific terms: "Let's go out somewhere and do something."

A man's thoughts and actions are more direct. He sees a pretty woman, and he reacts to her outward appearance: "Looking Meg up and down, Jefferson Birch could see that she was a good-looking woman."

A woman, for the most part, thinks in less direct terms. She sees a guy as what he could be: "He had the eyes of a dreamer and the smile that could melt a spring snow."

But I think the best explanation regarding the way men and women view the world is something I came up with when I was put on the spot during a local television talk show. The host, Paula Sands, asked me what I meant when I told her that my husband told me that I "wrote like a girl"—what was the difference between writing like a man and writing like a woman?

Beyond the glare of the studio lights, I could see the director motioning with his arm to wind it up (I'm no chimp). I blinked, not sure how to respond in the five seconds I had. Then it came to me like the blinding flash of a camera: "Men think, women feel."

I can't take all the credit for that line, but it all comes down to that—men think and women feel. Of course, I went on to say that this didn't mean that women had no brains and men had no feelings, only that we communicate in different ways.

When a man states his opinion, he usually begins by saying, "I think that we don't spend enough time thinking about our future."

A woman, on the other hand, usually attacks the same subject from a different angle: "I have always felt that present-day conditions hold the answers to our future."

Women tend to be more in touch with their emotions, and that ability will color a female character's narrative and dialogue. A male character's voice emerges from cognitive tendencies.

I try to keep all of the above in mind whether I'm writing about Jefferson Birch or Angela Matelli. And keeping in mind their differences has kept me on my toes. Which is kind of a difficult position to write in.

A Heroine for Me

Liza Cody

It was only when I got the first cheque that I realised the producers were actually serious about turning the Anna Lee books into a TV series. That was the moment I knew that I would have to give Anna Lee up to a quite different interpretation than my own.

I HAVE MY OWN IMAGE of Anna. Each and every reader has her or his own. All, probably, are different. That is what reading is all about—you make your own images, your own unique world, out of clues left on the page for you by a writer. It's a mind game.

TV does the opposite: it imposes its own image, its own world, its own interpretation on the viewer. A viewer is a lot more passive than a reader.

As one of life's blunderers, I try to avoid mistakes by learning from other people's experience. And, at this moment, I remembered what Peter Lovesey says about his TV experience. Although he was largely very pleased with the TV interpretation of his Cribb and Thackery stories, he found that it interfered with his own image of his own characters, and he was never able to write about them again.

This was a frightening thought, and I wanted to be prepared for the possibility that I might never be able to see Anna in my own way again. I wanted to have something else up my sleeve. I wanted someone else to write about. Someone completely different. Someone who no one in their right minds could possibly call a role model, or a good deed in a naughty world, or feisty, or bubbly, or, or, or any of the things Anna has been called.

And then, quite by chance I saw a poster advertising wrestling. Klondyke Kate's face was on the poster, glaring and snarling. Close by was another poster advertising . . . I can't remember, was it tights or cosmetics or records? But there was a model's face with an expression which said, "Oh please love me. Please approve of me." I looked at the two posters and decided to go to the wrestling.

So the first time I saw Klondyke Kate in person was one dark rainy night at the Bath Pavilion. The MC introduced her as "the Official British Ladies Wrestling Champion," but she didn't come out. The crowd howled. She was balking because the management got her music wrong. Someone in the back row yelled, "Play *Roll Out the Barrel.* She'll come out to that." Everyone laughed, but eventually she appeared. The first thing I heard her say was, "Shut yer mouth. Shut yer *dirty* mouth." This was before she reached the ring. She snarled her way through an unruly mob of hissing, spitting people, already winding them up, already threatening and playing dirty. The Ladies Champion was *not* a lady.

Wrestling is basic entertainment, rude in the old sense of the word and a wrestling crowd is not an opera crowd. The people who go to the fights are not there for subtlety or aesthetics. They want stories. They are a panto audience and they want to be part of the act. They need heroes and villains.

In the ring, Klondyke Kate is a villain, but she is a heroine for me.

She breaks all the rules. She is fat and she shows it off in a black leotard, under bright lights, in front of hundreds of jeering, sneering men and women. Most overweight hide. Klondyke Kate leans over the ropes and shouts, "What you looking at! Eh? Eh?"

She talks back. By no stretch of the imagination could she be called deferential. If you insult her she insults you in return. "My arse is prettier than your face," a man screams. "Come up and show us," Kate screams back.

"Ignore them," my mother used to say to me when I came home bleeding internally from some playground slight. "Show them you're above it all." I couldn't. I wasn't. I always made matters worse by fighting back. But like most little girls I wanted to be loved and approved of. So when I grew up I learned to control my temper. I taught myself to be nice. Most of the time. Women are supposed to look good, to behave well, to court love and approval.

Klondyke Kate doesn't. She glares across the ring at her little, perky opponent and shows no sympathy for her knee bandage. She will work mercilessly on that hurt knee later. She is not in the ring to show that women are the nurturing caring sex. She is there to win by fair means or foul—preferably foul. A villain is supposed to play dirty, and Kate takes the job seriously.

One thing that Channel 4's coverage of sumo has taught us is that fat people can be athletic. They can be very fast and very strong. Klondyke Kate is a fast, strong wrestler. She need not bite, choke, pull hair, stomp, or gouge. She could win fairly if she wanted to. She does not because it is her job to be the villain, and she is forced to be the villain because she is big and does not look pretty in a leotard. She does not look like what our culture demands of a heroine. She is not large-eyed, long-legged, glossy-haired, neat, or petite.

Not many women have the courage to be unpopular. It goes against our conditioning. We try hard to be acceptable. We try hard to look acceptable. If we are fat, we diet. If we're hairy, we depilate. If we are not pretty, we compensate with makeup and humour. If we are angry or ambitious, we hide it as far as we can. Kate does none of this.

I don't know if she would rather be the popular heroine. If she would, it doesn't show, and in any case nature didn't give her much choice. She makes the most of a bad job by becoming a beautiful villain.

So there she is in the middle of the ring, a barrel in black tights. She smashes, mashes, and crushes her opponent. The game little thing, pretty in pink, fights back. Kate becomes quite evil. She cheats blatantly. The crowd goes berserk. "Dirty slag!" they scream.

A little old man is so furious he bounds out of his seat and runs down the aisle to the ringside. The bouncers are waiting for him, but he stops short. He is beside himself with rage and probably hasn't moved that fast for forty years. "You . . ." he screams, "you . . ." Spittle flies from his mouth glittering like diamonds in the spotlights. He cannot think of anything bad enough to say. Finally it comes out: "You . . . you *bucket nut!*" he screeches.

"Come up here," she sneers at the hysterical old man. "We'll see who's got a bucket nut!" Kate's face—her bucket nut—says it all. It isn't a face to look at over the teacups. It's not the face of motherhood, sisterhood, or even Robin Hood.

But it is a face which makes a writer ask, "What on earth must it be like to be you? What makes you so brave? Why are you so angry?"

When I tried to answer these questions I found Eva Wylie. And I found that the little old man had given me the title to the first Eva book. That is the way it began.

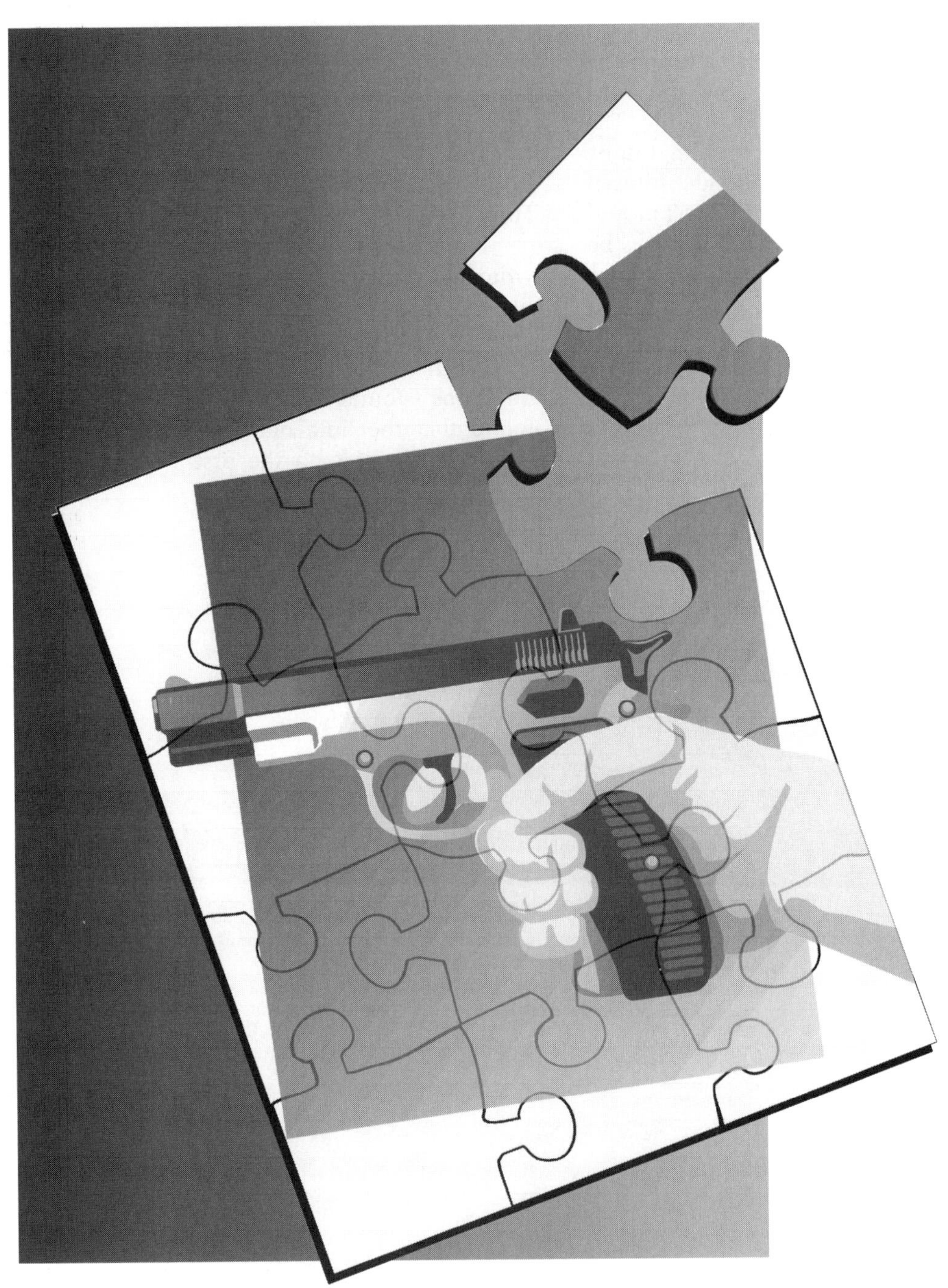

Interview with Minette Walters

Dean James

Few writers have debuted in the crime fiction field with the kind of attention that English writer Minette Walters has received. A former journalist and editor, Walters turned her skills with the written word to crime fiction, and her success was immediate.

HER FIRST NOVEL, *The Ice House,* won the John Creasey Award for Best First Novel from the U.K. Crime Writers Association. Her second novel, *The Sculptress,* won the Edgar Award for Best Novel from the Mystery Writers of America. Recently, her third novel, *The Scold's Bridle,* won the Gold Dagger (aka Best Novel) Award from the Crime Writers Association. *The Sculptress* was also nominated for the Anthony and Macavity Awards last year.

All three of Walters' novels offer the reader fascinating puzzles of "whodunit," but they offer the reader the tantalizing question of "whydunit" as well, since motivation for crime is of prime interest to Walters. Readers have quickly responded, as Walters's sales have risen dramatically since the publication of her first book. Collectors have taken note as well, since the first U.K. edition of *The Ice House* is now an extremely valuable commodity on the collectors' market. I corresponded with Minette Walters from her home in Hampshire, England, and we discussed her accomplishments and interests as a crime writer.

Has your background as a journalist been a help to you as a mystery writer? If so, how?

Yes, it was very helpful because I was an editor as well as a journalist. I worked on magazines for about seven years and learnt not only how to make ideas work for me on the page but, as an editor, I was also able to see where other writers were making mistakes. I saw the craft from both sides and that was a bonus.

Have you been a longtime reader of crime and mystery fiction? If so, do you consider that any particular writers have influenced the type of fiction that you write?

I think I read my first Agatha Christie when I was about ten years old. Crime has always been my favourite fiction genre because it demands reader participation. Crime writers involve their audience to a far greater extent than other fiction writers because we pose a riddle—Whodunnit?—which the reader is invited to solve. I have always enjoyed Patricia Highsmith's stories because I find her oblique way of looking at people very powerful. My favourite writer was not a crime writer but a writer of general fiction, Graham Greene. His characters struggle with eternal truths and, as I tend to do the same myself, I always empathise with them.

The victim in *The Scold's Bridle* was perhaps the most compelling character in the novel, and in the earlier two books we saw attention paid to "victims" of various kinds. How does this interest (if I've read it all correctly) fit in with your view of the contemporary crime novel?

Yes, the idea of the "victim" does intrigue me, perhaps because events can turn against any of us at any time. Who's to say what is waiting round the next corner? After my first two books I became increasingly aware that the dead have no voice. They can only be recreated through what other people say about them. In *The Scold's Bridle* I decided to give my murder victim a real voice, so I used extracts from Mathilda's diaries to allow her to speak for herself. This was peculiarly relevant because of the way she died, with "the rusted metal bit [of the scold's bridle] clamping the dead tongue still in the gaping mouth." However, it is not just the murdered person who is a victim, but also everyone closely associated with him/her, and that may well include the murderer. The idea that violent death can happen within a family or a close community without huge trauma being suffered by everyone concerned seems to me to be absurd. If nothing else, irrespective of police involvement, each individual is tarred with guilt until, and if, the murderer is discovered. In such circumstances, families and relationships fragment because belief and loyalty are stretched beyond endurance. These are the areas I like to explore in my stories.

Thus far each of your novels has contained an entirely new cast of characters. Why not write a series? What are the advantages, to the type of books you want to do, in *not* writing a series?

Oddly enough, it never occurred to me to write a series, probably because I realised that I would become bored very quickly with writing about the same people in every book. I enjoy the freedom of being able to write what I like, when I like, and how I like, without being shackled to specific people and places.

Which comes first for you with a new book—the characters or the plot situation?

I am very much a character-driven writer, so until my characters have found their voices I cannot really start a new story. Having said that, I always have a very clear idea of the sort of actions that the characters I am creating will perform. It may not be a fully developed plot at that stage, but it is certainly there in embryo.

In developing the plot, what is more important: who? what? or why?

Why, every time. I have been fascinated by what motivates people to follow particular courses of action (not necessarily murderous) since I was very young. Why does a murderer see taking somebody's else's life as a solution to a problem when it is clear to any objective observer that it can only create more problems than it solves? The fascination for me is always in the motive.

How important is it to you to keep your readers guessing up until (and sometimes after, as in the case of *The Sculptress*) the end of the book?

For me this is very important. Because crime fiction engages the reader actively throughout the story, it would be tedious for readers if their attention was lost too early. I hope I'm a good storyteller, and that means creating so absorbing a fantasy that no one wants to put it down until they've reached the end. However, it is not always *Whodunit?* that creates suspense. In *The Scold's Bridle* "why?" is as important as "who?"

Do you know the ending yourself when you start writing?

No. I have no idea who the murderer is when I begin a story.

Has your prison visiting had a significant influence on the way you view crime and criminals? (Perhaps you might also give a very brief explanation of just what "prison visiting" is for the benefit of American readers.)

Prison visiting is a voluntary occupation rather like hospital visiting. I had a letter recently from a man I had been seeing for some months who was moved to another jail to finish his sentence. He puts rather better than I can what it meant to him to have a prison visitor. "Talking to you every Monday evening has given me more confidence in myself, and our chats have made me take more notice of things and people around me." I should say that it was a two-way street. I gained as much from the conversations as he did. I suppose the most significant influence that meeting offenders has had on me has been my awareness (despite what newspapers might like us to think with banner headlines like "Animals" and "Scum") that you cannot tell murderers/rapists/child molesters/thieves just by looking at them. Often, you can't tell by listening to them either. If they maintain their innocence, it is very difficult indeed to know if they are telling the truth; even harder if you like them, because your natural instinct is to want to believe a friend. It explains why policemen try so hard for confessions. It's far more comfortable for everyone if a defendant admits his guilt. But the chances are that he is semi-literate, has grown up in an atmosphere of violence, probably has little or no contact with his family, and has no natural affinity with the social values set by the educated middle classes. The law tends to view everything in terms of black and white, while life tends to be a greyer affair where little, if anything, can be said to be certain unless you have an absolute belief in a god and his teaching. This whole area fascinates me. What is truth? How do you establish it beyond a shadow of a doubt? How far do our prejudices colour our perceptions? Is anyone all bad or all good? In a secular society, particularly one dedicated to the pursuit of wealth and materialism, how do you enforce a code of ethics which has no validity for people who perceive themselves to be excluded? All of which is fruitful ground for a crime writer, for it applies to individuals within families as well as to social groups.

In each of the three books thus far published, there has been significant

romantic tension between a couple. How does this element work for you as a component of the suspense of the novel?

I have great faith in the redeeming properties of love. However black a situation may be, where there is even the smallest spark of affection, tolerance, or kindness, then there is hope. The romantic tension that I put into my novels is a reflection of my own belief that love can only thrive where there is mutual respect, mutual understanding, and constant communication. I have severe doubts that love-at-first-sight is a good basis for a lasting relationship and am very unlikely to write anything so sweet and sugary into a novel!

Each of your novels published to date has won a major award from your peers. Is the pressure on for your fourth novel?

I felt the most pressure after I won the John Creasey Award for *The Ice House.* I had never written a novel before and I was afraid that the chances of winning another prize were minimal, particularly as the competition is so strong and getting stronger. Therefore, to win the Edgar for *The Sculptress* and the Gold Dagger for *The Scold's Bridle* was very thrilling. Of course I would love to go on winning—who wouldn't?—but I recognize that the competition is intense and three prizes are already more than I expected when I sat down to write *The Ice House.*

Can you give us any hints about your next book, or even the one after that?

My fourth novel is called *The Dark Room* and is to published next spring in the U.S. by Putnam's. As much as anything, it is a "what has happened" story. The challenge to the reader is to work out what went on in the month before the novel opens. It's a pacy read, and I enjoyed writing it. I hope that enjoyment will be shared by my readers.

Interview with Elizabeth George

Crow Dillon-Parkin

Elizabeth George is the author of eight novels featuring Detective Inspector Thomas Lynley and Sergeant Barbara Havers of New Scotland Yard. Lynley happens also to be the Eighth Earl of Asherton, and Havers is a working-class ex-grammar school girl with a massive chip on her shoulder.

These books are tightly plotted, evocatively located, and beautifully written; incidental characters are as fully realized as the main protagonists, and no matter how much the plots may twist and intertwine, the thread is never broken.

CDP: The first question I'd like to ask is: why crime fiction, and why England?

EG: Because when I first began writing I wasn't sure if I could carry off a novel from its beginning to its end and crime fiction had a natural structure that pulled me through, a linear structure with an established through line, and that appealed to me. Additionally, I taught a class called The Mystery Story, and the more I taught, the more I began to think "I think I could write one of these myself," so it's those two reasons that got me involved in writing crime fiction.

"Why England" is more difficult to explain. When I first started answering that question, I thought, well, I taught English literature, I traveled here a lot; in the sixties when the British influence was very dominant in American culture, I was a teenager, and I was profoundly affected by that, and I developed a real fondness for England based upon that. That's how I used to answer the question, but now I've realized that part of writing (this is going to sound as though I'm wearing a pyramid on my head!) involves the psychic connection, the spiritual soul connection between the artist and the material, if you're going to write well. I have a very strong emotional, psychic soul connection to England that I don't have to the United States. I can't explain why that's the case, but when I see certain locations in England, I feel immediately touched by them, and it's that feeling of being touched in a deep way that allows me to write about the place. I can't write about just any place in England; I can't just get in my car, drive someplace and say "Oh, OK, I'm going to set my story here."

CDP: So you don't go with a plot, you go

for a place?
EG: I go with the plot kernel, but for the plot kernel to germinate into a story, the place has to do it.

CDP: Because your sense of place is just stunning.
EG: Well, see, what I do is keep working at it until I find a place that's stunning to me, because not everything works for me. A certain amount of what I do is what we in the United States call a real crap shoot, where I've decided that I'm going to go to a particular section of the country for one reason or another and I single out a number of different towns, villages, great houses, places of historical or natural significance, and look at them in the hope that somewhere along the line one of them will work as a location in a book.

CDP: You write well about the English class system; is that another attraction?
EG: I find it interesting, because it's not analogous to anything in the United States, so it gives me an avenue to explore things. It makes the writing more difficult, because there are elements of the class system that would mean nothing to an American reader, but everything to an English reader; the type of cigarette somebody smokes, the type of car they drive, the type of simple vocabulary that's used—whether they call what I'm sitting on a sofa or a couch, or the room we're in a sitting room or a lounge—or what is the dread word you use for the bathroom, the toilet, lavatory . . . In the United States if you were to say, "I need to use the toilet"—well, nobody would say that anyway, 'cause we have all kinds of euphemisms for it [laughs], but not class-oriented euphemisms.

CDP: It seems to be the middle classes who cause the most trouble.
EG: In the books you mean?

CDP: In the books! The middle classes who think they know best. There's Lynley and his peer group and there's Havers putting her four penn'orth in when she thinks Lynley's got it wrong, but it's always these people who think that they're better . . .
EG: Mmm, I never thought about that. I suppose it's because I thought it was too much of a cliché to have anybody from either of the two ends of the spectrum be the ones that were committing the crimes . . . That seemed much more of a cliché to me, to have Lynley wading in because some peer of the realm has strangled his wife, or something. It doesn't mean that I won't do that someday, that has a lot of scope for plenty of fun between Lynley and Havers, but I hadn't considered it this far.

CDP: Are there things, the relationships between classes, and the relationships between the sexes, that are different in England, that might be more interesting to you?
EG: There's certainly vast differences in the way we look at class. Class in the United States is based almost entirely on money and education. So it's economics, it's not how old your blood is, I mean, people could care less how long your family has been in the country. If you're a success at what you're doing, that's what's admired in the United States. So, this British idea of [adopts horrified English accent] "Oh my God, he's in trade!", well, everybody in the United States has been in trade at one time or another, that's how the

country grew. So that's very, very different. I think we're a little bit more advanced with women's rights than you are in England. Women are still an oppressed minority in the United States, but it's not nearly as bad as it used to be.

CDP: How much of their (Havers and Lynley) back story do you have?
EG: Oh, I know a *lot* about these people! Some of it I know from the very first novel that I wrote, that was never published, and would never be published—it would be like, "Behave, or we'll publish this novel!" It's really, really [laughing] awful! But it has the back story on Lynley and his sister, and the death of her husband, Edward Davenport. So that's why I know about Judith and her predilection for slipping between the wrong sets of sheets.

CDP: Do you think it's fair to say that your books are more driven by character than by plot?
EG: Oh, yeah! Absolutely.

CDP: There's an article in *Writers News* that suggests that your plot style has shifted somewhat, with the last three books, in that the death that needs investigating isn't always the first thing that happens, and that gives you more space for exploring character.
EG: Yes, that's always been the important thing to me. Sometimes I move the murder up front to sort of get the ball rolling, but the creation and exploration of character was where my commitment was from the very beginning. I think I've gotten better at doing it, with each successive book, but that's always what I wanted to do. I begin with the plot kernel (the killer, the victim, and the motive) then the setting, and then I create the characters. That's a long process, designing them from the ground up, as if I were some sort of god, creating someone, not only physically and mentally but spiritually and psychologically, and historically. By the time I start writing about that character, I have a voice for them, an agenda, a through line, a pathology, and the person can emerge, much more realistically than if I were just putting a name on the page and saying "Now what?"

CDP: It seemed you suddenly got very topical, dealing with the tabloids, and parliamentary sleaze . . .
EG: Yeah, it was purely by chance that on the plane coming over to do this research, I opened up the British newspaper, and here was Tim Ye?—Yo?—and uh, a love child, and I couldn't believe my eyes—I was coming over here to do research about this MP with a love child, and it was playing out in the newspapers, even as I was doing the research! So it couldn't have been a luckier circumstance for me, because the tabloids did everything that I assumed that they would do, and my *God!* they were digging into his past, and I mean, good God! it was amazing!

CDP: The British attitude to sex is just so peculiar . . .
EG: Oh *yeah!*

CDP: In America, the press can just kill somebody's campaign, in a way that they can't here, because you've got the party machine behind you.
EG: Absolutely. That's what happened to Ed Muskie, when Richard Nixon was trying to set things up so that he was running against George McGovern, he had the dirty tricks

campaign going, and he ended up running against McGovern, who he wanted to run against.

CDP: Do you think you'd ever write something set in America?

EG: I've written one short story set in America, that's going to be published in an anthology this year. I was very pleased to come up with the idea for a short story, because I'm not a short story writer, at all. My philosophy has always been, why say it in a thousand words when you can say it in six hundred pages . . . It's hard for me to paint with broad enough brush strokes to be concise, it's real tough. In this instance I had an invitation to write something for an anthology at the precise moment that I had an idea for a short story, so I wrote it, and it takes place in southern California, in Newport Beach, close to where I live. I used a quirky little place on Balboa Peninsula where I have my detective have his office up above a place I used to get my hair cut, JJ's Natural Haircutting. I really did have to look for quirky places, there's not much quirkiness in that particular part of southern California. One thing that's helpful for me when I'm writing about England is that I notice the details, because it's a foreign country, but in the United States I don't notice the details because I see them every day, and details are an important part of setting, character, and plot.

CDP: How long do you have to spend somewhere, to get that feel?

EG: It depends on the kind of research I'm doing. For location research, hmm, it's about a week . . .

CDP: As little as that?!

EG: . . . to get the feeling for the place, yeah, about a week, and then I might go back a second time, to kind of fine tune it, and then I might go back a third time after I've got the rough draft done, just to make sure I've got everything correct. The harder things for me are the things that I can use for character details, because then you get into the kind of stores people shop in, the kinds of products that they buy, and what those products would say about them. In America, these are things I would just know, naturally, because I've lived there all my life. One of my students was writing a story, and she completely understood the idea of telling detail of character, because she said that the man and his wife were sitting at the kitchen table, wearing matching bowling shirts. That was it [clicks fingers] everybody in my writing group knew what the entire kitchen looked like. All she had to say was they were wearing matching bowling shirts, because it says everything about a class, a culture, everything, but that kind of stuff is ach! it's really, really difficult for me to know, so that's when I have to get on the phone, and call my friends, and say "OK, here's the situation, this is the character, what would they be eating, what would they be smoking," and my friends in England are very, very wonderful, very supportive, and really, really help.

CDP: You also deal a lot with the family, the problems in the family.

EG: Yeah, my books are about the family, and the dysfunctioning family, and I use the crime novel as a device to explore that. See, I used to read crime novels where no one was related to anybody, including the victim, and I thought it was strange that someone would die, and nobody was ever sad or came forward to claim the body. I thought this is sort of interesting, people die and no one's related to them. I didn't want to do that, I wanted to explore situations in which killer and victim had significant others, as well as the detectives. If a killing arises from a familial relationship, then obviously you're talking about a troubled family . . .

CDP: . . . murder doesn't happen in a family where everybody's getting on all right . . .
EG: . . . and besides, if everyone's getting along all right and communicating, it'd be a boring book, a white bread story where everyone's really nice and everybody gets along. You don't have any drama, you don't have any tension, you have no conflict so that would be pretty tedious.

CDP: Your books are whydunnits, not whodunnits?
EG: Yeah, it's more why than who.

CDP: You write to find out things, rather than to say things?
EG: Somewhat, certainly. Part of writing is to make it clear to me, and to the reader, why this was done, so that, if I'm successful, the reader understands the crime completely, rather than just have "she was killed because of the inheritance . . ." To have a psychological motivation, that I'm able to explain adequately, in the story, is important to me. You want your book to pass the refrigerator test. Alfred Hitchcock used to say that if the people who saw his movies didn't have any questions about the movies until they got home and opened the refrigerator, then it was a successful film. But, if they're saying "Hang on . . ." while the credits are rolling, then you've got a problem. I think with books you want to do more than that, you want it to linger, give the reader something to think about as well as being entertainment.

CDP: How far in advance do you work?
EG: Well, now I'm just writing the next one, the one that follows *In the Presence of the Enemy*. I'm about three hundred and fifty pages into that.

CDP: So you work quite fast? Well, it seems fast to me!
EG: I do five pages a day, so on the one hand that doesn't seem very fast, but then at the end of the week you have twenty-five pages. So I've written about a third of the book, well, maybe a little more than that, I'd like to bring it in at about eight hundred and fifty pages if I can.

CDP: Do you do much in the way of rewriting, or do you write it "in best" first time?
EG: Um, the first draft is the most difficult draft, 'cause subsequent drafts are generally polishing, they're generally not altering anything big in the story. So I take a lo-o-ot of time over my first draft, I'm pretty meticulous, I don't just sort of go, I'll slam it down on paper and then let my editor figure it out, or slam it down and hope that I can rewrite it later on. I try to get it as well done the first time through as I can, so that my work in second and third draft is fun, rather than agonizing!

It's Murder, Y'all

A Matter of Pedigree

Deborah Adams

No story begins on page one. There is always a convoluted ancestry of greats, grands, and twice-removeds that have intertwined to create the germ of the tale. Likewise, no writer comes to page one free of cultural and familial influences.

FOR SOUTHERNERS IN PARTICULAR there is strong social and historical pressure to create and share entertaining yarns. In our largely agricultural areas storytelling skills were honed among farm families who turned their isolation and the ability to survive it into a point of pride. To counteract loneliness and stave off madness (although some would say it wasn't *successfully* staved), these pioneers depended on each other for diversion. Family stories became an evening's entertainment—near-legends of heroic grandfathers who battled the hostile land to build homes, strong grandmothers who defended the hearth and hid the family silver while the men were away, and, of course, eccentric but charming aunts, uncles, and cousins who exhibited their own unique versions of bravery.

The stories were convenient and affordable pastimes, and they sustained us during the most difficult spells, so naturally a good storyteller was prized above gold. The tradition continued long after easy communication became widespread and families left behind the farms for crowded cities. Still, consciously or not, many of us understood that whipping up an entertaining account of some everyday event was an act every bit as important and patriotic as farming or fighting, and in our fondest dreams we were the creators of magnificent yarns that warmed the room and brought satisfaction to our kin. In recent years the mystery genre has been invaded by southern writers—a move that should come as no surprise to anyone with even a vague knowledge of our history. Of all the diverse groups in this country, those of us raised below the Mason-Dixon line are most likely to find satisfaction in a good mystery. While the popular old stories explored the human spirit or, as Faulkner preferred, "the human heart in conflict with itself," each was, in some way, a morality play.

It has been noted that southerners are the only Americans who know how it feels to lose a war, and much has been made of our reluctance to let go of that loss. We seem determined to cling to the harsh perception of ourselves as underdog—vulnerable weaklings fighting valiantly against a large and well-armed foe. But we manage to find in the David and Goliath tales some vindication of our stubborn self-definition, a reassurance that the small but clever scrapper can, indeed, defeat the more powerful enemy. It follows, then, that southerners would be drawn to the mystery story, the ultimate morality tale in which the small but clever amateur sleuth or lone, outnumbered law officer outwits and defeats a powerful villain.

Having found a fictional genre that fills our need for familiarity and optimism, we set out to make the form fit the tradition of all those comforting tales we grew up with. Southern fiction is so often explained by the superficial elements it contains. "It's a story about the region," critics say, "or written by someone *from* the region." The most important element, though, will inevitably be the unique and thoroughly human characters created by the southern author, and the female author has a particularly strong advantage here.

Keen perception of human behavior is a prerequisite for creating believable fictional characters, and this is a skill that is taught to our young ladies early. You see, there remains within southern society a rigid caste system, of which women are the caretakers. It is vital that we be able to size up a stranger within seconds, to understand where he or she stands in the social order, and how to behave toward that person. After a lifetime of practice, a feminine perception has developed that is so sharp, it eerily mimics psychic ability.

As writers, this allows us to collect and file subconsciously all the minute but telling quirks and ticks that add flesh to the character on the page. We instantly assign full pasts and rich presents to the shadowy skeletons in our minds—just as we immediately recognize (or imagine!) the life histories of everyone we meet.

The purpose of our novels is to explore the wealth of people who spring to life from our minds. When a southern woman sits down to write, she may begin with deliberately constructed plot, clues, and setting, but inevitably, with or without her blessing, the characters will take center stage, drawing the spotlight to themselves and directing the action of the story around their own personalities.

It seems to me, though, that the greatest strength we possess, and the one that so often *truly* defines a southern novel, is our immense appreciation for peculiarity. What some view as threatening abnormality, we call enchanting eccentricity. When literary legend Flannery O'Connor was asked why southerners so often write about freaks, she reportedly replied, "Perhaps it's because *we* can still recognize them."

In these politically correct times, I feel obliged to provide an explanation for that amusing comment, other than the obviously anti-Yankee one implied. Surely Ms. O'Connor meant to suggest that southerners have a wholehearted appreciation for aberration and therefore look closer to find—and admire—the freak in everyone.

How I Became Local Color

Toni L.P. Kelner

Have you ever said that somebody was acting as nervous as a long-tailed cat in a room full of rocking chairs? Or that somebody who wasn't too bright might be a few bricks shy of a load? Maybe you think that figures of speech like that are cute or even quaint, but it's just the way I talk. By now you're probably thinking that I'm a southerner, and you're absolutely right. I'm from North Carolina.

NOW BEING A SOUTHERNER is a funny thing. I don't think I realized just how southern I am until I moved to Massachusetts. I mean, I'm not any of those things that other folks *think* a southerner is. I'm not a southern belle, and I don't think mint juleps are fitting to drink, and I've never even met a member of the Ku Klux Klan. I grew up in a plain old everyday suburb and went to shopping malls and watched too much television, pretty much like anybody else. I couldn't be all that different from anybody up north.

At least that's what I thought until I got to Boston. Now my folks had warned me that Yankees aren't like the rest of us, that they have different ways. They weren't exactly sure what the differences were, but they were as sure as shooting that they were different. And as soon as I got here, it dawned on me just what it is. People up here talk funny.

First off, they talk as fast as all get-out, even when they're not in a hurry. And then they don't put r's in words where they're supposed to be, but make up for it by putting them where they don't belong. The really funny part is that they think the way *I* talk is funny. They say that the way I say "y'all" is cute, and they smile when I call my mama "Mama," and when I say, "That fellow must have been beat with an ugly stick," they laugh outright.

Now that alone would be enough to make me fit to be tied, but then they started trying to talk like me. What a mess they make of that! It sounds right foolish when someone who doesn't even know the difference between eastern North Carolina-style barbecue and western North Carolina-style barbecue tries to say y'all.

I had about decided that folks up here are just plain ignorant and I'd have to put up with it, when I got an idea. Maybe I could try and teach people some of the things they somehow missed out on, like how to talk right. Not by giving lectures or anything highfalutin' like that, but just by setting a good example.

So I made sure to always speak properly. When somebody tells me something I know doggone good and well isn't true, I go ahead and say, "That's your tale, but I'm sitting on mine." And when I've been standing in line at the grocery store for twenty minutes or more, I turn to the lady behind me to smile and say, "If that cashier was going any slower, she'd be going backwards." If I think the person I'm talking to is up to it, I'll even look at a real bright red car and say, "If he'd had another nickel, he'd have bought himself a *red* car."

Now this has been working out pretty well. My co-workers now ask me how my Mama is doing, and they've finally figured out that y'all is only used when you're talking about more than one person. My Harvard-educated husband even learned when it was appropriate to say, "It don't make no never mind." But I'm just one woman, and there aren't enough hours in the day to try and educate the entire state of Massachusetts, one person at a time. Let alone the rest of New England. So I decided to write a book so I could spread the word to those people I've not met personally.

Of course, a dose of molasses always makes the medicine go down better, so I knew I needed some kind of story to tell folks so they wouldn't catch on to the fact that they were being educated. And I've always loved a good mystery story. So putting it all together just made all kinds of sense.

That's why I came up with Laura Fleming, a North Carolinian like myself who lives in Massachusetts. When her grandfather gets hurt in an accident at the mill back home in Byerly, she hightails it back there to be with him. Only she finds out that it wasn't an accident, and when he dies, she sets out to find out who it was that killed him. Along the way, she has a run-in with the Klan and gets caught up in another murder and nearly gets herself killed. At least, that's what people are going to think that *Down Home Murder* (Zebra Books, ISBN 0-8217-4196-9, $3.99) is about.

What it's really about is what a North Carolina mill town is like, and what pulling socks is, and what it means to have five aunts and four uncles and more cousins than you can shake a stick at. And while I'm at it, I aim to try to teach people how to talk right.

Of course, I couldn't very well fit every little thing about the South into just the one book. After all, it took me my entire life to learn it. So Laura Fleming will be heading back to Byerly in "Gift of the Murderer," a short story set to appear in the Christmas anthology *Murder under the Tree* (Zebra Books, November 1993); and in the book *Dead Ringer* (Zebra Books, February 1994); and in another book I haven't quite finished with yet. Now don't you worry. There will be murders and blackmail and such in those books, too, so as to make the lessons more like fun. If people want to call all the important stuff in my books local color, that's not going to hurt my feelings one bit.

Of course I'm not expecting Laura's adventures to change the whole world right off. Yankees have been talking funny for an awful long time, after all, and those folks out in California aren't much better. Still, now that we've got Bill Clinton in the White House, it's not me who's got the accent anymore. Now is it?

Translating English Into . . .

Barbara Burnett Smith

I'll bet you have a gimme cap *somewhere in your closet.*

When it's hot, you probably enjoy a refreshing glass of ice tea.

And, when you redid your bedroom, finally throwing out the sixties waterbed, in all likelihood, you bought an entire bedroom suit.

IF THOSE TERMS SOUND perfectly natural to you, you probably live somewhere south of the Mason Dixon line. *More n' likely* in Texas, because those colloquialisms are as common around the Lone Star State as Johnson grass. As a Texas author I get to use them in my books. Or not.

Therein lies the challenge for writers—finding just the right balance. How many local colloquialisms can be offered up to the reader seems to differ depending on the locale being written about. Is it American or foreign, because that appears to be the key.

Take the British mystery novels as an example; based on the number of English authors who are extremely popular, one must assume that their regional language sells books. (The British-American dictionary for one.) Americans appear to be perfectly content to wade through a sentence like, "When I finished my ploughmen's lunch at the local pub, I went outside to discover I needed the jumper I always keep in the boot of my car." It takes a great deal of British to push us out of our tolerance zone, leaving us, figuratively, in the pub while the story races off elsewhere.

Australian-English has idiosyncrasies which appear to be taken in stride, as well. At dinner a female character admits to being "stuffed." American readers simply think the woman has eaten too much, whereas in Australia they know she is pregnant. Talk about a plot complication. Although no one seems too distressed by it.

Phrases from foreign languages also litter the mystery landscape causing hardly a ripple. French is considered *chic.* It can sometimes be titillating, even though most of us haven't any idea what the author is saying. Spanish adds its own unique spice. You can't pick up a book set in the Southwest without an "Ola, amigo." Even an author who is linguistically challenged, will at least have a character order a taco or enchilada.

What about computer jargon? It wasn't so long ago that surfing was done by blond youngsters on boards in the ocean. Now anyone can surf with a computer and a modem. If the baud rate is high enough. And we don't complain about protagonists who speak this new computerese.

Interestingly enough, though, we will only take so much of a character who says, "Hey, you dissen' me?" (Dissen' being American street talk for disrespecting.) The term *Bloody Hell* is charming to us. Saying *damnation,* on the other hand, is a sign of idiocy. What is the difference? It appears that we as Americans love most things foreign, including phrases. Unfortunately, it appears that we think any American accent is wrong unless it's ours.

Which means authors have the challenge of using just enough of those strange terms to transport us out of ordinary life and into a magical new world, without losing us on the journey. Copy editors become liaison people, requesting translation so the oddities are understandable to a universal audience. Bill Crider tells the story of a copy editor who questioned his use of the Texas accent in a book. The copy editor

wrote a note which said, "Do people really talk like this?"

They do everyday in Texas.

My own copy editor, a brilliant and charming woman, lives in the Northeast and often puts those little stickies with the words "Auth. What is this???" Then I get to do some explaining. For example, I've had to let her know that a gimme cap is a baseball-style cap given away free by the company that has their name or logo on the front. (The custom of giving these away to customers was particularly popular back in the days before the caps were.) Ice tea is known in other parts of the country as iced tea. (If you stop and think about the Texas version of the name, it makes perfect sense. After all, we don't have *cherried* limeades, or *Coked* floats.) As for that furniture in your bedroom, I suspect the term *suit* began as a badly pronounced suite.

Our world appears to be on its way toward homogenization, and who wants that? I'll settle for a little misunderstanding any day as long as we can have our own ways of speaking. It means that as readers, we have to enjoy the differences that come from out of country, as well as those that come from our bordering states. After all, we don't want people from Maine to talk the same as those from San Antonio, do we?

I certainly don't. No more than I'd want to travel to Egypt and find a gimme cap on the Sphinx.

Margaret Maron *Photo credit: Joseph Maron*

"I" Is Not Me

Margaret Maron

Recently, an irate reader took me to task for my last book, Shooting at Loons. *Offended when my first-person narrator remarked that someone was "not much taller than me," the reader acidly inquired if grammar were no longer important.*

"IT IS CLEAR THAT YOU DON'T know any better than to let your character—a judge with a law degree, for heaven's sake!—use bad grammar," he fumed, "but why didn't your editor catch it? Don't editors edit anymore?"

Fortunately for me, my editor is more astute than that particular reader. She knows the stylistic difference between an author's formal voice and a character's narrative voice and would never try to smooth away my "I" character's verbal idiosyncrasies. Nevertheless, that letter did make me stop and reconsider how, as writers, we often do use a first-person voice as a shorthand method to convey character and personality without actually having to spell them out.

The omniscient author's voice pays strict attention to the laws of grammar and punctuation; the narrative voice pays strict attention to the character of the "I" who is telling the story.

As someone who reads Fowler's *Modern English Usage* for sheer pleasure, I do know the difference between subjective and objective pronouns; and yes, I do try to use them correctly when writing third-person or formally. (Actually, Fowler prefers "Not much taller than me" over "Not much taller than I," which "strikes the reader as pedantic.") But that is neither here nor there. The truth is that when I write first-person fiction, I deliberately mimic language that will let my readers know this person's social class, present emotional status, and whether he is likable or mean-minded, brave or timorous, a whining pessimist or a cheerful optimist.

This is especially useful in the short story form where every word counts.

In my short story, "Deadhead Coming Down," no third-person description of an easily bored trucker can match the immediacy of his own voice saying,

> There's not one damn thing exotic about driving a eighteen-wheeler. Next to standing on a assembly line and screw-ing Bolt A into Hole C like my no 'count brother-in-law, driving a truck's got to be the dullest way under God's red sun to make a living. 'Specially if it's just up and down the eastern seaboard like me.

The trucker speaks in short blunt words and his coarse denial of his brother-in-law's worth foreshadows his truly callous actions in the story.

Conversely, when I wrote "On Windy Ridge," I hoped that the slower, dreamlike pacing and choice of elegiac language would help convey the image of a middle-aged mountain woman who possesses both intelligence and a slightly psychic sensitivity:

> Waiting is more tiresome than doing, and I was weary. Bone weary . . . but my eyes lifted to the distant hills, beyond trees that burned red and gold, to where the ridges misted into smoky blue. The hills were real and everlasting and I had borrowed of their strength before.

In *Shooting at Loons,* the novel that so exercised my overly pedantic reader, my narrator is Deborah Knott, a district court judge in her mid-thirties. Even though she knows better, Deborah is a breezily colloquial southerner who makes grammatical slips because she is the daughter and sister of semiliterate dirt farmers who

will use dialect, split infinitives, double negatives, sentence fragments, dangling participles, and a host of other colorful grammatical errors till the day they die. True, she has a law degree; true, she is a judge. Neither has turned her into a grammarian. (I was once sent to the principal's office because I would not agree when the English teacher insisted that it's was the possessive of it. She, too, possessed an advanced degree.)

With one foot in North Carolina's agrarian past and the other firmly planted in its high-tech present, Deborah is never going to "get above her raising." Not if I have anything to say about it.

After all, I have a classic precedent for claiming the right to a narrative voice that is not necessarily my own.

In a preface to one of his books many years ago, a certain writer used his formal voice to explain the technical side of creation: "In this book a number of dialects are used . . . The shadings have not been done in a haphazard fashion, or by guesswork, but painstakingly, and with the trustworthy guidance and support of personal familiarity with these several forms of speech." Then switching into his first-person narrative voice, that same author wrote, "You don't know about me without you have read a book by the name of *The Adventures of Tom Sawyer;* but that ain't no matter."

Had Mark Twain written the whole book as omniscient and highly literate author, *The Adventures of Huckleberry Finn* would be a forgotten piece of nineteenth-century esoterica. Instead he gave us Huck's distinctly ungrammatical "I" voice and the book remains a living, breathing masterpiece a hundred years later.

A Checklist of Southern Mysteries

by the Editors

Deborah Adams – *All the Blood Relations*

Mignon F. Ballard – *The Widow's Woods*

Rita Mae Brown & Sneaky Pie Brown – *Wish You Were Here*

Edna Buchanan – *Miami, It's Murder*

Susan Rogers Cooper – *Hickory, Dickory, Stalk*

Patricia D. Cornwell – *Postmortem*

Alison Drake – *Tango Key*

Tony Fennelly – *The Hippie in the Wall*

Mickey Friedman – *Hurricane Season*

Anne George – *Murder on a Girl's Night Out*

Charlaine Harris – *Shakespeare's Landlord*

Carolyn G. Hart – *Southern Ghost*

Joan Hess – *Death by the Light of the Moon*

Lynn S. Hightower – *Flashpoint*

Teri Holbrook – *The Grass Widow*

Kay Hooper – *Amanda*

Jody Jaffe – *Horse of a Different Killer*

Toni L.P. Kelner – *Trouble Looking for a Place to Happen*

Margaret Maron – *Bootlegger's Daughter*

A Checklist of Southern Mysteries
Continued...

Taylor McCafferty – *Pet Peeves*

Tierney McClellan – *Heir Condition*

Sharyn McCrumb – *MacPherson's Lament*

Barbara Michaels – *Be Buried in the Rain*

Elizabeth Peters – *Devil-May-Care*

J.M. Redman – *The Intersection of Law and Desire*

Sarah Shankman – *The King is Dead*

Celestine Sibley – *A Plague of Kinfolks*

Barbara Burnett Smith – *Writers of the Purple Sage*

Julie Smith – *New Orleans Mourning*

Patricia H. Sprinkle – *Death of a Dunwoody Matron*

Elizabeth Daniels Squire – *Who Killed What's-Her-Name?*

Kathy Hogan Trocheck – *To Live and Die in Dixie*

Susan Wade – *Walking Rain*

Mary Willis Walker – *The Red Scream*

Phyllis A. Whitney – *Woman without a Past*

Chris Wiltz – *The Emerald Lizard*

Sheryl Woods – *Hot Property*

SUE
GRAFTON

M

IS FOR MALICE

M Is for Malice by Sue Grafton

Why We Love Kinsey Millhone

Bev DeWeese

Sue Grafton, author of the well-known "alphabet" mysteries, zoomed onto the New York Times *Bestseller List as soon as* K Is For Killer *hit the bookstores. She's been there before. Last year, over five hundred people came out to hear Ms. Grafton when she appeared at Milwaukee Public Library. The audience saw and heard a witty, gracious, attractive woman talk about a female private eye called Kinsey Millhone.*

SUE GRAFTON CALLS KINSEY her alter ego, the person "I might have been had I not married young and had children." Her readers obviously consider the tough, independent Kinsey their friend. And therein may lie the extraordinary popularity of Sue Grafton's books. Incidentally, if you are one of the few who has not heard of the "alphabet" mysteries, the titles are as follows:

A Is for Alibi;
B Is for Burglar;
C Is for Corpse;
D Is for Deadbeat;
E Is for Evidence;
F Is for Fugitive;
G Is for Gumshoe;
H Is for Homicide;
I Is for Innocent;
J Is for Judgment;
K Is for Killer;
L Is for Lawless;
M Is for Malice.

What makes her mysteries so unique and so appealing to readers? First, Sue Grafton is a very good writer, and her early experience writing for television probably helped develop her undeniably strong sense of pacing and her ability to create a variety of complicated, intriguing characters. But I think Sue Grafton has four other enormous strengths as a mystery writer.

Her most obvious strength is the development of the character of Kinsey Millhone. Kinsey is a capable, sympathetic, realistically portrayed protagonist that many readers, especially women, simply consider a person they'd like to know. Sue Grafton has said that Kinsey is the woman she would like to be, at least part of the time. I think many readers feel the same way. And they also believe that, with a little hard work and discipline, they could become Kinsey Millhone. Kinsey is in her early thirties. She tends to stay there, something many of us would like to do. She graduated from high school, not college, and became a cop. But she felt too restricted in the police force, studied to get her private investigator's license, and now does a lot of consulting work for an insurance company, although she investigates other crimes too. Since her parents were killed in an automobile accident when she was eight years old, Kinsey has trained herself to be self-sufficient, physically and emotionally. She drives a VW bug and likes to carry some of her belongings with her, so she is always ready. Furthermore, she needs to feel in control of her life. As a result, she prefers small spaces, minimalist furnishings, few clothes, and no pets or plants. In fact, she lives in a one-room apartment with a loft bedroom. She doesn't cook, although she can create delicious peanut butter and pickle sandwiches, which alternate with her hard-boiled egg and mayo sandwiches. She enjoys wine and has a weakness for junk food, even though she knows those fats and chemicals are going to kill her. She doesn't like exercise, but she does jog because it's good for her. And she is wary of men. She's had a couple of failed marriages, and she intends to keep her independence.

On a less superficial level, Kinsey has an inner core of warmth and caring that probably reflects Sue Grafton's own personality. For example, Kinsey appears to be genuinely affected by the grief and unhappiness of many of her clients, though she does not let her emotions show or interfere with the performance of her job. In fact, Kinsey prides herself on being competent and fulfilling her contracts. And, unlike many people, she admits she likes to poke around in other people's houses and affairs. In summary, Grafton has created a woman that most men and women understand and like.

A second, sometimes overlooked, strength of Sue Grafton's books is her careful, consistent recreation of a time and place throughout the books. The streets, the bars, the beaches, and the restaurants of Santa Teresa are like our own haunts. We react to the temperature and the general weather conditions, and we know Kinsey will dress appropriately. We can do this because Grafton skillfully puts her readers in places that we can see and feel. There is also a strong linear sense to the novels; in other words, Kinsey and the readers remember her previous cases and clients. For example, in one novel, she is in physical therapy because of an injury in a previous book. This attention to detail has literally created another world that we enter each time we open a Grafton book. We feel at home there. Certainly, a believable sense of place is an important part of any well-crafted novel. But the places Grafton describes—a deteriorating trailer park; aging city buildings; seedy nursing homes; raucous, smoke-filled bars; Rosie's blue collar diner; millionaires' expensive homes; crackerbox suburban houses with weedy lawns; filthy, slum apartments—also evoke a strong intellectual and emotional sense of the segment of society she is describing. This sense of place adds a very satisfying texture that some mysteries don't have.

A third strength of the novels is a

sense of verisimilitude in the practice of the detective's trade. Sue Grafton has said that she has tried to experience whatever Kinsey does. She learned to shoot, she's attended autopsies, and she's carefully researched the reality of the murder methods she uses. When Kinsey is shot or slapped around, she feels it, often for several months. She has to take time out for bathroom breaks. She dresses for action, often in jeans and a turtleneck. And she always knows where her gun is, although she doesn't carry it constantly. Unlike some other detectives, when she shoots, she knows she has killed another being and she is not untouched by that. When Kinsey is trying to track down people, she goes to the county's public records division and digs through dusty files. She laboriously sorts through old newspapers and directories in the library. Using note cards, she methodically lays out what she knows about a case. This dual sense of competence and reality have a strong appeal for both men and women.

The fourth, and perhaps the most important, strength of Grafton's mysteries is the skill with which she delineates the psychology and tangled relationships of the victims and their family and friends. These victims are not simply cardboard characters that one can handily stab or poison; they often are people we and Kinsey have grown to like. In a similar fashion, the murderers are sometimes sympathetic, though their crimes never are.

Undoubtedly reflecting the troubles of our times, Grafton is especially adept at probing the conflicting loves and hatreds of the dysfunctional family. In *C Is for Corpse,* Kinsey is very drawn to a young man she notices in a local gym, Bobby Callahan. She learns he has narrowly escaped death in an automobile accident that has, however, left him physically and mentally impaired. When she talks to him, he hires her, saying someone is trying to kill him; but he can't remember what he knows that makes him so dangerous. In a few days, Bobby is killed in another supposed automobile accident. Kinsey wants to know why and insists on fulfilling her contract with the dead boy. As she talks to Bobby's family and friends, she realizes that there has been little real love in the Callahan family. The father has walked out, intending to find himself in an ashram. The mother has remarried and withdrawn from everyone, except Bobby. Derek, the stepfather, also seems very disconnected, even from his own daughter who is anorexic and regularly overdosing on drugs. The poignancy and sadness of this family almost overshadow the murder. Those qualities also make this a very memorable story.

In *K Is for Killer,* an attractive young girl, Lorna Kepler, is murdered and her mother wants Kinsey to find out what really happened. But, before she identifies the murderer, Kinsey uncovers the secret life of a pretty, bright teenager, who wanted to escape the dullness of her family and try all kinds of new experiences, including prostitution. And Lorna had apparently been a very successful call girl. Did her parents suspect she had a double life? Did her sisters know what she was doing? This portrait of a rebellious young girl who wanted to live on the edge surely touches the experience of many readers. And, again, a standard plot gains resonance and texture by the attention give to the psychological makeup of the victim and family.

E Is for Evidence is another story of a family that masks strong loves and hatreds for many years before these emotions explode, causing several violent deaths. Two sons and three daughters of a very wealthy family vie for control of the family business and for revenge against a father who didn't realize his actions were creating uncontrollable passions. Throughout this book, though Kinsey admits she has always felt a little depressed at Christmas, the portrait of family togetherness makes her feel lucky to be alone. Again, in *J Is for Judgment,* a disappearing husband ruins the lives of two women and his two sons. At the same time, Kinsey accidentally learns that some of her relatives may be alive, but she is very reluctant to become involved with them. She's seen families.

In *D Is for Deadbeat,* there is an extremely sad portrait of the psychological disintegration of the young son of a victim. In *G Is for Gumshoe,* an old woman, Agnes Gray, disappears and is eventually murdered. But the real victim is a little girl who grows up into a psychologically scarred, neurotic woman who can barely cope with life.

Grafton's novels are filled not only with the emotional fallout of crumbling families, but with the debris of marriages gone awry. In *A Is for Alibi,* a wife, convicted of murdering her husband, hires Kinsey to find out who really killed him. It seems any number of women and children had good reason to wipe him out. In *H Is for Homicide,* a violent petty crook essentially kidnaps his girlfriend and Kinsey, all in the name of love. But this is a love that is in partnership with beatings and violent death. Even Kinsey wrestles with the man-woman conundrum. In this series, Kinsey is attracted to a man who tries to kill her, she gives shelter to an ex-husband who betrays her to a murderer, and she has an affair with a cop who won't divorce his wife. Eventually, Kinsey Millhone has a brief, passionate affair with another private eye, but he leaves her. For obvious reasons, Kinsey is sour on marriage.

But, whether it's relationships between men and women, or parents and children, or sisters and brothers, probing the frailities of human beings gives an emotional texture to Grafton's books that is missing in some crime novels. Her skill at integrating these psychological insights into the novels and making them realistic rationales for plot and character are certainly one of the major strengths of the alphabet mysteries.

Finally, though a sense of humor may not be perceived as a strength, Kinsey's self-deprecating observations about herself give a marvelous seasoning to subjects that are intrinsically sad. For example, Kinsey's clumsy attempt to get herself dressed up for Vera's wedding strikes a chord among those readers who never quite look fashionable enough. (Vera doesn't think Kinsey's all-purpose black dress will rise to the occasion.) In *H Is for Homicide,* Kinsey becomes very enthusiastic about setting up fake accidents that she knows her co-workers will have to investigate. She also takes a great deal of pride in causing trouble for the new head of California Fidelity, who is going to fire her anyway in the name of cost efficiency. In *J Is for Judgment,* Kinsey gives us her version of a hooker prowling the hotel rooms. Kinsey and her readers are quite astounded when her victim rises to her rather klutzy seduction.

An empathetic protagonist, carefully realized settings, a sense of verisimilitude, and the psychologically astute portraits of victims and murderers, lightly seasoned with wisecracks, have created an enormously popular, entertaining mystery series. Good writing and perceptive observations on the human condition have made them very satisfying novels. Sue Grafton seems to have found the formula that pleases critics, garners awards from her peers, and creates stalwart fans. Just ask her readers. There must be over a million satisfied "users." And I admit I'm one.

Reprinted with the permission of *BookLovers,* A Jammer Publication.

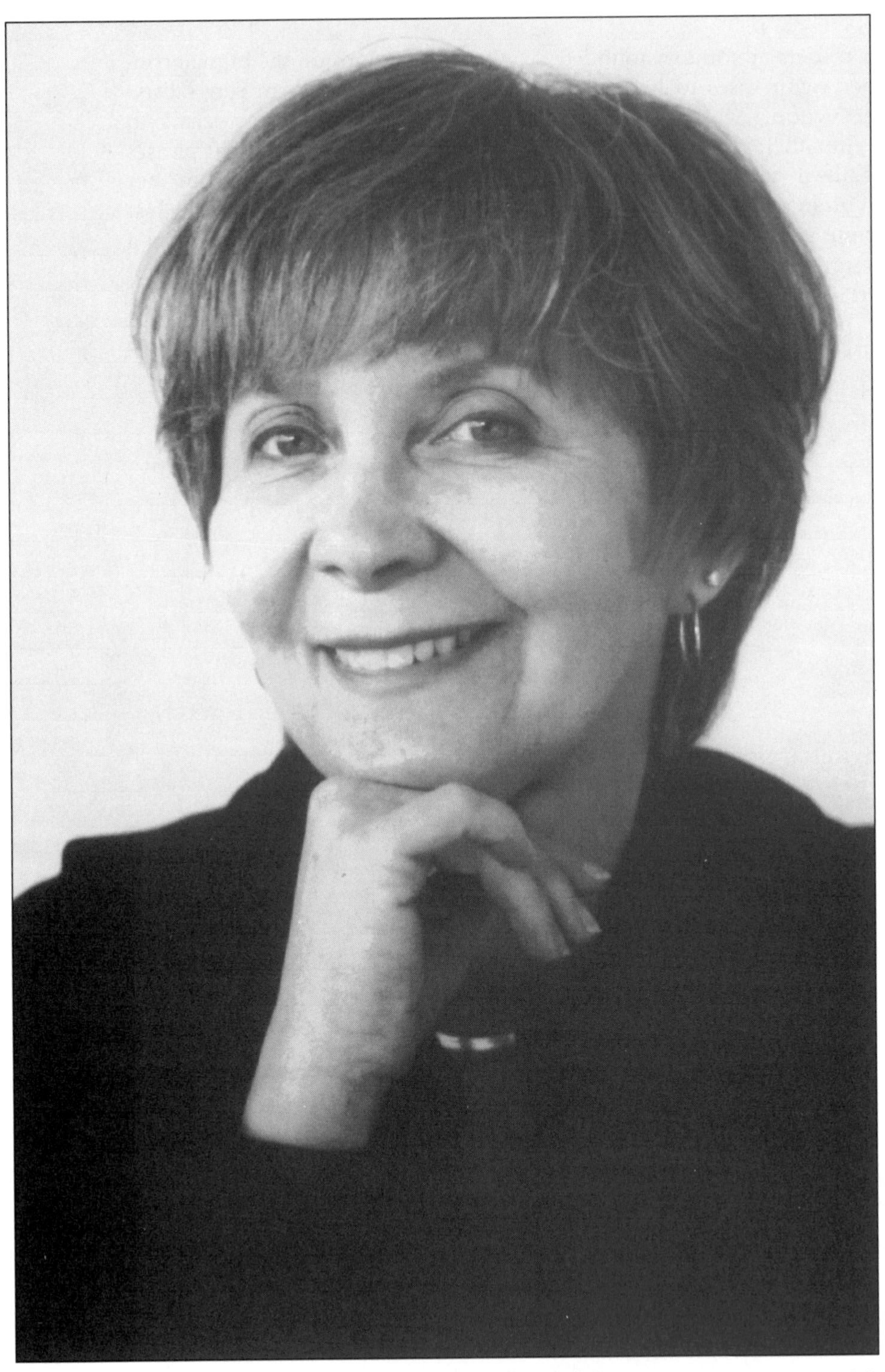

Janet Evanovich *Photo credit: Alex Evanovich*

Interview with Janet Evanovich

Adrian Muller

JANET EVANOVICH BURST ONTO the crime writing scene with the highly acclaimed *One for the Money.* Winning the CWA's John Creasey Memorial Dagger Award for the best first crime novel, it marked the start of a series featuring Stephanie Plum, a young New Jersey woman who decides to take up bounty hunting after losing her job in a downmarket lingerie store.

I met Janet when she was in Britain to promote her second novel, *Two for the Dough.* Sitting in a crowded patisserie in London, we talked about everything from who might play Stephanie in the film adaptation of *One for the Money* to how to make Rice Krispie Marshmallow Treats. The author starts by telling me about her background and how she came to start writing.

After majoring in art at Douglas College, New Jersey's state university, Janet Evanovich initially put her efforts into a career as an artist. After marrying she stopped painting and took "a whole bunch of really terrible jobs like Stephanie" to help finance her husband's university education. Then she became pregnant, had a daughter and later a son, and concentrated on being a mother. As the children became older she started having more time to herself and began looking for an artistic outlet. "In the interim of not actually having a career I discovered it wasn't that I loved painting so much, but that I just loved creating things. This was very enlightening to me because it meant that, whilst looking forward to a career, I really didn't need to restrict myself to being a painter."

Janet decided to try writing because she liked the idea of having a big audience. "When you do a painting a limited number of people will see this piece in the life of it. I had too much ego for that, I wanted to reach millions!" She chuckles at her last sentence and continues, "I tried a lot of things and failed. I tried writing children's books, and I wasn't any good at that; I tried journalism, and I was really crummy at that; and then I decided—it was bizarre idea—I would write a novel! I wrote this very strange book about a fairy who was living in this scary forest in Eastern Pennsylvania and . . ." Confused, I interrupt and ask if she is talking about one of her children's books. Janet bursts out laughing as she explains that since the book was about a pornographic fairy, no, it was not for children. Unsurprisingly, that manuscript was turned down as was her following one. Knowing their children were looking forward to going to college, Janet realized her husband's occupation, good as it was, would not be enough to pay the college fees. Not wishing to give up her writing for jobs she was not interested in, she did some research and came to the conclusion that she might break through by writing romantic novelettes. The market had a huge turnover, and it was not necessary to have an agent. "I had never read any romance novels because as an art major you don't read 'trash.' I went out and literally bought and read about a hundred romance novels, finding I liked them because they were fun, they were very positive, and they had a lot of good qualities. I analyzed them, trying to figure which ones I liked, which I didn't like, and what I wanted my book to be about, before deciding that I was going to try writing the short contemporary romances. Then I sat down, wrote one, and sold it!" Smiling at the memory of how easy it was she says, "I had become a romance writer."

Janet says it was a good place to start because, having no literary background, it gave her the chance to work with a lot of editors, thereby learning and improving her writing skills. She also gained maturity as an author and, by the time she started work on *One for the Money* five years later, she felt she had found her voice as a writer."

Working on her ninth romance—she wrote twelve—Janet became bored and wanted to branch out. Believing her style did not suit a long novel, she decided to continue writing genre fiction, which she felt was more appropriate for a shorter book. She had recently started reading crime fiction, discovering Robert Parker and Elmore Leonard, and realized it met many of her requirements. "I was really influenced by Robert Parker because what I wanted to do was write a very fast entertaining read, which is exactly what he was doing. He was writing these very simple linear books, with snappy dialogue and an irreverent voice. I liked that. The other thing that appealed to me was that the P.I. novel is one of the few areas where it is acceptable to write in the first person. I really wanted to write in the first person because it was a good vehicle for my kind of humor, which was has this very conversational tone." With a grin Janet grudgingly admits that, in the expanding market of crime fiction, a further attraction was the prospect of her book reaching a very large audience. "Apart from good writing skills, finding a gap in the marketplace is what ultimately makes you a success. I felt like I could move into crime fiction, take some of the things that I knew I did really well as a romance writer, like sexual tension and physical humor, and use them in a mystery novel."

By now Janet had acquired an agent who suggested that, for her first crime novel, she write a police procedural. Feeling it would require specialist knowledge she did not have, Janet searched for over a year before finding a concept that suited her abilities. "My intention was to try to find something where I could come up to speed with my protagonist. I wanted to have some honesty in this character, just in terms of understanding her. Then, one day I walked through the den and my husband was watching *Midnight Run,* a movie about a bounty hunter starring Robert De Niro and Charles Grodin. I just immediately knew that's what I could do." After finding out bounty hunters really existed,

Janet managed to meet and talk to some of them but did not do any active research, "Because," she says, "nobody wanted to drag this middle-aged housewife around, chasing some guy who had shot people." Looking at the author, who is wearing black jeans, trainers, and a bomber jacket, I am not so sure that I cannot imagine her out there with Stephanie, chasing criminals on the loose. "I got to be friends with a couple of bounty hunters and tried to figure out what kind of people they were. It turned out that they fly by the seat of their pants, responding to all sorts of situations. They look at a bond agreement, see who's put up the bond, or trace people who are important to the felon. Then they start from there. They stake that person and wait for this guy to come visit his girlfriend." Janet also went to Trenton, New Jersey, the location of the Plum books, and spent some time with the police. Apparently the area is not as crime riddled as it is in the novels, and the author admits to having fictionalized some of the settings as well. "You don't want to invade people's privacy, and I also wanted to create my own world, but some things are pretty spot on. I get fan mail from people in New Jersey all the time saying they recognize places, so there must be something there."

Apart from *Midnight Run,* Janet also wanted to use some of the things that she liked best on television, and when borrowing from television she borrowed from the best. Most prominent is probably the influence of *Moonlighting.* "I looked at *Moonlighting* and I felt it just had a great formula. It looked like a mystery, it had all the structure of a mystery, but it was actually a romantic comedy. I loved the love/hate relationship between the two characters and that was one of the things that I set out to do in my book." The love/hate relationship in the Plum series is between Stephanie and Joe Morelli. It all started when Stephanie was six years old and was not allowed to be the train when playing "choo-choo" with eight-year-old Joseph! Morelli (it is worse than it sounds!). Ten years on and Joe strolls back into Stephanie's life and into the bakery where she works, just long enough to take her virginity behind a case of chocolate eclairs. Her revenge comes three years later when, driving her father's Buick, she clips Joe and breaks his leg. Stephanie's excuse that it was an accident is never really accepted because she jumped the curb in the car and followed Joe down the sidewalk. When Joe jumps bail in *One for the Money,* he becomes one of Stephanie's first cases, hardly improving their relationship. Yet mutual lust is a hard thing to ignore, so surely it can only be a matter of time before they hit the sheets again? "Well, I'm going to delay it as long as I can because I think that's the fun of it. What I discovered as a romance reader was that as soon as they actually did "it," the tension was all over for me. The chase is what I liked. So even if Stephanie and Joe ultimately do the deed it's not going to be a romance, something's going to go wrong somewhere along the line."

Further inspiration for the books comes from *Barney Miller, M*A*S*H*,* and *Cheers,* not only for the humor, but for structure as well. "One of the things I realized was that these programs had a very large cast of characters which they could draw from. I looked at writers like Sue Grafton and Sara Paretsky, and I love their books, but they have their protagonist out there almost all by themselves. I thought this would make writing an arduous job. I couldn't imagine myself being so talented that I could carry a long term series exclusively with this one person." Apart from establishing the series's characters like Stephanie's parents, Grandma Mazur, (ex)prostitute Lula, and Stephanie's mentor Ranger ("This here's gonna be like Professor Higgins and Eliza Doolittle Does Trenton"), *One for the Money* focuses on Stephanie and Joe. The importance of the supporting characters becomes more apparent in *Two for the Dough*. Grandma Mazur especially has her moment in the limelight and, armed and ready, she knows how to draw attention. "By using these characters, it helps me to make each book just a little bit different. I really was worried about making it boring for the reader, concerned that they would feel like they were reading the same book over and over again but with a different crime. I didn't want that to happen. So book number two, in losing some of the emotional impact of scenes in the first book, doesn't have some of the grit that the first one had, but I think it is very funny. Only time will tell if I'm successful, but I thought that by bringing out these different characters the whole tone of the books would reflect that, keeping the series fresh." Stephanie & Co. will make their third appearance in *Three to Get Deadly*, published in the U.S. early next year. This time it is the reformed Lula who comes to the forefront, and Janet calls it her "street book." The humor comes from Lula and her street mentality. She sort of puts Stephanie to shame with her bravado. She's just out there with her chest out front, when in reality she knows she's even less competent at bounty hunting than Stephanie is."

Finding that, as with other female crime writers, some of the violent scenes in Janet's books feel very menacing and real, I ask her if she would agree that women authors are better at portraying violence and its disturbing effects. "A lot of the people who have reviewed my books have said that they felt there was a theme running through them of violence against women, when in fact it was not an intentional theme for me. I think maybe women are more vulnerable to violence, or maybe I should say that we look at them as being more vulnerable." She stops to ponder the question further and then continues, "My two favorite authors right now are Robert Crais and Michael Connelly, and I frequently have a very strong sense of the danger when their protagonists are in jeopardy. I've just read the latest Robert Crais, called *Sunset Express*, and he had a fight scene in there that has got to be the best I think I've ever read. I definitely was worried about this guy. So I'm not so sure if it's a gender thing rather than a male or a female writer being really good at their craft."

Stephanie is a big lover of junk food, frequently indulging in greasy take-outs, chocolate, and Rice Krispie Marshmallows Treats. I ask the author how her heroine manages to stay in shape, how she will age, and what are Rice Krispie Marshmallow Treats? "Oh you're kidding! You've never had those? Oh you've been so deprived!" Janet gives me the recipe and says, "Stephanie has a hard time buttoning the snap on her pants, but she does keep pretty active." As for the matter of aging her characters, the author says Parker's Spenser was never the same for her from the moment he started wearing bifocals. "I'm not aging Stephanie at the rate that the books appear. There was a year and a half between the first book and second book, but in the story line it's only months. I'm going to continue with that because I like this thirty age. There's a lot of vitality to it. Stephanie still has all of these things in front of her so that she can be brash and have all of this bravado."

By now Janet Evanovich has a firmly established routine when writing her books. Getting up at around seven o'clock, she will have breakfast before walking her dogs. Saying her best time for writing is in the morning, she then works at her computer for four to five hours before breaking for lunch. Then she works out, or walks the dogs again, getting a little exercise before writing for the rest of the afternoon. In the evening she will help cook a meal with her husband and her son. If she is on schedule she will take the night off, but more often than not she has fan mail to answer. Plotting a book is equally well established. "It takes me about a month to think about the plot, doodling and outlining it in my mind. By that time I know what the crime is going to be—that's the first decision I make. Then I decide who the bad guy is. At this stage I can usually see the beginning and the ending of the book. What I do then is to make a little time line. I know that my book is going to have approximately seventeen chapters, and about twenty pages to each chapter. Then, on a pad, I write maybe three or four sentences about each chapter. This is what I start from, and I revise as I go along. If I have real good quality writing time, where I'm not interrupted, then I think it takes me about five to six months to write one of the books."

One for the Money has been optioned for a feature film—and not inappropriately, the person working on the screen play was a long-time scriptwriter for *Cheers*. Despite horror stories like *V.I. Warshawski*, Janet is not overly concerned about how the end product might look. "My feeling is that nothing but good can come from a movie. I don't care if they change Stephanie Plum to a man or some little old lady. The book will still get all of the exposure that a movie gives. Then people go out and they buy the book and judge it on its own merit." The author is not sure about who she would like to see as her heroine. I mention Michelle Pfeiffer (think *Married to the Mob*), Elizabeth Perkins, Marisa Tomei, and Sandra Bullock, adding that the latter might be too young to play the thirty-year-old Stephanie. Apparently the last name strikes a chord. "Sandra Bullock might be a little young now, but by the time they get to make the movie she could be forty!"

In the meantime, all fans can do is kick back with the paperback edition of *Two for the Dough*, out in August, and wait for *Three to get Deadly*, which is expected early next year.

Brief Appearances

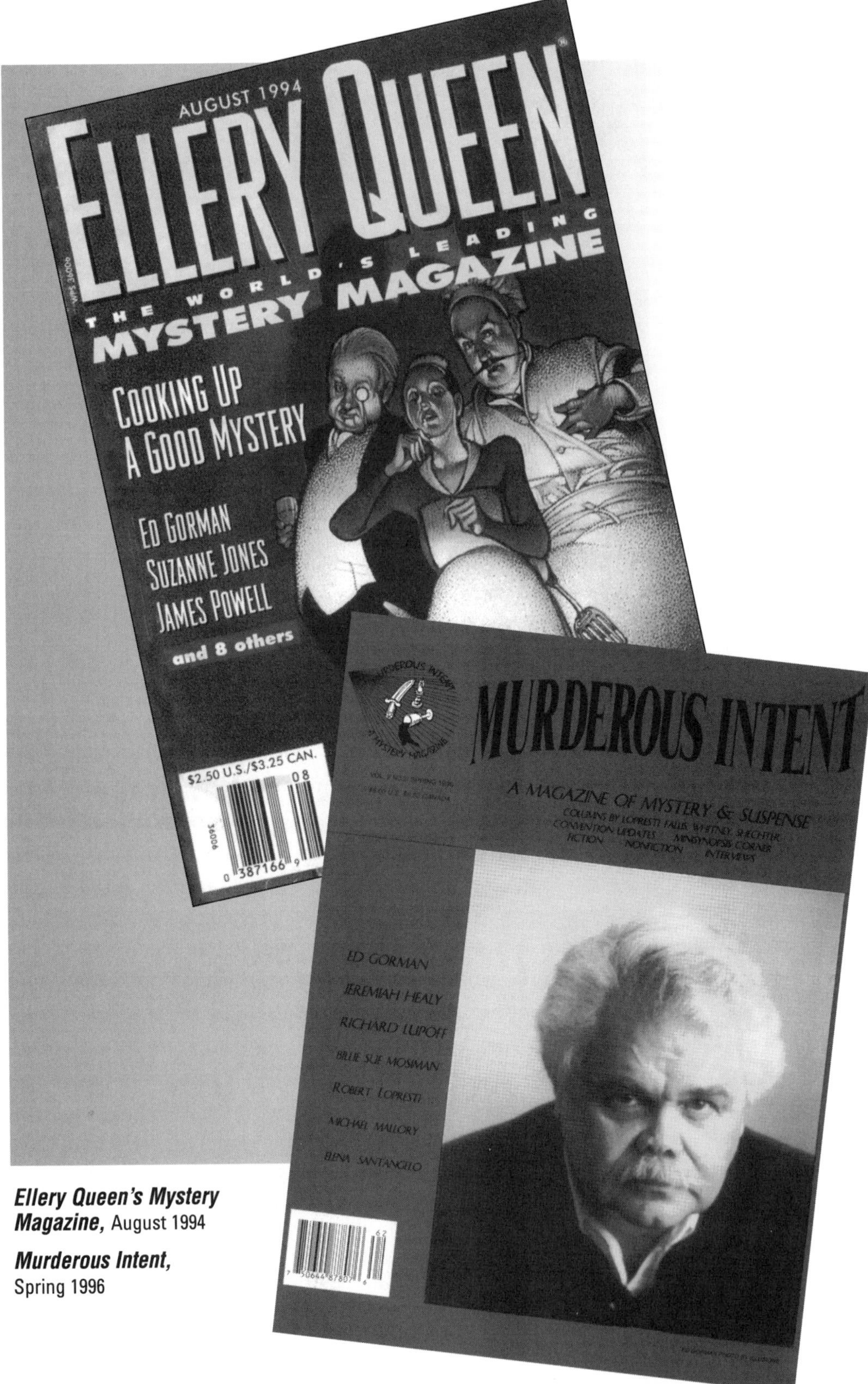

Ellery Queen's Mystery Magazine, August 1994

Murderous Intent, Spring 1996

Short and Sweet

Edward D. Hoch

If any more evidence was needed that the decades of the 1980s and '90s have been the age of the female mystery writer, the book you now hold should be the final proof. In the United States more women are writing mysteries, and reading them, than ever before.

THE BEST-SELLING MYSTERY WRITER in America, and perhaps the world, is Mary Higgins Clark. The most critically acclaimed mystery writers in England are P.D. James and Ruth Rendell.

Women writers are not yet quite so visible in the field of the short story as in the novel. During the period 1980 to 1995 only three women won MWA's short story Edgar Award while six women walked off with the Edgar for best novel. Still, Marilyn Wallace's popular *Sisters in Crime* series produced five volumes and numerous other anthologies were devoted to women mystery writers.

It was through various anthologies that I first became acquainted with the work of three women writers who began publishing novels in the 1980s. They are P.M. Carlson, Wendy Hornsby, and Carolyn Wheat. Even today I know and admire them mainly through their short stories. Each has pursued a distinctive course, and the bulk of their shorter works might be characterized individually as historical, hard-edged, and procedural.

P.M. (for Patricia McEvoy) Carlson published her first novel in 1985. She holds a Ph.D. in the psychology of language and for a time taught at Cornell University. Her first ten novels brought a pair of Edgar nominations and other nominations for Agatha, Anthony, and Macavity awards. She is a past president of Sisters in Crime and has held various positions in the Mystery Writers of America.

Although the first of her books, *Audition for Murder* (1985), is set in 1967, it is more of a memory novel than a true historical mystery. Rather it is Carlson's short stories featuring Victorian actress Bridget Mooney which represent the historical mystery at its fascinating and well-researched best. An early Bridget Mooney story "The Father of the Bride; or, A Fate Worse Than Death!" (in *Mr. President, Private Eye,* 1988) teams her with President Ulysses S. Grant in a mystery involving his daughter's White House wedding in 1874. "Death Scene; or, The Moor of Venice" (*Sisters in Crime,* 1990) takes place on a Shakespearean theatrical tour in 1880—81. Continuing her unique and flavorful titles, Carlson's "The Dirty Little Coward That Shot

Mr. Howard; or, Such Stuff As Dreams Are Made On" (*Sisters in Crime 5,* 1992) deals with the killing of Jesse James in 1882, while Bridget is performing Shakespeare in Kansas City. One of the best of the series, set against a background of the Brooklyn Bridge construction, is "The Eighth Wonder of the World; or, Golden Opinions" (*Deadly Allies II,* 1994). Lately Bridget has crossed paths with Thomas Edison in "Put Out the Light; or, The Napoleon of Science" (*Malice Domestic,* 1995) and famed actress Sarah Bernhardt in "The Rosewood Coffin; or, the Divine Sarah" (*Crimes of the Heart,* 1995).

Bridget Mooney, clever and saucy in her narration, is a series character one looks forward to meeting again. In the increasingly popular sub-genre of the historical mystery, P.M. Carlson has skillfully combined the world of the early American theater with the history and crime of the period. The result is a unique treat for readers.

I speak of Wendy Hornsby's short stories as being hard-edged rather than hard-boiled because they are not about policewomen or female private eyes. To my knowledge she has never used a series character in her short fiction, though her first novel in 1987 launched one of two series she has published to date in the longer form. Many discovered her talent for short stories with her Edgar-winning "Nine Sons" (*Sisters in Crime 4,* 1991), a tale to startle and disturb the most experienced readers.

Though she holds graduate degrees in ancient and medieval history, Wendy Hornsby seems to prefer the present in her fiction. She followed "Nine Sons" with another hard-edged tale, choosing this time an urban setting rather than the rural locale of her Edgar winner. "High Heels in the Headliner" first appeared in *Malice Domestic 3* (1994), belying that series's reputation for coziness. In it, a woman mystery writer turns to a homicide detective for help in her research, with unexpected results. During the same year, Hornsby published a completely different type of story, "New Moon and Rattlesnakes" (*The Mysterious West,* 1994). Set in the desert of southern California, it is more novelistic in tone and plot, but with the same hard edge we've come to expect. Wendy Hornsby's short story output has not been large, but we seek out each one, as we might look for nuggets of gold.

The short stories of Carolyn Wheat are procedurals of a very special sort, usually involving a woman lawyer or policewomen with more than their share of problems. Occasionally she focuses on a male police officer or a nonprofessional, but always with a difference. Wheat's first novel, a 1983 Edgar nominee, introduced Cass Jameson, like her creator a Brooklyn attorney with the Legal Aid Society. Cass has appeared in at least one short story, "Three-Time Loser" (*The Armchair Detective,* Fall 1990).

When not writing about lawyers and police officers, Wheat occasionally attempts something entirely different, as in "Cousin Cora" (*Sisters in Crime 2,* 1990) and "Life, For Short" (*Sisters in Crime 4,* 1991). The former is the more successful of these, a fine dark story of childhood on an Ohio farm. But it is with her police stories that she excels. "Crime Scene" (*Sisters in Crime,* 1989) introduces rookie police officer Toni Ramirez, involved in her first homicide. In the course of the brief investigation she learns something of the art of detection, and of life. A quite different policewoman is transit sergeant Maureen Gallagher in "Ghost Station" (*A Woman's Eye,* 1991), who must battle her own alcoholism as well as crime in the subways. One of Wheat's rare stories told from a male viewpoint, "Undercover" (*Murder Is My Business,* 1994), is also one of her best. Set in 1967, when the times were different, it deals with an ex-cop on disability retirement who fakes an alibi in a homosexual bar to cover his part in an arson and murder. As I wrote when I reprinted this story in my *Year's Best* anthology, Carolyn Wheat is one of our most daring and dependable writers.

They are names to remember next time you're glancing over the contents page of an anthology or a mystery magazine. P.M. Carlson, Wendy Hornsby, and Carolyn Wheat—you can't go wrong with any of them.

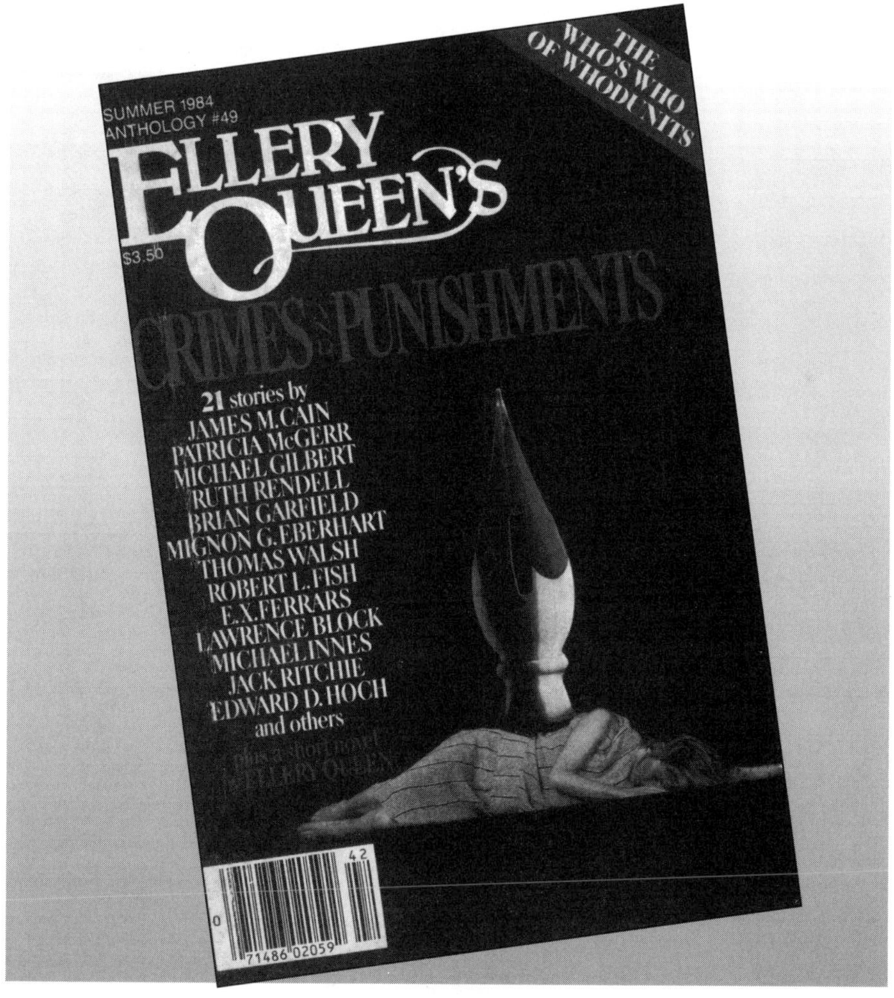

Ellery Queen's Crimes ands Punishments, Summer Anthology 1984

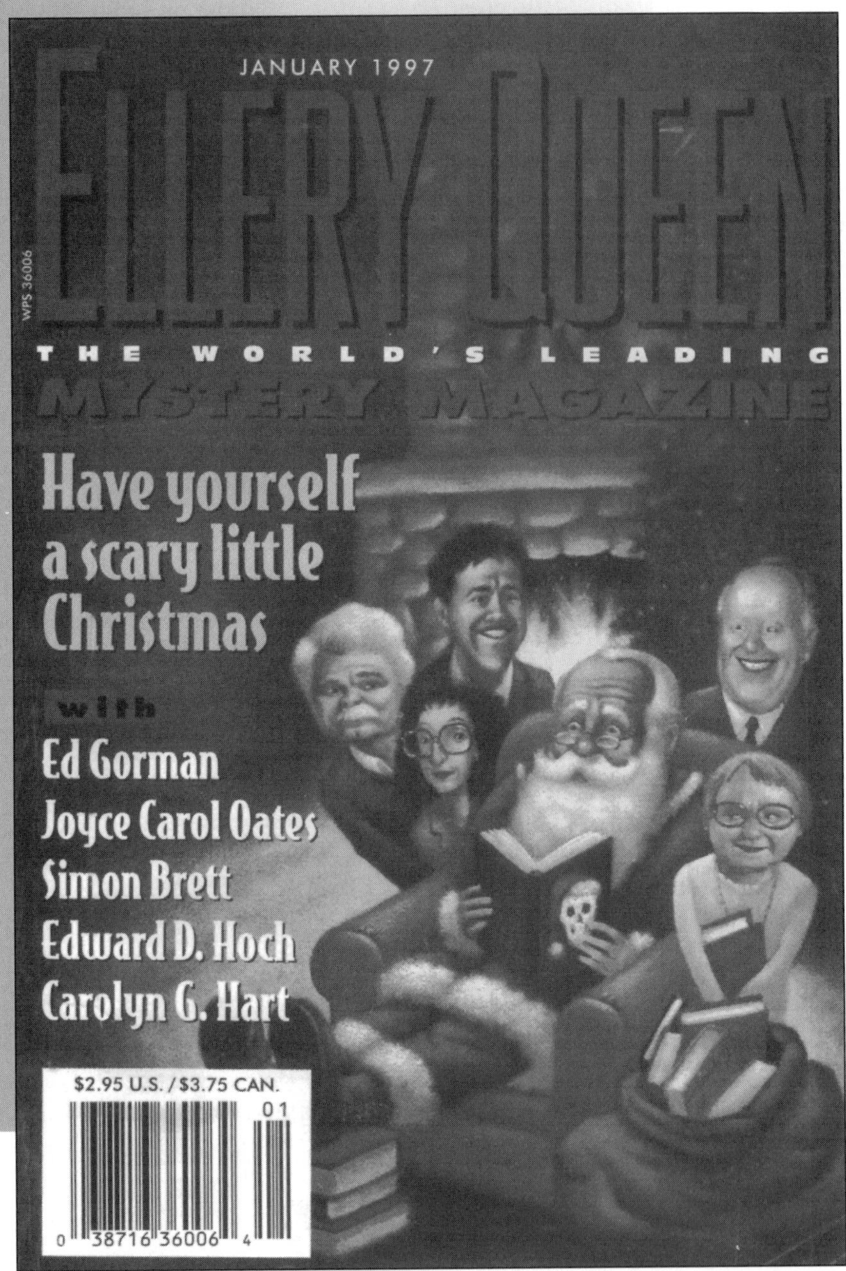

Ellery Queen's Mystery Magazine**,** January 1997

The Long and Short of It

Jan Burke

Why bother writing short stories?" a novelist friend asked recently. "There's no money it."

HER ATTITUDE ISN'T SURPRISING, especially when you understand that she's never felt the desire to write a short story—money or no money. I know short story writers who've never felt the desire to try novels but who have tired of being asked when they are going to write one. Because novelists usually receive greater financial rewards and more public recognition than short story writers, even those who write both novels and short stories often find themselves devoting their writing time to the form that will bring in the bucks. When talking to relatives and friends, they'd rather say, "I've written a book" than "I've written a story."

The short story deserves higher regard than it currently enjoys. Mystery short story writers have often been on the cutting edge of the genre. Edgar Allan Poe's Dupin, generally regarded as the first fictional detective, appeared in three stories dating from 1841. Sherlock Holmes almost always solved his cases in a few pages. Dorothy L. Sayers, Agatha Christie, Rex Stout, and Ellery Queen are among the many classic mystery novelists who also wrote short stories.

When hard-boiled detectives first appeared in print, it was not in novels but in *The Black Mask*—in short stories which introduced readers to Dashiell Hammet, Raymond Chandler, Erle Stanley Gardner, and others.

Short stories, for all their brevity, can be powerful. There are noir stories by Cornell Woolrich, Shirley Jackson, and James M. Cain which may only take an hour to read, but are as chilling as anything you'll ever read in novel form.

More recently, Nancy Pickard's "Afraid All the Time" and Wendy Hornsby's "Nine Sons" sent shivers down my spine—two stories which appeared in Marilyn Wallace's excellent Sisters in Crime anthologies, a series which brought new attention to women mystery writers. Maxine O'Callaghan's Deliah West was one of the first contemporary female private eyes—and she debuted in a short story.

Although the market for short stories has narrowed for all forms of fiction, mystery still boasts a relatively strong one. *Ellery Queen Mystery Magazine* and *Alfred Hitchcock Mystery Magazine* reach hundreds of thousands of readers worldwide. *The Red Herring, Murderous Intent, Over My Dead Body,* and others offer additional opportunities for writers. Anthologies, which tend to feature stories by novelists and established short story writers, have expanded the mystery short story audience. There are even online publications featuring mystery short stories.

Are short stories easy to write? No. Isabel Allende has compared writing a short story to shooting an arrow. "You only get one shot, and you have to have the right speed and tension or you'll miss the target completely." A writer who adopts Allende's attitude will, I believe, find short story writing both challenging and (if the arrow hits the target) exhilarating.

Short stories writers aim at targets as varied as those of novelists. Some intend only to entertain or to provide a puzzle with a wicked twist. Some gleefully strike fear in our hearts—make us keep the lights on at night. Others describe worlds outside our experience, or make us take a closer look at our own lives. In any of these cases, though, the short story is not simply a "little idea" or a novel that didn't reach puberty.

For me, writing both short stories and novels allows me to stretch as a writer. Some plots require the kind of time and space a novel allows, and writing a series provides even more room for the characters to evolve.

Certain aspects of my series have been defined from the beginning: Irene Kelly, the protagonist, is a contemporary amateur sleuth who tells the stories in first person. She works as a reporter. Frank Harriman is part of her life, as are her sister and her friends. She lives in southern California. She has characteristics (loyalty, stubbornness, a sense of humor) that are as familiar to me as her voice. Each novel is written with these elements in mind.

With short stories, though, nothing is previously established. I can write in third person, from a male point of view, about a different time or setting, about a sleuth with a different occupation. I can write in a different style—perhaps the story will be darker than my novels usually are, perhaps lighter. Perhaps the protagonist will be less sympathetic than Irene is, perhaps more so. Perhaps the story will be told from the point of view of a rhinoceros. Short stories allow me to try any of these differences without tying up the kind of writing time which would normally be required to write a novel outside the Irene Kelly series.

If I finish a draft of a novel, write a short story and then return to the novel, I find I can approach the rewrite from a much better frame of mind. I've taken a break, explored another fictional world, spent time with other characters, written in other voices. I can return to Irene Kelly's world feeling refreshed and ready to make changes.

The experience of writing short stories and novels undoubtedly differs among writers, and my own may not reflect those of other writers. These differences are, I believe, part of what keeps the genre alive. Consider the amazing variety one finds in the mystery short stories and novels produced since Poe first penned "The Murders in the Rue Morgue" more than one-hundred fifty years ago. Think of the characters we've met, the worlds we've traveled to, the problems confronted. It isn't difficult to remain optimistic about the future of the mystery, in all its forms, at any length.

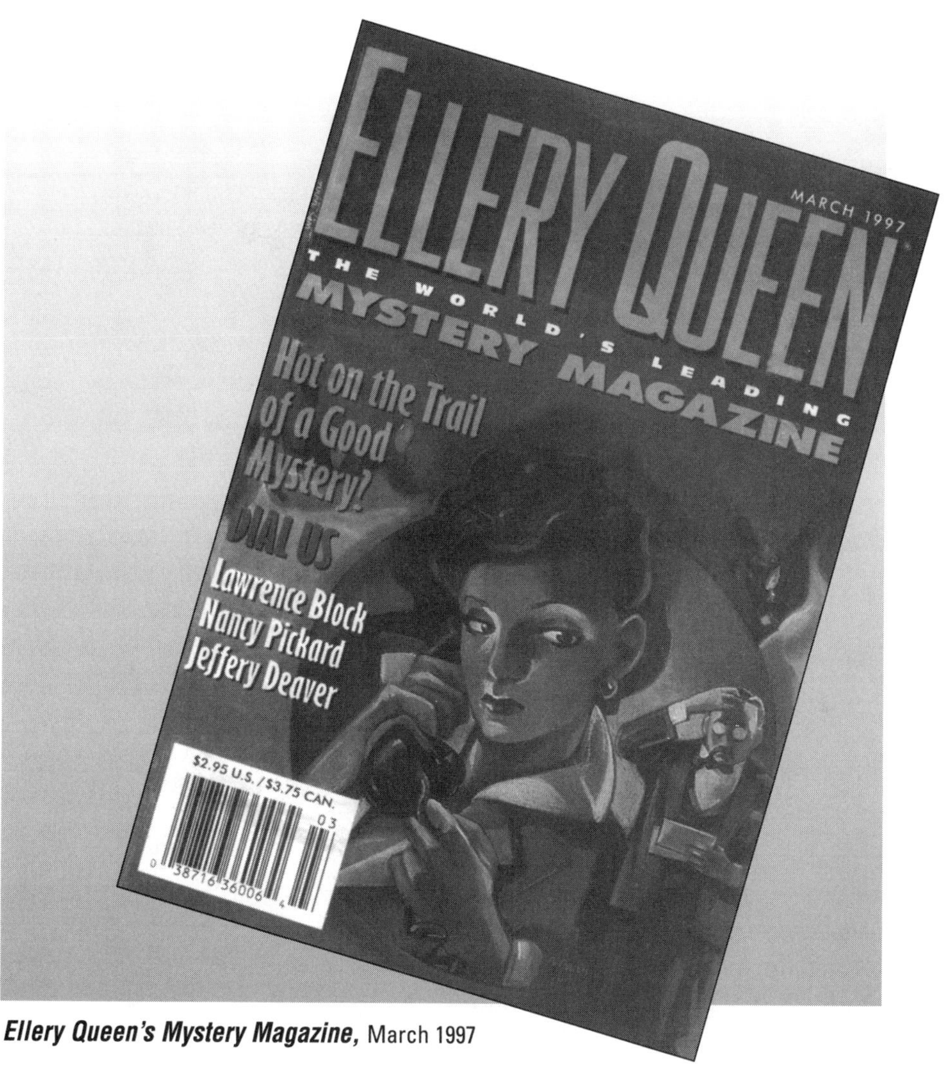

Ellery Queen's Mystery Magazine, March 1997

Nancy Pickard *Photo credit: Roy Inman*

Interview with

Nancy Pickard

Jeffrey Marks

NANCY PICKARD WASN'T SURE that her readers or her editor would accept her last book. Yet, *I.O.U.*, the seventh book in the popular Jenny Cain series, won an Agatha and was nominated for an Edgar. The novel is Jenny's search for answers to the bankruptcy of the family business and her mother's subsequent deterioration into mental illness. With this moving and emotional story, Nancy has heard from her fans, telling of their own mothers' deaths.

Amidst hundreds of these fans, I had a chance to catch Nancy at Malice Domestic shortly after she won the Agatha for *I.O.U.*

JM: When did you start writing?

NP: I started writing professionally as soon as I got out of college. I have a journalism degree from the University of Missouri. I went to work at a local newspaper where I was a reporter and editor for two years, which was long enough to tell me that I was not cut out to be a reporter and editor. But I did things that turned out to be helpful to me as a crime novelist—like cover city council meetings and get to know cops and politicians, I discovered that your main function as a new reporter is to get yelled at a lot and starve. So, I went to work for Western Auto where nobody screamed and I made more money. After three years writing training programs there, I realized that I was not cut out for the corporate life either. You could say that what I did for the first fifteen years of my career was to eliminate from my life all the things I didn't want to do. As someone recently pointed out, now my life consists of embracing what I want to do.

JM: What happened after Western Auto?

NP: I took off and traveled in Europe with my boyfriend for a few months and then came back and discovered that I could make a living freelancing. So I did that for about thirteen years. The first year I freelanced I cut my income exactly in half and increased my workload about twice but had three times as much fun. I felt productive in those years, but the work didn't have any particular meaning at its core. Eventually, that began to wear me down. Then one day I was frankly overcome by a desire to do nothing but write fiction for the rest of my life. I quit my paying job, cold turkey. I read everything on the craft of fiction writing that I could. I set regular office hours. Actually, within a month I had sold my first short story to Ellery Queen's "Department of First Stories."

JW: Wow, that is good.

NP: I finished the first novel quickly too and got the first agent I approached—Meredith Bernstein, who is still my agent and pal. Then real life set in, and it was one rejection after another for about a year and a half. That first novel never sold, thank goodness. Having the advantage of already being a professional writer, I compressed my struggling years into a year and a half and eventually Avon bought *Generous Death,* which was my second book and first published novel.

JM: You mentioned before you set regular office hours. What are your work habits?

NP: When I started out, I did set regular hours. That was before I had a child. I think, if nothing else, setting regular office hours helps control the rest of the people in your life. You don't say "I'm writing," you say "I'm working." I worked regular hours in a very businesslike sense, until my son was born in 1983. Then I had the luxury of being able to work my writing schedule around his schedule. I had him kind of late in life—when I was thirty-eight—so I think that I was more appreciative than I would have been at a younger age. I wrote *Bum Steer* when he was in Kindergarten, and he was only gone two and a half hours a day. By the time I took him to school and got him back, that left only about an hour and a half to work. I feel as if I wrote that book in fifteen-minute increments. I used to admire people who hold down another job while they write. It finally dawned on me, I have been doing it.

JM: You were talking, too, about your time when you were trying to persevere and get published. Do you have any advice for new writers?

NP: The best advice I ever got was from a writer who said if you ever encounter someone who makes you feel like not writing, run like hell. I think it's essential, particularly when you are starting out, to be surrounded by people who have your best interests at heart. That can be defined as telling you the truth, but telling you in a way that doesn't devastate you. I had one creative writing course in my life, and the teacher was so vicious that it kept me away from fiction for years. Now I understand that the problem wasn't that I couldn't write, the problem was that he was a jerk.

People will come up to published writers and they will say, "I should write a book and if I had the time I would write it." That makes us grind our teeth. The best answer I have for this is Kevin Robinson. Kevin Robinson is the new mystery writer at Walker who wrote *Split Seconds* and *Mall Rats.* Kevin is paraplegic. He writes his novels with one finger. I don't want to hear anybody talk to me about time. Time is not the issue; desire is the issue.

I always have a feeling when I am talking to a new writer that he or she will make it, if they talk to me about rewriting. There are a lot of wonderful first drafts sitting in closets at home and they'll never sell because their authors won't dedicate themselves to the task of rewriting. Most published writers who I know feel the real writing comes from the rewrite. The creative first draft is exhilarating, but the book doesn't begin to be a book until you rewrite and rewrite and rewrite it.

JM: You once wrote copy for funeral

homes, and you used part of that for *No Body.* What other experiences have you used in some of your books?
NP: I was married for a long time to a cattle rancher and that was the basis for *Bum Steer.* I wrote *Dead Crazy* because I have a friend in Kansas City who runs an outfit devoted to helping former mental patients make a transition back into society. I had heard her talk about how difficult it is to start halfway houses, I knew that, too, from my newspaper experience. Whenever you have a governing body with a proposal for a halfway house, particularly if it is for mental patients, what happens is that craziness of the clients seeps out into the neighborhood and makes everybody crazy, a perfect milieu for a mystery.

JM: How much of Jenny is you?
NP: Oh, probably a lot. It is getting harder to deny. Jenny is rather like a younger sister or a good friend. Eventually, she will be more like a daughter because I am aging more quickly than she is! We aren't identical. She's got a different tone to her. At least, I think so, but what do I know? She looks different, walks different, and talks in a different accent. In my consciousness, she's a very distinct person from me. I would be foolish if I didn't say that we share a similar sense of humor, identical political views, and things like that, because obviously we do. It is funny writing a character who is ten years younger. I'm not sure how that works. I guess it's funny writing a character who is any age you are not. I may be writing Jenny as I wished I had been at that age, more straightforward, more bold, just more.

JM: You have done so many different social concerns through all your books. Is there one that is particularly close to you?
NP: It must be mental illness because it keeps recurring. I wouldn't have known that if you would have asked me to after the first book or even the sixth. I'm a kid of the sixties. My interest isn't in bells, like Dorothy Sayers, or guns or horse racing. It's in social issues, and so I can no more avoid talking about them in my books than I can avoid having blue eyes. When I started doing social issues, I was aware that it hadn't been done much in mysteries. Now it is fairly common, I think, and it's simply a reflection of the fact so many of us who are now middle-aged went through the sixties and came out of it with that particular kind of consciousness. I didn't want to be known as the social-issue-of-the-week writer, however, which is one of the reasons I wrote *Bum Steer.* Just to have fun.

JM: Since you were talking about women in mysteries, can you tell us about Sisters in Crime and your involvement in it.
NP: I look at Sisters in Crime now and what I see is potential. As big as women's mystery fiction has become, it's only the tip of the iceberg. Sue Grafton and Sara Paretsky are really proving this with their enormous first runs and great sales. I personally think that all those women out there who grew up reading Nancy Drew are our potential audience and most of that audience has not been tapped. Critics sometimes say our detectives, Jenny for instance, are Nancy Drew all grown up. They mean it pejoratively. When I hear that, I laugh to myself and think, go right ahead and "Carolyn

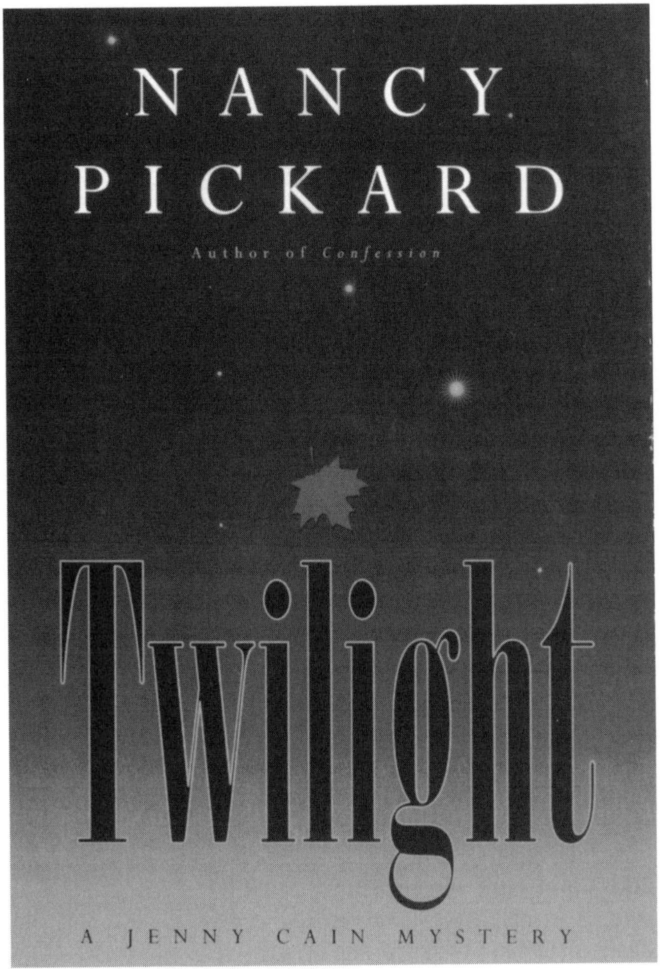

Twilight
by Nancy Pickard

Keene" me. I think, say that as often as you want and as loud as you like. If you strip away certain silliness of the plot, for instance the fact that her father hands her a gun, and says, "Here, Nancy, you may need this", and you strip away the extremely unfortunate antisemitism and racism, what you've got left is a hell of a brave, smart, young woman who is a model for anybody. I think that whatever it is that attracted those millions of us readers to Nancy Drew as we were growing up, those qualities still attract us to books we read now. Most of those readers still don't know that the books exist that give them back that heroine.

Sisters in Crime frequently gets described as a writer's organization and it ain't. The reason it gets described that way is because our board is made up of mostly writers and that is because the writers have the influence to do what needs to be done and also because writers started it. But it's primarily readers, probably ten to one, all of them potential readers for all of us, brothers and sisters.

JM: How did you become involved in the Virginia Rich books?

NP: The story is that shortly after my first book was published, I happened to read Virginia Rich's first book and I really liked it. I wrote to Mrs. Rich because there were certain similarities in what we wrote and in our lives. Her husband was a rancher and my husband was a rancher. She lived and set a lot of her stuff on the East Coast, I don't live on the East Coast but that is where my series was set up. So I wrote to her and told her I liked her stuff and that I was a new mystery writer, too. I got back the most gracious note. She said among other things she was working on a book called *The 27 Ingredients Chili Con Carne Murders.* I was thrilled to hear from her, she sounded like the nicest person. Sometime after that I heard that she had died. Years passed, but her three books, the books that she had written, continued to be popular, continued to remain in print. A lot of people didn't know that she had died, and they were also angry when they found out. We readers get so mad when our favorite authors have the nerve to up and die on us. How dare they!

JM: So how did you become involved in writing the "Rich" books?

NP: Her husband was going through her papers and came across boxes of notes, ideas for future novels. He had approached her editor at Delacorte and suggested continuing the series. The editor approached my agent who called me out of the blue and said how would you like to write a mystery called *The 27 Ingredient Chili Con Carne Murders*. I figured to was fate. I needed a break from Jenny. The Jenny books are written in first person and the Eugenia Potter books are written in third. I liked the idea of writing from an older woman's point of view, before I got to be too much older and it was my own point of view. One of the disadvantages of having me write the book is I don't cook. I had to get the recipes. Virginia had written about forty pages of manuscript. It was mostly first draft that she wouldn't have kept. There were place descriptions, however, I put into the book which are pure Virginia and which I couldn't have done. There is a fairly lengthy description of a tostada buffet, for another touch of her writing. There is a relationship between Mrs. Potter and her old college boyfriend who comes back into the picture and some of her memories of first knowing him, the first time they meet again, some of that is from the pages Virginia wrote. I tried to keep some of her characters' names although they aren't the same characters. If I could get Eugenia Potter right, then it would still be Virginia's book and the rest would roll in place.

JM: Sounds most intriguing and we'll look forward to it.

[This interview was first printed in *The Armchair Detective* in April '93 and edited for this publication.]

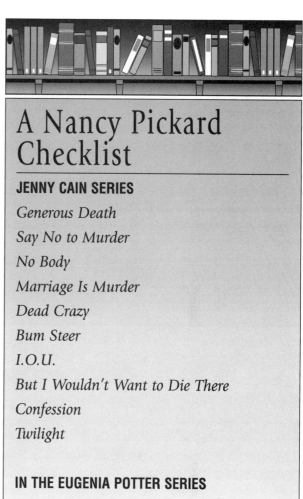

A Nancy Pickard Checklist

JENNY CAIN SERIES

Generous Death

Say No to Murder

No Body

Marriage Is Murder

Dead Crazy

Bum Steer

I.O.U.

But I Wouldn't Want to Die There

Confession

Twilight

IN THE EUGENIA POTTER SERIES

The 27 Ingredient Chili Con Carne Murders

Forthcoming—'98

The Blue Corn Murders

Get Them While They're Young

Joan Lowery Nixon *Photo credit: Alexander's Fine Portrait Design, Houston, Texas*

Murder She Writes: Joan Lowery Nixon

Mary Blount Christian

When entering the office of Joan Lowery Nixon, one is immediately struck with the wealth of awards that occupy shelf and wall space. Four Edgar statues, their mournful expressions identical, share space with her more than one hundred titles.

OVER HALF OF THOSE titles are mysteries. The walls display plaques and certificates verifying that her readers consider her the very best. Young readers in six states voted *The Other Side of Dark,* her 1986 Edgar for Best Juvenile, their favorite read of the year. Five other titles won in statewide contests in California, Colorado, Indiana, Iowa, Nebraska, Nevada, Oklahoma, Utah, and Virginia.

Joan recalled reading her very first mystery novel around age seven. "I still remember the shock, surprise, joy, excitement. It was hard to believe that anyone had come up with such a wonderful plot. I was hooked."

Although reared in Hollywood, she was never starstruck. "I saw that those glamorous people learned one line at a time and took forever to get it right. It was the writers who made the stories come alive."

When her own children were young, she expressed her interest in writing for children. "Kathy and Maureen [her two oldest daughters] told me that the book had to be a mystery, and I had to put them into it."

Joan prepared for the project by reading "stacks" of mysteries for the eight-to-twelve age group. At that time there was only one book on writing for children, one written by Phyllis Whitney. "I practically memorized it," she said.

That first manuscript, *Mystery of Hurricane Castle,* was published by Clarion in 1964, and she has been writing for children and teens ever since.

Her main characters are all female and all admirable role models for readers. "They have all been strong individuals who make their own decisions, set high standards, and respect themselves and others," she said. They haven't changed."

Joan includes murder in her young adult mysteries. *The Kidnapping of Christina Lattimore,* 1980 Edgar for Best Juvenile, was the exception. In it, Christina is kidnapped but escapes early in the book. The real story is her search for the perp and her own self worth, an important theme throughout Joan's stories.

The Seance (1981), *The Other Side of Dark* (1986), and *The Name of the Game Was Murder* (1994) are the other three Edgar winners. She has been nominated five additional times, including *Spirit Seeker,* for 1996.

Her mysteries with a western historical background, *High Trail to Danger* and *A Dangerous Promise* were nominated for Spur Awards from the Western Writers of America in 1992 and 1995 respectively. Two of her nonmysterious books won Spurs.

Mother of four and grandmother to thirteen, Joan understands the influence of stories on children. She does not use murder for her eight-to-twelve mysteries but prefers to deal with disappearance, burglary, white collar crimes, etc., and to balance that off with a healthy dose of humor. If she does include a murder, it's off-scene. "No gore," she emphasizes. "Ever."

In her young adult mysteries she may let the main character see the body but she avoids any vivid detail. "Detailed descriptions of gore would show a lack of respect on my part for my readers' ability to share the story with me," she explains. She feels that, "A book is a combination of my words and my readers' imaginations."

Her energy for the written word seems boundless. A young adult mystery, *Don't Scream,* and an eight-to-twelve mystery, *The Shadow Man,* are scheduled for publication in 1996 with Delacorte. Disney will release six more titles in her "Casebusters" series, and several of her short stories are scheduled for anthologies in the fall of 1996.

The authenticity in her books is no accident. Joan takes her research seriously. She was living in Corpus Christi, Texas, when she wrote *The Stalker.* "I made an appointment with the public relations officer in the police department. He took me through the places I asked: the homicide department, the court where one of my characters would be arraigned, etc."

It was a deputy in the sheriff's department, who finally heeded her pleas to see inside the women's jail. "But he took my pen apart and examined it; then he said I could take nothing but a small pad of paper. I was examined, and the steel doors clanged behind me. We took an elevator upstairs, I was examined again, and then I was taken to the jail. Another set of steel doors clanged shut. It was a horrible feeling."

In Houston, she was using an actual murder case as a springboard for *Whispers from the Dead.* Assuming that no one would be at the crime scene, she parked her car blocking the driveway and proceeded to sketch the scene for purposes of a memory jog later. "Suddenly, a car loomed up on my left. It was the stepmother of the murderer—someone I thought had helped to cover up a second murder. Naturally, she wanted me to move my car so she could get into her driveway, but the scowl she gave me was frightening. For an instant I almost panicked, wondering if she knew what I was doing and why. There we were—just the two of us on an empty cul-de-sac." Joan knew that no one had come when the victim had screamed and screamed and that one neighbor had even hidden instead of calling the police. "Believe me, I got out of there in a hurry!

"Mysteries give children a chance to be brave," she said. "They challenge the readers' powers of deduction, and they provide good plots, exciting reading, and great fun. If I were to name something that I hope my mysteries leave children with on the last page it would be a feeling of self-worth."

In *The Kidnapping of Christina Lattimore,* the main character's last remarks are, "I know what is important. I am. It's a great feeling."

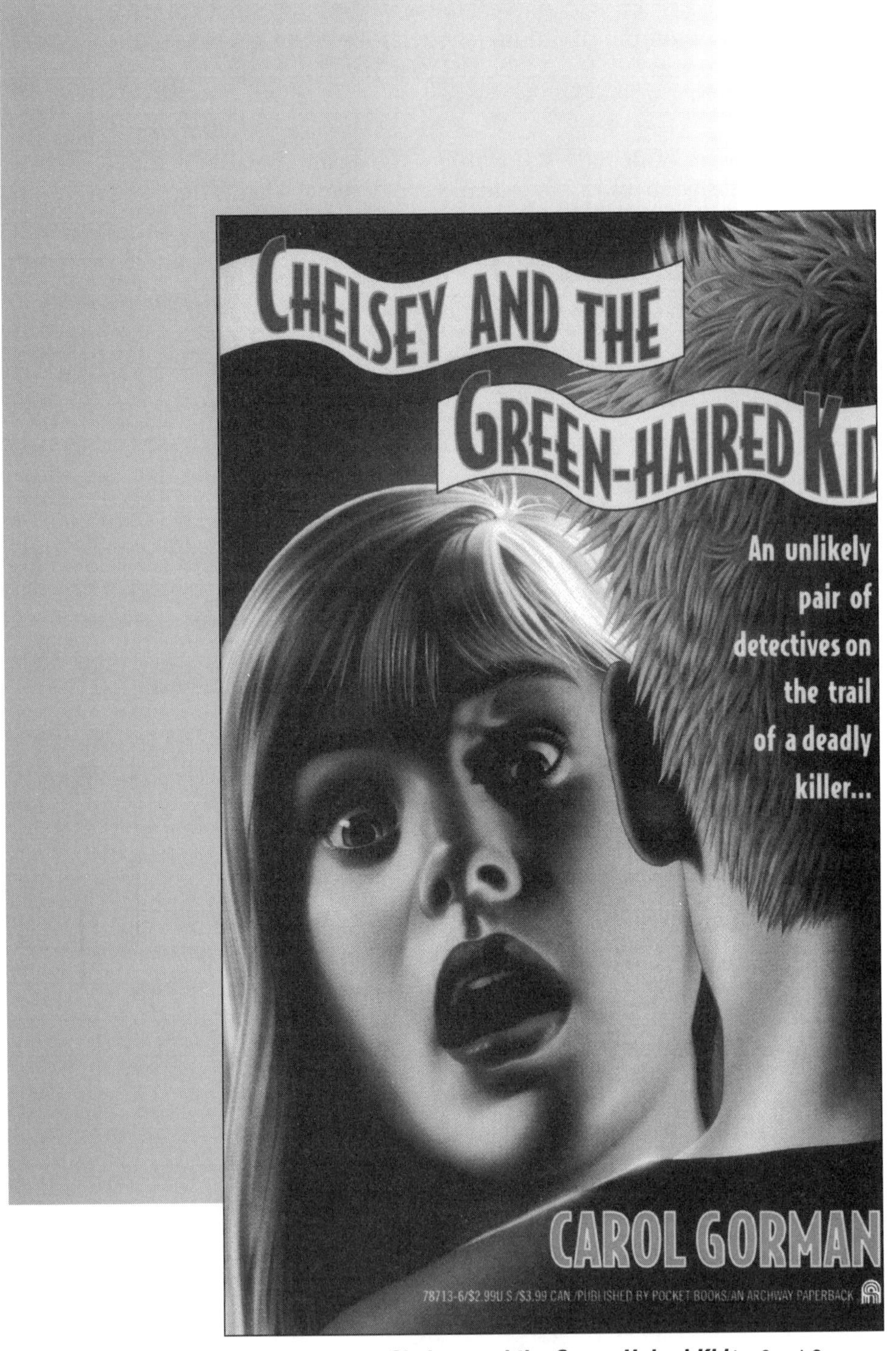

CHELSEY AND THE
GREEN-HAIRED KI
An unlikely pair of detectives on the trail of a deadly killer...
CAROL GORMAN
78713-6/$2.99U.S./$3.99 CAN./PUBLISHED BY POCKET BOOKS/AN ARCHWAY PAPERBACK

Chelsey and the Green-Haired Kid by Carol Gorman

Pathways, Pointers, and Pearls

Interview with Carol Gorman

Carol Crowley

Carol Gorman, YA and middle-grade novelist, taught language arts and starred in musicals including Peter Pan *and* West Side Story *before turning to full-time writing.*

SHE WAS ENCOURAGED BY husband Ed Gorman (mystery writer, editor of *Mystery Scene* magazine, and fellow SinC member) to try writing books. Her second juvenile, *T.J. and the Pirate Who Wouldn't Go Home,* sold. *Die for Me* and *Graveyard Moon* were IRA Children's Choice and YA Choice winners. *Chelsey and the Green-Haired Kid* received the Ethical Culture Book Award, appeared on three state young readers' lists, was selected for *Ladies' Home Journal*'s "How To Get Your Kids To Love Books," and was named an ALA Recommended Book for Reluctant Readers. *Jennifer-the-Jerk Is Missing* was praised by Kirkus as "a cozy comic mystery . . . daring and clever . . . suspenseful as well as funny . . . a pleasantly thrilling escapade." Booklist commended Carol's well-drawn characters, good humor, and refreshing sense concerning pre-teen issues. Another YA novel, *Back from the Dead,* was featured on National Public Radio.

I met Carol for tea and talk recently in Cedar Rapids, Iowa to learn more about her writing, acting, teaching, and also the SinC Mysteries for Minors Speakers Bureau which she coordinates.

CC: How did the Mysteries for Minors Speakers Bureau come about?

CG: It materialized from a discussion among juvenile writers led by Joan Lowery Nixon at the SinC Conference in Houston. It's a cooperative effort to connect us with teachers, librarians, and booksellers and to get our books before more young readers. Our promotional packet includes YA author bios and lecture topics. It also includes the SinC *Books-in-Print* and information brochure, plus our catalog *Kids Love Mysteries.* Because the bureau is a new endeavor, I have urged members to notify me of positive results they experience from our promotional effort.

CC: What benefits do you realize from the time and effort you invest in school visits?

CG: Getting into the schools allows me to eavesdrop on conversations, see interactions between the kids, how they dress, and find out what's currently considered "cool." Another thing I've found beneficial is to take neighbor children out for french fries. Away from their parents, they open up and talk to me about whatever I ask. I used one topic gained in such conversation in *Dork in Disguise.*

CC: I understand you taught at University of Iowa's Summer Writing Festival. Your subjects?

CG: "Writing Humorous Novels for Seven-to-Twelve-Year-Olds," and "Writing Middle-Grade/YA Novels." We discuss opening hooks, characterization, dialogue, and structure. I learned structure by outlining mysteries chapter by chapter to identify where characters and problem were introduced, where complications occur, how to begin and end chapters. Ed suggested mystery writers that I should read to learn structure, but the two he mentioned most often were Margaret Millar and John D. MacDonald. If you are looking for well structured YA mysteries, pick up any of Joan Lowery Nixon's novels. Lois Duncan's suspense novels are good to study, too.

Speaking of mystery and suspense, in children's books publishers don't usually distinguish between the two. Any story dealing with a crime is categorized as a mystery. My experience has been that children's editors generally don't know the difference. That can cause problems now and then. I'll give you two examples, but first let me explain the difference.

In mystery novels, the reader generally doesn't know who committed the crime until the end when the main character, who has acted as the detective, unmasks the killer. (There are other types of mysteries than the who-dun-its, and in these books, there is a mystery at the core of the story that the character must unravel.) In suspense novels, the reader usually knows the identity of the killer fairly early in the novel. Suspense frequently involves a race against time. The heroine is working fast to prove who the killer is before the killer closes in on her. (I wrote a suspense novel, and the first two editors we sent it to turned it down saying, "But I know who did it!")

There is a convention in adult suspense fiction that introduces a character in the prologue. We get to know that character, what her hopes and dreams are, and we assume she's the main character. She's killed at the end of the prologue. The beginning of the first chapter introduces the real heroine who will track down the killer. This is how I started my novel, *Die for Me.* The first editor we sent it to turned it down, saying, "You can't kill off your main character!"

CC: What writers do you admire for their mastery in specific areas such as creating and maintaining suspense, characterization, plotting, and voice?

CG: I read writers of both adult and YA fiction to learn elements of writing. No one builds suspense better than Dean Koontz. I love the humor of Joan Hess, Sharyn McCrumb, and Elizabeth Peters. I just read a delightful book, *The Persian Pickle Club,* by Sandra Dallas, that used humor and character very well. Two YA's I've read recently that have vivid, delightful characters are *The Orphan's Tent* by

Tom De Haven and *Flyers* by Daniel Hayes. I loved the plotting and characters in *Mr. Was* by Peter Hautman. I'm reading a book right now that has a lovely, stylish voice, *The Cuckoo's Child* by Suzanne Freeman. I'm sure we'll be hearing a lot more from this first-time novelist.

CC: Do you have a theme firmly in mind when you begin a novel? Have readers responded with a recognition of your theme's significance and what it meant to them?

CG: The only time I started a book with a theme in mind was when I wrote books for a religious publisher. My intention is always, first, to tell a good story. Themes do emerge in the writing of the book, and I certainly am aware of them, and I use them. But to start out with a theme in mind, I think, increases the danger that a writer will sound preachy. Kids can spot that right away, and it really turns them off, as it does me. Yes, I've heard from readers and teachers who say they've gotten into interesting discussions in class while reading my books. That's always gratifying.

CC: When you begin the novel process is there one ingredient or facet that serves as a lightning rod to attract the other vital components to your creative mix?

CG: I don't intentionally start out with one element, but usually the first thing that occurs to me is the setup or the hook. I can think of only one exception. With *Die for Me,* I thought of the motive first.

CC: Your current book project?

CG: I'm reworking a novel, about a fictitious girl in 1910 who gets a job at the triangle Shirtwaist Factory, a sweatshop that burned killing 146 young immigrant women. This book is certainly a turn in the road for me. Until now I have written mysteries and light, humorous, coming-of-age books This brings up another point that I learned the hard way. I'd been reading *A Tree Grows in Brooklyn* as I started writing my book. *Sarah,* like the heroine *A Tree,* is a slice of life that focuses on characters and their relationships in a historical setting, and the pace is leisurely. Writer friends of mine who are astute readers (and honest with me) loved *Sarah.* But I couldn't sell it the way it was. "Too slow," one editor said. "It will have to move more quickly to keep children turning those pages," another said. So you see, I was influenced by a wonderful book that's very much out of fashion. I pointed to a middle grade historical novel published just six years ago that moved very slowly. It didn't matter. Editors *this year* want fast-moving historicals. So it's important to keep up on current books.

CC: Have you taken time out from writing for any recent stage performances?

CG: No, but I played a security guard in the movie *Mommy's Day,* a black comedy written and directed by mystery writer Max Alan Collins in Muscatine, Iowa. It was great fun; the whole town got involved.

CC: Have you any pearls of wisdom for those of us trying to achieve that first published novel?

CG: Read and analyze the best. I studied Joan Lowery Nixon, Lois Duncan, and Katherine Paterson.

F as in Fascination

Don Sandstrom

The selection of Faye Kellerman as the 1997 Left Coast Guest of Honor is appropriate not only for her ten excellent novels, but also for the fact that she is a Left Coast Author—Left Coast by adoption. Faye Marder was born in St. Louis, Missouri, and married Jonathan in 1972. The couple are the parents of four children. Reinforcing the Left Coast connection is the fact that Faye is also a graduate of the University of California at Los Angeles with an A.B. in Mathematics and a D.D.S. She also is a Regents Research Fellow in Oral Biology.

THE LEFT COAST CONNECTION for Ms. Kellerman has significance for me as well. First, it was in 1988 following the San Diego Bouchercon that I was attracted by a copy of *The Ritual Bath* at the Los Angeles Airport. I found it to be a fascinating debut novel and became an instant Faye Kellerman fan. Webster defines "fascinating" to mean: "1. to transfix and hold spellbound by an irresistible power; 2. to command the interest of; 3. to be irresistibly attractive." I use the adjective in all three meanings and apply it to the next nine novels as well. For the second Left Coast applicability, fast forward to the 1991 Bouchercon at Pasadena where I was again fascinated by the author in person as she and her husband discussed their writings and their life. All this by explaining my objectivity in composing what is intended to be a sincere tribute to a remarkable author/lady.

Her series novels have several plusses working for them. Although billed as "A Rina Lazarus/Peter Decker Mystery," each of the nine is a police procedural with the added fillip of the love affair, and the subsequent marriage of Rina and Peter as a subtext. Another large plus is the incorporation of the doctrine and practice of Orthodox Judaism in the series—but always in context. Rina and Peter are not merely characters on a page; they are as human and understandable as they are likable. The same is true for the third lead, Marge Dunn, who until Peter's promotion in the latest book, was his partner, but still Rina's good friend. Rina is not an amateur sleuth, although in the seventh book, *Sanctuary*, she does accompany Peter to Israel and helps him in his investigation, since she speaks Hebrew and he does not. Rina had also lived in Israel at one time.

Still another plus is the variety of plots, locales, and crimes in the series. Ms. Kellerman does not write boilerplate novels. A large plus for me is the authentic dialogue. It is always in character and utterly believable. It is also the means by which she unfolds each story; often as much as 90 percent (my estimate) presented via realistic dialogue. This attribute as well as the other ingredients of her stories bespeak her solid research and enrich her striking storytelling ability.

In 1989, her one non-series novel, *The Quality of Mercy,* was published. Truly a fascinating tour de force based on several months of intensive research in England, it is basically a historical story with a marvelous heroine, Rebecca Lopez, daughter of Queen Elizabeth's personal physician. Doctor Roderigo Lopez was a historical figure, who was drawn and quartered at Tyburn in 1594, having been found guilty of plotting to poison the queen. In a note at the end of the book, Ms. Kellerman suggests the doctor could have been the inspiration for Shylock in Shakespeare's *Merchant of Venice.* The fictional Shakespeare in this book is passionately in love with Rebecca who is involved with her family in smuggling Jews out of Spain to escape the Inquisition. As in her modern novels, her Jewish characters have a deep faith and she brings to life the customs and practices of the conversos in a crypto-Jewish community in sixteenth-century England. There is also a mystery involving the murder of Shakespeare's close friend with Rebecca helping the playwright find the culprit. Fanciful, but as I said above, still a fascinating story.

During this same decade—1986-96—Ms. Kellerman has also written several short stories. Her "Holy Water," published in *Deadly Allies II* (1994), was selected by mystery short story expert Marvin Lachman as one of the best stories of that year. Frankly, I haven't a clue on how she does all that she does, but am awfully glad she does. I am indeed honored to have been asked to write this fan letter to one of my favorite authors.

Hidden Treasures or Buried Trash?

Illustration © 1997 Desert Isle Design

Recycling in the New Millennium

Susan Rogers Cooper

The year was 1985 and my fledgling writing career was floundering.

THREE YEARS BEFORE I'D sold my one and only romance attempt called "Listen to Love" to an audio house. After the check for my hundred-dollar advance cleared, the house went belly-up and my first publication never had the chance to gather dust on the shelf. A year later, I sold a story to a "literary" anthology that folded before I even got the check.

Since then I'd mailed out partial chapters and synopses to every publishing house in the United States and Canada. My new goal in 1985 was to receive enough rejection slips to finish wallpapering the bathroom.

That's when my husband—my partner in all things—came to me saying he had a great idea for a mystery. Since I read mostly mysteries, I wasn't opposed to writing one, as long as my husband could put in all those pesky little extras like clues.

He had written on the back of a grocery receipt a list of the names of his characters and a brief outline of the plot, which had something to do with militant fundamentalists and greatly resembled a recurring nightmare of his about white-robed reactionaries chasing him through the woods.

I took the characters, Willis and E.J. Pugh, and his plot, and started working. I was about one hundred pages into the book when I started being visited by a guy named Milt Kovak. Milt never rang the doorbell or called on the phone. No, he's a lot more devious and insidious than that. He would worm his way into my mind and begin to talk, and the louder his voice got the better.

So I started cheating on my husband. First I would take an hour out of my day to work on the first Milt Kovak book, then it became two. Before I knew it, Willis, E.J., and the militant fundamentalists were hiding in the back reaches of the computer while I spent my days blithely carousing with my buddy Milt.

After one hundred and fifty pages of the first Milt book, I confessed all to my husband. He was very modern and sophisticated about the whole thing and agreed to start sharing our lives with the pudgy, fiftyish deputy sheriff from Oklahoma.

Wonder of wonders, that first Milt book, *The Man in the Green Chevy,* was sold rather quickly for this business to St. Martin's Press, Inc. I went on to write three more books in the Milt Kovak series, but something kept nagging at me.

There was absolutely nothing wrong with the Willis and E.J. characters—or the E.J. and Willis characters, as I came to think of them. No, the problem had been that the plot sucked.

I went back and reread the one hundred pages of my first mystery and found that they worked. What didn't work was the outline that concluded the book. So I ditched that, reworked it, and *One, Two, What Did Daddy Do?* was published by St. Martin's Press in 1992—and was named one of the best books of 1993 by the editors of *Mystery News.* (I know there is a discrepancy in there somewhere, but let's try to ignore it.)

Avon Books picked up the paperback rights to *One, Two, What Did Daddy Do?* and the reprint came out in the summer of 1996, followed in the fall by the second in the series, a paperback original, *Hickory Dickory Stalk.* In June of 1997, the third of the series, *Home Again, Home Again,* came out, again as a paperback original by Avon.

Conclusion: Something was salvageable from that first mystery; the characters, the opening scenes, the basic theme of life in suburbia and the trials and tribulations of husbands, kids, pets, and lawn care.

Okay, so there are no white-robed militant fundamentalists, and Willis Pugh never gets to run through the woods with ammunition strapped to his manly chest, an AK-47 under one arm, and E.J. scantily clad clutching the other. But I've come to the obvious conclusion that that's not my style. It never would have worked for me.

In recycling, E.J. and Willis Pugh have found a new voice and a new life, one fraught with just as many dangers, but the kinds of dangers we all might face some day: the loss of loved ones, the fear of living in the nineties, and the ever-present worry of not being able to keep what you have and hold dear close to you.

And this works for me.

Funny You Should Ask . . .

Barbara Burnett Smith

AFTER *WRITERS OF THE PURPLE SAGE* came out I went on tour in all the typical places, but I also went to Brady, Texas. (It's not too far from Purple Sage.) While there I got a phone call from a former neighbor who asked me to stop by his house. When I arrived he handed me a battered navy-blue folder, and inside was the original manuscript of my first book! I had loaned it to him almost twenty years ago.

Tale of a Post-Feminist Gothic

Carole Nelson Douglas

Shocked by an incident of English bigotry witnessed during a college trip to Ireland, I began One Faithful Harp *in 1965. The early chapters called a drawer home for eleven years while I pursued a newspaper reporting career. Finally, bruised by repeat engagements with the glass ceiling, I finished the novel for my own entertainment in 1977.*

ENTER WRITER/PLAYWRIGHT GARSON Kanin, a satisfied interview subject, who offered to take the completed ms. to his publisher. A historical mainstream Gothic novel was the kiss of death during the peak of the bodice-ripper boom, but mine sold. Renamed *Amberleigh* after the protagonist, it debuted in 1980, was reissued by my current publisher in 1993. Both behind its market and ahead of its time, *Amberleigh*'s narrative threads and themes still stitch together my novels today: character-driven fiction using women's and social issues to lend mainstream substance and psychology to genre elements like mystery and romance. *Amberleigh* even has a key animal character, a heroic Irish wolfhound named Boru who does in the murderer "doggy" style.

First Manuscript?

My First Manuscript

Jan Burke

I WAS LUCKY; MY first manuscript was published. My first manuscript, not to be confused with my first attempt at a novel. When I was in the eighth grade, I was supposed to write a short story for an English class. I asked if I could write a novel instead. It was going to be on Micronesia. I had never been to Micronesia, knew no one from Micronesia, had never seen a film or read a book about Micronesia. But it looked interesting on a globe—all those islands. I don't think I got more than five handwritten pages done. Didn't write the short story either. Lesson number one: you have to actually write something.

I do have an unpublished manuscript. I wrote it after I was published. It has a central theme that is guaranteed to cause any editor to make a face—a cross between a "don't make me laugh" face and a "don't make me sick" face. Someday this story will be incredibly commercial. It isn't now. But I'll have to rewrite it anyway, because I've cannibalized portions of it for other books. Rugby players aren't the only ones who eat their dead.

First Manuscript

Lynda S. Robinson

WHERE IS IT? In the attic of course. It was a space opera, and it was too long and too dramatic and much too anthropological for science fiction at the time. I put it away and kept writing. I think that's the difference between a professional and a wannabe. You have to keep writing, keep improving, and not let rejection discourage you.

Luckily, I had a wonderful family who kept urging me on, especially my husband. Unluckily, for years I had to hear about that blasted first manuscript and how good it was, how I ought to rewrite it and send it out again. "It was much more interesting than this other stuff you're writing, although that's good, too sweetie." Now I'd like to burn it, but I'd get into trouble.

My First Manuscript?

John Lutz

I DON'T KNOW BUT if I find it I will burn it.

First Manuscript

Wendy Hornsby

MY FIRST MANUSCRIPT: I worked on my first book, *No Harm,* in Raymond Obstfeld's novel workshop. When I decided it was finished, Raymond handed it to his agent, who agreed to take me on. I was rejected twice, then bought by Dodd, Mead for hardcover publication. Not much of a story, is it? Except of course that Dodd, Mead closed its doors shortly after the book came out. But it was a book, and that's all that really mattered.

First Manuscript

Gayle Lynds

MY FIRST MANUSCRIPT? Its manuscript box, battered and squished, lies at the bottom of a pile of research and my first mystery, also unpublished. My first novel was a so-called literary work, which chronicled in painful abundance my philosophy of self-inflicted victimization. As you can tell, there wasn't much action and no suspense and certainly no humor. Are we surprised that it didn't sell? Nope. Are we glad now that it didn't sell? You bet!

My First Manuscript

Mary Blount Christian

TO ANSWER THE BURNING question about the first, unpublished manuscript! I have a file drawer (recently expanded to two) called R.I.P. However, I occasionally raise the dead and with a fresh eye revise or combine two and often sell them. If a manuscript zombies out a second time, I may just rescue a character or idea that I liked in it. The first draft of the first manuscript I ever wrote I keep handy; I reread it before teaching a class. It reminds me that there is no such thing as hopeless—only clueless!

My First Mss

Anette Meyers

Coming of Age With Peaches and Pears, my first ms, was, obviously, an autobiographical novel, about a Jewish girl growing up on a chicken farm in New Jersey during World War II. It is still dear to my heart although remains on a shelf in my closet, along with another ms about the theater, which I never submitted anywhere. Nearly twenty years have passed since I had some interest in *Peaches and Pears* from two major publishers and each time it waned when an editor was purged.

The Big Killing was the first mystery I'd ever written, It turned into my Smith and Wetzon series. I finished it in September of 1986, sold it and a second one—not yet written—to Bantam in January of 1987, without an agent, and I was finally published in June of 1989.

My First Mss

Ed Hoch

WHAT HAPPENED TO MY very first unpublished manuscript? I was writing stories all through high school for my own amusement without submitting any of them for publication. The earliest I can clearly remember was one in which the president of the United States would sneak out of the White House at night to solve mysteries. This was in 1946 when I was sixteen. In March of 1947 *Ellery Queen Mystery Magazine* announced the winner of its second contest: "The President of the United States, Detective" by H.F. Heard. The story was futuristic and nothing like my idea, but it convinced me I could become a writer. That early manuscript is long gone but not forgotten.

My First Mss

Billie Sue Mosiman

WHAT HAS HAPPENED TO my very first manuscript? I have it somewhere, in some box stuffed away, who knows in what shed or cranny. It was shown to six publishers over a year's time by my very first agent and then I took it back and shut it away forever. I knew it wasn't good enough.

My First Manuscript

Elizabeth Daniels Squire

MY FIRST UNPUBLISHED MANUSCRIPT—at least, that I remember—was a *New Yorker*-type short story in which absolutely nothing happened but the relationship between a boa constrictor and members of a dysfunctional family.

I still like that story. Maybe if I redid it now, and had one member of the family train the boa constrictor to kill on command, the thing would sell.

Also, in the third novel in my Peaches Dann series, *Memory Can Be Murder*, I recycled an unusual murder weapon that showcased a character flaw in each victim. That weapon came from an early unpublished you-know-what. Never waste anything that resonates.

Now, can anybody out there tell me how to train a boa constrictor?

Mary Wings *Photo credit: Ponch Hawkes*

Interview with

Mary Wings

Adrian Muller

EMMA VICTOR, THE LESBIAN sleuth in the series of crime fiction novels by Mary Wings, was born in the Netherlands. Well, maybe not born, but she was certainly created in the small European country that borders on Germany, Belgium, and the North Sea. Mary had come to Holland for a two week holiday, fell in love with a woman who was living in a communal squat in Amsterdam, and ended up staying for eight years. In that time she learned the language so well that my question about her reasons for writing crime fiction was met by a reply in near-perfect Dutch: *"Ik had taal heimwee*—I was language lonely." Being half-British, half-Dutch myself, Mary and I are both happy for the opportunity of speaking our "foreign" language. In the London pub where I am interviewing the author, people around us look slightly bewildered at the noise emanating from our table, the conversation alternating between English and the strange guttural noises that typify the Dutch language.

Mary has fond recollections of Holland, a mellow country where, for example, it is not uncommon to personally handmake umpteen cards to be sent out announcing the birth of a baby, or to invite people to a party. "Dutch people tend to set aside time for doing creative things and I really liked that. Had I stayed in America," the author says, "I never would have written the novels. Everyone seems so ambitious in the States. If you write a book there it has to be a best-seller. To write for pleasure is almost unheard of."

Mary Wings found her creative writing outlet shortly after she decided to stay with her girlfriend in Holland. Her initial inability to understand everything spoken in the Dutch language led to a revealing self-discovery. The would-be author was attending a dinner party, enjoying what she believed to be a charming description of someone's holiday, only to later find out that the topic of conversation had been the Dutch occupation by Germany during World War II! "It was then that I realized I had a vivid fantasy world. When you live in a foreign country, and only have a limited understanding of its language, you tend to be very much dependent on your own imagination. That is how I came to start writing. I think I wrote the novels because I was homesick."

I am amazed to hear that Mary

Wings wrote the first two Emma Victor novels while she was in Amsterdam. It turns out that the realistic description of Boston in *She Came Too Late* and the San Francisco locale of *She Came in a Flash,* the second book in the series, came from memory or from books out of the public library situated on the *Prinsengracht*—one of Amsterdam's many canals. "Many people have said that they can feel the warmth of the sun when reading my novels. The reason there was so much sun in my books is because it rained so much in Holland. I suppose that writing was like a cheap flight to San Francisco."

Mary readily admits that Emma Victor is her alter ego, and that a large part of the enjoyment in writing the series comes from the fact that her protagonist allows her to do many of the things she would like to do as well. One of the author's major influences was Raymond Chandler but, when setting out to write her first crime novel, she decided it was high time that women were allowed their share of the fun and made her protagonist female. Not that the author's sleuth immediately stepped into the hard-boiled footsteps of private eye Philip Marlowe. In *She Came Too Late* Emma works for the Women's Hotline, and only becomes involved in crime because she feels guilty for not having arrived in time to prevent the death of one of the helpline callers. The reason that *She Came Too Late* is the only novel in the series to be set in Boston is because someone recognized the person the fictional murderer had been based on. "I couldn't allow that to happen, so I relocated the setting of *She Came Too Late* from San Francisco to Boston in an attempt to disguise the person I had written about. That's the trouble with crime fiction: you have to be careful if you base the murderer on a real person."

The question of whether Mary is bothered about being known as "the lesbian author with the lesbian private eye" is not one she can easily answer. The tag has both pros and cons. Wings feels that part of the reason that the manuscript for *She Came Too Late* was snapped up by the Women's Press, a British publishing company that is still first in releasing the books, was because she was the first author in Europe with a lesbian private eye as a leading protagonist. "Nowadays you can write a beautiful novel, and it still won't be published. My book was unusual, but I don't only write for the 'unusual' community, I want to reach the rest of the world as well. There might be people who put the books back on the shelf because they see the word 'lesbian' and that's a shame. It's sort of how I think about racism: if you participate in it you lose a lot, you don't learn about other worlds."

A brief question on whether "gay" is the current politically correct term for the lesbian and gay male community turns into an interesting discussion. There is some kind of resolve when Mary says, "It is easy for people to use the word 'gay'. It's a non-threatening word, it is one syllable, and it means happy. Whereas 'lesbian' has a Latin feel to it, like 'thespian'. It almost sounds like a medical phrase, I suppose lesbian women prefer to be called 'lesbian' because we sometimes feel overwhelmed by the male gay world. If lesbian women are called gay, I think it is because a lot of heterosexuals are comfortable with the word."

Unfortunately, the lesbian

author/protagonist tag is still the main source of interest for many journalists. "They interview me because I am an interesting story, the lesbian detective writer, but I need my books to be reviewed saying there is something for everybody in them." It doesn't help that Mary's novels often can't be found under "Crime Fiction" or even "Gay Literature,", they are frequently tucked away in "Gay Lesbian Detective Literature." "I'm in this tiny, tiny, little slot," the writer says sadly. A further reason for Mary's novels attracting attention is because they do not shy away from describing Emma's love life. "The books really exist on a lot of different levels, and I put sex in them because it happens in a lot of other suspense writing as well. However, in the same way you don't want to overwrite the blood, guts, and gore, the other thing you don't want to do is to overwrite the sex. If it is well done, it just adds a further aspect to what is an exiting story." The author recalls an occasion when she was on a promotional tour in Britain and a woman verbally attacked her for including descriptions of Emma making love. "She said, 'so you *admit* you want to make people excited. Why do you want to make people excited?' To which I replied, 'Why not?' I write for myself and my friends when I write, and I just try to be honest."

The author went through a weekend of hell as part of the research for the second Emma Victor novel. In *She Came in a Flash* Emma is on holiday in California but ends up looking into the death of her best friend's sister after her body has been found in the San Francisco Bay. When clues lead to the Vishnu Divine Inspiration Center, Emma goes undercover to find out what the connection is. In order to realistically describe the Inspiration Center, Mary spent a weekend at a Bhagwan retreat. "To fit in I borrowed red underwear, red sweaters, red socks, everything. It was a nightmare and I described it quite literally in the book. People throwing up, screaming, freaking out. It was very confessional, like everyone trying to have had the worst car accident. They keep you busy every second and it's supposed to be really great. You didn't have a chance to think or react to anything. It was like being back in kindergarten."

On the advice of a colleague, Mary had written the second Emma Victor novel before *She Came Too Late* was published. "If your first book receives good reviews, you end up competing with yourself. So, because my friend said the second book is always more difficult, I wrote the follow-up before the first one appeared." A wise move, as it turned out, because it took four years before Mary's third book, a gothic novel called *Divine Victim*, was published. The writer's block was largely due to what the author describes as "a culture shock to my own culture." The bizarre experience occurred when Mary was on what was supposed to be a brief visit back to the States. "I was so used to being in the *Jordaan* section of Amsterdam that in San Francisco many things felt foreign to me. The brown bags for carrying groceries, strangers saying, "Hi, how are you?" I would think, "How are you? You don't even know me!" I tried so hard to adapt to the Dutch way of living that I had become a stranger in my own country. It was such a shock that I decided to move back to the States. For a few years I was a real mess. I was dreaming in Dutch, speaking in English. I decided that the only way I could continue with Emma Victor was to write *Divine Victim.*" The author has described *Divine Victim* as the Stephen King version of *Lesbians Who Love Too Much,* and says it was influenced by Daphne du Maurier's *Rebecca,* had Rebecca been a lesbian. "It's about a woman in love with someone who doesn't always treat her well. Despite being a critical success, lesbian women stayed away in droves. They only wanted novels that featured positive role models."

When Emma Victor made her comeback in *She Came by the Book,* the intervening years had brought about a change in her character. Somewhat apprehensively I mention that, contrary to the earlier books, Emma seemed to have acquired a sense of humor and is less critical. Mary laughs out loud, "Yes, you are right. Emma has become less Dutch." The author goes on to describe a typical Dutch habit used for starting a discussion. "In Holland someone might say, 'Why did you say something like that?' in such a manner that it will take someone aback. It might not be intentional, but it can come across as very aggressive. *She Came by the Book* is much more out of myself and out of my own sensibilities, I think. These days I feel that Emma comes out of the end of my fingers and on to the paper. She's much more like me," As the title suggests, *She Came by the Book* has a literary setting. A murder occurs at the opening gala of the Howard Blooming Lesbian and Gay Memorial, Howard Blooming being a flamboyant politician assassinated some twenty years earlier. Mary says that this Emma mystery was the most fun to write because "the real secret of *She Came by the Book* is that this novel challenges everybody's idea of what is gay and what is straight." To say anything more would spoil the surprise.

Strangely enough, now the author has started writing crime fiction she has stopped reading much of it. "I tend to keep a few things around by friends, people I know, people I have heard of. Right now I am reading Val McDermid, who I think is really good. The last time I was in Britain she said, 'You've got to write straight books, you will reach a much wider audience,' but I can't do that because I realize that what I really want to do is describe this gay and lesbian community in San Francisco."

In between writing books the author has organized classes for people interested in writing crime fiction. She calls them "The Mary Wings Magical Mystery Weekends," and her eyes light up when she discusses the project. "Boy, do I like giving that writing class. People were asking me questions on how to write these books, so I thought, "I'm going to construct a little 'fun weekend' with all these crazy things I make these people do, like treasure hunts." One of the things you have to do when you write suspense is to draw out that one moment. In order for people to realize how to do that, I hide little skeletons. Once they have found them, they have to take twenty steps back and, in every step forward, they have to build up and describe the suspense." Mary also uses newspaper articles about real murders, getting the participants to describe the points of view of the murderer, victim, witnesses, etc. There is also a lesson called "How to

Write Prose Like a Camera." Part of this class involves a showing of the 1946 film *Lady in the Lake,* in which all the action is shown from Philip Marlowe's point of view. "How they did that was by making the camera Philip Marlowe's eyes. The audience only see him when he stands in front of a mirror. It is that feeling of being there, the 'first-person camera work,' that you should be able to conjure up as an author. When people see the film they understand what I mean right away." People with a variety of backgrounds have taken the class and one person, Robyn Vinten, has had a short story published in *Reader, I Murdered Him, Too,* a Women's Press crime fiction anthology. "It is called *The Man in the Hat,* and it is very good," says Wings, adding , "What I really try and get people to realize is that language is something that you discover, and language is there for you to use. It's fun. It's really, really fun."

The author has also tried her hand at writing some film treatments for what she calls "film and TV money." "It pays well, but they go through millions of committees and nothing ever happens. God forbid, if one of my books was made into an American movie. I would take the money and close my eyes." No doubt some of these experiences will find their way into *She Came in the Castro,* the fourth Emma Victor novel. "*She Came in the Castro* is about film and the film industry, set in and around San Francisco's Castro Theater. The reason *She Came Too Late* was such a success, I think, was because it was largely set in the gay and lesbian community. To put Emma in a different kind of community didn't feel right, it wasn't really what I wanted to do. So I decided to place all of the books in the gay and lesbian community where, of course, everyone can be as nasty as anywhere else."

Mary Wings concludes happily, "I have decided to keep going on with the Emma series, and I am so glad to be back in America."

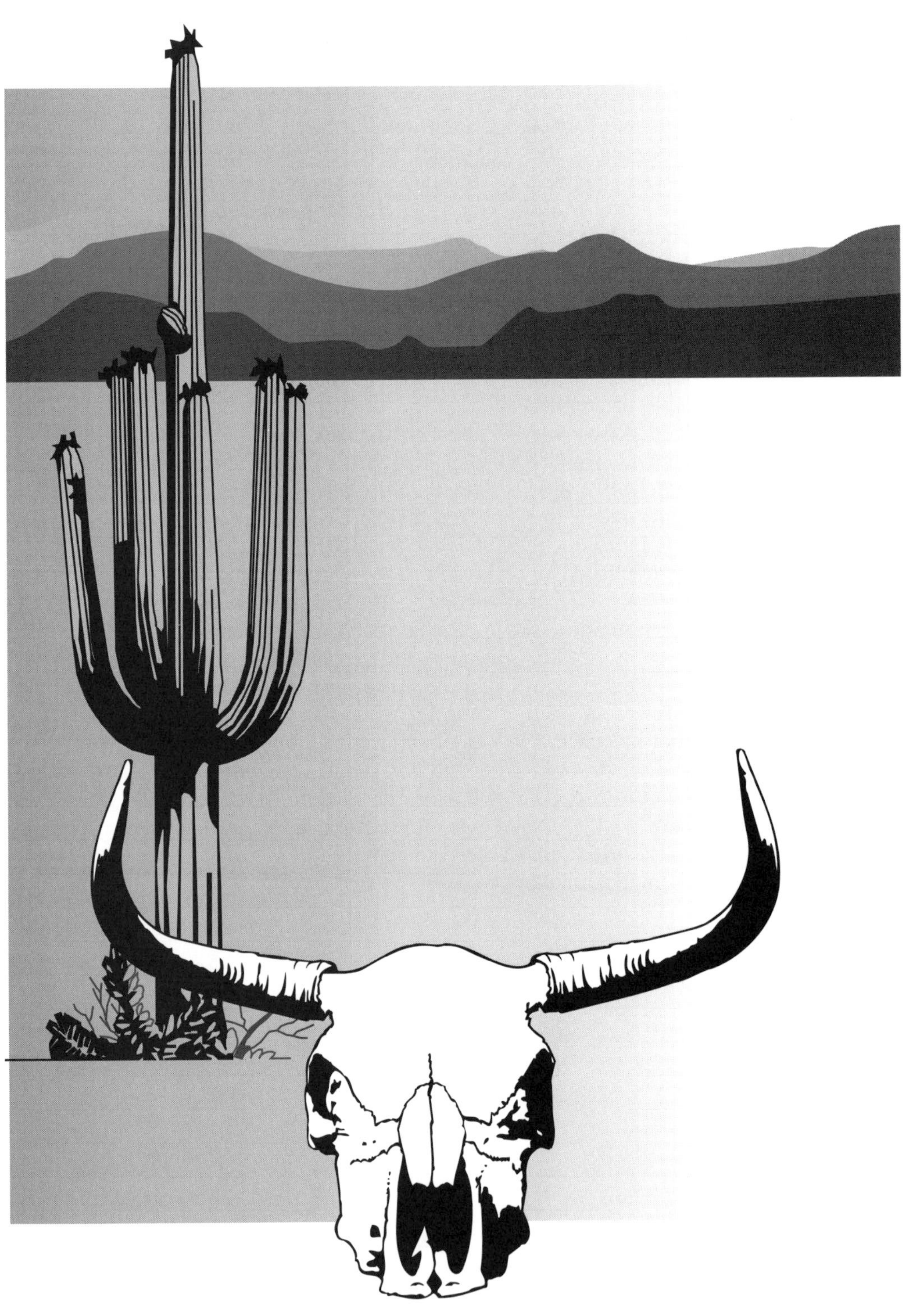

Interview with

J.A. Jance

Rylla Goldberg

J.A. (JUDY) JANCE AND I are definitely an odd couple, if one judges by appearances. She is tall, elegant, blonde; I'm short, no longer thin, and am learning to like gray hair. So much for looks. In the ways that matter, Judy and I have several things in common: we love stories (she tells them, I read them); we love hats and wear them often; and we both know what it's like to survive loving someone who is an alcoholic.

I met Judy nearly five years ago when I was working at an alcohol and drug abuse outpatient treatment center in Seattle. I was invited to be a guest co-host on "Straight Talk," a new radio talk show on the subject of recovery. The producer, a Philip Marlowe wannabe, accepted my idea of doing a piece about alcoholic fictional detectives who enter a recovery program. I suggested we start with J.A. Jance, whose protagonist, Seattle homicide detective J.P. Beaumont, was in treatment at an Arizona alcohol rehab ranch in *Minor in Possession.* I hoped she would talk about Beau's addiction and recovery. Happily, she was entertaining and articulate on the air (many people become monosyllabic when the mike is turned on) and the show was a wonderful success.

In the eleven years since Judy's first Beaumont book was published, her repertoire of mysteries has grown to include short stories in magazines and anthologies, three novels in her Arizona series featuring Joanna Brady, and a baker's dozen of Beau's adventures (number thirteen, *Name Withheld,* was released in January 1995).

PS: Beau is still in recovery.

You seem to enjoy the business side of producing books, and you participate in a variety of marketing and promotion activities here and elsewhere. Members of your family pitch in to help and they seem to enjoy it, too. Was it difficult at first for you to make the transition from writer to marketer? Since at any given time you are working ahead of—or even in a different series from—the book being promoted, do you have to remind yourself sometimes that *it's Tuesday so I must be in Rome?*

Actually, after ten years in life insurance sales, the initial transition was from marketer to writer and then back. I grew up in a large family, the daughter of a life insurance salesman and a full-time homemaker. I started in sales early—homemade jewelry, Girl Scout cookies, newspaper subscriptions, and all-occasion greeting cards. In our family, selling was everybody's business with my mother dishing out the "leads" about new folks in town over the breakfast table. Once my first book was published, I took up where my mother left off. I'd do signings with my two kids—nine and ten—handing out brochures on the sidewalk or in the parking lot. To this day, either I or some member of the family, calls our list—a thousand-name data base—to announce the arrival of a new book and to invite people to the grand opening event.

And as far as juggling multiple balls, my ability to do that comes from growing up in a large family. Living in a household with two parents and seven children with only one two-doored bathroom teaches focus in a way nothing else can.

Speaking of promotion and travel, how much of the year do you spend thinking about, researching, and writing a book compared to the amount of time required to market it? When your first book was published did you think it would be like this eleven years later, that so much time and energy would be spent to sell a book after all you went through to create it?

I think a lot of new authors come to this business thinking their responsibility ends once the writing and rewriting are all done. At the time my first book was published I had no idea how much of the selling job would be mine as well. For the first nine books, there was almost no publisher-paid touring, and only one out-of-state trip to L.A. Nonetheless, every book still had a minimum of thirty signings. Many of those were in the local, Puget Sound area. The ones that weren't—Arizona, California, Oregon, and Idaho—were accomplished on our own time and our own nickel, often making use of my husband's hard-earned frequent flyer miles. The bottom line is that those initial signings, publisher supported or not, helped create my very local fan base.

Early on, the job was 50/50—50 percent writing and 50 percent promoting, including speaking to any number of civic groups. Now, as the publisher picks up more and more of the slack, I'd say the division is more like 60 percent writing/40 percent spending time with my fans.

Computer technology allows you to keep writing almost anywhere. How about the times when the plane is late, a road is closed, or some other obstacle forces a change in plans?

I have a little laptop that goes in and out with me. Actually, I was a very early adopter of laptop technology, starting with a dual floppy that I bought second hand from a real estate appraiser who wanted to unload the computer in favor of a pickup truck. Since then I've worn out three Toshiba laptops and have used them everywhere. When I bought my first computer in 1983, I could look up words in my dictionary faster than I could do it with the computer since I had to exit one program and call up another in order to use either the spell-checker or the Thesaurus. In twelve short years, we really have come a long way, baby.

Are you planning to distribute you books electronically, perhaps via a network or on CD-ROM? Do you think this method of distribution will be the norm in the future? Aside from copyright protection, which is a prime concern, do you think electronic distribution will open the flood gates to poor writing and leave

the better quality writing and paper publishers scrambling for markets and readers?

At this point, other than audio-taped versions of my books, I have no plans of stepping onto the information highway where I would no doubt end up as cyber roadkill. I use computers all the time, but right now I can't see how CD-ROMS will ever compete with an ordinary book for ease of use, privacy, and plain old convenience. I went on a weekend trip to a cabin once, expecting to do some last-minute editing on a manuscript. It turned out, though, that the cabin ran on propane and my computer did not. So, rather than working on my manuscript, what did I do instead? I read somebody else's book. The propane lights didn't make any difference when it came to reading words on the printed page.

How do you manage your writing, family, and social schedules? Is this easier or harder to do now than it was when all or some of your children were home?

Friends and family are very important. Both my husband and I had first spouses who died in their early forties. We came away from those tough experiences with absolute knowledge that life is not forever, so if it comes to a choice between doing something with family and friends and doing work, family and friend are going to win every time. Between us Bill and I had five children when we married in 1985, and four of them were still at home. Now that they're all out on their own, scheduling—and mealtimes—are much easier to manage, but there were any number of books that were written in a household that contained a husband, four kids, three dogs, and no fence. Once again, growing up in a large family saved my life. I learned to concentrate by doing homework on a bench at the kitchen table with the ebb and flow of life swirling around me.

You are very much a public figure in our community. Do you wish sometimes that you could be anonymous when you and Bill go out in public? For example, do restaurant owners or other merchants respect your privacy?

It is a little disconcerting to run into the grocery store in a pair of sweats and have people pointing me out over the stacks of fresh vegetables. It happened in Costco just this last weekend. Still, to have perfect strangers come up to you in the store aisle to tell you how much they love what you do is a real blessing. After all, there are lots of jobs where that *never* happens. For instance, whoever stopped a parking enforcement officer on the street to tell them how much they appreciate what the officer does?

***Writer's Digest* recently asked a panel of published writers to name the "most influential writer of out time." A majority chose Ernest Hemmingway. Which four or five writers have influenced you the most? Has that list changed in the years you've been writing fiction full time?**

Reading Frank Baum's *Wizard of Oz* in second grade was enough to convince me that I wanted to be a writer. I was a voracious reader as a child, racing through the Nancy Drew, Hardy Boys, and Judy Bolton mysteries as well as every Zane Grey western I could lay my hands on. I eventually went on to Mickey Spillane and John D. McDonald. In terms of writing a series, I'd have to say that J.P. Beaumont owes a whole lot to McDonald's Travis Magee.

What books or which writers do you read now, compared to what you read before Beau entered your life?

James Lee Burke, Lawrence Block, Lindsey Davis. Right now, though, I'm lost in an eight-hundred page Rosamund Pilcher. I think writing a series allows the same kind of connection to the characters that you get from one of those long family sagas. The only difference is, if you read in bed and fall asleep in the process of reading one of my books, you don't risk hurting your nose the way I might with Pilcher's *Coming Home.*

Speaking of writers, were there other writers in your family before you? Are any of your children writing or being published?

I was the first person in my family to go to the university. My father attended a teacher's college for a year. One of his instructors encouraged him to consider doing some writing, but the Depression and any number of children precluded his following that advice. So perhaps, then, the genetic inclination was there, but so far none of my children is showing any particular bent in that direction.

Who, besides writers, have been heroes to you or exerted the greatest influence on your life?

Because her vision was so poor and the family could not afford to pay for glasses, my mother was forced to drop out of school in seventh grade to go to work as a maid in Minneapolis. Despite her own lack of formal education, she encouraged me to get all I could out of school, including offering to let me skip some of the household chores in favor of taking extra classes in high school. Without necessarily realizing what she was doing, that tactic put me on a college prep track, and it's paid big dividends in the long run.

Along with many of your readers, I believe *Hour of the Hunter* is the best novel you've written so far. Are you planning any other non-series books? If yes, when? If no, why not? How about writing in another form, such as a screen or stage play?

Hour of the Hunter was a real departure, and it's also my personal favorite. I've written a sequel, *Kiss of the Bees,* that is currently in a publishing scheduling limbo, but it will be out eventually. Meantime, both the Beaumont and Brady books continue aspace, letting me do what I've always wanted to do which is write books. As for screenplays or plays? I don't do windows and I don't do screenplays, either.

The poems published in *After the Fire* are offered to anyone who is going or has gone through emotional trauma. The rage and pain were very real to you when you wrote them. (They have a healing effect on me.) But that was a dark time in your life. What about now? Do you use poetry to express the emotional highs, too? If yes, are you planning to publish any of these poems?

"I'll live with nothing rather than with less. The flame is out. There's nothing left but ash."

The emotional desolation in those words from the title poem speak to anyone who has loved and lost. You're right, the poetry was written at a very dark time in my life. Those bits of verse, jotted off on spare scraps of paper in the dark of night, acted as little pressure valves for me as I dealt with the grim realities of being married to a man who was dying of alcoholism.

However, it was doing a poetry reading of *After the Fire* at a widowed retreat where I met Bill, my second husband. He and I have just celebrated our tenth anniversary, so I can assure you that the poetry had a very healing effect on my life as well. Writing was a way of pouring out my soul at a time when no one was listening. Now, living a life that can best be described as happy as a clam with a loving, listening partner, I find that someone has turned off the poetry switch in my heart. I, for one, think that's just as well.

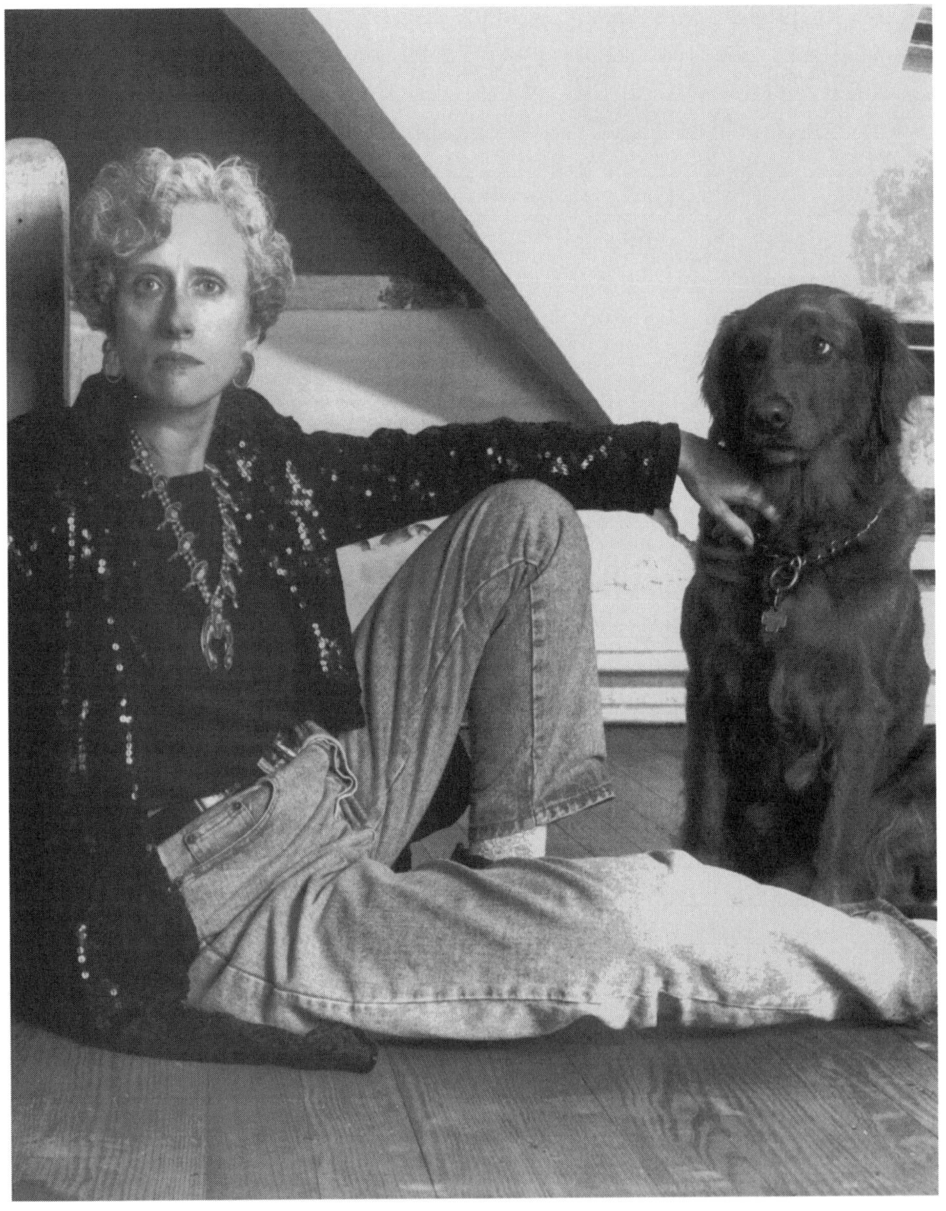

Sara Paretsky *Photo credit: David Carter*

Interview with
Sara Paretsky

Dean James

FEW WRITERS HAVE HAD the impact upon the whole genre of the mystery novel which Sara Paretsky has had. In 1982, she published the first in her series of novels about Chicago private investigator V.I. (Victoria Iphigenia) Warshawski. *Indemnity Only* was not the first novel written by a woman about a contemporary private eye, for Paretsky followed both P.D. James and Marcia Muller by several years, and also in 1982 Sue Grafton published her first Kinsey Millhone novel. What made Paretsky immediately distinctive, however, was the strong feminist voice of her character and her interpretation of the conventions of the classic hard-boiled private eye novel. V.I. Warshawski has a passionate attachment to justice, and she fearlessly does what she feels she must in order to see that justice is done. Another distinctive feature of the series is the setting itself, Chicago, for Paretsky makes the city, its history and its politics an integral feature of each story. V.I.'s cases often pit her against corrupt institutions, and in this way we see the private detective battling against great odds to ensure that personal justice is not sacrificed for the sake of corporate profits.

Sara Paretsky's novels frequently appear on the best-seller lists here and abroad, and *Blood Shot* (published in the U.K. as *Toxic Shock*) won the Crime Writers Association Silver Dagger in 1988. In addition to her writing, Paretsky was also a significant force behind the founding of the organization, Sisters in Crime and served as its first president. From her home in Chicago, she graciously answered my questions about her career and her forthcoming works.

Which writers, if any, have influenced you in your conception of the mystery novel?

When I started my first novel, *Indemnity Only,* I followed the conventions of the hard-boiled form as laid out by Chandler and refined by Ross MacDonald, rather slavishly. This meant, among other things, that I gave my heroine a confrontational relationship with the police, built the action towards a physical confrontation between the thugs and V.I., and ended the book with the heroine alone and depressed. As time had passed, my work has become much more interior, responding to my own evolving vision of human and social issues, and largely ignoring the ways in which other writers solve the problems that we all confront.

One of the distinctive qualities of your books is the strong emphasis on the

moral and political ethos which V.I. represents. How does the "form" of the mystery novel suit the purposes of what you want to say in your books? Why is this medium more effective that another might be?

The mystery is ideally suited for addressing social issues. The crime novel is the place where law, justice, and society naturally intersect. This does not mean that every crime novel needs to deal with these issues, nor that every crime novel deals well with these issues, but that if social and justice concerns are on your mind a crime novel is the natural place to address them. In Saul Bellow's *The Dean's December*, Bellow fulminates about the problem of crime in Chicago through an extended reminiscence or flashback of his main character while the man is in Romania. The structure is awkward at best. It is possible to show the effect of a terrible crime on ordinary people's lives as Rosellen Brown does in *Before and After* but that is a much different kind of novel.

How do you balance the "issue" with the "entertainment" factor?

First and foremost I am a storyteller. The issues that I deal with are ones that I think of naturally and which wed themselves naturally to the story I am telling. The books which seek only to explore an issue are, in my opinion, quite arid. Novelist Carol Anshaw remarks that writers sometimes get wedded to an idea—perhaps welded to an idea would be a better way to put it—and that that idea then strangles the work. I believe that this is a real pitfall and one which I work hard to avoid.

Chicago is very much a "character" in all the books. How crucial is the setting, in your mind, to each of the books? Which does setting influence more, the characters or the plot?

I first came to Chicago in the summer of 1966 to do community service work on the south side. That was the summer that Martin Luther King, Jr. tried to work for open housing in Chicago. It was a vital and frustrating time in the life of the city. The life I experienced in the neighborhoods that summer, the struggles of ordinary people to make a decent life for themselves and their children, the cynicism with which banks and realtors treated the neighborhoods, all made a lasting impression on me. That summer informed my view of the difficulty that ordinary people have when faced with large and pitiless institutions. For that rea-

son, Chicago dominates the way in which I think about life, power, and justice. In that way the city influences both characters and plot equally because both depend on the size, the impersonality and yet the vitality of life in the neighborhoods.

V.I. is a complex character, who has grown tremendously since her first appearance. What qualities in her do you most admire? Which ones frustrate you? (Does she ever refuse to do what you want, for example?)

When I started the series I was so lacking in confidence in what I might do that I gave V.I. all the qualities of the typical loner hero—she is alone, an orphan and without lasting attachments. It soon became clear to me that this was a most arid landscape for my own vision, and other characters began to populate the scene, most notably Lottie and Mr. Contreras. V.I. values integrity and loyalty above all other traits. These are both her strengths and her weaknesses because they lead her to pursue justice in a passionate way that hurts the people that she is closest to. For instance, in *Tunnel Vision* it was my intention that she and Conrad would stay together. Yet, in the course of the book, I found that her independence, her impatience, and her single-minded pursuit of the truth threw a major wedge between her and him. I don't know what she can do to resolve those very painful issues in her life.

What sparks a novel for you and makes you say, "Yes. *This* is what I want to write about?"

I don't know how to answer this question. Sometimes the idea of a character—as Hattie Frizell in *Guardian Angel*—and sometimes the mind-boggling scope of corporate corruption—as happened in *Blood Shot*—will have that kind of an effect on me. But I can't identify ahead of time what will happen that will make me want to tell a story.

What are the challenges for you as a writer to maintain an interest in a series character? Do you ever want to give V.I. a vacation for a few years and do something different?

A series character has to keep changing and also have conflicts that are not resolved. For instance, if V.I. ever resolved the tension that she experiences between her need for intimacy and her need for independence, it would be hard for me to imagine how to keep the series going in other than a wooden way.

Rex Stout wrote seventy very suc-

cessful Nero Wolfe stories by telling in some ways the same story of Wolfe and Archie over and over. That is what gives those books their abiding appeal—the comfort of stepping into that unchanging world on Tenth Avenue. My books are more interior. They come out of the emotional and social issues that I am wrestling with at the time that I write them. It would not be possible for me to keep that kind of stasis in my own work because my writing is so personal. That does not mean that it is better, just that it is mine. And yes, not only do I want to give V.I. a vacation in order to keep the voice with which I tell her stories fresh, but I am about to do so. Dell is publishing the collected V.I. stories, including an original novella—*Grace Notes*—in November. After that I will be working on something completely different.

What has surprised you the most, or perhaps brought you the most pleasure, with regard to your career as a writer, in the thirteen years since *Indemnity Only* was first published?

The wide appeal of V.I. to readers of many ages, both sexes, and diverse backgrounds, both in the U.S. and overseas, has brought me enormous pleasure. I feel honored by the support of this wide range of readers, and I try to live up to my obligations to them.

Do you have any regrets over the movie which starred Kathleen Turner as V.I?

Both Ms. Turner and I wish that script had been stronger and less slapsticky. However, the movie brought pleasure to millions of viewers and it had this major redeeming feature: it is one of the few feature films to have an action figure who is female and who does resolve her own problems without needing to sacrifice all for love in the end.

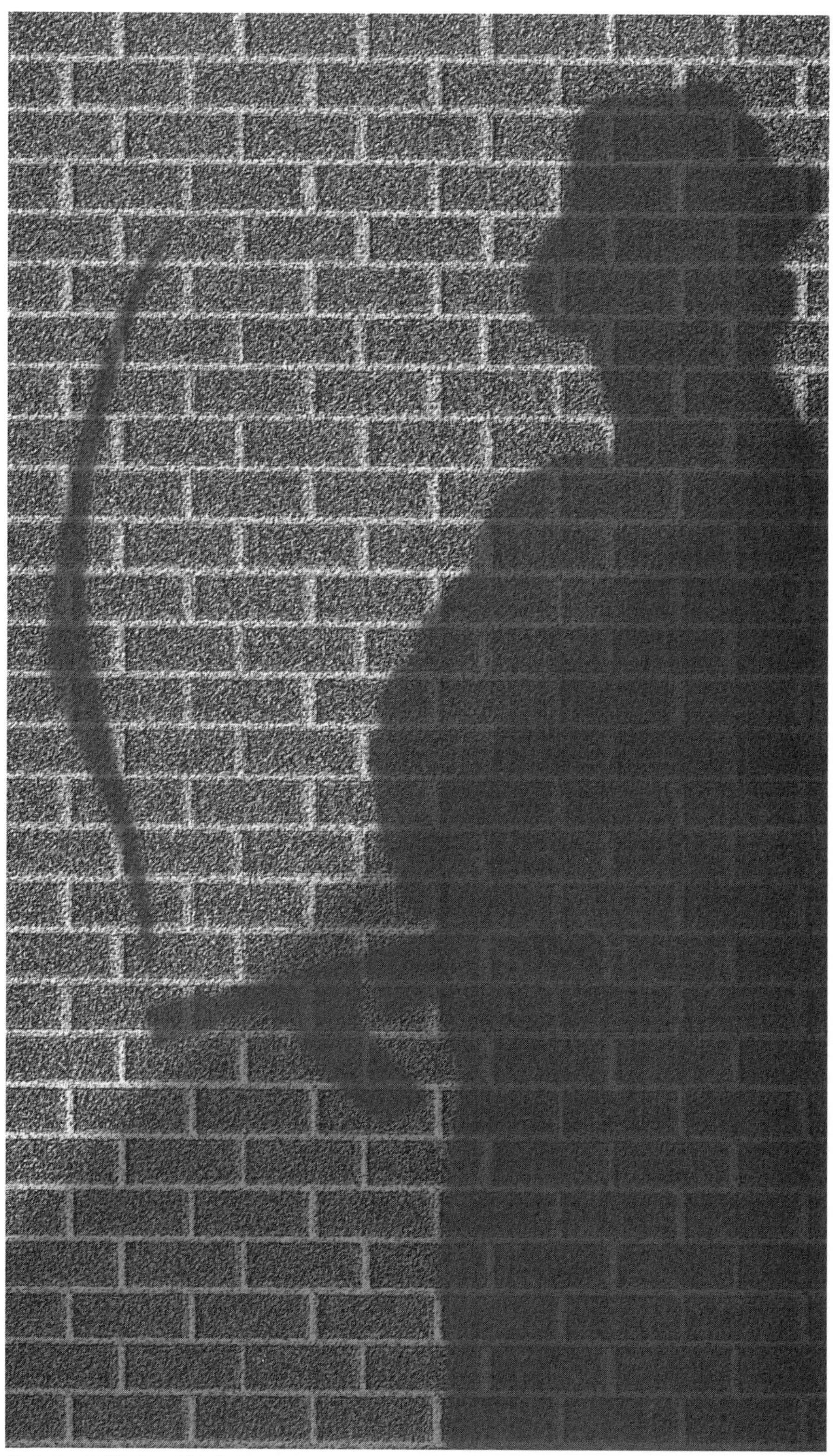

Deadly Allies

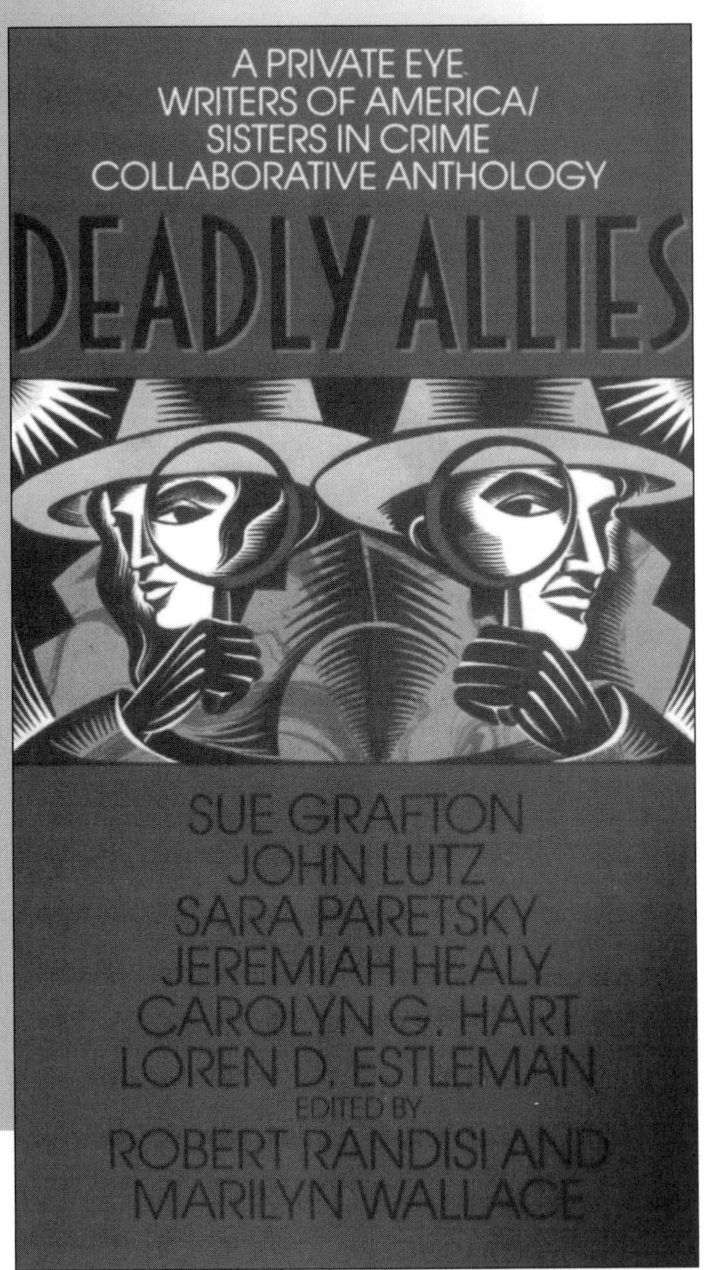

Deadly Allies
A Private Eye Writers of America/
Sisters in Crime collaborative anthology

Chipping Away at Affirmative Action

P.M. (Pat) Carlson

When Sisters in Crime was founded seven years ago, the U.S. mystery field was basically an affirmative action program for men.

PUBLISHERS GAVE MEN SPECIAL encouragement to write mysteries: they accepted twice as many men's books for publication as women's.

Reviewers gave men special encouragement: the *New York Times*, for example, reviewed five times as many mysteries by men as by women.

The major mystery organization, Mystery Writers of America, gave men special encouragement: for decades, the Edgar Award for Best Mystery Novel had never gone to an American woman.

It's not that these folks said, "Hey, today I guess I'll go favor a man mystery writer over a woman mystery writer." As in the rest of society, many people in the mystery field just assumed, without thinking, that men's ideas and men's books were more important and interesting and "universal" than women's. The rest followed.

Sisters in Crime was formed by women who challenged this assumption. We set out to educate ourselves about the problems. We gathered facts. We counted books and reviews and Guests of Honor and awards, and we told people what we'd learned.

And we kept reading, and writing, wonderful mysteries, and told people about them too.

We're still at it, always with the accent on the positive. This year a marvelously energetic and sensible Steering Committee worked with many other Sisters on many things—a White House mystery library, new local chapters including a GEnie electronic chapter, a Sisters in Crime miniseries scheduled for Lifetime TV, new attention from chain stores,

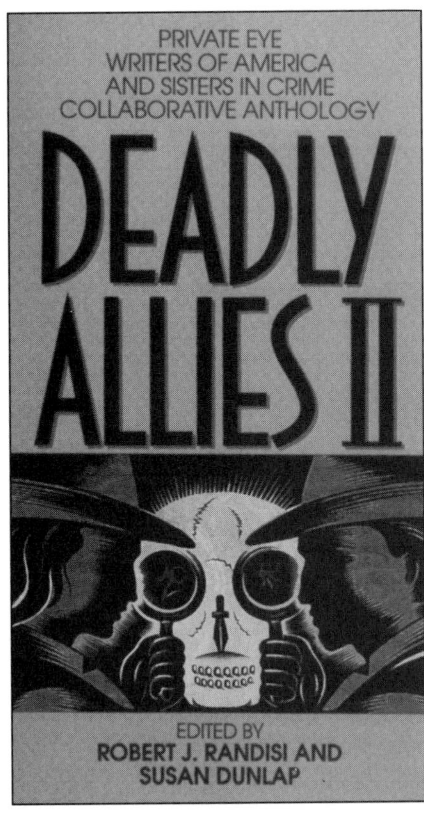

***Deadly Allies* II**
A Private Eye Writers of America/ Sisters in Crime collaborative anthology

a galvanizing speech from Sara Paretsky at the Toronto Bouchercon, a quarterly newsletter (special thanks to Margaret Maron!), and too many more to list.

To me as a writer, one of the most important things about Sisters in Crime is less tangible. As other Sisters show the breadth and depth and delight that our mysteries can provide, I get the courage to dig deeper and range wider too. So a special salute goes to these splendid writers and to the wonderful readers, booksellers, teachers, and librarians who affirm the importance of the funny, sad, inspiring, enraging, thoughtful, delightful stories that women have to tell.

In addition to wonderful books and an organization full of brains and talent and incredible energy, Sisters in Crime has two big pluses in the campaign to educate the public and the publishing industry about women's contributions to mysteries. First, supportive readers have been buying and loving mysteries by women all along, and new fans appeared when the word went out that these books are available. Our positive approach made the pie bigger. Second, while we often put other things first, most of us Americans want to be fair. Yes, Virginia, even publishers. Even reviewers. Even Mystery Writers of America.

We're making progress. In 1992, 40 percent of mysteries published were by women. Men are still favored, but now a mystery is not twice as likely to be by a man, it's only one-and-a-half times as likely to be by a man.

Our Book Review Monitoring project showed a market increase in fairness on the part of many newspapers. It's still true that where there is favoritism it almost always favors books by men, but it's clear that many papers are much more fair.

And for the second time in these seven years, an American woman won the MWA Edgar Award for Best Novel.

It's not yet time to quit, but we're chipping away at the mystery field's affirmative action program for men. The progress is real. And so are the friendships and joys of working together to make our favorite corner of the world a little fairer.

President Salutes Past, Looks to Future

Annette Meyers

As we begin celebrating our tenth anniversary year, Sisters in Crime membership has reached 3,200 worldwide and continues to grow rapidly. One-third of us are published authors. We have forty-two chapters: thirty-nine in the U.S., two in Canada, and our newest chapter is in Hamburg, Germany.

WE ARE MOST PROUD of our beautiful, twice-a-year *Books in Print* catalogue, with great covers by Trina Robbins and printed by Gavin Faulkner. It has been so successful in celebrating our authors that other writers' organizations are following our lead.

This year the catalogue was sent to more than ten thousand wholesalers, distributors, libraries, independent bookstores and chains. The pull-out insert listing our authors who write young adult and juvenile has been incredibly effective.

So where do we go from here?

Eve Sandstrom is ending her service as editor of the newsletter. She has done a fabulous job. Ruthe Furie will be coming on as editor this month. We are going to redesign and restructure the newsletter to create an easier-to-read, more professional publication. You'll begin to see the changes in the next issue.

The newsletter connects us to each other and to what's happening in the field. Use it. Make it work for you. Highlight what's important to you. Cut out the appropriate items, conference dates, deadlines, pin them up where you'll see them every day. It works!

We are going to concentrate on opening channels to editors and publishers. Last year, sixty-three million mystery and detective novels were purchased (an increase of six million from the year before).

Mystery and detective novels represent 12.5 percent of all adult books sold. There are mutual benefits that can come from just meeting on the "bridge."

Patty Sleem is our new *Books in Print* editor. We're designing a new registration form, which should help clarify the information we need for your listing.

When you get the form, send it back quickly. It costs you nothing. You don't want to be left out. Libraries and bookstores all over the world read *Books in Print* and use it as a guide for ordering books.

Vicki Cameron, Patty Sleem, Barbara Burnett Smith, and Janice Steinberg have joined the board. Vicki is our troubleshooter and is working on the proposed 1999 Writers Retreat. Barbara Burnett Smith takes over for Marlys Millhiser, coordinating our growing chapters. Janice Steinberg is special interests groups coordinator.

Board member Patti Sprinkle is always available for publicity advice or with ideas.

If something works for you, tell us about it.

Beth Wasson, our executive secretary, is our good-humored, steady lifeline.

She knows what's happening.

We want to hear from you. That goes for all the membership, whether you are an author, editor, agent, librarian, or a reader. Let us know what you're thinking. Let us know if you're interested in volunteering for one of our special projects.

For Sisters in Crime, this has been an amazing ten years. From our first year with our first president, Sara Paretsky, our goals have not changed. We still advocate the level playing field.

We are an inclusive organization. Sisters in Crime promotes all types of writing in the mystery/suspense genre, from cozy to hard-boiled, true crime, nonfiction, novels, and short stories.

I am honored to take the helm as president at this particular time and look forward to an exciting year of working together, a year dense with reading, writing, selling and camaraderie.

Best wishes for the holiday season and a very happy, healthy New Year.

Former Presidents Lead Celebration

Eve K. Sandstrom

Sisters in Crime began its second decade with a salute to its first at a tenth anniversary celebration October 12.

DURING THE ANNUAL MEETING held in conjunction with the celebration, 1995—96 president Elaine Raco Chase said that SinC now has 3,200 members.

"We're more than Sisters in Crime," she said. "We have quite a few brothers . . . Everybody's mystery novel stands on its own. We're not after replacing all men authors."

Members present also elected Annette Meyers 1996-97 president, heard reports from officers and committee chairs, and acted on routine business.

Other new officers are Sue Henry, vice president; Medora Sale, secretary; and Mary Lou Wright, treasurer. Board members-at-large will be Patricia Houck Sprinkle, Barbara Burnett Smith, Vicki Cameron, Janice Steinberg and Patty Sleem. Thirty-one mail-in ballots were included in the election count.

Founder and first president Sara Paretsky contributed champagne and orange juice mimosas for the 320 members who attended the breakfast meeting held during Bouchercon 27 in St. Paul Minnesota.

Paretsky was one of eight present and past presidents who were at the celebration. Also taking part in the tenth anniversary tribute were former presidents Margaret Maron, 1989—90; Carolyn Hart, 1991-92; P.M. Carlson, 1992-93; Linda Grant, 1993-94; and Barbara D'Amato, 1994-95. Only two former presidents Nancy Pickard, 1988-89, and Susan Dunlap, 1990-91, were unable to attend.

D'Amato recalled that she was warned that her year was likely to be a tough one, because by 1994 SinC had become strong enough to make some segments of the mystery world feel threatened.

"But it turned out to be an easy one," D'Amato said. "It was the year many groups began to see that what we were doing worked, and instead of opposing us, they began to adopt many of our programs."

In brief remarks, Paretsky recalled the twenty-six women who gathered for breakfast at the Baltimore Bouchercon in 1986 to discuss common concerns of women mystery writers and readers. Among these, she said, were the prevalence of graphic violence against women in "what passed for" mystery novels and the disparity in the numbers of reviews received by men and women writers.

Paretsky led a toast to Sisters in Crime and its first ten years. "Let us pledge that we will never again know another season of silence," she said.

Photo credit: Vicki Cameron

Saluting the first ten years of Sisters in Crime's history at the annual meeting were eight of the writers who have served SinC as president. From left are ***Annette Meyers,*** *1996–97;* ***Margaret Maron,*** *1989–90;* ***Barbara D'Amato,*** *1994–95;* ***Carolyn Hart,*** *1991–92;* ***P.M. Carlson,*** *1992–93;* ***Sara Paretsky,*** *1987–88;* ***Linda Grant,*** *1993–94; and* ***Elaine Raco Chase,*** *1995–96.*

The Private Eye Writers of America "A Very Personal Reflection"

Robert J. Randisi

It was January of 1982 when the first issue of the PWA newsletter, Reflections in a Private Eye, *came out. It was mailed to forty people. Included, on the last few pages, was the first roll of PWA.*

HERE ARE THE NAMES that appeared on that roll: Franklin Bandy, Lawrence Block, Terry Beatty, Max Byrd, William E. Chambers, Max Collins, William L. DeAndrea, Loren D. Estleman, William Campbell Gault, Stephen Greenleaf, Edward D. Hoch, Richard Hoyt, H. Edward Hunsburger, Stuart Kaminsky, Joe R. Lansdale, J.J. Lamb, Elliott Lewis, John Lutz, Dennis Lynds (Michael Collins), Don McGregor, Richard Meyers, Stephen Mertz, Marcia Muller, Warren Murphy, Maxine O'Callaghan, Percy S. Parker, Talmage Powell, Bill Pronzini, Robert J. Randisi, James Reasoner, Bob Shayne, Jory Sherman, Lewis Shiner, Ross Spenser, and Chris Steinbrunner. Nonactive members at the time were Billy Palmer, Michael Seidman, and Bruce Taylor. There were also two names on a mailing list, people who were not members but who were receiving the newsletter: Isadore Haiblum and Elmore Leonard.

I had started PWA earlier, in 1981, and on the first page of this initial issue of the newsletter I explain why. To boil it down, I had been corresponding with most of these people for some time, and the letter writing was getting to be a chore. I decided to *organize* us so that I could communicate with everyone through a newsletter. Also, I created

PWA logo by Terry Beatty

the "Shamus" Award to honor and recognize P.I. writing, which I felt, at the time, was not being properly acknowledged. I sent a letter to about twenty of the people whose names appear above, asking them to send me a quarter if they were interested in another mailing, to cover postage. I received twenty-five cents from Block, Collins, Estleman, Greenleaf, Hoch, Kaminsky, Lansdale, Lutz, Lynds, Muller, Murphy, Pronzini, Reasoner, and some others. The list blurs sixteen years later, but to the best of my knowledge these were the "charter" members of PWA. Over the course of about half a year that membership swelled to include all the names you see above. I asked Bill Pronzini to serve as our first president, while I served as vice-president. I did this because I considered Bill to be not only one of the biggest influences on me as a P.I. writer, but one of the most recognizable names in the field. He gracefully agreed to serve a two-year term. (I did not become president myself until 1997.)

PWA's newsletter, *Reflections In A Private Eye*—affectionately referred to as R.I.P.E.—continues to be published and is edited by the current vice-president of PWA, Jan Grape. Contact Jan for questions about joining at 11804 Oak Trail, Austin, TX 78753-2319, Tel: 512-339-1615, Fax: 512-339-1696, E-mail: Jangrape@aol.com

You will doubtlessly notice that on the original list of PWA members there are only two women, Marcia Muller and Maxine O'Callaghan. However, I soon approached Sue Grafton, Sara Paretsky, and Linda Barnes to join, and in time Sue was elected president. Marcia Muller later served as a vice-president, and still later (1993) received the Life Achievement Award. She has the distinction of being the only woman, to date, to be presented with it. I'm sure at least two more—Sue Grafton and Sara Paretsky—will follow sometime later in their now relatively young careers.

At present there are ninety-two active male members of PWA, and fifty-two female members. We have published two anthologies, *Lethal Ladies I* and *II*, which have featured short stories by only female members, and two previous anthologies, *Deadly Allies I* and *II*, were published in collaboration with Sisters-in-Crime, all of which illustrates that PWA never has and never will be a gender-segregated organization. We will continue to count among our members some of the best "writers" of P.I. fiction in the genre, male or female.

We have, and always will be, Deadly Allies.

* * *

Bill Pronzini was the first in a long line of high profile presidents: Lawrence Block (one year), Michael Collins (one year), William Campbell Gault (one year), John Lutz, Sue Grafton, Jeremiah Healy, Les Roberts, Parnell Hall, and myself followed. The position began largely as a figurehead one at that time—by design—requiring only that the president "say" he or she was president in their bios, and attend the awards ceremonies.

It was not until Jeremiah Healy became president that the office became "active," and this was by Jerry's design. He proceeded to serve for two years not only as president but as an ambassador at large, talking about PWA wherever he went, carrying applications for membership with him.

When Jan took over as editor of *R.I.P.E.*, Sue Grafton was the president and Jan asked Ms. Grafton if she would write a brief "president's message" for each issue. Sue agreed and the president's column continues.

As for the "Shamus" Award, it was first presented at Bouchercon in San Francisco, and it has been presented at Bouchercon ever since. The winner of the first "Shamus" for Best Novel was Bill Pronzini for *Hoodwink*. Bill accepted, and he himself cried "fix" before anyone else could.

(To illustrate how the "fix" is in regarding the "Shamus" Awards, I have been nominated three times, but not since 1984, and I have never won.) The only other categories at the time were Paperback Original—*California Thriller*, by Max Byrd—and our Life Achievement Award, "The Eye," which went to Ross Macdonald. The award was accepted by Dennis Lynds. A year later the Short Story category was instituted, won by John Lutz for "What You Don't Know Can Hurt You" (read that title carefully); three years later the First Novel category was born, won by Jack Early (Sandra Scoppetone) for *A Creative Kind of Killer*.

The award has gone on to be much sought after and respected, won in several categories by such names as Sue Grafton (three times), Lawrence Block (four times), Max Allan Collins (twice), Jeremiah Healy, Ben Schutz, Jonathan Valin, Ed Gorman, Earl Emerson, Marcia Muller, and others. The Life Achievement Award has been presented to, among other, Mickey Spillane, Bill Pronzini, Marcia Muller, and John Lutz.

In 1995 we published a collection of the first twelve "Shamus" winning short stories in an anthology called *The Eyes Still Have It* (Dutton/Signet). PWA has published, since 1984, nine anthologies altogether—all edited or co-edited by me—and will continue to do so in an attempt to always provide a steady market—in a "fluctuating" marketplace—for the short form.

In the early years of PWA, luncheons were held in New York during MWA's Edgar Week at a restaurant called Bogie's. The owners, Billy and Karen Palmer, were mystery enthusiasts who went on to become writers themselves and the owners and operators of "Bogie's Mystery Tours." In those days they catered to a mystery crowd, with authors' photos and dust jackets adorning the walls along with Humphrey Bogart posters and memorabilia. They made their restaurant available to use for our luncheon, a purely social gathering where little or no business took place. Bogie's, the restaurant, no longer exists, but we are grateful to Billy and Karen for supporting us for so long, and we wish them continued success as they go forward with their other endeavors.

However, a PWA luncheon also takes place at each Bouchercon, and will take place at each EYECON (discussed later). At these luncheons a bit of business is done, including the announcement of the winner of the PWA/St. Martin's Press First P.I. Novel Contest. They remain, however, a way for members to get together on an informal basis where they can do some catching up.

In 1986, we presented the first winner of the PWA/St. Martin's Press First Private Eye Novel contest *An Infinite Number of Monkeys* by Les Roberts. This contest was conceived in a conversation between Bill Pronzini and myself, and proposed to Thomas Dunne of St. Martin's Press, who immediately took us up on it. The winner receives a ten-thousand-dollar advance, and is published in the United States by St.

Martin's Press, and in England by Macmillan London, Ltd. Les Roberts has gone on to publish nearly a dozen P.I. novels in two series—"Saxon" and "Milan Jacovich"—and, of course, eventually became president of PWA.

Other winners who have become recognizable names in the field are Gar Anthony Haywood, Karen Kijewski, Janet Dawson, Ken Kuhlken and others who are rapidly making a name for themselves. The most recent winner, as of this writing, was Charles Knief for *Diamond Head* (SMP, 1996).

The contest continues to be held annually. Interested parties may write for rules to PWA/St. Martin's Press Contest, St. Martin's Press, 175 Fifth Avenue, New York, N.Y. 10011.

In that first newsletter I announced that we would someday have our own convention, and I dubbed it EYECON. Well, the first EYECON was finally held in Milwaukee, Wisconsin, in July of 1995, chaired by PWA member Gary Warren Niebuhr, with Sue Grafton as our first guest of honor. It was a smashing success, and will give rise to further EYECONS in the future, although as of this writing the next one is not scheduled. The only thing we were sure of when discussing future EYECONS was that we wanted to keep it special, and not have it every year.

The first six years of PWA were rocky, to say the least. The biggest reason was that I was doing the whole thing myself. I was editor of the newsletter, Awards and Membership Chairman, chief cook and bottle washer. Every dirty "little" job that had to be done—organizing the luncheons and the awards ceremonies at conventions, mailing the newsletter—fell to me, and I almost crumbled beneath the weight. But at the halfway point the organization hit its stride, and others came on board to help me and I'd like to thank them: Dick and Jackie Stodghill, our earliest membership chairs; Martha Derickson, our current chair; Max Allan Collins, our longtime Awards Chairman, and Ed Gorman, the current chair; and most notably Jan Grape, longtime editor of R.I.P.E., current vice-president, and ever available strong right hand. All the dirty jobs seem to fall to her, now, and she seems to handle them with grace and ease.

My thanks to all of you.

* * *

PWA remains a small group, at last count around 200 members, 150 of whom are active P.I. writers, the others publishing professionals and serious devotees. We also have an international membership with writers such as Liza Cody and Michael Z. Lewin (England); Marele Day (Australia, and a "Shamus" winner); and Peter Sellers and Howard Engel (Canada). The Membership Chair at this time is Martha Derickson, 407 W. Third St., Moorestown, N.J. 08057.

We remain a small group, very nonpolitical, as we exist simply to foster and promote the P.I. genre. There are other organizations which are far larger than ours—MWA, Sisters in Crime come to mind—who may have loftier goals, but as founder, permanent executive director, current president and creator of the "Shamus" Award I take great pride and satisfaction at where PWA is now, fifteen years later, and I have no doubt we will continue to prosper—and, okay, grow a little—as time goes on. Already the P.I. novel appears with regularity on the best-seller lists, the banner carried for years by Robert B. Parker, Sue Grafton, and Sara Paretsky, but others are fast approaching as the P.I. novel continues to grow and mature in the hands of able professionals, all of whom are colleagues, and many of whom are my friends.

When I edited the very first PWA anthology, called *The Eyes Have It,* I opened my introduction with a quote that is still very applicable: "With a little help from my friends . . ."

I would like to thank all my friends for the support they have given to me and to PWA over the years. How often do dreams come true? You all helped mine to do just that.

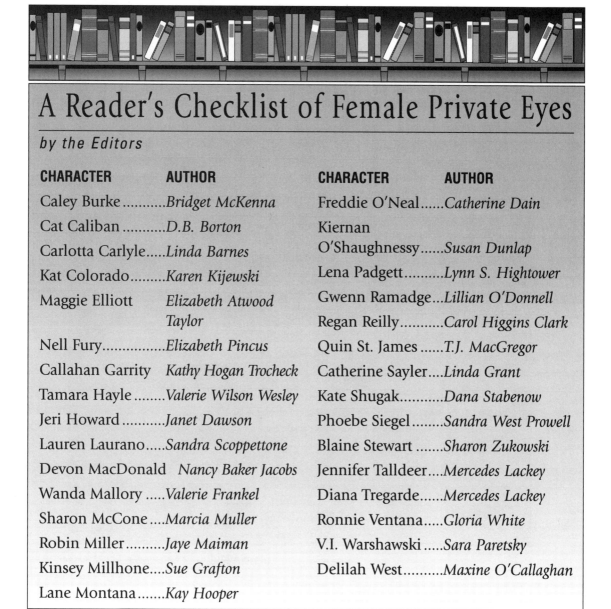

A Reader's Checklist of Female Private Eyes

by the Editors

CHARACTER	AUTHOR
Caley Burke	*Bridget McKenna*
Cat Caliban	*D.B. Borton*
Carlotta Carlyle	*Linda Barnes*
Kat Colorado	*Karen Kijewski*
Maggie Elliott	*Elizabeth Atwood Taylor*
Nell Fury	*Elizabeth Pincus*
Callahan Garrity	*Kathy Hogan Trocheck*
Tamara Hayle	*Valerie Wilson Wesley*
Jeri Howard	*Janet Dawson*
Lauren Laurano	*Sandra Scoppettone*
Devon MacDonald	*Nancy Baker Jacobs*
Wanda Mallory	*Valerie Frankel*
Sharon McCone	*Marcia Muller*
Robin Miller	*Jaye Maiman*
Kinsey Millhone	*Sue Grafton*
Lane Montana	*Kay Hooper*
Freddie O'Neal	*Catherine Dain*
Kiernan O'Shaughnessy	*Susan Dunlap*
Lena Padgett	*Lynn S. Hightower*
Gwenn Ramadge	*Lillian O'Donnell*
Regan Reilly	*Carol Higgins Clark*
Quin St. James	*T.J. MacGregor*
Catherine Sayler	*Linda Grant*
Kate Shugak	*Dana Stabenow*
Phoebe Siegel	*Sandra West Prowell*
Blaine Stewart	*Sharon Zukowski*
Jennifer Talldeer	*Mercedes Lackey*
Diana Tregarde	*Mercedes Lackey*
Ronnie Ventana	*Gloria White*
V.I. Warshawski	*Sara Paretsky*
Delilah West	*Maxine O'Callaghan*

Marcia Muller *Photo credit: Tom Graves*

A Visit with Marcia Muller

Jan Grape

JG: In the recent release of the McCone short stories you mention how you came up with the name of Sharon McCone. Will you recount that for us?

MM: Sharon is for my college roommate, and McCone is for the late John McCone, a former head of the CIA.

JG: Was the first manuscript you wrote published?

MM: No. I wrote my first book at age twelve, and as an adult I wrote another unpublished manuscript.

JG: Was that one a private eye?

MM: Yes—Sharon McCone. I'd fallen in love with the mystery and the private eye novel after reading Ross Macdonald. I soon found Chandler and Hammett as well. Two American women authors I admired were Lillian O'Donnell and Dorothy Uhnak. They write about strong, tough women characters—what I wanted to write about.

JG: There's four to five years between *Edwin* and *Question.* How did you keep from being discouraged?

MM: By continuing to write. I think during that period editors didn't think a female private eye was realistic, but later they realized there actually were female detectives, as well as that people wanted to read about strong women characters. Speaking of discouragements, in college my creative writing teacher told me I'd never be a writer because I had nothing to say. And it was true; I was only nineteen. As a result, I went into journalism.

JG: Do you think Sharon and Kinsey and Delilah West and V.I. Warshawski made mystery readers more aware of how the genre would change with the addition of strong women writers?

MM: Yes and no. I think what they did was make readers who were interested in writing in the genre more aware and encouraged women to enter the field. For instance, Nancy Pickard has said she read us and was inspired to try her hand at a novel.

JG: Do you think there was any influence on women writers of, say, the Nancy Drew books?

MM: Those stories influenced all of us who read them. For me, it wasn't so much Nancy Drew as Margaret Sutton's Judy Bolton books. They were the cornerstone of what I read in children's literature. They were what made me read adult mysteries.

JG: The appealing thing about Nancy Drew is that she was an independent

young woman and went out and solved these cases herself. As a young girl that impressed me.

MM: That's what impressed me about the Bolton books. I went back and reread them because I was doing an article for *Femmes Fatale*. I discovered similarities to Sharon McCone that I hadn't known existed. For instance, Judy had a boyfriend who was a pilot.

JG: I think your characterizations are superb and your plots "ain't" bad either. Do you think knowing Sharon as well as you do makes things easier?

MM: Definitely. I can be writing a scene and I don't have to concentrate on her reactions, on what she's going to do or say or think. Instead I can concentrate on the other characters, the setting, the pacing. Half the time when I write dialogue between her and the ongoing series characters—whom I know equally well—it just flows. Very often she simply takes over.

JG: You just write it.

MM: I just write it. She knows exactly what she wants to happen, and it's going to happen regardless of what I may have planned.

JG: Sharon seems to deal with more realistic situations with each book you write. Do you think perhaps writers today are more perceptive of the "realistic issues" of life?

MM: I can only speak for myself and, to some extent, for Bill, because we have similar approaches to our fiction. I'm certainly more perceptive now than I was early on. Realism is important in the mystery because we ask our readers to believe in some fairly preposterous situations, such as the private eye finding murder victims over and over. The more firmly the books are grounded in reality, the more the reader is able to suspend disbelief. For that reason, I follow procedure rigorously. I've had private eyes and attorneys compliment me on the books' accuracy, which is very pleasing because I'm trying to give my readers as much of the real world as possible.

JG: How do you keep a story fresh for you and Sharon? You never write the same book, that's one of your strengths, and I wonder how you do it.

MM: I did write the same book. If you look at the first three McCone novels, you'll see they have similar structure. I was very much into formula. With the sale of the third one, Bill told me, "Maybe you ought to think about varying your plots." After that, I broke away more with each book. I've discovered I have a low tolerance for boredom, and I figure if I'm bored and just going through the motions, the reader is going to be bored and stop going through the motion of buying the books. I try to do something different each time, with the subject matter or structure. For instance, in *The Broken Promise Land,* I brought in Sharon's assistant, Rae Kelleher, as a second first-person voice. In the book released in summer of '97, *Both Ends of the Night,* I open the parts with all-dialogue segments between Sharon and her flight instructor; what they're talking about relates thematically to what happens in the following section.

JG: I planned to ask you about the flying lessons.

MM: The flying lessons have been fantastic. It's been like going back to college; I've had to learn weather, aerodynamics, radio communication, the internal combustion engine. And how to keep the damn thing straight on the runway. It's been a real growing experience, and it's given me an insight into a whole world that I didn't know existed. The people in that community have been overwhelmingly supportive. The people at our little airport knew I was writing a book, and they were immensely helpful. My flight instructor read all the parts of the book that pertain to flying. She even corrected my typos!

JG: How great. Will you continue?
MM: At this point I don't know. I don't see myself buying a plane and zipping around the country, but on the other hand I'd be unhappy if I couldn't fly occasionally.

JG: It's quite a diversion from sitting in front of a typewriter, too.
MM: Oh, yes. I found out about things I didn't know were there. For example, I knew there were geysers in the hills east of here, but I didn't know until I flew over them that Pacific Gas and Electric has harnessed them to pumping stations. I told Bill about that, and he used it in his latest "Nameless Detective" novel.

JG: Hey, that's cool.
MM: "Nameless" says Sharon told him about them, of course.

JG: Sounds as if you're having a really good time. Let's talk next about how Sharon is dealing with her family lately. Is that going to continue?
MM: That family . . . It's a dreadful family, totally dysfunctional. The continuing story of the Savage family goes on; I go into how the children are dealing with their parents' divorce. I'd love to bring back her brother John; he's one of the few people who doesn't take any nonsense off of Sharon. I don't know about her brother Joey; he's dumb as a post and not a very interesting person. But the parents and the other sister—they'll be back.

JG: I was going to ask if you do your own research, but it's obvious from the flying that you do.
MM: I do, but I also have an assistant who helps. She's online, so I can ask her to find out almost anything, and the next thing I know I have a huge folder of information. She then zeroes in on the specific aspect of a subject that I need. But I do all my on-site research myself.

JG: Do you visualize a big plan in your head for the next two or three books?
MM: Not usually. Sometimes I panic when I'm halfway through one book and haven't yet gotten the idea for the next. But lately I've come up with enough of a personal angle on the ongoing story that I can see where the series is going. I actually have the first scene of the book after the one I'm working on now written in my head.

JG: Okay. Now the next two questions deal with your office and what your writing day is like. Do you have a big businesslike office? Or a messy one?
MM: It's a small, messy office. Sometimes I get it organized, usually after I finish a book or at the first of the year. It has a lot of strange stuff in it. There's a stuffed gorilla hanging from one of the beams.

JG: Well, that's different.
MM: I used to wish I could dress up in a gorilla suit on Halloween, rent a

limo, and go around and pick up my friends from their offices for lunch. It was a weird fantasy that I never carried out. One of them gave me the gorilla. As for the writing day, I usually start out at about eight-thirty or nine in the morning, work until eleven-thirty, then go to the post office. Then I'll come back to work in the late afternoon and go on till around seven.

JG: Is it not great to have a superb writer husband to bounce ideas off of and talk about writing?
MM: You bet it is. I've learned more about writing from Bill than I probably did in all six years of college. When I started out in the business, I was learning while actually making a living at writing, and I had to do both very fast. Bill's help was . . . well, I can't place a value on it. And of course now I've come along enough that I can return the favor. We kick ideas around and read each other's work in progress.

JG: Do you accept his criticism well?
MM: I can take it because he never says anything that isn't justified and usually has an idea of how I can fix a problem. Sometimes I grouse and grump at first because it involves work. I'm the world's laziest person.

JG: Aw, I don't know. I thought I was. But I'm sure when he criticizes it's something that makes sense to you and he knows how to tell you.
MM: Right. He never says anything really nasty.

JG: Tell me about your fan mail. Do you get Crayola printing on Big Chief tablets? Or scented stationery?
MM: By and large, my fan mail is pleasant. Usually typed and businesslike or written on good stationery. More than half of it comes from men, and the only letters I don't answer are the occasional abusive ones.

JG: My next question was if you have any idea of the number of male and number of female readers, but you say more than half of your mail is from men.
MM: I think it's about equal—the men just are more prone to write. More and more I encounter couples who both read me. It's gratifying to see that, because it means Sharon rings true to both genders. Since Hy Ripinsky has appeared, I've noticed the men identify with him.

JG: Any words of wisdom for aspiring writers?
MM: Sit down in front of the keyboard and write at least one page a day. Write every day. Write more than a page if you can. Keep at it, be patient. That's really what it's all about. It's a tough business, but people still break into it all the time.

JG: Okay, the fun questions. What do you wish you had written?
MM: Better than I have.

JG: Who do you like to read?
MM: That's one I can't answer, because I don't want to leave anybody out.

JG: Bill Pronzini. He's your favorite author, right?
MM: Of course.

JG: What music do you like?
MM: Country, classical, and jazz.

JG: What's your favorite color?
MM: Depends on what it's on. Red on cars, yellow in kitchens. Quiet colors

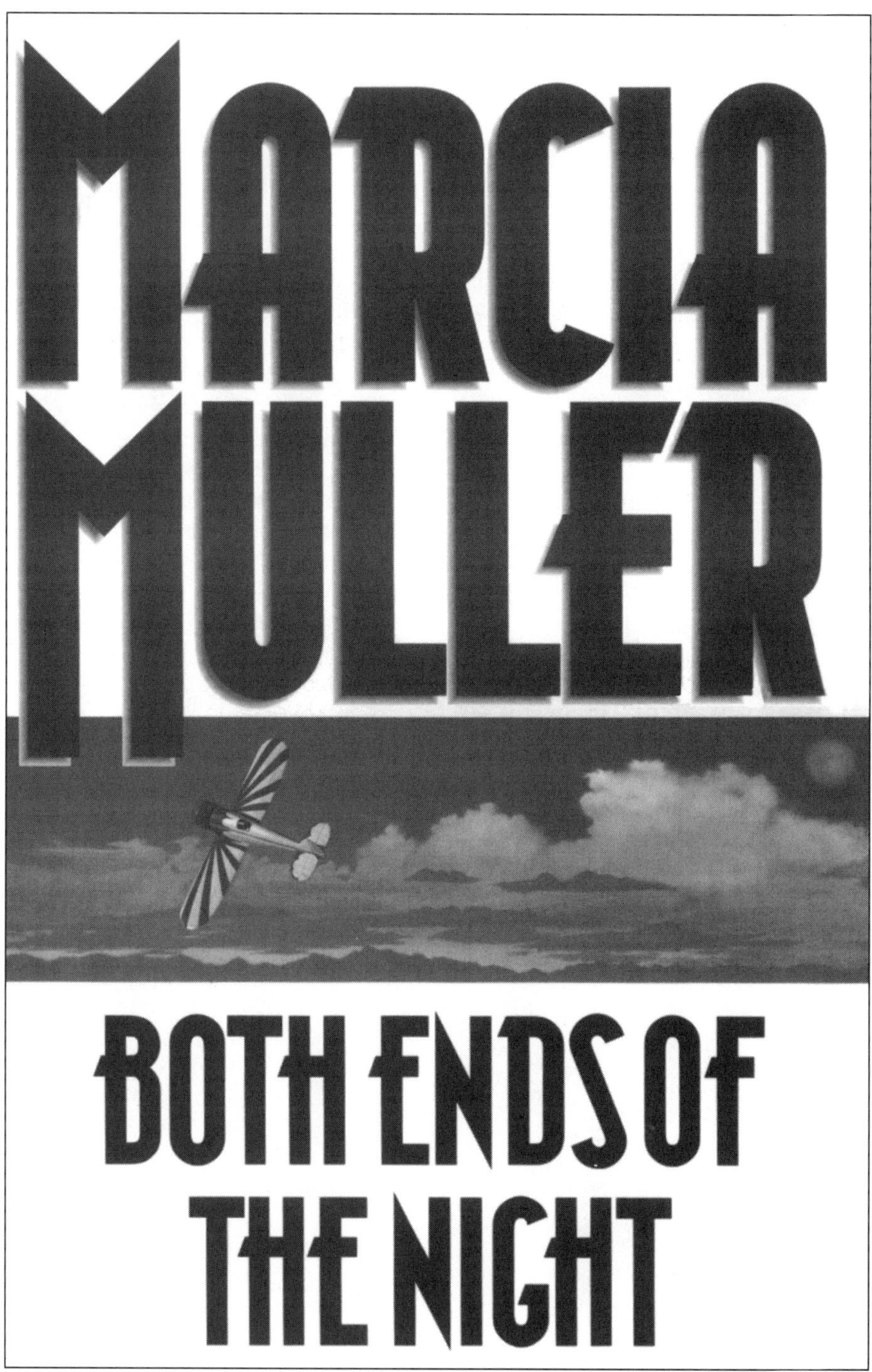

Both Ends of the Night by Marcia Muller

like blues and greens elsewhere. Green and purple on me.

JG: With whom would you like to be stranded on a desert island?
MM: Bill Pronzini. He would keep me sane.

JG: If you could live anywhere in the world—where would you want to live?
MM: What I'd like is a second home overlooking the Pacific Ocean.

JG: What does your best friend say about you?
MM: My best friend is Bill. One of the things he frequently says is, "You're weird, sir."

JG: What do you do to relax?
MM: I work with scale models. I've finished a model of Sharon's home. I dig in the garden. Watch old movies. Swim, when the weather's right.

JG: What's a "great evening" for you? Dinner out? Bill cooking dinner for you?
MM: Actually, it's the two of us cooking an Italian meal together, complete with his famous garlic bread. And some nice music and a good bottle of wine. Maybe watching an old movie and ending up soaking in the hot tub.

JG: Sounds good. What do you wish an interviewer would ask you, and pretend I just did.
MM: What I wish you would have asked me is, "What questions are you glad I didn't ask?" I would answer, "Where do you get your ideas? Why is Sharon McCone a woman? When are you going to write a real book?"

JG: That pretty well sums it up. Tell me again the title of the next book due in summer of '97.
MM: It's called *Both Ends of the Night.* The one after that is called *While Other People Sleep.* The latter is one of Bill's titles.

JG: And *Both Ends* is . . .?
MM: Mine.

JG: Great. And thanks. I appreciate your taking the time from your busy schedule for this.

A Marcia Muller Checklist

THE SHARON MCCONE NOVELS

Edwin of the Iron Shoes
Ask the Cards a Question
The Cheshire Cat's Eye
Games to Keep the Dark Away
Leave a Message For Willie
Double (With Bill Pronzini)
There's Nothing to be Afraid Of
Eye of the Storm
There's Something in a Sunday
The Shape of Dread
Trophies and Dead Things
Where Echoes Live
Pennies on a Dead Woman's Eyes
Wolf in the Shadow
Till the Butcher's Cut Him Down
A Wild and Lonely Place
The Broken Promise Land
Both Ends of the Night

THE JOANNA STARK NOVELS

Cavalier in White
There Hangs the Knife
Dark Star

THE ELENA OLIVEREZ NOVELS

The Tree of Death
The Legend of the Slain Soldiers
Beyond the Grave (With Bill Pronzini)

A NON-SERIES SUSPENSE

The Lighthouse (With Bill Pronzini)

TWO SHORT STORY COLLECTIONS

The McCone Files
Deceptions

Does Crime Ever Pay Enough?

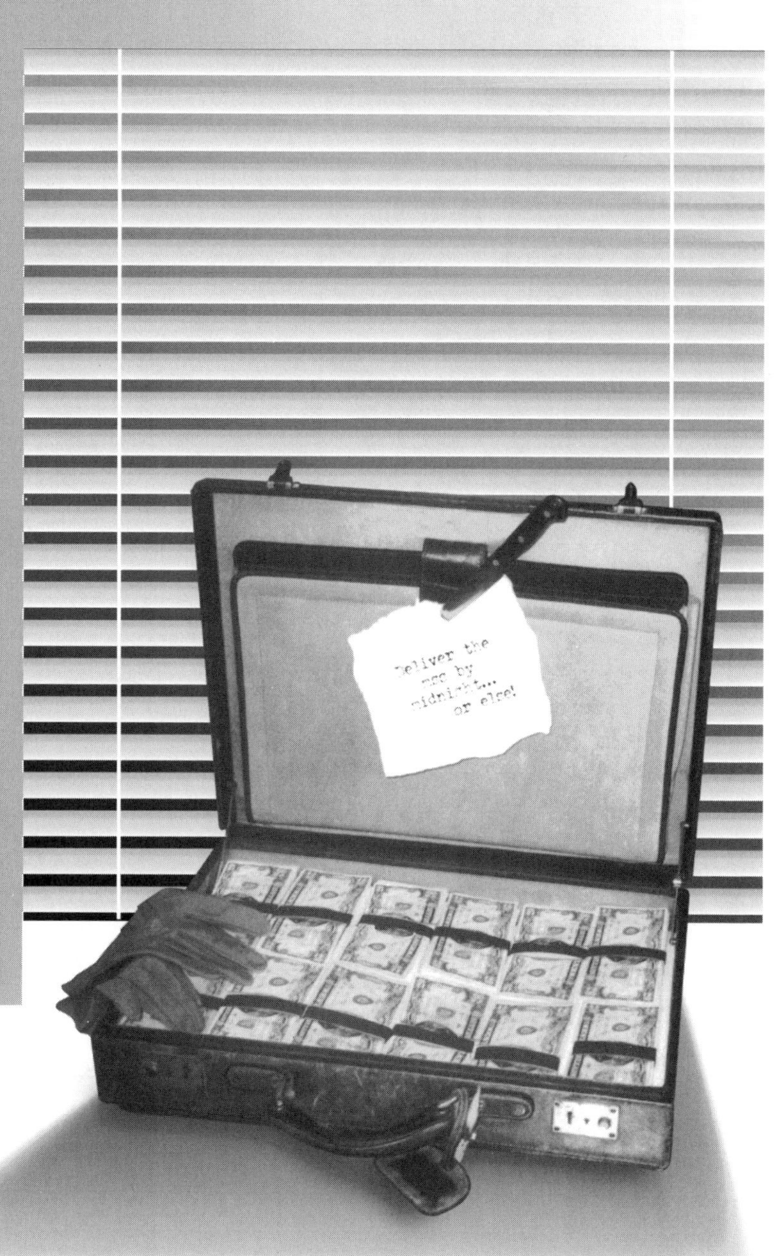

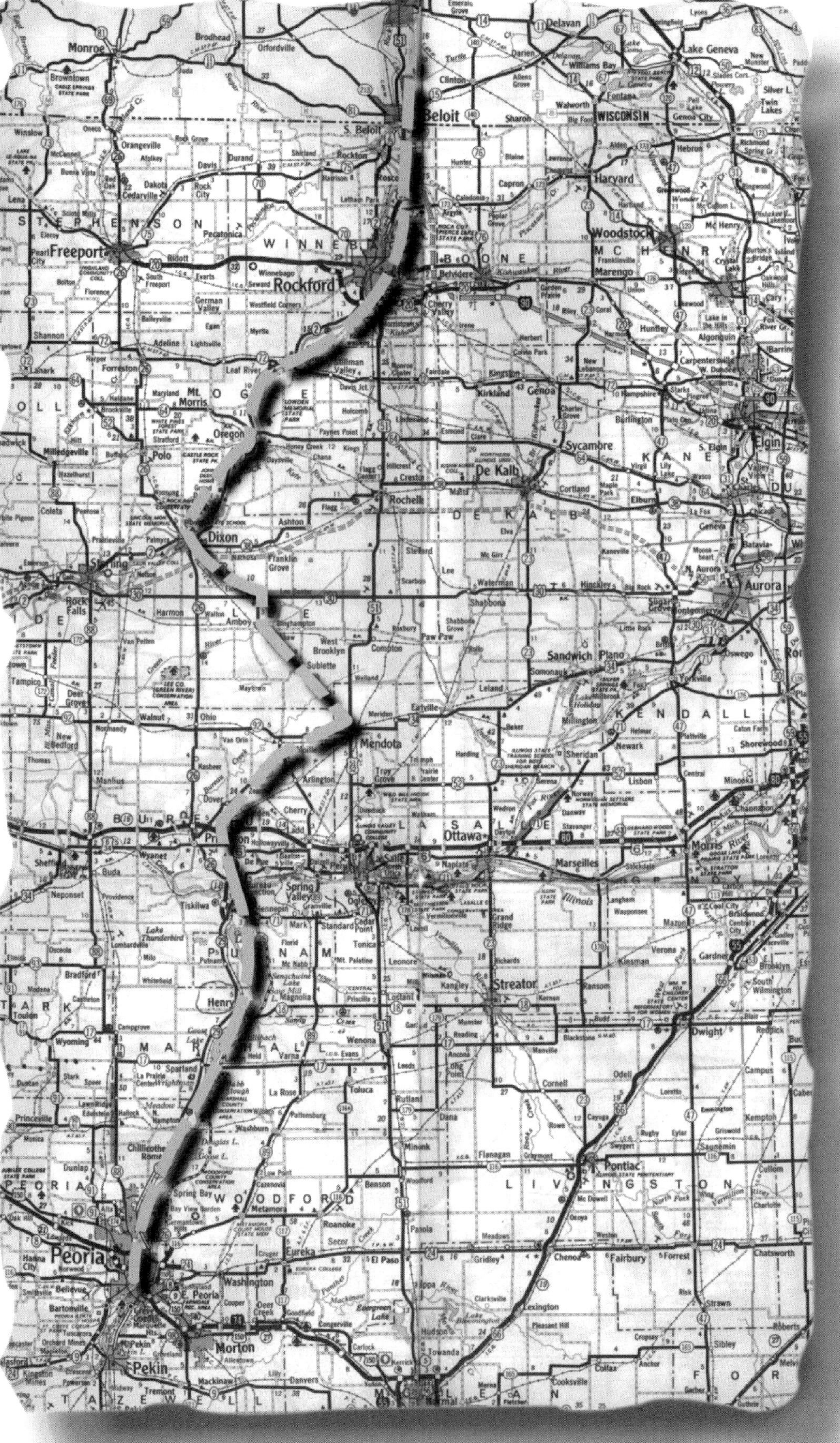

Monroe
Brodhead
Orfordville
Delavan
Lake Geneva
Beloit
S. Beloit
WISCONSIN
Harvard
Woodstock
Freeport
Rockford
Belvidere
Marengo
Elgin
Oregon
Rochelle
De Kalb
Sycamore
Dixon
Sterling
Rock Falls
Amboy
Aurora
Sandwich
Plano
Mendota
Ottawa
Morris
Princeton
Streator
Henry
Dwight
Pontiac
Peoria
Pekin
Morton
Washington
Eureka
El Paso
Chenoa
Fairbury
Lexington
Normal

On the Road Without Charles Kuralt (or Throwing Up in Madison)

Marlys Millhiser

Well, I've just returned from two book tours nearly back to back and since you all know me so well by now you won't be surprised to learn that I'm just brimming with cogent thoughts and half-baked notions about self-promotion.

TO WIT:

1. *We are sending the wrong people on booktours!* The people who really need to get out into the real world are in marketing, sales, publicity, editing, and agenting. Leaving New York for a few days to visit a mystery convention or two and hide from fans in case they're wannabes with a suitcase full of book proposals does not give a true picture of anything valid as far as markets are concerned. Speaking at writers' conventions out in the boonies or visiting ABA or ALA or talking to salesmen who have talked to area reps who have talked to bookstore staff doesn't cut it either.

2. One of the newer wrinkles in the constant battle to prove oneself promotable to an indifferent publisher is to *hire a New York publicist* or second best one in your area who will be more affordable or one in the area in which your book is set. (I talked to a mystery bookstore owner who has hired a local publicist for her store!) I talked to two writers on the road who have done so. One

hired a New York publicist for two months to create publicity opportunities in two cities—Minneapolis and Chicago. The publicist alone cost him six thousand dollars and so far has garnered him signings he probably could have lined up himself and radio and TV interviews and a newspaper feature he probably couldn't have. Is it doing any good? That's a difficult question to answer when you can't get reliable figures on print runs and sales. But the purpose here is more than just selling books. It's attracting attention from marketing departments more interested in pushing bigger names than yours. And this guy now has at least a verbal promise from his publisher to pick up some of the publicist's costs. Then again, he's single and earns enough to pay his living expenses with an unrelated and more lucrative writing job. The other writer lives in the Midwest and her series takes place in the Northwest. She's hired a Seattle publicist.

Makes you wonder if soon only the wealthy will be able to hold onto publishing contracts and if book proposals will come to include a separate page stating how much authors propose to spend on their own publicity campaigns. But, lest we forget, nobody's making these authors do this and as much as we all like to consider ourselves unique and our prose a cut or four above everybody else's, writing skills are not all that rare in our society and what these writers are trying to do is to stand out in a very crowded field in hopes that Lady Luck will take notice.

3. *Book tours are probably most helpful for hardcover books,* and although there is an accumulative effect as an author's titles in print increase in number (if she's lucky enough to land a paperback publisher who keeps titles in print) an author would have to sell hundreds of mass market titles at each stop to make much of a blip on the sales charts. Met another author on the second tour who had just discovered while signing that a five-year-old original paperback was in a third or fourth printing but still had not earned out. This author has a tough time believing bookstores are just now returning a five-year-old title but has to pretend he's not being frigged over.

4. *Is it all worth it?* Or would an author make better use of his time and energy staying home and writing, depending upon chance or the lure of an active fantasy life to attract Lady Luck? Like most people, I'm a lot better at asking questions than answering them but I can say I'm glad I took these tours. For one thing, the experiences—walking into a brand-new bookstore in Chicago unannounced and finding my book there and offering to sign stock. Calling ahead to a Dalton's in Las Vegas and offering to sign stock and walking down the mall later to find the signed books displayed face out at the front of the store. If there's one time of the year someone's likely to buy a hardcover, it's before Christmas. Of meeting fans, old and potential, who would probably never make it to a convention. Of meeting bookstore managers and staff face to face. Of doing a solo talk and reading in a crowded bookstore on a corner in Albuquerque on a Saturday night and realizing that people who'd simply wandered in to browse, had stopped to peer at me

over the stacks and were listening! Many stayed to ask questions. Some even joined those who had come to hear me in buying copies of my book. Of spending an afternoon riding around one of the worst sections of Chicago in the back of a police car with two of the most charming young plainclothes cops you'd meet this side of a TV screen and coming upon two robberies in progress within ten minutes! (Their commander is a mystery writer. Need I say more?)

5. *Yeah, but would I do it again?* That's a little harder to answer. On the Midwest tour I traveled with two other writers and we hit one mystery bookstore that'd had something like twenty-eight mystery writers come through since Bouchercon. We had a good crowd for our panel but were disappointed in the number of books sold on the spot. Bookstore owners everywhere had us sign all their copies in stock and assured us that they would sell before Christmas. They are uniformly kind and wonderful people, they're book people after all, but they must also be business people to survive and, no matter what you've heard, signed books can be returned and are. My traveling cohorts and I wondered if at least the mystery bookstores might be burning out on author signings, panels, and talks—straining the base of loyal readers and attendees. Let's face it, the local Sisters in Crime groups can only buy so many books and most of them are busy trying to write their own. The postcard with the book cover on the front has become passe, have the author dog-and-pony shows at mystery bookstores done the same? We did two of those at general bookstores which didn't fare much better. Different types of bookstores appear to

demand different methods of attracting buyers to the lonely writer at the cardtable stacked with books.

6. Another wrinkle is to forget about the big picture and *blanket the region* in which you live and/or have set the book. Blitz every bookstore, novelty shop, newspaper, radio, TV, cable source in a region of one to four states. Why sell five thousand hardcovers nationally if you can sell twenty thousand locally? Okay, unless you are among the anointed you may not get those size printings in the mystery these days, but you get the idea. And it makes sense. Just one problem. If you're doing all this you aren't going to have time to write. It takes nearly as much writing time to set up one of these tours as it does to do it! I don't know about you but if I go long periods without writing I become "dislocated." (Too many years on the muse drug maybe.)

7. *So, okay, Millhiser, what's the bottom line here?* I'm afraid it's the bottom line. A writer cannot afford to promote his own books and he can't afford not to. It's certainly not going to make him a better writer. But it could make him a writer who can continue to publish.

If this all doesn't make sense it's probably because I'm feeling dislocated.

8. Oh yeah, throwing up in Madison. Somewhere in the Midwest there was *a violent flu bug* that attacked our murderous little trio in a stealth so subtle it didn't zap us until we were almost through the tour. But it got two of us within a half hour of each other in Madison, Wisconsin, and we spent half a day in the local emergency room getting rehydrated intravenously. We blamed the mustard dip at the heavenly pot luck served us by the local mystery readers who welcomed us so graciously and may we burn in Hades for being so cruel because after our last "gig" in Minneapolis two nights later the third in the trio (who had not, repeat *not* eaten the mustard dip) threw up halfway back to Chicago.

9. But the bottomist line of all is—I had a blast. (Maybe because I was touring with two crazies—D.R. Meredith and Jean Hager.)

Retrospect

Joan Hess

My first mystery novel, Strangled Prose, *came out eleven years ago as we speak. Such a babe (okay, maybe not a* babe *babe) in the woods I was back then, fully expecting to be rich and famous, fawned over by adoring fans, courted by talk shows, wooed by Hollywood. My hair* was *natural back then, dear readers, and my accent discernible, if not mellifluous.*

IT'S BEEN QUITE A rollercoaster ride since then, mostly wonderful, occasionally so gawdawful that I wanted to renew my teaching certificate and vanish back into the quagmire of lesson plans and milk money. For your amusement, I present eleven of the more memorable experiences I've had as an author over the same number of years. I can only pray things settle down in the future.

1) Thanks to a conscientious US postal worker,

I found in my mailbox a letter addressed to me—but only with my name and hometown. No street address, no zip code. It turned out to be from a woman in Ohio who sounded exactly like Mrs. Jim Bob, warning me that I'd better "mend my ways" or face divine retribution.

2) I give up.

Over a three-month period some ten years ago, I received a half-dozen anonymous postcards from cities all over the country. Each had a cryptic crossword clue referring to my books. No one ever claimed responsibility. When the moon is full, I still go outside and howl, "Who are you?"

3) If only I'd been writing about Robert Redford.

One sunny, innocuous afternoon, I was writing a scene in which Claire went into a house during a thunderstorm and the power went out. My power went out. You tell me.

4) Where have all the buildings gone, long time passing?

Sharyn McCrumb and I had a gig on the University of Washington campus in Seattle. Having consulted a map (you knew mystery writers were

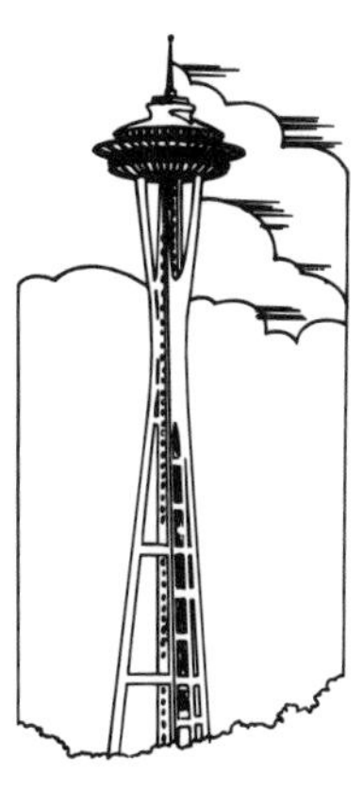

cunning, didn't you?), we zipped over the bridge from Bellevue and into the campus. We saw trees, lawns, flowers, shrubs, and gravel paths—but no buildings. Increasingly perplexed but assuring each other that they had to be somewhere, we drove on winding roads for a long while until we spotted a pedestrian and stopped to ask. He informed us that we were in the arboretum. Oh.

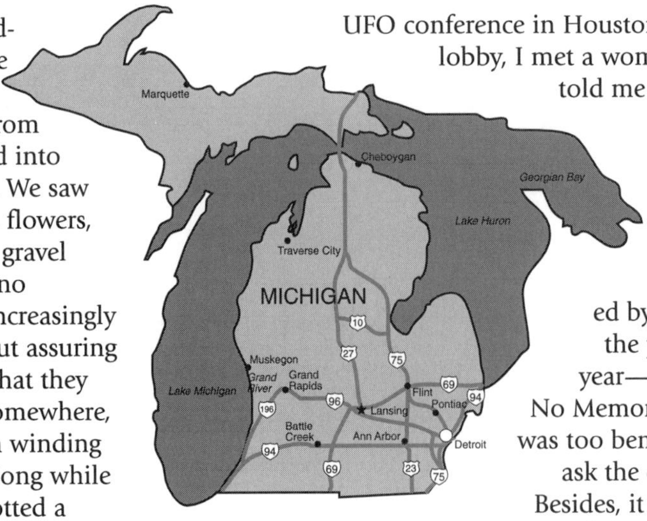

5) Dismality.

Sharyn, Dorothy Cannell, and I were visiting various bookstores in North Carolina, and while pondering a map, I happened to notice that we would be in the proximity (well, sort of) of the Great Dismal Swamp, and more specifically, the East Dismal Swamp, which supposedly was on the west side of the GDS. I insisted that we set aside time for an outing. Margaret Maron, who might have been shaking her head just a bit, bade us a misty farewell, and with intrepid Julian Cannell at the wheel, we went forth on a grand adventure. And never found the East or Great or any other swamp. Locals who should have been waist-deep in muck had never even heard of the swamp. Many hours later we found a lake. We saw a frog. End of swamp story.

6) Beam me up, Scottie.

In the course of research, I went to a UFO conference in Houston. In the lobby, I met a woman who told me that she and her roommate had been abducted by "them" the previous year—and had No Memory of it. I was too bemused to ask the obvious. Besides, it makes a much better story.

7) The grass is always greener in the other time zone.

One mellow spring day, Dorothy and I drove from Chicago to Kalamazoo to present a panel at Jim Huang's bookstore. We took back roads, drank iced tea, plotted short stories, and ever so cleverly arrived forty-five minutes early. When Jim came dashing out to the sidewalk, we were flattered by the warmth of his welcome. Except we were fifteen minutes late. Kalamazoo was at one time the Celery Capital of the world, by the way.

8) It should have happened to Stephen King.

At an informal gathering of the Whimsey Foundation at Malice Domestic, the suite door burst open and in stormed Brother Verber, in robe and collar, to berate me for the wicked, wanton ways of the denizens of Maggody. As proof, he thrust into my hand a plastic bag of evidence purportedly gleaned from ditches; my delicate nature precludes relating further detail. This was one of the few times I've been speechless. This does not mean, however, that I won't seek revenge in the future, Mr. Allen Simpson. I've heard it's best served cold. Like goose liver.

9) Sheep wars.

This would require such a lengthy and possibly incoherent explanation that I lack the fortitude to tackle it. Barbara Mertz (aka Barbara Michaels and Elizabeth Peters) is the worthy opponent, and it's in its fourth year. Last exchange to date, Mertz to Hess: a framed print of a gang of murderous sheep thundering down a country road; Hess to Mertz: a copy of *Buddhism for Sheep*. It's not over till the fat lady bleats.

10) Be careful what you wish for.

Finally, the glamorous author tour. One morning I had breakfast at the Beverly Hills Hilton, then twinkled at numerous bookstore signings in LA. The escort took me to the airport that evening, and I decided rather than have a tuna sandwich there, I'd wait until I was in the hotel in Sacramento and could take off my shoes, mix a drink, and order room service. I arrived at eleven o'clock. No room service. Cheetos are not glamorous, but they can be damn tasty.

11) So I said to Kate Jackson.

The reality is that I was pathetically inarticulate at the time, and mostly gurgled and gulped (and probably drooled). The Maggody series had been picked up as a possible television series, and I took my kids to the set to watch the filming of the pilot. I found myself in the middle of the tiny town that had been superficially converted to Maggody. Ruby Bee's Bar & Grill was on one side on the road, Estelle's Hair Fantasies on the other. The Flamingo Motel. The city limits sign (population 755). The Maggody Police Department. I stood on the yellow line in the middle of the road and gaped; it was pure luck that I wasn't hit by a chicken truck. CBS declined to order further episodes, but I met Kate Jackson all the same, hee hee.

Now that I consider all this, I can take another eleven years of it. Maybe.

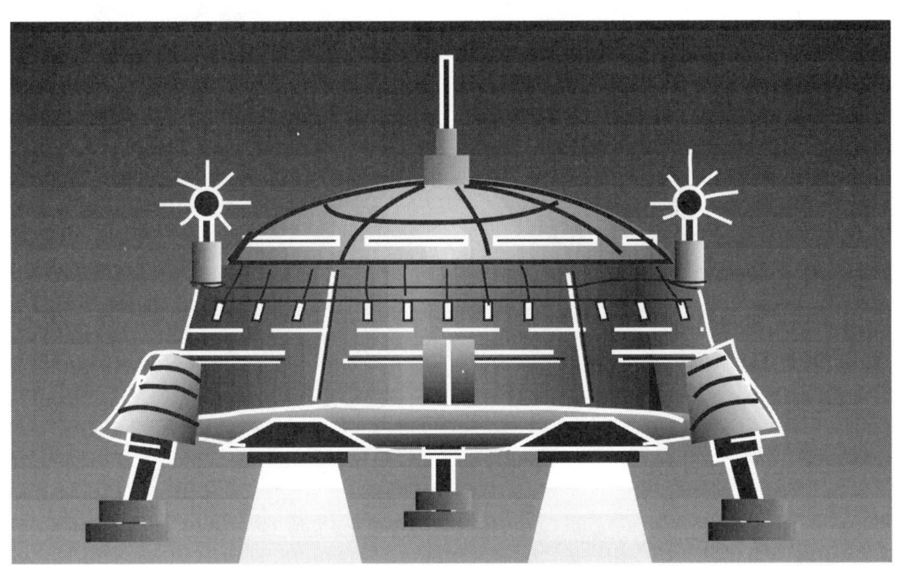

Mary Wallace Walker *Photo credit: Constance Abby Photography, Dallas, Texas*

An Austin Country Mouse

Mary Willis Walker

An author going to ABA is like a simple country mouse arriving in the big city to peddle her homemade cheese and discovering that millions of other mice with cheese to sell have gotten there first and set up marquees with blinking lights and elaborate cheese displays and they're all giving away free samples. The place looks like Times Square on New Year's Eve; it's huge and glittery and all around her are pyramids of Camemberts and Monterey Jacks, and the scent of melted Brie is being blown through the vents.

E*VERYONE* IS SELLING CHEESE.

It's all pretty exciting for a country mouse who loves cheese and cheesemaking, but she is daunted to see just how much cheese is out there in the big city.

And she's a little starstruck because lots of these other mice are very glamorous celebrity mice who could probably sell cheese to lactose-intolerant dieters. So she can't help feeling a bit discouraged. After all, she is just a country mouse, ignorant of the business, unable to sing or dance or play an instrument, dressed in her usual wrinkled homespun, middle-aged and—she hates to admit it to herself—but as she looks around, she sees that she is . . . well . . . kind . . . of . . . mousy.

So what's a mouse to do?

Well, she came to the city to sell cheese, so she gives away free samples just like everyone else. Now you'd think that giving away cheese would be easy, but there's so much cheese here in the city that even *giving* it away is competitive. Right next to her, handing out her American cheese, is a glamour-mouse with sleek ears and the longest, slenderest tail, whose picture has been in all the magazines, and she's been in the *movies* even. There are long lines to sample her cheese because girl-mice are hopeful it will make them look like glamour mouse. And there's another mouse giving away samples—he's bald and been to prison—but he's very famous for having made lots of money and people want to try his Swiss in hopes *they* will learn how to make lots of money. There are TV cameras and flashbulbs popping and reporters clustered around these celebrity cheese mongers. And very long lines to sample their cheese.

But the country mouse is pleased to see that some mice stand in line to sample her cheese, too—her favorite sharp cheddar. And they say they like it! She is flattered and thinks this is not so bad after all.

But when she gets back home, the country mouse wonders if it makes sense to go on making cheese when so many other mice are doing the same thing. Maybe she should take up needlepoint or gardening, but needlework is a yawn and she hates getting her paws dirty. So she goes back to work on a brand-new Limburger she's had in mind, because, dammit, she loves to make cheese and anyway, it's the only thing she's fit for.

There's Not Much Mystery Here . . .

Barbara Peters

No book celebrating the distaff side of American mystery writers would be complete without a few words about the role of the mystery bookstore. Specialty crime emporiums have been on the scene for just three decades. Although modest in size, they have wielded a powerful influence in shaping readers' tastes and authors careers by hand-selling and promoting books, stocking a broad selection of titles across the genre, providing a forum for authors and readers, or groups of readers, to interact, and staving off the suffocating standardization of the superstores. In 1996 they number about eighty and network the country. Why such an explosion?

IN 1989, WHEN I was contemplating a career change to bookseller, a look round quickly convinced me that only in crime would a misspent life be an asset. More importantly, a survey of the bookselling scene brought the realization that opening a specialty bookstore would be the best, if not the only, way for a modest independent operation to survive the coming bookstore wars. Anyone who had watched the demise of the small grocery store or the neighborhood hardware company could see that the independent general bookstore was subject to serious attack. The explosion of information and of publishing would make it harder to master and manage inventory; the economies of scale derived from centralized buying and processing would be hard to beat; and the capital to invest in key locations, fixtures, and computer systems would be difficult to raise. And what would be the place of the author in the superstore environment?

It seemed to me, judging from my years of dedicated hanging-out and book-buying at the pioneering mystery emporiums in New York City when I traveled there on business, that in selected specialist areas like mystery, the big players would actually be at a disadvantage. The techniques that work when addressing economies of scale are ineffective when working with the specialist publisher or small press that can't put enough books into play. In-depth knowledge is possible in a limited universe, impossible in the general. Books that need long-term shelf life or hand-selling can't pay their way in a big operation. And authors are going to stand out by special placement and promotion. In short, I could see that the specialist could take advantage of the opportunities left on the table by the generalist, whether chain store or independent, large or small, and win at its own sort of game. And I think that is exactly what is happening.

It is clear, however, that the mystery bookstore must early make an election as to what it's going to be, a business, or a hobby, for many decisions will dramatically differ depending on the owner's goals. Either end is perfectly legitimate.

What is it that the mystery bookstore must do? Basically, its job is to provide access to the whole range of titles available in the genre. Obviously this gets into problems of definition and personal taste, but I think the reader who comes to the mystery bookstore should expect to find nearly all of what is reasonably termed "mystery" on the shelves. In my store, this is very broadly defined. In others it may be less so. To this day I am the book buyer for the store, and our collection reflects my taste and prejudices, but it is a very broad-ranging, multi-faceted assemblage, and gender neutral. My staff contribute as they will, and we remain responsive to customer comments and requests. Some of our most successful books were suggested to us by others.

How do we provide access to this wealth? For most mystery bookstores, the best weapon is a newsletter or catalog. Hand-selling and staff recommendations in the store. Displays. Special shelf areas. Book signings, a discussion group, articles and lectures, whatever it takes. People expect a mystery bookstore to know the field and to provide access. They hope for wide-ranging and unusual selection. They demand a vertical cut through the whole range of the genre—from used books to collector books, from classics to current, from backlist to future releases—and through the whole range of bookselling services. And mystery readers want special services, like signed books, access to authors, special events, an enjoyment in being entertained, a sense of participation in the community, a sense of being-in-the-know, and a sense of being valued.

And then we made the really amazing discovery! We aren't really in the book business, we're in the show biz. To do our job right, to bring readers and authors together physically or through print, we've become part of the entertainment network. And network is a key word, because it's through developing electronic networks that we're finding new ways to do this. I am convinced that the future lies online, and that right now we can't conceive what the form of that future will be. It's exciting, and frightening, to wonder if we'll be outmoded by the electronic marketplace in ten years time.

It's difficult to overestimate how important the role of the author is in all this activity. Not just in writing the books, but in promoting them, validating them, and establishing a hands-on connection with readers through personal appearances or signing books off-site. There have been a lot of surprises since we got underway, most of them pleasant.

One is to find that nearly everyone in the mystery book business loves it, finds it fun, is supportive and cooperative, and in general generous. Meeting authors at first filled us with apprehension—and we were sometimes graceless—but when we got over our fright we discovered what a great bunch they are, and that many of them were finding the business of being an author as challenging as we were finding the business of bookselling.

When I got into the game, men were publishing the majority of mysteries, about 70 percent or 586 of the 1988 titles, according to recent figures published by my bookselling colleague Jim Huang, also editor of *The Drood Review.* Since then, the percent has dropped to 66.8 percent in 1991, 56.7 percent in 1994, and 56.0 percent in 1995. Jim remarks that in paperback publishing, "which is more sensitive to market demands," the percent has changed from 71.1 percent male/25.3 percent female in 1988 to 49.9 percent/48.5 percent in 1995. Thus the number of books coming out in a given year come in even numbers from men and women authors. There is no doubt that not only the writing activities but the tireless promotional activities of women writers—the business of being an author—and the effect of lobbying groups like Sisters in Crime and the publication of bibliographies and review media, have been the key. In this, the mystery bookstore has played a major part.

In 1992, some mystery booksellers decided to band together to create the Independent Mystery Booksellers Association to promote awareness of their activities and to lobby for helpful terms. As of March, 1996, IMBA had fifty-three active members. Thirty of the stores are owned by women, and another thirteen have one or more members of each sex as partners or associates. Many have urban locations, but some do not. Nearly all depend upon in-house publications, author appearances, discussion clubs, and other events to attract and nurture business. We've come a long way since Dilys Winn opened up in an Upper West Side garage. Despite her long retirement, Dilys recently reopened in Key West with Miss Marbles Parlour, proving that the good mystery bookseller really loves it, the genre and the job. And correctly identifies both. And makes it happen. There's really no more mystery to it . . .

Mysteries by men and women, 1988-1995

FIRSTS

(mystery titles first published in the U.S., in any format)

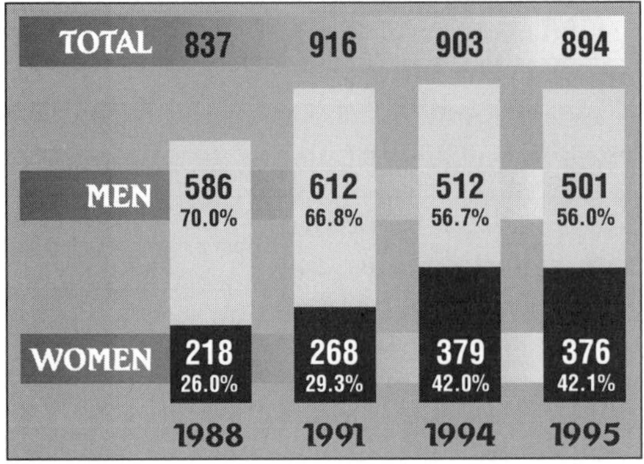

PAPERBACKS

(titles published in paperback, original or reprint)

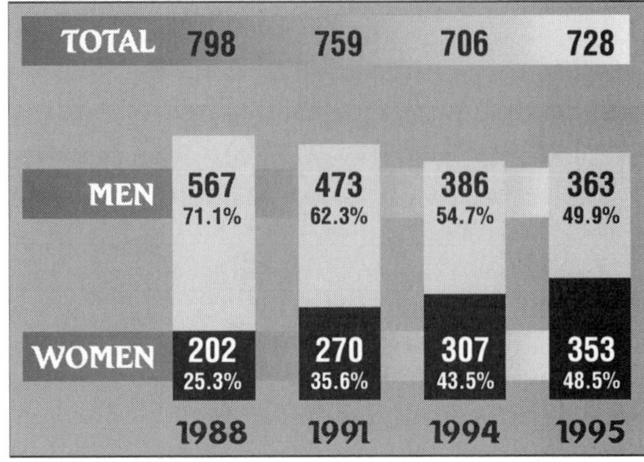

NOTE: Figures for 1995 are preliminary. Percentages do not add up to 100 due to books by both men and women, and authors we were not able to identify.

Since 1988, the Drood Review *has tracked the number of mysteries published each year. These figures reflect the dramatic growth in the number of titles by women. Paperback publishing, which is more sensitive to market demands, is now nearly evenly divided between men and women authors.*

—Jim Juang

Collecting Women Authors

Jean Swanson

Mystery novels by women writers have become increasingly collectible. Collecting first editions may once have been the hobby of the wealthy gentleman, but now anyone with a reasonable budget, enthusiasm, and a keen eye for books can do it.

THE TYPICAL PLACE TO begin is with first editions in hardcover of your favorite writers. Many people like to collect all the works of a writer, and this is a good starting place. You can buy systematically or haphazardly, in whatever way gives you pleasure. You might also want to collect books that have become famous for their collectibility—like the early works of Sue Grafton and Sara Paretsky.

But before we can set out on our scouting trip for rare books, it's good to know a bit about collecting.

There are three main ways in which a book becomes collectible. A book is hard to find. It is in very fine condition, especially for its age. It is desirable to collectors. So the basic criteria can be boiled down to: scarcity, condition, and demand.

Scarcity

In general, books only become valuable when they are hard for the collector to find. They may have been printed in a limited edition from the start, or the publisher may have ordered only a small print run. The book may have been widely available many years ago, but now only a few good copies can be found.

Collectors usually want the first edition of a novel. This is the first group of books printed and sold. If a book is popular, the publisher may order the printer to print a second printing, and so on. Look carefully at the back of the title page of the book. Does it say first edition? Or first printing? Does it have a line of numbers like this:

10 9 8 7 6 5 4 3 2 1

If it does, and all the numbers are present down to one, you probably have a first printing of the first edition. If the 1 is missing, you have a second printing, and the book is probably much less valuable. If the numbers go down only to three, you have a third printing, and so on.

Look at the inside flaps of the dust jacket. Does it say "Book Club Edition" anywhere? If so, you have a specially printed and bound version of the book that has been made for distribution to members of a book club. These books are more widely and cheaply produced than ordinary hardcovers, and are generally not of value to the collector.

Collectors often like books that have been published in small editions, perhaps five thousand copies or less. It can also be worthwhile to look for books published by small publishing houses or by publishers who don't usually publish mysteries. Recent examples are Margaret Coel's *The Eagle Catcher* and Virginia Lanier's *Death in Bloodhound Red,* both first novels published in modest print runs by small presses.

In recent years, first novels printed in fairly small editions have become valuable collectibles if the writer makes it on to the best-seller lists or gains critical acclaim for a later book. So if you think a hot new writer is going to hit the big time, go out and buy a copy of her first novel, fit a plastic cover on it, and put it, unopened, on a wooden bookshelf. Which brings us to a discussion of condition . . .

Condition

The business of rare books is all about condition. A scarce book in terrible condition, with a book plate pasted in, library stamps on the title page, and no dust jacket, is not going to be worth much even though it's scarce. So keep your collection in excellent condition and watch out for flaws when you're buying books.

First of all, look at the book's jacket. It should be in fine shape, with no tears or chips. Jackets with the price clipped off bring down the price of a book. Books should not be exposed to bright sunlight, or their jackets will fade (especially on the spine), and the edges of the pages will fade as well. If possible, book jackets should be protected with a plastic book cover. These are available from library supply dealers; ask your local librarian or favorite bookseller where to buy them.

Don't buy ex-library copies as collectibles. Buy them for reading copies only. These usually have markings that bring down the value of a book. If you buy a book from a remainder table in a bookstore, it may have a remainder mark somewhere on it. The most common remainder marks are a slash of black Magic Marker on the bottom of the text block, or the word "remainder" stamped on the end of the book. These marks take quite a bit off the value of a book; book dealers may mark the book down by 25 percent or more from its collectible value.

If you want to read your collectibles, don't turn down pages to mark your spot, don't attach Post-it notes to pages, don't put bookmarks (especially metal ones) between pages for long periods of time, and don't write comments in your books. Read carefully and try to avoid damaging the jacket or text. Don't read while eating spaghetti!

Don't keep books, including vintage paperbacks, in tightly closed plastic bags where condensation might gather. Don't repair rips in pages or the jacket with Scotch tape. Unless you are an expert at book repair and conservation, it's best to leave these alone or take the book to an expert.

Don't have the book rebound

unless it's done by a conservation expert. If you want the names of conservators, call your local university library and ask for advice. But it's best to take the book first to an expert rare book dealer and have it appraised. Book repair is expensive.

Demand

A great book by a great writer is a collectible *only* if it is in demand as an artifact, not just as a text. If you simply want to read Anne Perry's books, for example, you might buy them in hardcover or paperback, or borrow them from a library. A collection of Anne Perry's mysteries is valuable in itself only if there are collectors who are interested in her books for their intrinsic value.

So how can you tell what writers are in demand? You can start with award winners, especially winners of the several awards for best first novel. The major awards in the mystery field are the Edgar (perhaps the most prestigious awards), the Agatha, the Anthony, the Shamus, and the Macavity, plus the Crime Writers Association Gold and Silver Dagger awards in Great Britain. Even paperback original winners of these awards can become collectible.

There weren't many American women winners of Edgar best novel awards until the 1990s. Recent award winners like Julie Smith, Mary Willis Walker, and Minette Walters are now very collectible. The Agatha Award (given by the Malice Domestic convention members) has been won by authors like Elizabeth Peters, Carolyn G. Hart, Sharyn McCrumb, and Nancy Pickard. All of these writers are certainly worth collecting.

Another way of finding out about hot new writers is by keeping up with the gossip on the DorothyL discussion group on the Internet, or talking to fans at mystery conventions about rising stars in the field. Look especially for first novels, or early novels by writers now gaining fame or winning awards.

Good sources for information about women writers (besides this book) include: *By a Woman's Hand: A Guide to Mystery Fiction by Women*, by Jean Swanson and Dean James (second edition; Berkley, 1996); *Great Women Mystery Writers*, by Kathleen G. Klein (Greenwood, 1994); *Silk Stalkings*, by Victoria Nichols and Susan Thompson (Black Lizard, 1988); and *The Woman Detective: Gender & Genre*, by Kathleen G. Klein (University of Illinois, 1995).

Women Writers

An easy way to categorize some of the most collectible women writers is to organize them into the following categories. But it's as tough to organize mystery writers as it is to herd cats, so you may find that the dates of some books by these authors overlap into adjoining categories.

The Early Days (1860s–1919)

There are so few Victorian mysteries now available that most of them are collectible, if they can be found in good condition. This is an area of increasing interest to collectors and scholars, so books are gaining in value and becoming more elusive.

Some writers to look for are: M.E. (Mary Elizabeth) Braddon, Anna Katharine Green, Jeannette Lee, Marie Leighton, Marie Belloc Lowndes, Baroness Orczy, C.L. Pirkis, Seeley Regester (Metta Victoria

Fuller), Mary Roberts Rinehart, Carolyn Wells, Mrs. Henry Wood.

The Golden Age (1920–39)

British and American women writers in this group are highly collectible. Prices may be very high for first editions, even first American editions, of Christie, Allingham, and Sayers in particular.

Some writers to look for are: Margery Allingham, Agatha Christie, Margaret and G.D.H. Cole, Georgette Heyer, E.C.R. Lorac/Carol Carnac, Ngaio Marsh, Gladys Mitchell, Dorothy L. Sayers, Kay Cleaver Strahan, Phoebe Atwood Taylor, and Josephine Tey.

War and Post-War (1939–1976)

Women mystery writers of the 1950s and '60s in particular have been a relatively neglected area of collecting, and so may bear further investigation by astute collectors. Prices have gone up in recent years for Rice, Highsmith, and Hughes.

Some writers to look for are: Leigh Brackett, Christianna Brand, Gwendoline Butler/Jennie Melville, Vera Caspary, Elizabeth Daly, Dorothy Salisbury Davis, Doris Miles Disney, E.X. Ferrars, Patricia Highsmith, Dorothy B. Hughes, Emma Lathen, Elizabeth Linington/Dell Shannon, Margaret Millar, Patricia Moyes, Lillian O'Donnell, Craig Rice, Mabel Seeley, Juanita Sheridan, and Mary Stewart.

Modern (1977–)

Collecting modern firsts is a risky business or hobby. They are much more variable in price, and it's hard to predict if a writer will hold on to her reputation over the years or will be forgotten. Caveats aside, it's also a lot of fun—like rolling the dice in Las Vegas!

Some writers to look for are: Sarah Caudwell, Liza Cody, Patricia Cornwell, Lindsay Davis, Frances Fyfield, Elizabeth George, Sue Grafton, Martha Grimes, Carolyn G. Hart, P.D. James, Karen Kijewski, Jane Langton, Margaret Maron, Sharyn McCrumb, Marcia Muller, Sara Paretsky, Anne Perry, Elizabeth Peters/Barbara Michaels, Ellis Peters, Ruth Rendell, and Julie Smith.

Some of the most collectible authors of recent years are: Nancy Atherton, Nevada Barr, Diane Mott Davidson, Janet Dawson, Janet Evanovich, Wendy Hornsby, Laurie King, Sharan Newman, Abigail Padgett, Sandra West Prowell, Lynda Robinson, Kate Ross, Judith Van Gieson, Mary Willis Walker, Minette Walters, and Valerie Wilson Wesley.

A Sample of Collectible Mysteries by Women Writers:

Barnes, Linda. *Blood Will Have Blood* (New York: Avon, 1982)

Barr, Nevada. *Track of the Cat* (New York: Putnam, 1993)

Braun, Lilian Jackson. *The Cat Who Could Read Backwards* (New York: Dutton, 1966)

Cannell, Dorothy. *The Thin Woman* (New York: St. Martin's, 1984)

Caspary, Vera. *Laura* (Boston: Houghton, 1943)

Caudwell, Sarah. *Thus Was Adonis Murdered* (London: Collins, 1981)

Cody, Liza. *Dupe* (London: Collins, 1980)

Cooper, Susan Rogers. *The Man in the Green Chevy* (New York: St. Martin's, 1989)

Cornwell, Patricia. *Postmortem* (New York: Scribners, 1990)

Davidson, Diane Mott. *Catering to Nobody* (New York: St. Martin's, 1990)

Davis, Lindsey. *Silver Pigs* (London: Sidgwick & Jackson, 1989)

Ferrars, Elizabeth. *I, Said the Fly* (London: Hodder & Stoughton, 1945)

George, Elizabeth. *A Great Deliverance* (New York: Bantam, 1988)

Gilpatrick, Noreen. *The Piano Man* (New York: St. Martin's, 1991)

Graham, Caroline. *The Killings at Badger's Drift* (London: Century, 1989)

Green, Anna Katharine. *The Golden Slipper and Other Problems for Violet Strange* (New York: Putnam, 1915)

Hager, Jean. *Night Walker* (New York: St. Martin's, 1990)

James, P.D. *An Unsuitable Job for a Woman* (London: Faber & Faber, 1972)

Kelly, Nora. *In the Shadow of Kings* (London: Collins, 1984)

Kijewski, Karen. *Katwalk* (New York: St. Martin's, 1989)

King, Laurie. *A Grave Talent* (New York: St. Martin's, 1993)

Langton, Jane. *The Transcendental Murder* (New York: Harper, 1964)

Lathen, Emma. *Banking on Death* (New York: Macmillan, 1961)

Marsh, Ngaio. *Overture to Death* (London: Collins, 1939)

McDermid, Val. *The Mermaids Singing* (London: HarperCollins, 1995) (first printing with missing pages)

McMullen, Mary. *Strangle Hold* (New York: Harper, 1951)

Michaels, Barbara. *The Master of Blacktower* (New York: Appleton, 1966)

Monfredo, Miriam Grace. *Seneca Falls Inheritance* (New York: St. Martin's, 1992)

Moyes, Patricia. *Death on the Agenda* (London: Collins, 1962)

Muller, Marcia. *Edwin of the Iron Shoes* (New York: McKay, 1977)

Neely, Barbara. *Blanche on the Lam* (New York: St. Martin's, 1992)

Orczy, Baroness. *The Old Man in the Corner* (London: Greening, 1909)

Page, Katherine Hall. *The Body in the Belfry* (New York: St. Martin's, 1990)

Paretsky, Sara. *Indemnity Only* (New York: Dial, 1982)

Peters, Ellis. *A Morbid Taste for Bones* (London: Macmillan, 1977)

Rendell, Ruth. *Wolf to the Slaughter* (London: J. Long, 1967)

Rice, Craig. *Trial by Fury* (New York: Simon, 1941)

Sayers, Dorothy L. *Gaudy Night* (London: Gollancz, 1935)

Smith, Julie. *Death Turns a Trick* (New York: Walker, 1982)

Thomson, June. *Death Cap* (London: Constable, 1973)

Van Gieson, Judith. *North of the Border* (New York: Walker, 1988)

Walters, Minette. *The Ice House* (London: Macmillan, 1992)

Wolfe, Susan. *The Last Billable Hour* (New York: St. Martin's, 1989)

An Independent Mystery Press . . .

Barbara Peters

The nature of bookselling, already shifting when I opened The Poisoned Pen in 1989, has rapidly evolved under the pressures of a more and more competitive marketplace featuring aggressive merchandizing techniques, nontraditional bookselling outlets, electronic technologies, and the dizzying expansion of the Internet for retail and resources. Coping in a faster paced, less profitable environment where the mystery midlist is shrinking, it is no longer possible for the bookseller to stand still and survive.

CONSOLIDATIONS AMONG MAJOR PUBLISHERS driven by the star system and by the chain-dominated distribution system and the gradual demise of the independent general bookstore under attack by economies of scale and the tactics of robber-baron bookselling corporations push all of us—authors, publishers, booksellers, and readers—toward centrism and subject us to subtle yet dangerous forms of censorship. What are we to do? While the specialty or niche bookstore has its own armor and its own audience, and may even benefit from the current system as cited in my article on mystery bookstores elsewhere in this volume, it must still overcome the forces in play to survive and to serve its constituency—defined here as mystery lovers.

One weapon in the speciality bookseller's arsenal is to go beyond breadth of inventory to create unique inventory. Small press books, imports, collector books, and other rareties will lure customers and keep them coming back. Why not take it a step further and publish books for the mystery audience? A glance around Barnes & Noble last year reminded me that it has been producing its own books for years, and presumably at a profit. We've had great success selling titles from very modest operations like Dennis McMillan Publishing and Write Way Press. Why not catch the tide and try it ourselves? Thus, Poisoned Pen Press was born in January 1997.

What kind of books are suitable for a specialty mystery press? There are many possibilities, but one that immediately struck me is books from the vanishing backlist. Too often a customer discovers an author, wants to read earlier books, and is frustrated. Shelf life for many titles, particularly paperback originals, can be less than a year. Reprints of titles that have dropped out of print, or making paperbacks from hardcover books deemed unlikely to attract a true mass market audience, would not only improve specialty bookstore inventories, they would be a real service to the vanishing midlist author or to the author who has an audience but will never be a star.

Another possible range of titles lies in classic crimes, books by masters of the genre that can still attract a modest number of readers. Customers of specialty stores should be able to enjoy these treasures. And their enjoyment can be enhanced by some quality reference works and biographies as well, books that could also find their way into libraries and schools where there is an expanding interest in crime fiction as a literature worthy of study. I've tested this myself by joining the faculty at Arizona State University where I introduce undergraduates to American detective fiction, and use as the text the first book published by Poisoned Pen Press.

This to me came about almost by accident. In another shot from our customer service bow, The Poisoned Pen began a series of annual crime symposia focused on specific themes under the generic title, "AZ Murder Goes . . ." Our first event in February 1996 was "AZ Murder Goes . . . Classic," current crimewriters lecturing on past masters. The fourteen authors, having prepared talks, supported the idea of publishing the collected papers. Why not start here? we thought, and plunged into the mysteries of editing and production, emerging with *AZ Murder Goes . . . Classic: Papers of the 1996 Conference* just in time for "AZ Murder Goes . . . Artful," the February 1997 event. We've a lot to learn about the procedures, technologies, and economics of publishing on a small scale, but we're now committed to a series of volumes and we've field-tested the book and find it does the job we want it to do in the classroom and for mystery fans. We're also committed to a series of reprints of books by authors we admire we can't otherwise obtain.

Clearly we haven't learned enough about small publishing to speak with further authority. We can offer some perceptions that, if true, should promote our venture. If authors perceive a benefit in increased exposure and increased marketability of current books by building upon past publications, then acquisitions costs can be modest. Desktop publishing makes layout an in-house option. Fortunately, advances in printing technology support the concept of limited production or printing-on-demand. Warehousing is minimal, especially if returns are ruled out. Web pages—our own and others, electronic bulletin boards, the Independent Mystery Booksellers Association network, and our own publications provide a marketing channel. Without the giant overheads of the giants, higher unit production costs can be tolerated. Thus the standard trade terms can be offered, making it possible to not only offer the books to the whole range of mystery bookstores but giving the author wider exposure.

While ideally a specialty press should make a profit, for us Poisoned Pen Press is a labor of love. It should be a means of serving authors and a way to attract and keep customers. Bottom line: if the bookstore profitability is enhanced, then the press has done its job if it breaks even.

My own view is that the current publishing system will only grow larger, that medium-size presses, authors, and bookstores will be squeezed out. Inevitably, new, smaller presses must arise and fill in—just as more niche bookstores will balance superstores. While technology on the one hand has accelerated the growth of Goliaths, it can support the Davids as well. By targeting a limited objective while assuming a modest risk, we hope to test technologies and the marketplace with Poisoned Pen Press without jeopardizing The Poisoned Pen. Perhaps when the next edition of *The Fine Art of Murder* publishes, we'll know if we judged rightly.

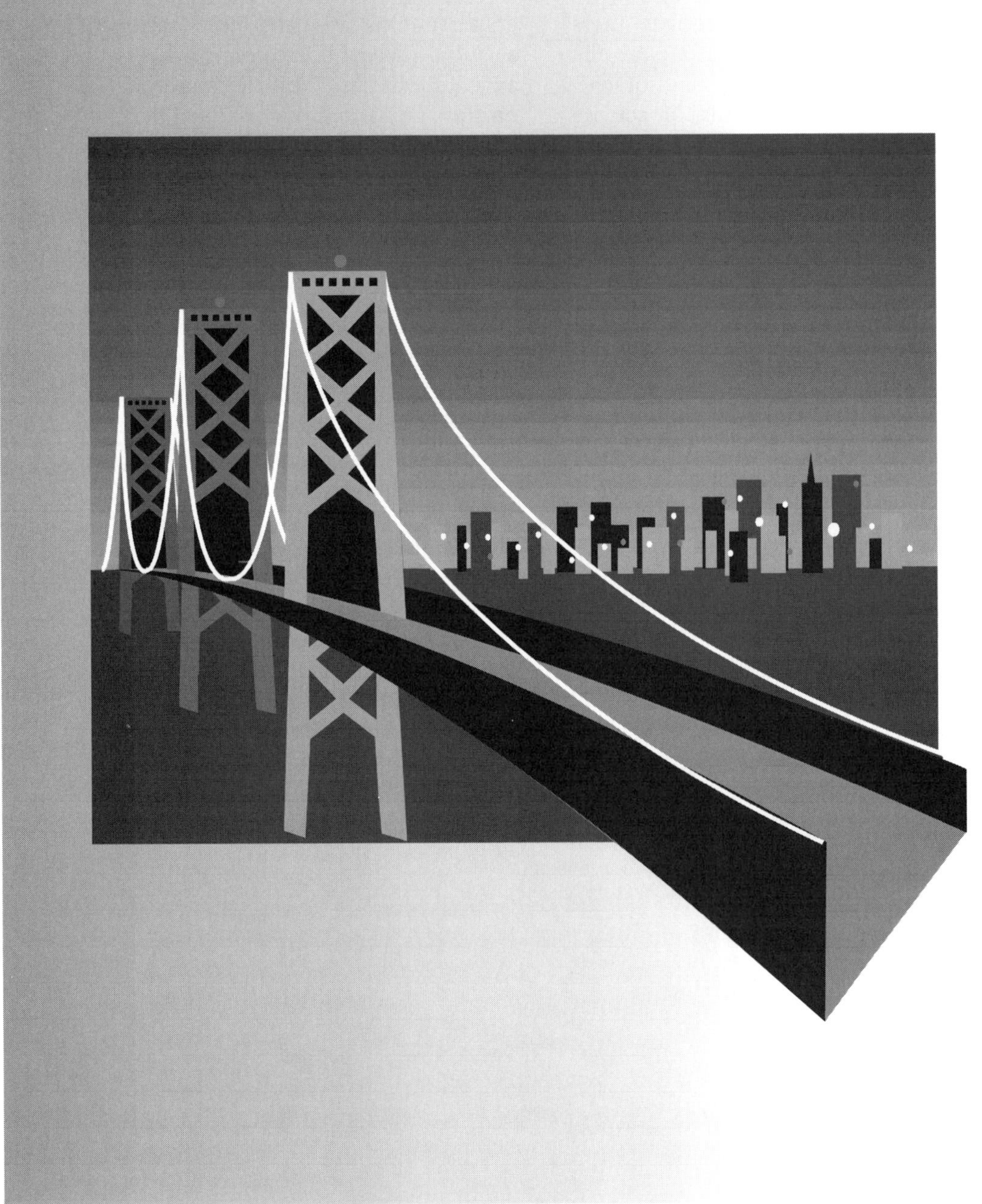

Interview with
Laurie King

Dean James

WINNING AN EDGAR FOR Best First Novel from the Mystery Writers of America happens to very few writers, and in 1994 it happened to Laurie R. King, a third-generation Californian who published her first novel, *A Grave Talent,* with St. Martin's Press in 1993. *A Grave Talent* introduced a compelling main character, a San Francisco homicide detective named Kate Martinelli, with a secret to hide. Trying hard to keep her personal life from interfering with her job, Kate walks that fine line like many contemporary women. Not content, however, with creating one distinctive series character, in 1994 King published *The Beekeeper's Apprentice* (also St. Martin's), and this book introduced to the world the extraordinary young Mary Russell, who literally stumbles across Sherlock Holmes in a Sussex field in 1915. This book has recently been nominated for an Agatha Award for Best Novel by the members of Malice Domestic, the mystery convention devoted to celebration of the traditional mystery.

Both novels are forthcoming in paperback from Bantam Books, *A Grave Talent* this summer and *The Beekeeper's Apprentice* in January 1996. King has published her third novel, *To Play the Fool* (St. Martin's), which records a further case for Kate Martinelli. Amidst her touring to promote this book, Laurie King graciously answered my questions from her home in northern California. Fans of her work will find much to savor in her answers.

Why did you choose to write mysteries, rather than some other type of fiction?

If by "choose" you mean a deliberate, conscious choice, I never did *choose* to write mysteries. The first piece of fiction I wrote was a futuristic sort of novel, where I kill off nearly all the men (nothing personal, Dean) and leave a decimated population of women. Oddly enough, the title I eventually gave it was *Daughters of Men,* and as P.D. James has since then published her *Children of Men,* which also presents a future of limited fertility and a decimated population, mine may not be published for a very long time. At any rate, a year or so later I was visited by Mary Russell, and the choice of genres was decided for me. I continue to write mysteries because I feel at home with the basic structure, the skeleton on which a writer may hang so many and varied bodies—like the sonnet, I suppose, or the haiku, as compared to the free verse of mainstream fiction. There's also the freedom to create, in effect, a story thousands of pages long, by working in a series.

What is your conception of the mystery novel? Do you consider any writers to have been of significant influence upon your view of what a mystery novel is (or can be)?

I don't write whodunits, and I rarely read them. (Similarly, I can't stand crossword puzzles, word games, or logic conundra, and the only time I do a jigsaw puzzle is on Christmas or Thanksgiving, when I become compulsive and ill-tempered until it is complete.) To me the point of a mystery novel is not the solution of the crime, but how the crime affects the people around it, how the protagonist wrestles with restoring order to the universe, and how the lives of the main characters and the solution of the mystery interweave. As for influences (assuming that admiration creates an influence), I would have to say Dorothy L. Sayers, for the elegance of her language, Josephine Tey for her slyness in twisting the genre to her purposes, and Peter Dickinson for his sheer bloody brilliance.

You have a master's degree in theology. How does this background inform your conception of the moral dimension of mystery fiction?

I'm not quite sure how to answer this. Obviously morality is an unstated assumption in both "god-talk" and in the mystery genre, but I don't know that an academic degree in theology has a whole lot to do with morality. Perhaps it would be safe to say that I have always been interested in humankind's relationship with the divine, both theoretical and practical, and whereas with the M.A. I was looking at the development and history of that relationship, the broad spectrum as it were, in writing mystery novels I can delve into the specifics of how an immoral act (although that seems an awfully weak description of murder) affects us all. Applied theology, perhaps, or even practical morality.

On the other hand, my background in theology certainly has influenced the topics in the stories, which range from the Trickster archetype I wrote about for my bachelor's thesis (used in *To Play the Fool*) to the investigation of the feminine aspects of God that was the topic of my master's thesis (used in the second Mary Russell story, *A Monstrous Regiment of Women*, due out this summer) and the question of women in the leadership of the early Church (using a purported letter from Mary Magdalene in which she calls herself an apostle, a third Mary Russell story to be published in 1996).

Your first published novel, *A Grave Talent*, won the Edgar for Best First Novel. Has the award made a significant difference in your career thus far?

Of course. People return my phone calls after the third or fourth time now, instead of after five or six tries.

The main character in *A Grave Talent* is a lesbian. Was that a deliberate choice on your part?

As you may have guessed by now, there are few deliberate choices on my part in the development of a novel. Looking back I can see the various threads that led to a character being one thing or another—Mary Russell, for example, had to have an American element in her background in order to excuse the occasional slips in vocabulary and attitude, but when she introduced herself, she simply *was*. Similarly, Kate Martinelli was to have a close relationship with an older man, her partner Al Hawkin, but without the dimension of sexual attraction, and although it is very possible to have simple friendship between the sexes, making her unequivocally a lesbian made the limits clear from the start. Or nearly the start, because I took some time getting around to describing her home life. However, this is all hindsight; in the process of writing, she simply (ahem) came out that way.

In police work, as in many spheres of life, women are often treated as outsiders. As a lesbian, Kate Martinelli has a double mark, in a way, against her, even in San Francisco. How do you think this perspective affects your work? Or does it?

Although the San Francisco Police Department is less encumbered with homophobia than other departments, as you say, it's still there, and before you ask: no, last time I asked, there were no women homicide inspectors. So of course this is one source of pressure for Kate, and I am finding it coming heavily into the third in the series, which I am now in the process of writing.

I read in another interview that, even with the second book in the series, *To Play the Fool,* you have begun to tire of Kate Martinelli and her partner, Alonzo Hawkin. Is this true? If so, why? What about these characters no longer challenges you as a writer?

I was fed up with them after *A Grave Talent,* much less five years later when I wrote *To Play the Fool.* Every time I finish a book I'm sick and tired of the characters I've just spent several months following around the page. I wouldn't say there is no challenge left in them, and in fact future books continue to take shape in the back of my mind. Kate is, however, a more limited person than, say, Mary Russell, simply because she's more real and the situations in which she finds herself have to be more firmly rooted in humdrum daily life of the late twentieth century. In a sense, she is more of a challenge because I have to work at the Martinelli books, whereas the Russell & Holmes books tend to write themselves.

In *To Play the Fool* you make reference to another case, the "Raven Morningstar" murder, which sounds fascinating. Is this anything we're likely ever to see in print?

I don't think so. It was put in as a means of tying *Fool* in to *Grave Talent,* the Morningstar case being the means by which Al Hawkin pulls Kate back onto the job at the end of *Grave Talent.* However, it's obviously a depressing and distressing case, with a disastrous ending, and is hardly the thing, if I were to write it up, that most people would want to read. Too *noir* for me, so I will probably just leave it a tantalizing but unknown episode. However, anything is possible.

With your two main characters, Kate Martinelli and Mary Russell, you have unusual women with strikingly different points of view. How does each of them represent your ideas of the roles of women in their respective worlds?

Mary Russell is the embodiment of the New Woman of the early twentieth century, when women had run England during World War I and, with the vote, anything seemed possible. Kate Martinelli is the practical outcome of that great new beginning, at the far end of the century when the revolution has revolved, ending up in just hard work and variations of the same problems there were to begin with. Ironically, Kate is much more vulnerable to male oppression than Mary Russell is because Mary is so immensely self-contained and because Mary is, after all, in a country that had a tradition of such remarkable individuals such as Gertrude Bell and Mary Kingsley, coddled Victorian women who found themselves wandering the Arabian desert or the West Africa tropics, unaccompanied except by hired native men. The American continent has produced its share of eccentric women, but not, I think, such striking examples.

Where did Mary Russell come from? Was the notion to match her with the "great" Sherlock Holmes there from the start?

God only knows. Again, using hindsight, I think she had her beginnings in an upsurge of feminist sentiments triggered by a television production of one of the Holmes stories, the feeling that really, this much-vaunted man was only using skills possessed by any woman who has a child over the age of two, and many women who were not mothers at all. Call it common sense or feminine intuition, when it is found in a male it is considered extraordinary. And yes, she needs Holmes as her counterpart: he represents the height of Victorian, masculine thought, whereas she is the embodiment of modern feminism. Equal brains, different settings, different times.

The relationship between Mary and Sherlock in *The Beekeeper's Apprentice* is quite warm, and many readers have already suspected that the relationship is destined to bring them even closer. Does the "M.R.H." with which Mary ends her "Author's Note" mean what all we readers think?

We shall have to wait until I decipher future manuscripts to be sure, but I doubt it means what you think. I really can't imagine that Sherlock Holmes would go so far as to adopt her, do you?

St. Martin's told me that Mary's next adventure, *A Monstrous Regiment of Women*, is due out late this summer. Would you care to give your fans any more tidbits about further exploits of Mary Russell and Kate Martinelli?

A bit of gossip? Very well. *A Monstrous Regiment of Women* is based on a treatise by the long-suffering John Knox, the full title of which was "The First Blast of the Trumpet against the Monstrous Regiment of Women," in which he rails against women rulers in general and his own disapproving queen in particular. My own *Monstrous Regiment* involves a charismatic woman religious leader in the early twenties, a time just after the First World War when so many young men had been killed or disabled and the women they might normally have married were called, in the press, "surplus women." So flattering. Mary Russell gets involved with this woman's community, tutoring her in the feminine aspects of God that can be found in the Bible, and finding her more appealing than the continually ill-tempered and irritating Holmes. There is a murder, and a kidnapping, and a lot of fog. The next Kate Martinelli book I am now trying to write, not an easy thing when I'm also supposed to be travelling the country and talking about *To Play the Fool.* Nonetheless, a page at a time I am putting together a story about Kate and particularly about Jules Cameron, the young girl who appears in the end of *Grave Talent* and whose mother is involved with Al Hawkin. The name at this point is *With Child,* and it's due out, assuming I finish it, next February. And yes, Lee is in it too. And Lee's mad Aunt Agatha. And a homeless boy named Dio. And a raccoon named Gideon . . .

Charlotte MacLeod *Photo credit: Grace Desjardin*

Interview with Charlotte MacLeod

Dean James

MENTION THE NAME "CHARLOTTE MacLeod" to a traditional mystery fan, and said fan is guaranteed to smile, for Charlotte, whether writing under her own name or that of Alisa Craig, has brought many a smile per book to her readers. (I wonder, is there a smiles-per-book measurement, an SPB? If so, Charlotte would probably get the highest "octane" rating available.) Charlotte MacLeod wrote a number of books before 1978, when the first Peter Shandy novel, *Rest You Merry,* was published by the now sadly defunct Doubleday Crime Club. The following year, Doubleday published the first Sarah Kelling novel, *The Family Vault,* and the second Peter Shandy novel, *The Luck Runs Out.* Alisa Craig first appeared in 1980, again with Doubleday, with *A Pint of Murder,* the first of the Madoc Rhys novels, and in 1981 with *The Grub-and-Stakers Move a Mountain,* the first of the Grub-and-Stakers novels.

Charlotte's wonderful combination of humor, delightfully dotty characters, and zestful word play quickly brought her a large and loyal following among mystery readers. She has also been honored by her peers with an Edgar nomination for Best Novel for 1987's *The Corpse in Oozak's Pond,* as well as nominations for her juvenile mysteries. In 1986 she received a lifetime achievement award from Bouchercon, and in 1991 she was Guest of Honor at Malice Domestic. Ever gracious and witty, Charlotte answered my questions in her inimitable fashion from her home in Maine.

You had written a number of different kinds of books before *Rest You Merry,* the first Peter Shandy novel, was published. Had you always wanted to be a mystery writer?

"Always" is a big word. I must have been all of ten years old before I decided to become a mystery writer. Mysteries were what I liked best and there were never enough of them in our little branch library, so I decided I'd better write some to fill the gaps. Actually most of the nine hardback books published before *Rest You Merry* were YA (young adult) mysteries; in fact Atheneum published one called *King Devil* at about the same time as Doubleday turned Professor Peter Shandy loose on an unsuspecting world. I did three more after that, one of which, *We Dare Not Go A-Hunting,* was nominated for an Edgar, but I have done no more since 1984 and probably never will.

From previous conversations, I know

you've always been a great reader. Do you consider that any particular writers have influenced your conception of the mystery novel (or have influenced the type of mysteries you chose to write)?

I've read so much for so long that it would be impossible for me to pick out any special role model, though Mark Twain and Jane Austen would have to be on the list, along with a few dozen others. Perhaps you'd better make that a few hundred. Anyway, I wasted a lot of time trying to play the sedulous ape. Then one day I decided "The hell with this. I'm just going to write what I want in the way that I like it. At least that will give me one satisfied reader." I had a wonderful time with *Rest You Merry,* it sold well,* and taught me to mind my own business. *(P.S. it still does.)

How did Peter Shandy come to be? Did he come first, or did Balaclava and its environs come first?

It was Peter who put me in my own back yard to cultivate my rutabaga patch. With me, the characters always come first. I can't get going on a plot until one of them comes up with the magic key to the secret garden.

The Curse of the Giant Hogweed **was a hilarious departure, in some ways, from the rest of the Shandy series with its time-travel element. Did you consider that you were taking a risk by doing something so audacious in a traditional mystery?**

I had no expectation that *The Curse of the Giant Hogweed* would ever appear in published form and wouldn't have cared if it hadn't. After the sudden death of the real "Max Bittersohn" I was left, as one partner has to be, feeling that half of myself had been ripped away. My recourse was either to languish on a couch like a Victorian matron with the megrims or grab a shovel and start digging. That was when I discovered how the law of balance really works. I was so far down in the depths that it was going to require a chunk of looniness the size of a meteorite to hurl me up out of the pit.

It has been often, tritely, and truly said that when one door closes, another opens. One of the dear friends with whom I have been richly blessed sent me a clipping about a giant hogweed plant that had escaped from somebody's garden, gone hog wild, and was invading the hedgerows of Britain like the mongol hordes of Genghis Khan. I've always had an over-developed funnybone, I recall having gone into hysterical giggles at my grandmother's funeral and having to pretend that I was overcome with tears, not because I hadn't been fond of her but because the unaccompanied soloist was singing flat.

A forest of giant hogweed on the march through the dark ages with three members of the Balaclava Agricultural College faculty who had metamorphosed into a bard and two druids seemed like a reasonable proposition under the circumstances in which I found myself, and it was. I still reread the book occasionally and wonder why the flaming perdition a book that gives the reader some therapeutic guffaws should be less respected than the doom and gloom and blood and guts that get ladled out under the guise of realism in literature.

One of my favorite supporting characters in the Shandy books is Catriona McBogle, who first appeared in *Vane Pursuit.* Is there any truth to the rumor

that she was inspired by an (in)famous mystery writer who's a good friend of yours?

I cannot imagine why you take Catriona McBogle to have been modeled after some infamous writer alleged to be a friend of mine. All my friends are persons of vast erudition and impeccable breeding, loaded with gentilesse and savoir-faire, and kind to animals. They are also witty, charming, and tolerant of nice young men who send them provocative questionnaires. (But only up to a point, so don't push it, Sonny.)

The Sarah Kelling Bittersohn books have a very different setting, Beacon Hill and the Boston Brahmins. How did Sarah originate?

For some years, while I was struggling to find my own voice in the adult mystery field, I had been wanting to try something about a widow who lived on Beacon Hill and took in boarders. She went through several metamorphoses and many drafts before it dawned on me that I ought to provide her with an adequate background. This led to my writing *The Family Vault,* which was supposed to be an introduction to *The Withdrawing Room* but wound up being taught in a course on the mystery at Radcliffe College.

***The Family Vault,* the first Kelling book, is very funny with its portrait of a dotty Beacon Hill family. But it is also a very affecting story of a young woman dealing with the loss of a beloved spouse. Was this difficult to write, to balance the comedic aspects with the very real emotions of loss that Sarah experiences in the book?**

Since I am unhampered by a college education, it has never occurred to me to give a conscious thought to balancing the comedic aspects with the *vey is mir.* I just write it the way it feels right and if it doesn't, I try again.

Max Bittersohn is a great character, the perfect foil for Sarah. How did he come about?

It was never my intention to stick young Sarah Kelling with an elderly husband who meant well but had not the strength of will to break away from his vampire of a mother, even though Alexander was such a sympathetic character that my then agent begged me with sobs and cries to spare his life. But I can be ruthless. Max Bittersohn was the right man for her, pulling her free of the Kelling web and helping her to find a new life.

How did Alisa Craig originate?

After [the Doubleday] Crime Club had given a favorable reception to the first few Charlotte MacLeod novels, my editor asked me to write more books under a pseudonym. This, it appeared, was standard procedure, but I didn't want to play.

Then it occurred to me that this could be an opportunity to write books set in Canada, where I was born and for which I'd always had a chauvinistic fondness even though I'd been brought to the Boston area as a baby. Since I'd collected a drawerful of unfinished manuscripts by then and learned how a mystery should be put together, it was not too hard to furbish them up and send them to my agent. They all sold under the pseudonym Alisa Craig.

Many Canadian mystery writers find it difficult to get published in the United States because American publishers seem to think American mystery readers

aren't interested in Canada. You certainly have proven them wrong with your two series set in Canada. Do you think mystery readers really have such a geographic bias?

All I can say is that when Avon started publishing my Alisa Craig novels in paper, they wrote a blurb that left out any reference to Alisa Craig's Canadian origin. When I remonstrated, I was told that somebody in the merchandising department had claimed nobody wanted to read about Canada. It took a good deal of arguing even to get them to mention Alisa as a "Canadian-born writer who lives in Maine." I think the bias is all in the New York office, and I hope they'll wise up and quit acting so provincial.

Characters in all your novels have wonderful names, some of them delightfully outrageous puns, like Rovedock (in *The Bilbao Looking Glass*) or Dittany Henbit, for example. Have you always enjoyed playing with the language in this way?

Playing games with language is an endless delight. Most of my readers enjoy the crazy names; those who don't can always go off somewhere and read Elmore Leonard.

Many of the women in your novels have what I would call a "pragmatic" feminism. They aren't the overt and political feminists which some writers employ, but they are intelligent, capable, able to think for themselves, and forceful when necessary. Do they collectively (or singly, in any particular example) represent your own ideas on the subject?

In February 1944, I was hired just out of art school to be a staff artist and copywriter for a Boston-based supermarket chain, for the sole reason that it had been impossible to find anybody else. As mine was technically a man's job, I got privileges other female employees didn't have, such as being allowed to stay on the job from 9 A.M. to 11 P.M. getting the next day's ad out and dining on peanut butter and crackers filched from the buying department. I stayed in advertising for a long time, doing a man's work and being treated as one of the guys. My overall feeling, after years of research, is that, by and large, men have a tougher time of it than women do. Too many of them were running scared all the time and lacked women's versatility in dealing with a variety of tasks. Not to rain on Sisters in Crime's parade, but I used to feel sorry for the poor souls.

Humor is obviously a very important element in your writing. Do you ever find yourself convulsed with laughter (the way your readers are) over something you've written?

Certainly. I enjoy my own books, and naturally I convulse as easily as you do. Maybe easier. Why not? I've done the work, I might as well get in on the fun.

What gives you the greatest satisfaction from your work?

There's great satisfaction in getting paid, but I do honestly think that what I love best is the writing. And the readers, bless their hearts.

You've recently published a biography of Mary Roberts Rinehart. Why did you choose her as the subject of your first biography?

I'd been wanting to write a biography just to see whether I could, and I chose Mary Roberts Rinehart because she was such a many-faceted character, because I'd always enjoyed her mysteries, and because it galled me that she'd been so totally overlooked when Agatha Christie was getting so much attention at her centennial.

Would you repeat the experience and write another biography? Why or why not?

As to whether I'll ever try again, I just don't know. Having to stick to the facts makes it slow going sometimes.

Why, in your opinion, do mysteries remain so popular among readers today? Why do you think traditional mysteries, or "cozies," as some people call them, remain so popular?

While fads in mysteries seem to come and go, the traditional novel of manners with an aura of crime about it just keeps on cozying up to its many, many fans and climbing to the tops of the balance sheets as usual. You know more about this than I do, Dean . . . I'll leave it to you.

Your most recent book is *Something in the Water,* a Peter Shandy novel. What can we expect to see next, from either Charlotte MacLeod or Alisa Craig?

Now in the process of production and slated for May 1995, is *The Odd Job,* a new Sarah Kelling Bittersohn story in which our favorite Bostonian is going to be a mighty busy lady. On my agenda and even partially written is a Peter Shandy story that doesn't yet have a title. This book is not scheduled by Mysterious Press until 1996 but I'm having such a lovely time with it that I don't want to stop.

Many thanks to Charlotte for taking the time to talk about her work!

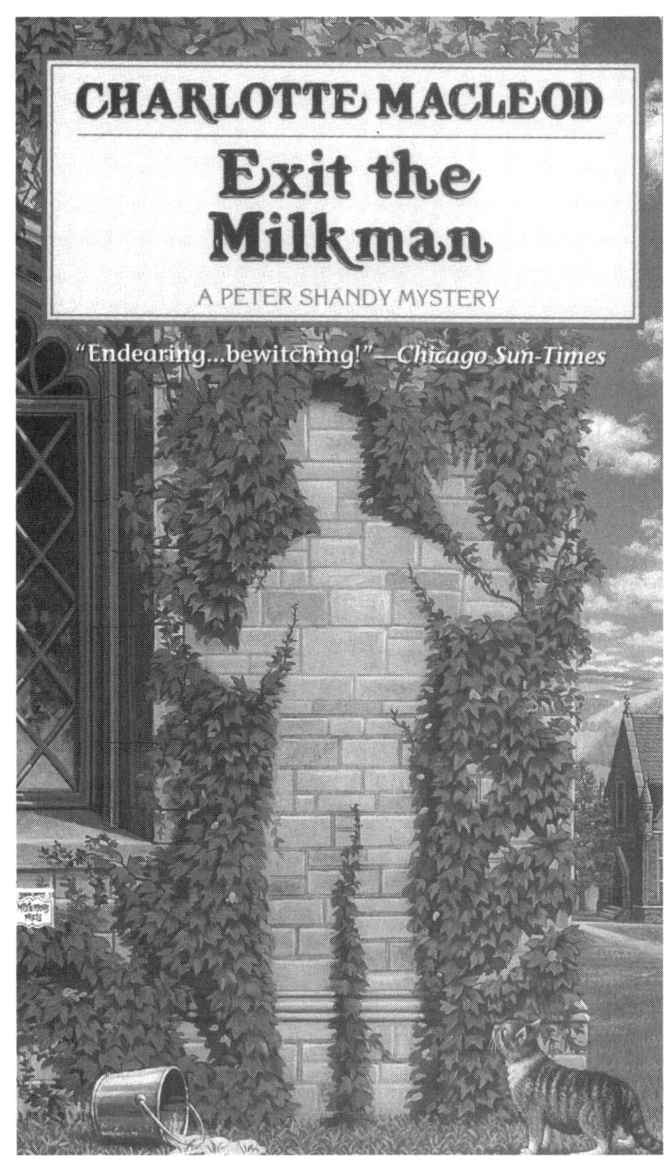

Exit the Milkman
by Charotte MacLeod

Contributor's Notes

CHARLES CHAMPLIN is the author of several books and is also the retired book editor of *The Los Angeles Times.* Mr. Champlin now has more time to write articles about the pioneering women of msytery and definitely more time to read.

ROBERT J. RANDISI has written twenty-seven novels in the Mystery/Suspense genre, as has edited fifteen anthologies. His newest novel, *In The Shadow of the Arch,* will be published by St. Martin's Press in January of '98. He is the founder and current President of the Private Eye Writers of America, creator of the Shamus Award, and co-founder of *Mystery Scene Magazine.*

BILL PRONZINI has been a full time writer since 1969. He has published more than forty novels, including three in collaboration with his wife, Marcia Muller and twenty-three in his critically acclaimed "Nameless Detective" series, four non-fictions and scores of short stories, articles, essays and book reviews. He's edited or co-edited numerous anthologies. Published in thirty countries and eighteen languages, Bill has been nominated for an Edgar Award five times, has won two Shamus awards and the Life Achievement Award, "The Eye" from PWA. Bill also won the Grand Prix de la Literature Policiere from France in 1988 for his novel, Snowbound. He lives in northern California with his wife and his collection of books and pulp magazines.

BILL CRIDER by day is the mild-mannered chair of the Division of English and Fine Arts at Alvin Community College. By night, he dons his red cape and blue tights to patrol the streets of the city, fighting crime and making sure that the traffic lights don't begin blinking before 10:00 p.m. He also has written over thirty horror, western and suspense which includes his mystery novels with three different series characters and has won an Anthony award for Best First. His collection of old mystery paperbacks long ago took over all available space in his home.

GEORGE KELLEY is a well-known writer of reviews and articles about mystery fiction. He donated 28,000 volumes of mystery, adventure, and detective stories to the State University of New York at Buffalo's Lockwood Memorial Library for the George Kelley Paperback and Pulp Fiction Collection.

JEFFREY MARKS is the author of a biography of Craig Rice published by Libraries des Champs Elysees and the editor of a dog-mystery anthology due out in 1998 from Ballantine.

ED GORMAN writes multi-genre books and stories and his mysteries have been described as "a combination of John D. MacDonald and Jim Thompson." He has won the Shamus, the Anthony and been nominated for the Edgar and the Golden Dagger. Three of his novels are in preparation as feature films. He is the editorial directory of *Mystery Scene* magazine but still finds time to read the "good old stuff."

THOMAS LEITHEC – is the Mystery Editor of Kirkus Reviews. When he's not setting his readers straight about great and not-so-great mystery fiction, he's doing the same thing for his students at the University of Delaware, where he teaches literary theory and directs the film studies program.

NANCY PICKARD has won numerous mystery awards for her short stories and novels and probably best known for her Jenny Cain series. She was chosen by the estate of Virginia Rich to finish Ms Rich's last novel. A former reported and editor she is a past president of Sisters In Crime. She lives in Kansas with her son and still admits to the Nancy Drew influence as she continues her writing.

MARCIA MULLER broke new ground when she introduced Sharon McCone, the first hard-boiled series featuring an American female Private Eye in 1977. She's the author of over twenty novels and a respected anthologist and critic of mystery fiction. She's been nominated for the Edgar, won the Anthony and the Shamus and been the recipient of "The Eye" Lifetime Achievement Award from the Private Eye Writers of America. Her most recent Sharon McCone books, *Broken Promise Land* and *Both Ends Of The Night* moves Marcia and Sharon into the thriller, best-selling status.

MARGARET MARON is the author of two mystery series and numerous short stories and her books have been nominated for every major award (except the Shamus) in the American mystery field. Her Bootlegger's Daughter in the Judge Deborah Knott series won the Agatha, the Edgar, the Anthony and the Macavity Awards in 1993. Margaret is the Past Persident of Sisters In Crime, and actively participates in MWA, is the current President of the American Crime Writers League but more importantly has a beautiful new granddaughter. She lives with her husband, Joe, in North Carolina and knows the country and the people she writes about quite well.

SHARON ZUKOWSKI has experienced a varied professional life—stockbroker, founder of group homes for mentally retarded adults, temporary secretary—all which gives her a unique perspective on life and colors her fiction with reality. Her P.I. series featuring Blaine Stewart also gives her an opportunity to tackle tough contemporary issues such as surrogate mothers, fertility clinics, animal rights, covert government operations and terrorism. Sharon also utilizes her love of travel to Key West, Washington DC, the Carolinas and other locales in search of truth and fiction.

LYNDA S. ROBINSON has a doctoral degree in anthropology with a specialty in the subdiscipline of archaeology and the author of several historical romances. Lynda's new mystery series is set in ancient Egypt with the fifth book coming out in 1998. She will serve as a "literary study guide" on a tour of archaeological sites in Egypt. Lynda lives in south central Texas hill country with her husband, Wess.

SUSAN WITTIG ALBERT is the author of five China Bayles herbal mysteries, two non-fiction books on women's issues, and (in her former incarnation as an English professor) too many critical essays to count. Writing under the pseudonym of Robin Page, she and her husband, Bill Albert, have created a series of Victorian historical mysteries featuring Kate Ardleigh and Sir Charles Sheridan. Together they also have written over sixty novels for young adults. Susan and Bill live in the Texas Hill Country.

ELLEN HART has created two popular mystery series. The first stars Minneapolis restaurateur Jane Lawless and her flamboyant sidekick, Cordila Thorn, which has been nominated several times and has won the Lambda Award for Best Lesbian Mystery. The second series features food critic and journalist Sophie Greenway.

KATHY PHILLIPS practicers law in North Andover, Massachusetts, where she also sells first edition mysteries and thrillers by mail to libraries and collectors as "Time and Again Books." She is the buyer of new trade books for Spenser's Mystery

Bookshop in Boston, and her reviews appear regularly in *The Drood Review, Mystery Scene* and *The Women's Review In Books.*

JERRY SYKES is a regular contributor to *A Shot In The Dark, Crime Time* and *Mystery Scene.* He made his fiction debut in *Love Kills* and has since sold stories to *Love Kills Again* and *2019.* He is also the editor of a forthcoming anthology of short crime fiction based around the millennium.

PAUL DUNCAN is the founding editor of *Crime Time* magazine, author of a graphic novel *Second City,* interviews crime writers for *The Third Degree.* He's lives in England and is currently working on a biography of Gerald Kersh.

TERI J. WHITE has published seven suspense novels, two of which have been made into film in France, and a number of short stories. Her first novel, *Triangle,* won the Edgar A. Poe award for Best Original Paperback. She is an avid science fiction fan and a passionate Anglophile.

BILLIE SUE MOSIMAN is the author of eight novels of suspense and more than one hundred short stories. Her novel, *Night Cruise,* was nominated for an Edgar Award and her novel, *Widow,* was nominated for the Bram Stoker Award. Her latest project was an anthology of mystery stories edited with Martin Greenberg, *Death In Dixie.* Four more regional volumes of mystery stories will follow soon from Rutledge Hill Press. Billie tries constantly to live down her "you don't look tough enough to write such tough stories" image.

CAROLE NELSON DOUGLAS is the multi-genre author of thirty four novels and writes two award-winning series. *Good Night, Mr. Holmes* initiated four historical mysteries about American diva Irene Adler, the only woman to outwit Sherlock Holmes, and was a *New York Times Notable Book.* Feline supersleuth Midnight Louie's *Cat In A Crimson Haze* won the Cat Writers' Association 1995 Best Novel Award. *Cat In A Diamond Dazzle,* a 1996 CWA finalist was along Mostly Murders's Top Ten Traditional Mysteries of 1996. Midnight Louie's eighth case is *Cat In A Golden Garland* and owns too many cats to name them all.

GAYLE LYNDS is a former newspaper reporter, and the author of *Masquerade, Marionette,* and *Mosaic,* all suspense thrillers with female heroines. *People* magazine named *Masquerade* their "Page Turner Of The Week." Ms Lynds has been a magazine editor and a think-tank editor with top secret security clearance. Her fiction delves into the underworlds of spies, the backrooms of politics, and the board rooms of power. She lives in Santa Barbara with her mystery writer husband, Dennis, (aka Michael Collins.)

JULIE SMITH is a former reporter for the *New Orleans Times, Picayune* and the *San Francisco Chronicle,* has written seven novels featuring Skip Langdon. The first in the series, *New Orleans Mourning* won the Edgar for Best Novel. Julie recently married and moved back to New Orleans where she lives in an 1830s Creole town house with its very own ghost and serial murder story.

ELEANOR TAYLOR BLAND is the author of the Mattie MacAlister mysteries. Mattie broke new ground in that she's a mother, a widow and the only black female cop in Lincoln Prairie, IL. Eleanor is a CPA in her other life and lives is suburban Chicago.

ELIZABETH DANIELS SQUIRES is a veteran journalist from a distinguished southern family, who has covered murders and murder trials writes a series of mysteries about absent minded sleuth Peaches Dann, and highlights the amazing ways of human nature under stress, not graphic violence or police procedure. Her short story, "The Dog Who Remembered Too

Much" won the 1997 Agatha Award.

JOYCE CHRISTMAS is the author of two mystery series. The first features the aristocratic English sleuth Lady Margaret Priam. The second series stars retired businesswoman Betty Trenka. Joyce was co-Guest of Honor at the 1997 Cluefest fan convention in Dallas, TX and she's been known to wear a tiara on occasion.

BARBARA PAUL writes mysteries, science-fiction, and a web page. Her latest mystery in the Marian Larch series is *Full Frontal Murder,* her latest sci-fi story is "Earth Surrenders" in *First Contact,* and her constantly growing web page can be found at http://www.lit-arts.com/bpaul.

CAROL HARPER is an ardent mystery fan currently living in Beijing, China. She reviewed mysteries for many years for *Alfred Hitchcock Mystery Magazine* and has long served as Associate Editor of the *Mystery Readers Journal.* Carol also served on the committee and later chaired the Agatha Awards Committee for Malice Domestic.

WENDY HORNSBY won a Edgar for her short story, "Nine Sons" and writes a series featuring Maggie McGown, a TV investigative reporter. The native Californian lives in Long Beach where she teaches history at on the college level and takes care of her two teenagers—recently sending one off to college.

GAR HAYWOOD is the Shamus Award-winning author of two highly-acclaimed mystery series, one featuring hardnosed private investigator Aaron Gunner, who works out of present day South Central Los Angeles, and the other series features Joe and Dottie Loudermilk, the Airstream-owning pair of retirees who solve crimes as they see America, one highway off-ramp at a time.

JOAN HESS is a fifth-generation resident of Arkansas and the author of more than twenty comedic mystery novels in the Claire Malloy and the Maggody series. She has won the American Mystery Award, as well as the Agatha, Macavity, and Drood Review awards. She has served on the national board of Mystery Writers of America, chaired the Edgar best novel and short story committees, and is a past president of the American Crime Writers Association. She has no discernible Southern accent and her hair is not natural.

JOHN LUTZ is the Edgar and Shamus Award winning author of two P.I. series, one featuring Fred Carver and the other Alo Nudger. He also wrote the suspense novel *SWF Seeks Same* which was made into the highly successful film, *Single White Female.* Recipient of the Life Achievement Award from PWA, his most recent novel is *Lightening,* featuring Carver. John is a Past-President of Mystery Writers of America.

WENDI LEE is another writer who likes to go against the grain. Her first p.i. series featured Jefferson Birch, a male P.I. in Hollywood in the 1930s. Her current series features Angela Martelli, a female P.I. living in Boston.She also write historical fiction and westerns. Wendi lives in Iowa with her husband, Terry and stays busy with her recently adopted daughter.

LIZA CODY writes the Award winning series featuring Anna Lee, a British investigator which as been made into a British TV series. Her latest series features a female wrestler "The London L'Assassin," Eva Wylie who is completely opposite from Anna Lee and even considers Ms. Lee as "The Enemy."

CROW DILLON-PARKIN is an artist and photographer by profession, began writing for *Crime Time* is now the current editor of that magazine and is also currently writing a first novel, *Holiday.*

DEBORAH ADAMS is a reformed Southern belle, who gave up ballgowns and bouffant hair to write mysteries. Her series is set in the mythical town of Jesus Creek, TN. The first in the series was nominated for an Agatha and she's been nominated for an Agatha and won a Macavity for her short story. Deborah still lives in TN with her husband and stays busy corralling her youngsters. In her spare time she writes and rides horses.

TONI L.P. KELNER is a transplanted Southerner, who has lived up North for ten years, and even gave birth there, but still talks like a Southerner. In between playing with two-year-old Maggie, the first Yankee in her family, Kelner writes the Laura Fleming mysteries. The fifth in the series *Tight As A Tick* will be released in January of 1998.

BARBARA BURNETT SMITH is a former broadcaster who spent sixteen years in radio, much of that time on the air. She also worked in news, production and sales, winning several awards for her writing. Now she is the author of series set in Purple Sage TX. Her first, *Writers of the Purple Sage,* was an Agatha nominee for Best First. Currently in the series is *Mistletoe From Purple Sage* which takes place in Austin. In her left brain life, Barbara is a consultant trainer for corporations and state agencies, teaching primarily in the area of communication. In her spare time she voices radio and television commercials, and serves on the national board of Sisters In Crime. Barbara lives in Austin with her husband and visits her son and grandson in Houston quite often.

BEV DEWEESE is a librarian at the Milwaukee Public Library and one of the founding members of the Cloak & Clue Society. Bev reads everything and reviews books. She was programming chair for EYECON'95. Bev also is interested in the theater, her cats and science fiction, which is understandable since her husband is Gene DeWeese who writes sci-fi.

ADRIAN MULLER is a freelance journalist specializing in crime and mystery fiction. As well as producing a number of features, interviews and reviews he also has regular columns in both *A Shot In The Dark* and *Mystery Scene* magazine.

EDWARD HOCH is an Edgar winner for Best Short Story and Past- President of MWA, who has published over 800 stories and more than forty books. His stories have appeared in every issue of *Ellery Queen Mystery Magazine* since 1973 and he edited *The Year's Best Suspense Stories* for twenty years. His stories have been published in twenty-five countries and several have been adapted for television. He lives in Rochester, NY with his wife, Pat.

JAN BURKE is the author of five novels featuring southern Californian newspaper reporter Irene Kelly. The first, *Goodnight, Irene,* was nominated for both an Anthony and Agatha. Her short stories have won the Macavity and the EQMM Reader's Award. She has been a history researcher, freelance writer, manufacturing plant manager and some forgettable occupations. Jan currently lives in Southern California with her husband. Tim, and dog, Cappy, and now occupies herself with full time writing.

MARY BLOUNT CHRISTIAN was asked by her teacher as a young fifth-grader to stand up in front of her class everyday after lunch and tell a continuing suspense story involving other children in the room. The young storyteller quickly learned that her audience stayed interested if the tale had plenty of action. After a career in journalism she began writing children's mysteries including the critically acclaimed and highly popular "Sebastian, Super Sleuth" a doggy p.i. and stories like *The Double-Double Cross.* Mary also writes children's historical stories. She's a part President and one of the founding members of the Southwest Chapter of MWA. She's lives in Houston, TX with her husband, George and tells stories to her grandchildren and never ever lies about her age.

CAROL CROWLEY is currently the president of the Rocky Mountain Chapter of Sisters in Crime where she also edits the newsletter and interviews mystery writers.

DON SANDSTROM is a a life long mystery fan. He's had articles published in *Mystery Scene, Deadly Pleasures, The Armchair Detective* and other mystery fanzines. He's a knowledgeable collector and voracious reader. He was fan Guest of Honor at the 1993 Bouchercon in Omaha and the first Magna Cum Murder con at Ball State University. Don lives in Indianapolis.

SUSAN ROGERS COOPER has written eleven books in three series: The E.J. Pugh series, The Milt Kovak series and the Kimmey Kruse series. Susan is a founding member of the Heart of TX chapter of Sisters In Crime. She lives in Austin with Don, her husband of twenty-five years.

RYLLA GOLDBERG lives in Bellevue WA across the lake from Seattle. Her mystery writing includes essays, interviews, and book reviews. Rylla also constructs crossword puzzles and other word games for children and adults. Her mystery crosswords appear in *Mystery Scene.*

ANNETTE MEYERS spent sixteen years as a headhunter on Wall Street and sixteen years on Broadway working as assistant to Hal Prince and combines both milieus in her Smith and Wetzon series. She and husband Martin using the pseudonym Maan Meyers also writes The Dutchman series. Her story stories have appeared in numerous anthologies. Annette is the current (tenth) President of Sisters In Crime, holds memberships in MWA, PWA, The Author's Guild and is on the Executive Council of the International Association of Crime Writers.

EVE SANDSTROM has drawn on her professional and cultural backgrounds, adding imaginary crimes and characters, to create fictional plots grounded in reality. Her new series, which opened with *The Violence Beat,* features a newspaper reporter and uses Sandstrom's twenty-five-plus years in the newspaper business to create a setting. Her first series, the three "Down Home" books, is laid in the ranching country where Sandstrom has lived for nearly forty years.

MARLYS MILLHISER is the author of four books and five short stories in the Charlie Greene series and six previous novels—one of which, a classic, *The Mirror* was recently reissued in trade paperback. Marlys is also intelligent, witty, loyal, faithful, trustworthy, nice, sweet, lovely and a girl scout. She lives in Boulder with her hunky husband, David.

MARY WILLIS WALKER spends a great deal of time sitting alone at a keyboard in a darkened room making things up. In this way she has to her amazement turned out four books—An Agatha winner and Edgar winner and a Hammet Award winner. *Midnight Hags* is forthcoming in 1998. Mary plans to continue doing this as she is unfit for anything else. She lives in Austin, TX and only refers to herself in third person when writing bios.

BARBARA PETERS – owner of the Poisoned Pen bookstore in Scottsdale, AZ is a co-founder of the Independent Mystery Booksellers Association and creator of the Dilys Award. She has hosted and chaired writer's conferences such as Left Coast Crime and now the third annual AZ Murder Goes Alternatively and she recently began a publishing business to reprint nearly forgotten mysteries. In her spare time she travels and writes articles about book selling.

Index

—C—

—D—

—E—

—F—

—G—

—N—

—O—

—P—

—Q—

—R—

—S—

—T—